Evaluating Administrative Performance: Current Trends and Techniques

by
Elio Zappulla, Ph.D.

Star
PUBLISHING COMPANY

Star

PUBLISHING COMPANY
Belmont, CA 94002

Typesetting — M. Anderson
Graphic Arts — D. B. Hurd

Printed in the United States of America
ISBN: 0-89863-059-2

Contents

FOREWORD
by
Terrence E. Deal
Harvard University

Writing the foreword to an anthology is like trying to set the scene for a wine-tasting. It's hard to describe the contents adequately, it's even harder to imagine how people will experience the various offerings as they try them out. The only reasonable contribution that a foreword might attempt to make is to create an ambience, to set the stage for what follows. And since the complexities of leadership are akin to the subtleties of wine, the setting can influence significantly what we conclude. It is in that spirit (so to speak) that I want to try to embed what you are about to sample in a broader context of some issues in administrative evaluation.

Evaluating Administrators: Why Bother?

In a historical, or cross-cultural, context, it seems puzzling why we would need evidence to establish how well our educational leaders are performing. Tradition would tell us that they were, of course, performing adequately — they have a moral responsibility to do so. Given no evidence to the contrary, they must be doing the job. Charismatic ideas would focus our attention on special qualities of school leaders. If someone has character, personal attraction, or worthy goals, *ipso facto* his or her leadership must be sound. One's magic charm intact, why question the performance?

But in times like ours, both tradition and charisma have paled before a robust blossoming of rational assumptions. And in the ebb tide, most institutions and their leaders are being asked to prove they make a difference, to show that they produce results. Believing is no longer seeing; most people want it the other way around. We are paying attention to the evaluation of educational administrators because people doubt their "virtues." We may disguise that fact with the rhetoric of improvement, justification, or other reasons why we should now evaluate administrative performances. But our current interest in evaluation cannot be separated from the general decline of faith in public schools. We are bothering because people are bothered. And we have to be careful that our efforts to upgrade evaluation don't bother them even more.

The Quirks of Leadership

Leadership under any conditions is like punching a feather pillow while people keep looking at how well the trains are running. You know the resistance; they want to see some results. The connections are difficult to describe or trace.

In schools, the Rube Goldberg chain between superintendents' and principals' actions and student learning is classic. In theory, you make a policy; a teacher reads it and conforms; your reasoning was sound, and test scores go up. In fact, you create a policy, and what happens thereafter would cause most systems analysts to reconsider their profession. If anyone implements your suggestions, you question their motives. If test scores go up, you probably haven't the foggiest idea why. A seasoned administrator shared with me a maxim for administering schools: "If it flies, shoot it; if it falls, claim it." Given the segmented character of schools, there is some real wisdom in those words. It's hard to support the thesis that there is a direct and measurable link between what administrators do and the behavior of teachers and students or what is learned in school. But if administrators don't control what happens, what role do they play? The answer seems obvious: they are actors on a stage; they set the tone, create the ethos, establish the climate, reinforce desired values. The daily dramas inside schools or school districts require an appearance on behalf of a superintendent or principal. Without their part, the script doesn't make sense. The entire production loses its vitality and meaning. Kids and teachers begin to wonder what they are doing and why. They need clues and look to the administration to provide them.

The presence of administrators on stage is even more critical to the audience. Parents and local communities look to administrators for signals that tell them how well the drama is being performed. The heroic portrayal reassures; a weak performance causes concerns. The audience knows what it wants; the administrator's performance is the focal point of their attention — in telephone conversations, in public, at formal occasions. Administrators are judged on how they appear, because what they have accomplished is impossible to determine. While this is true in all organizations, it's particularly true in schools. Even a losing season for a baseball manager can be offset by dramatic outbursts at a poor call from an umpire or by the imposition of a heavy fine on a wayward player. Imagine what parents look for when they hear that the public schools are failing.

As we move to strengthen the system used to evaluate the school administrator, the quirks of leadership need to be considered. Many lists of criteria ignore the dramaturgical aspects of being a principal or superintendent. The lists overlook the fact that an administrator's performance is always going to be determined more by rumor, gossip, and appearance than by anything else. To design an evaluation system that eliminates the subjective side of administration cancels out 90% of what is important. Eliot Eisner has advanced the idea that the process of evaluating schools should resemble that of judging art. And since the leadership is still more of an art than a science, a connoisseurship approach to administrative evaluation may need to be considered alongside other efforts.

Schools are quirky places. Leadership is always difficult to define and measure. Both of these facts need to be taken into account in evaluating administrators — for their professional development or in order to assure the public that schools are accountable.

Walking the Tightrope:
The Substance and Ritual of Administrative Evaluation

Deep in their hearts, most administrators would agree with the profile sketched above. But agreement begs the main issues. What do we do to evaluate administrators at a time when people want evidence of effective performance? How can we devise a system that provides feedback that helps administrators perform better? How can we help administrators in their efforts to improve education for their students? — or conditions for teaching?

These are questions for which there are no clear answers. As we struggle to create new approaches to evaluate administrators, we balance precariously on a tightrope with two ways to fall. We can design sound, rational systems approaches with substance that try to measure style. Or we can consider the task a ritual for internal and external consumption, ignoring the practical needs that evaluation must address. The first alternative plunges us into a spiral that will undoubtedly upset the delicate social equilibrium of schools and reinforce administrators for doing things that will cause trouble — for everyone. The second opens schools to criticism that they continue to pull the wool over the eyes of the public — protecting weak administrators and doing nothing to help marginal cases improve. Either spells disaster, the only real solution is to balance on the wire somewhere between the two.

The Anthology as a Balancing Pole

The present collection of readings is written by people whose ideas and judgment I respect. Some are practitioners; others are scholars. I don't agree with everyone, and would not expect anyone to agree with me. (I don't even completely agree with the article of mine that's included!) The book's appeal is multiple: it creates a dialogue between the different positions, tries to outline the role of district leaders and principals and the problems both face; presents concepts and details of current approaches to evaluating administrators, tells how to implement evaluation procedures without creating chaos, presents a number of useful forms, and shows some of the parallels between the experience of schools and the business world in evaluation. If there is a bias to the collection, it errs in the direction of being too rational. That's why this foreword is somewhat off the wall — stressing the expressive side of administration and schools. The secret to creating new systems of administrative evaluation is to walk the balance between what we know to be true and what could be. It's the problem of doing something without overdoing it. Balancing the two is the key to administrative evaluation.

The foreword has tried to create the setting for sampling a variety of ideas in order to walk the tightrope between irresponsibility and over-responsibility. What follows should help. Enjoy, and be guided by your own taste buds. There is no substitute for the judgment and instruction of experienced superintendents and principals.

Cambridge, Massachusetts
1982

INTRODUCTION

The idea for this book originated during the 1980-81 school year when I was asked to help develop a procedure for evaluating administrators in a Long Island, New York, school district. In the course of looking at what other school districts were doing about this question, I began to realize that while a number of them have developed some workable evaluative procedures, the great majority do not yet seem to have given the question of administrator evaluation the serious attention it deserves. Furthermore, in researching the available literature on the subject, I noted that the sources offering the kind of information needed to devise an evaluative system were widely scattered among a variety of publications (if, indeed, they were published at all) and were often difficult to obtain.

It occurred to me that school personnel in districts around the nation who were also seeking to evaluate their administrators in a systematic way could be helped by a single text that assembled current ideas and practical suggestions on the subject. When I suggested the idea to publisher Stuart Hoffman, he received it enthusiastically and asked me to edit such a book. The present work is the result.

While compiling the material for this book, I kept in mind a number of assumptions about evaluation. Chief among these is the assumption that whatever purposes are assigned to evaluation, the main one, surely, is to improve the educational process in the school or district — no matter what other purposes are stated, valid though they, too, may be.

I have, however, observed that even as instruments of evaluation are theorized about in the literature or are developed and used in the field, there seems to be a peculiar failure to make this purpose the lodestar. In fact, evaluation of administrators is often used for purposes that are quite divergent from, if not at complete variance with, the notion of improving education, though such improvement may occur fortuitously. Often, evaluation is done primarily for less noble motives — perhaps to demote, or get rid of, an administrator.

I repeat that using evaluation for purposes other than that of improving the quality of education is not necessarily invalid. My point is that, as the tools of evaluation are made, honed, and used, focusing on the most important goal and keeping it firmly in view will do more good than using those tools for some ancillary end. Good for whom? Why, for the children, whom the entire educational apparatus allegedly exists to serve, to whom it owes its very "raison d'etre," and to whom it is, after all, ultimately responsible.

Another of my assumptions is that it is vital to see clearly how the administrator's job influences the quality of the educational program. Evaluation is made all the more difficult when the waters are muddied by confusion about what administrators do, or are supposed to do.

One reason for this failure in perception is that the administrator functions outside the classroom, where, we all assume, the actual learning takes place. The classroom is viewed, quite properly no doubt, as the center of the educational system, the almost sanctified locus where the student is prepared to absorb what the teacher is ready to dispense. What, after all, does the administrator have to do with that process by which knowledge is somehow transferred into receptive young minds? When the administrator's role is thus neither clearly understood nor accurately perceived, methods and criteria established to measure how well the role is played lack validity.

When teachers are observed, on the other hand, the things they do are more readily observable, more easily seen, and the relationship between these things and "education" is more obvious. An administrator entrusted with the mission of writing up a teacher evaluation can obtain the data he needs simply by walking into the classroom where the teacher is at work. There the teacher may be seen in direct contact with the students; her methods of imparting knowledge may be witnessed, recorded for later analysis; the teacher's rapport with the class is apparent to the observer's eye; the room is often filled with teacher-directed student projects and displays, tangible evidence of the teacher's inspirational power or instructional know-how — or the lack of these. When all the necessary data have been gathered, there is surely a reasonable possibility (at least, this is how the theory goes) that a fairly accurate appraisal of the teacher's performance can be drawn up, despite preconceptions or misconceptions, and barring, of course, ineptitude on the part of the observer.

The kinds of jobs that administrators perform, however, and the relationship of those jobs to instruction do not easily lend themselves to the kind of scrutiny that can yield data for evaluation from the teaching staff. But although it is more difficult to determine the effects, for good or ill, that administrative performance has upon the education of children, I believe it is inarguable — another of my assumptions — that administrators significantly affect the quality of education. And while the effects may not be so immediately apparent, they permeate the educational environment and reverberate profoundly throughout the particular educational organization.

At least one aspect of what administrators do plays a larger role than most people would imagine in determining the quality of teacher performance: they help set the tone for learning in their district or building. By their attitudes, by actions both subtle and overt, they create an atmosphere that can be conducive to sound learning or can act as a damper on the enthusiasm of both teachers and learners. The truth of the commonplace needs to be emphasized: leaders who are positive, energetic, kind, resourceful, and knowledgeable create conditions favorable to learning.

I do not wish to indulge in hyperbole on this point. Obviously the quality of the educational program depends upon many factors besides the capacities of the school leaders. Board policies, the effectiveness of individual teachers, community problems, budget restraints, and many other things are stirred into the educational pot; each of the ingredients will help determine what the final product will taste like. But, if I may continue the metaphor, the administrator is the chief cook, and while he may not be able to control the quality of every ingredient, he is certainly in a good position to greatly improve, or even ruin, the sauce.

In view of this, it is apparent that the more attention we pay to the job the administrator is doing and the more clearly we perceive the real influence of that job upon the process of education, the more meaningful and valid the evaluation of administrator performance will be. If that is so, the concomitant result will be a better educational program. The theory is that if we can evaluate properly, we can properly prescribe remedies for shortcomings in performance, and the remedies will hopefully bring in their train the general improvement in the educational process that I spoke of earlier as being the main purpose of evaluation.

The administrator's importance in the educational process makes the evaluation of his performance not only advisable but indeed mandatory. That is another of my assumptions. However, still another one lies behind it: the assumption that in any system supported by public funds there must be some sort of accountability — to use a much-overworked word. Board members and trustees have a duty to the public to determine how effectively the district's employees are working, how much they are contributing to the improvement of education. The public wants, and indeed deserves, some assurance from the board that the money it so agonizingly pays out in the form of property taxes, most of which goes toward school employee salaries, is being used to pay the best people for doing the best job, to put it in simple terms. But the simplicity of the statement does not detract from its fundamental validity. And it has never been more valid than in this era of economic downturn.

Additionally, since administrator salaries have, in our time, come to be perceived as high in comparison with teacher salaries, not to mention the average salaries of the people in the community at large, there is now perhaps a greater inclination to scrutinize administrative performance. And let us make no mistake about it: the power of the public in the domain of education is considerable. While the "vox populi" may not exactly be equivalent to the "vox Dei", it is certainly not the "vox clamantis in deserto." On the contrary, the voice of the public is heard, and usually listened to attentively, by every administrator. No doubt the zeal with which the public frequently makes its voice heard at school board meetings is given added impetus because of public frustration over not being able — in its own, perhaps inaccurate, perception — to have a similar large voice in other branches of government. It boggles the mind to consider to what degree local government might improve it it, too, were to become the target of that same public enthusiasm.

Yet another of my assumptions is that the process of evaluating administrative performance must take into account the position in which administrators find themselves in the hierarchical structure of the world of education. In this age of teacher activism, for example, administrators are subject to pressures from below in ways that were unthinkable a few decades ago. At the same time, they are pressured from their superiors in the administrative chain or by the board of education itself. Meanwhile, out in the community lies the public, ready to exert pressures of its own.

Such pressures, naturally, go along with the job. While they make the task of the administrator more difficult to accomplish, since often these groups can send conflicting messages to the administrator about what he should or should not be doing, we must be realistic in admitting that, given the present ambience in education, such pressures are not likely to disappear soon, let alone relent. Nor am I completely convinced, frankly, that we administrators would necessarily do a better job if the pressures were suddenly to vanish.

My point is that any evaluation of the administrator must recognize not only the complexity of the administrative task but also the fact that such tasks are made even more complex and more difficult to accomplish because of the words, and actions of groups and individuals both within and without the walls of the school building. The evaluative process cannot, therefore, consist solely of an examination of the superficiae of the administrator's job. We are dealing, after all, not so much with easily measurable things as with a complicated set of circumstances. No administrator does his job "in vacuo"; he is always in the spotlight. And the glare of that light sometimes blinds him so that he cannot always do his job with the clarity of purpose and intensity of concentration we expect from him. Our judgments of his work should therefore be tempered by a sympathetic recognition of his peculiar predicament.

I believe that the majority of the works chosen and written for this text implicity or explicitly share many of the assumptions which have guided my own thinking about evaluation. And I do not think this is solely because I am the one who did the choosing. The assumptions under discussion run through the literature of evaluation like leitmotifs in a Wagnerian opera. I believe, too, that the authors' sensitivity to these (and other) assumptions has helped make their suggestions for evaluation well balanced and workable. The evaluative systems they outline and their perceptive comments on the entire evaluative process can yield a good understanding, both theoretical and practical, of administrative performance.

The material in this book is divided into five parts. The first makes some observations about the role of the school district leaders, from board members to superintendents and other administrators. In this section the authors try to shed some light on the administrator's world, reminding us, sometimes amusingly, of the problems that beset those who would lead the schools. Part II gives an overview of the kinds of evaluative systems that are currently being, or have recently been, used in a number of school districts throughout the nation. It is instructive to learn how different schools are handling the question of evaluation.

Part III contains a large number of works written by people knowledgeable about setting up and implementing evaluation systems. Some of the articles present general concepts around which an evaluative process may be constructed; other are meticulous in spelling out the details of establishing such a process. In both cases the ideas are sound. Taken as a whole, all the works in this section are a veritable mine of information on ways to go about making judgments about how administrators are doing their job. Some of the works were written expressly for this book; most of the others, though they originally appeared elsewhere, are of comparatively recent vintage and reflect current thinking.

Part IV consists of a number of forms that may be useful in doing evaluations.

Finally, because we in education sometimes forget that people in other fields may have something important to teach us, I have included in Part V examples of some concerns about personnel evaluation with which managers in the business world are currently preoccupied. Their experience may give us a clearer idea of how best to use the tools of evaluation.

* * * * * * * * * * * *

In preparing this book, I have been helped by a number of people, all of whom contributed in some way to making it better than it might have been and none of whom are responsible for any of its shortcomings.

I am particularly grateful to Stuart and Debora Hoffman for their constant encouragement and support. My thanks also go to Jeannine Cook, Phyllis Akins, Ruth Bussiere and Colleen Kennefick of the Emma S. Clark Memorial Library in Setauket, New York, who were extremely helpful in obtaining materials and information of all kinds; to Naida Dewey for assistance in typing, and to the staff of the library of the State University of New York at Stony Brook for valuable assistance in locating hard-to-find articles and authors.

Finally, words are too weak to express my gratitude to my wife, Lynette, for her sound advice, devotion and understanding, and to my children, David and Eve, for their marvelous forbearance.

Elio Zappulla
Stony Brook, New York

PART I

Looking at Administrators

It's a Bird!
It's a Plane!
It's Super-Principal!

Gilbert R. Weldy

Gilbert R. Weldy entertains us with an account of several days in the life of an imaginary super-hero, Mark Grant, Super-Principal. Reading of his exploits, we are reminded that the job of leading a school often seems to require the kind of superhuman capabilities that, alas, only few of us possess. Those who have experienced, or closely observed, the duties and responsibilities that characterize the principal's job will smile knowingly, for Weldy's portrait of Grant isn't quite so fanciful as it appears. Weldy is himself a principal - at Niles North High School in Skokie, Illinois.

The opening sentence of most any professional article about the principalship today will declare how changed, how challenging, how demanding the role is. The National Association of Secondary School Principals says the principal is a curriculum analyst, executive, interpreter, manager, mediator, ombudsman, scholar, strategist, and a teacher of teachers. Has anyone suggested that to meet the demands of today's principals, he would have to be a Superman? Everyone remembers Superman.

"Faster than a speeding bullet, more powerful than a locomotive, able to leap tall buildings in a single bound, he was the strange visitor from another planet who came to earth with power and abilities far beyond the abilities of mortal men. He could bend steel in his bare hands, change the course of mighty rivers. Disguised as Clark Kent, mild-mannered reporter for the *Daily Planet*, he fights the never-ending battle for truth, justice, and the American way."

Superman? A Super-Principal? Do you suppose . . . ? What if . . .?

* * * * * *

Mark Grant, Principal of Lincoln High School, was *not* an ordinary man. When he had first decided to undertake the responsibilities of administering a high school, he knew that ordinary knowledge, skill, and perceptivity would not be sufficient. He was not a believer in the occult, but he learned quite by accident of a medium who could help him secure the extraordinary sensitivity and power which principals need if they are to succeed.

The ritual was relatively simple, but mysterious and unwordly. He submitted to the influence, and following a brief spell of unconsciousness emerged transfigured, feeling exhilarated, renewed. The experience was indeed a transformation, from mortal human being Mark Grant to a unique and unprecedented being - to be known in this account as Super-Principal.

In appearance, Mark Grant did not change. He appeared to be conventional enough. His modest business suits and jackets were only occasionally brightened by modishly colorful shirts and ties.

Beneath these undistinguished outer garments, however, lay the secret of his unusual power — an undervest of ordinary gray which blended inconspicuously with any ensemble he happened to wear. The secret of his unusual gift was in the lining, a most special radiant material which infused his being and transformed him whenever he chose to put it on. It was only when he wore the remarkable undervest that Mark Grant became Super-Principal. When not in use, the undervest was secured safely in a secret desk drawer, lined with lead.

Miraculous powers were not always required. Mark Grant used them judiciously and sparingly, lest his unnatural powers be exposed and his effectiveness destroyed. When he sensed a situation calling for Super-Principal, he closed and locked his office door, instructed his secretary not to interrupt, and donned the magic vest under his more conventional attire. Only he knew the miraculous transformation which electrified his senses, super-charged his energies, magnified his powers, and turned him into Super-Principal. No one knew; no one suspected that the man was any more than an unusually capable, perceptive, clever human being. No one imagined that by donning an unobtrusive vest the man was transported to a state of super sensitivity, of super intelligence, of super memory, of super strength and agility. This and more was Mark Grant when he became Super-Principal.

* * * * * *

On a Monday when Mark Grant arrived at his office and reviewed his calendar for the day, he knew that it was going to call for Super-Principal. Without a second thought, he arranged for his privacy with his secretary and removed his jacket to slip into the uniform of Super-Principal. When his outer attire was again in place, he felt the warm surge of power and sensitivity from the miraculous garment. As Super-Principal, he called for one of his most unique resources — cloning. Super-Principal left his office to have coffee with some visitors and to acquaint them with plans for their visitation. He was congenial, hospitable, and enthusiastic. He appeared simultaneously at a meeting of counselors who were chafing with criticism about their function and role. He was insightful, calm and reassuring. Unknown to the others and at the same time, he also left the building to join his colleagues at the district office in a special meeting to develop a new policy affecting his school's graduation requirements. He demonstrated his wisdom, his persuasiveness, and ability to see the future. Finally, at the far end of the building, he joined a class where he observed a new teacher. To the new teacher, he was attentive, helpful and supportive.

Two hours later, Super-Principal returned to his office to continue the activities of a day that was far less demanding — as the singular Mark Grant.

* * * * * *

When the deans left his office one afternoon that week, Mark Grant knew that he was going to have to do something to help them curtail the demoralizing use of illegal drugs among students. Particularly was he being challenged to find methods of identifying and apprehending the drug pushers and suppliers. It would take a superhuman effort to break through the conspiratorial web of secrecy, deceit, and treachery that surrounded drug activity in the school. It looked like a job for Super-Principal.

No one saw Super-Principal leave his office. He had told his secretary that he would take no calls, that he did not want to be disturbed for an uninterrupted hour, while he worked on an extremely sensitive project. It was true. No one would know how sensitive the project or how easily it was to be accomplished by Super-Principal, who had used his abnormal power — to make himself invisible.

He stationed himself in the boy's washroom where he knew the drugs were passed. He stood unseen while deals were made, money exchanged hands, drugs were discussed and appointments made. When the dealers left, Super-Principal moved on the parking lot, noting names, faces, license numbers, and remembering times and places for the sales. From there he went to the student lounge where he stood literally within the circle of malefactors as they engaged in their heinous offenses.

Back in his office, Super-Principal prepared his plan of attack. He called the deans, the security officers, the local police (some of the parking lot habitues were not students). He told them that it had been his good fortune to come into some information whose source would have to be confidential but which should help them "bust" the drug activity. He named the names and places. He described the modus operandi. He identified which were the sellers, the pushers, the buyers, the users.

The next day, three non-student pushers were arrested in their cars with neat packages of grass and pills, not very well hidden. Six students were apprehended at the door, pockets bulging with their "deliveries." Twenty-two more who awaited the stuff at three locations in the building were gathered up, parents called, and the process of counseling begun. Many marveled and admired, but no one dreamed that the "bust" was the result of the miraculous power of Super-Principal to make himself invisible.

* * * * * *

On another day later that week, Mark Grant prepared for a conference calling for mediation between a student and her parent with a teacher who had accused her of cheating. The situation was explosive. Hard feelings had already been aroused. The student had been threatened with a failing grade. The situation called for unusual diplomacy and insight. It seemed like an occasion for Super-Principal and his uncanny ability to know always when someone was — or was not — telling the truth.

Mark Grant was prepared when the participants arrived. As Super-Principal he was relaxed and confident. He knew that his super powers would lead him to the truth. His extra sense was more reliable than a polygraph. It invariably helped cut through all the pretense, hedging, posing, and outright prevarication.

The mother and daughter were hostile and belligerent. Their denials were adamant and vociferous. The teacher was defensive and stubborn. He was certain of what he had observed. The student was insistent that no cheating had occurred. The parent insisted that even if she had cheated, it did not deserve a penalty of failure in the course.

Because of his unusual powers, Super-Principal knew what to do. The student had not planned to cheat, but she had seen answers on her neighbor's test paper inadvertently and used the information to improve her performance. She was not an habitual cheater. She was a good student customarily, self-reliant and trustworthy. The teacher was inclined to be quick on the trigger and at the conference was privately wishing that he had not gone so far with his threat of failure. Super-Principal calmed the troubled adversaries and soothed their hurt feelings. He acknowledged their differing perceptions of the incident. He explained how the teacher must act upon what he believes has happened in his class. After all, the teacher is not a mind reader. He showed the girl why her actions had aroused the teacher's suspicions. He took the teacher off the hook by suggesting that he consider failing the student for the questionable examination only and not for the term. He cautioned the student about her suspicious actions. All were relieved. Super-Principal's objective approach and sense of fairness impressed the antagonists. They were relieved.

The student was penitent. The teacher felt the principal's support. The conference closed; the participants exited; and after a moment's privacy, Super-Principal became Mark Grant, principal once again.

* * * * * *

The school's homecoming activities were reaching a climax as the week wore on. Students and faculty were building up spirit, making plans for the big weekend and the big game. The only thing that was in question was the team's chances of winning the game. The confidence was not there. The team's tradition was a losing one. The coaches were inclined to make excuses. The morale of the team was shaky. Their attitude seemed to be that they always needed a big break, but it never came.

Mark Grant, reflecting on how much a victory in the big game would revitalize the spirit of the school, unify the student body, bring pride and a sense of accomplishment to the entire community, decided that this was a task for Super-Principal. It would take his unique ability of hypnotic suggestion to bring about the needed transformation in the outlook and performance of the team — and the coaches.

The time for intervention was a problem. Would the coaches consent to have the principal join them in the locker room before the game? Having the principal speak to the players formally before the game was unprecedented. It might not be acceptable. It was Super-Principal, not Mark Grant, who approached the coach on Friday and asked him if he would mind if the principal addressed the team for a few minutes before the homecoming game. The coach was agreeable. He was even grateful. *His* anticipation began to heighten for the game.

Super-Principal joined the team in the locker room after they suited up, waiting for their final instructions and their pre-game "pep" talk. Super-Principal was appalled at the apathy. The players seemed stunned and defeated before the game began. Some actually appeared frightened. Others were bored, hardly prepared for a maximum effort.

The coach introduced Mr. Grant (Super-Principal) rather perfunctorily, saying he had asked to have a few words with the team before the game. It was Super-Principal who stepped forward and before saying a word, looked intently into the eyes of every player and every coach. The players sensed that something unusual was happening. They raised their heads to meet Super-Principal's eyes. They sat up straighter. Their muscles tensed in a state of readiness. Not a word had been spoken. Every eye and ear was prepared for Super-Principal's "few words." The words came easily and quietly. They flowed through the room, soothing, but electrifying. The players were spellbound. Super-Principal spoke of their preparation, of their determination, of the necessity for a supreme effort, of their individual and collective challenge, of the satisfaction of doing one's best. He transmitted the confidence he had in their ability to defeat their opponent. He described how they would achieve the victory. They hung on his words; they began to respond — to move inwardly. He built their rapport as a team. He asked each one to look into the eyes of his team mates and join each one in a spirit of determination and will to win. It was no ordinary locker room pep talk. The team was transformed. They knew what to do. They knew they could win — would win.

It was Super-Principal who watched from the stands, sure that he had accomplished his task, but ready to join the team at half time if he was needed. He was not. The team won its biggest victory of all time — thanks to the persuasive hypnotic power of Super-Principal.

* * * * * *

Mark Grant was pondering what he should do about Miss Bellicose. It was a serious dilemma. The complaints about her from students and parents were escalating. He knew that there must be some foundation for their reports, that they complained that she was sarcastic, unreasonable, demanding, unsympathetic. She was inclined, they said, to put students down, to degrade them, to threaten, to humiliate them. She was unwilling to provide help. Her attitude was, "Here is the material; it's your responsibility to learn it." Some students went so far as to say she was emotionally ill, that her meanness and insensitivity was a fairly recent personality change.

Mark Grant and the department chairman had each visited Miss B twice during the preceding month. They both visited the class from which most of the complaints came. They saw none of the behavior students had reported. Miss B was virtually a model of thoroughness, good organization, fairness, and concern. They could find no fault with her teaching performance and saw no evidence of her failings. Three students came together the day following one visit and told Mark Grant that Miss B had really put on a show when he visited her — that she really had her controls on and that the class he observed was far from typical of her recent behavior.

Mark Grant received calls from parents whom he knew and trusted, whose children, whom the parents trusted, assured them that Miss B's behavior was getting more bizarre by the day. Mark Grant called Miss B to his office and told her of the complaints and the severity of the charges. Miss B was shocked and hurt. She absolutely and categorically denied that she was guilty of any of the abuses students had described. She assured Mark Grant of her interest in her students, of her dedication to the teaching profession, of her loyalty to the school and its principal. She asked him to come and see for himself. He reassured her that in his recent visits he had not observed any of the behavior students had described.

He began to wonder if the students, for some unknown reason, had conspired to engage in some cruel joke on Miss B.

Mark Graant was deeply concerned, worried for the welfare of the children and for the health of Miss B. He was prohibited from observing Miss B secretly or from using any electronic devices to monitor her classes. There seemed to be only one way to find the truth. Mark Grant closed his office, arranged for his privacy, and donned the gray vest of Super-Principal. Only then could he, with his extraordinary power to see and hear through any barrier, observe poor Miss B at her natural (or unnatural) self.

Super-Principal stood inconspicuously in the hallway across Miss B's classroom . Her students entered and took their places. His first clue that all was not as Miss B had pretended occurred as she called roll and found Bill absent. She remarked, "I suppose that hop-head is stoned out of his mind downstairs in the john?" Super-Principal did not have to watch and listen too much longer. The students' worst complaints were true. Miss B was, in fact, experiencing severe personality problems. All of her worst feelings and prejudices were openly expressed. She was on the verge of breaking. He observed physical signs of emotional collapse.

Mark Grant brought Miss B to the privacy of his office at his first opportunity where he quietly and firmly told her he was relieving her of her duties until she could rest and seek professional help and recover her good abilities as a teacher. Miss B was relieved and thankful. The tension lifted. She confessed that she could not understand, explain, or control her own behavior. She recognized that Mark Grant had saved her from professional disgrace, that he had saved her students from her vagaries. Super-Principal once again had saved the day.

* * * * * *

Mark Grant was not looking forward to a meeting of dissident students and their indulgent parents scheduled for that evening. This would be his third meeting, his third effort to try to understand their feelings, to get a handle on their complaints. He had not been able to ascertain their motives or to appreciate their personalities. He knew that their thinking was vague and confused. As he tried to clarify and to close on their ideas, the ground for their arguments shifted and discussions deteriorated into disorganized ramblings and redundancies.

The impression he had was that the students and parents only knew that they were unhappy, "turned off" by the usual educational activities, and seemed to enjoy being discontented. He had no idea what an acceptable, satisfying alternative would be.

Mark Grant went to the meeting as Super-Principal, knowing that he would need more than the ordinary knowledge, communication skills, and perceptivity. As Super-Principal his knowledge was encyclopedic, his analytical ability keen and accurate, his skill for synthesis and planning infallible.

The group assembled as usual, dour and complaining. They were an unhappy, confused assemblage, feeding on each other's most negative experiences. The most vocal ones took off in their usual style, carping and criticizing. Super-Principal knew it would take a miracle to cut through the hostility, the unreality, the neurotic ramblings of this group's thinking. He decided he had better perform one.

Building on his superior knowledge of all the creative educational thinkers from John Dewey to James Coleman and of all the White House Conferences and Kettering Commissions, he quickly reviewed his copious knowledge of learning styles and educational psychology. He drew upon the sound research that was applicable to this time and circumstances. Super-Principal stepped to the chalkboard and began a presentation of brilliant rationale for a series of educational alternatives that went to the very heart of the disenchantment. He built the program on sound, articulate, measurable instructional objectives. He described the format, the method, the teaching materials. He cut through red tape and bureaucracy to streamline an organization that assured accountability. After an hour of amplification on his ideas, the eyes in the group lit up with understanding, the heads began to nod in assent. The troubled visages relaxed. The hearts warmed to an educational innovation that all could support and help implement. Every person present could see where he or she would fit in. Everyone had a meaningful piece of the action.

Super-Principal returned to his office to record the substance of his creation which would await the time for presentation and acceptance by the governing board. He made his way home, relaxed, and somewhat weary, but fulfilled.

* * * * * *

A school principal's role seldom calls for the physical strength and agility of Super-Principal, but Mark Grant did find his unlimited endurance, his invulnerability, his flashing speed (faster than a speeding bullet) to be most useful on rare occasions. On all occasions which might conceivably call for his super strength and speed, Mark Grant donned his miraculous undervest as an act of preparedness.

It was a fire alarm, an occasion for the utmost alertness and preparation. It was Super-Principal who slipped out of his office door, notified the security staff, quickly scanned the monitoring system, and took his station by the main entrance where he could supervise the evacuation. Students and teachers were leaving in their usual brisk, orderly fashion. The evacuation was complete in less than three minutes, as Super-Principal received the all-clear signals from his staff members. He walked to the entrance to observe the fire equipment arrive since this *was* an emergency and the direct signal to the fire station brought the local fireman and equipment to the scene. Super-Principal heard the sirens and stepped out on the front steps to direct the firemen to the area of the alarm.

As he saw the hook and ladder truck come down the steet, he sensed that the driver was having some difficulty. The huge truck was traveling too fast. As it approached the school driveway, he could see that it would negotiate the corner. Instead the cumbersome vehicle careened wildly, bumped violently over the curb, losing two of the firemen riding on the ladder trailer. The red mass of steel, hoses and ladders headed straight across the front campus where the students had assembled clear of the building and the driveway. No one saw the flash of action that was Super-Principal racing to the truck in a split second, leaping to the driver's seat, and miraculously bringing the huge behemoth under control just before it reached the screaming students. Fortunately, as Super-Principal, he was able to disappear from the scene.

The confused driver never could coherently relate what had happened, either when he blacked out as he neared the school or how the hook and ladder truck was halted just before crashing and crushing into the helpless students. The mystery was never solved. Super-Principal returned to his school to marvel with the others about the fortuitous circumstances that had saved the lives of his students.

******

Mark Grant used his marvelous talents wisely. In all times of need for super-human talents and insights, so often called for from modern-day principals, he was careful to use his unusual powers only in behalf of his students' welfare — or as he saw it — in the "unending battle for truth, justice, and the American Way."

The Head Nut,
or Reflections on School Leadership

Roland S. Barth

As a school principal, Roland S. Barth has had ample opportunity to experience leadership at first-hand. In this meditative, often eloquent, essay, he attempts to define for us what leading a school really means. "All too many schools . . . ," says Barth, "are characterized by high anxiety and low productivity . . . Leadership for me is attempting to establish within a school conditions of low anxiety and high productivity." I think readers will find his examination of the quality of leadership both thoughtful and original. Roland S. Barth is a Lecturer in the Harvard School of Education and is the author of "Run, School, Run," published by Harvard University Press.

"The Head Nut, or Reflections on School Leadership" by Roland S. Barth. From *Run School Run*, Harvard University Press, Cambridge, Massachusetts, 1980. Copyright © 1979 by the author. Reprinted by permission.

I was once asked to describe how I provide leadership as a school principal. The question surprised — and disturbed — me. It was at once a very obvious, very difficult, and very personal query, and one to which I didn't respond well at the time. But I've thought about leadership a good deal since, and I'd like to try again to answer that important question.

There are many theories of leadership, complex models by which outsiders explain the inner workings of complex organizations. In concrete situations, however, I find that leadership arises from the interaction between a person and a context. It is different every time; seldom does it fit a particular model. Ultimately, I believe, leadership is best defined not by the leader, but by those the leader attempts to lead. Leadership is in the eyes of the led. A principal's firm, decisive formulation of rules for playground behavior, for example, will seem a courageous act of leadership to some, but others may see the same judgment as autocratic or even tyrannical. There is nothing inherent in a decision that qualifies it as an act of leadership or a lack of leadership.

– 11 –

WORKING FOR INDIVIDUALIZATION

All of us attempt to be democratic. In practice, that usually means trying to provide equitable treatment or opportunity for everyone. Unfortunately, such a goal makes us preoccupied with a search for uniform policies that will work for everyone. When we find something that looks like such a policy, we engrave it in stone. I find the quest for a way that works for all teachers or all parents in a school no more realistic than a quest for a way that works for all children in a class. The only difference is that children are more likely to submit than adults. Group solution of individual problems leads to grouptalk and groupthink, to passive compliance and active resentment. Attempts to lead by achieving consensus may result in a majority of tired hands raised above tired heads late in an afternoon faculty meeting, but when everyone reappears in the morning, little remains of that consensus beyond a vote recorded in the minutes. Proceeding as if lasting agreement exists on such a tenuous basis I find both hazardous and foolish.

For me, leadership has been a process of individualization rather than collectivization. If agreement genuinely emerges from discussions and debates, I will acknowledge it — in fact, I will delight in it. But I prefer to assume there is no consensus on *anything* in a school, that each individual sees the world through a unique "Swiss cheese," and the holes in one person's Swiss cheese line up with the holes in someone else's about as often as the planets are aligned. Occasionally, I am pleasantly surprised; I am seldom disappointed. It was four years before I called for a vote in a faculty meeting. The issue was coffee. The result: some teachers wanted a common pot, some a machine; others wanted to bring in instant coffee, tea, or soup and wanted only hot water. And still others argued that coffee and tea were malnutritious drugs and should not be allowed in schools. Teachers' feelings about education are at least as disparate as their feelings about coffee!

I think schools function better when we minimize rather than maximize the search for unanimity. Rather than finding or creating consensus, I derive greater satisfaction and success from constantly talking with individual teachers to find out what each needs — and how close I can come to fulfilling those needs. One teacher may want a principal to produce authoritarian efficiency and mandate clear rules and procedures. Another needs support for his or her own innovations with no interference. When I must make a general decision, I do it in a careful, limited fashion, in a way that will affect as few, not as many, as possible. For me, then, leadership is a constant search for the unique conditions under which each person best works, learns, and grows, and for the means — within my own limits and the limits of the school system — to provide those conditions.

LEARNING WHICH PROBLEMS ARE PROBLEMS

I used to lament, "If only someone would take care of all these intrusive demands of the job — memos, budgets, parents, discipline — then I could be a great principal." But I gradually realized I was acting like the teacher who moans, "If only someone would remove all the troubled, troublesome children from my class, I'd be a great teacher." In both cases, the supposed obstacles to performing the job *are* the job. They represent not a barrier, but the means, the occasion for exercising good teaching and good administration. The task is to somehow come to terms with these difficult elements of the job and sort them out, not to pretend one can eliminate them.

I remember when we first bought our rambling, running-down farm in Maine. We felt overwhelmed by the number of problems and tasks demanding immediate attention. We worked frantically, finding neither much fun nor much success. But over the years, I have discovered a taxonomy of difficulties. A few problems go away if left alone (the irregular line of stone posts supporting the shed evened up after the spring frost heave); some remain but don't get worse (the ugly asphalt shingles someone nailed on the end of the barn), and some at first scream for repair, but gradually become all but invisible as you get used to them (the cracks in the plaster of most of the ceilings in the house).

Some problems, on the other hand, present growing uncertainties, like a portion of the stone foundation in the cellar that buckles inward at a cataclysmic angle. I remember fifteen years ago predicting that the wall would collapse at any minute and bring the house down with it. To date, however, there has been no shift in either wall or house. I have discovered that the house sits on a generous 10" x 10" sill supported, in turn, by a large, intact section of granite wall, testimony to the over-kill with which nineteenth-century craftsmen constructed their buildings. I have come to accept the advice of the elderly native who, giving the threatening wall a kick, muttered, "If it falls in, then you can fix it." Indeed, why spend a month working on a wall that may not need attention during my lifetime? Why risk creating new problems, like rupturing the sewage line that passes through the wall? This kind of analysis of problems leaves time and energy to attend to the real crises, the ones that *will* get worse if you leave them alone (the major leak in the barn roof is one).

Like managing an old farm, I find leading a school is knowing — or guessing — which problems are which, learning to ignore the "maybe" problems and the cosmetic problems so we can come to terms with those that will grow more severe if we wait. In some ways a school is a fragile house of cards, but I generally find healthy institutions as resilient as healthy people, and just as capable of dealing with difficulty. Most schools are protected with as much structural redundancy as an old farm house. They have a life of their own that does not depend on administrative coddling.

LEARNING TO WAIT

If we have learned anything about educational change over the years, it is that substantive, lasting change comes only with the personal growth of educators. Personal and institutional growth take time, and the waiting can be worthwhile. Even instability, friction, and conflict are worthwhile, as long as gorwth continues. We who work in schools need to have ideals, to keep our eyes on a star, but we also need the patience to ask not, "How far are we from the star?" which is a depressing and painful question, but rather, "How much closer are we to the star today than we were last week?" The incremental growth of individuals, while less dramatic than sudden institutional reform, is more satisfying and lasts longer.

REDUCING FEAR

Leardership for me is reducing fear so that those in the school may grow. No one learns well or works well under conditions of fear. Each of us has personal fears, fears that cannot be eliminated. But principals can reduce rather than contribute to the fears of others so they do not become debilitating. I'm learning there are incentives for improving teacher performance that are more desirable than fear. I'm learning when to be a conductor of information from the world outside and when to be an insulator, shielding teachers and students from pressures. By and large, I think it is essential for teachers to know what is going on. But do they need to know things that produce great anxiety and little benefit? Does it do a teacher any good to know that the central office is thinking about eliminating a teaching position? Does it help children learn to be told they will repeat fourth grade if they don't learn?

I know schools characterized by high productivity and high anxiety (elite preparatory schools, for instance); I know schools characterized by low productivity and low anxiety (many so-called free schools, for instance). All too many schools, of course, are characterized by high anxiety and low productivity, a losing combination all around. Leadership for me is attempting to establish within a school conditions of low anxiety and high producativity for both children and teachers.

SELECTIVE RISK TAKING

Leadership is learning to recognize risks in which the odds are good and the stakes are high. There are times when we must assume we have authority whether it has been explicitly bestowed on us or not. If we use responsibility successfully, the chances are we will not be challenged. If we don't, we've risked and lost.

Faced with accountability on all sides, principals frequently must choose between, on the one hand, taking risks that violate established policies in order to provide what we believe is good education for children and good working conditions for teachers; or, on the other hand, minimizing risks by becoming cautious, sometimes almost catatonic. The former course offers educational responsibility with the danger of legal irresponsibility; the latter offers legal responsibility at the expense of educational responsibility. Unfortunately, legal and educational responsibility are not always congruent.

Selective risk taking, then, is like working on an old car. I once asked a neighbor who was helping me rebuild the engine on a Model A how much I should tighten a head nut. "Stop a quarter-turn before you strip it," he said. That is an apt way to think about school administration. I want to stop a quarter of a turn before I strip the organizational nut. But of course, I've got to strip a few before I know my strength, the mechanical advantage of the wrench, and how much the nut can take. It's a while before I know exactly how far to turn. In the meantime, risks will be taken and nuts will be either too loose — or stripped. Schools are places where principals, too, can learn.

INDEPENDENCE AND INTERDEPENDENCE

And for me, perhaps above all else, leadership has meant independence and interdependence. We principals often find it difficult to delegate or to trust. But we can't do all, and we certainly can't do it all well. Just as important, if we try to do it all, then no one else gets a chance to do any of it. Leadership is recognizing teachers with strong leadership characteristics as future colleagues, rather than present threats, and sharing with them as much responsibility as we both can manage in the day-to-day running of the school. Enlisting teachers as leaders involves all of the elements discussed above — individualizing, waiting, reducing fear, and taking risks.

Most principals have in their bottom drawer a few marbles of power that come with their appointment and even more that they earn as time goes by. Some principals play these marbles alone — they determine what happens. Others don't play at all, making few decisions themselves and allowing others to make even fewer. I try to play all the marbles all the time. Sometimes I play by myself (when I evaluate teachers, for instance); some marbles I give to others to play (like the teachers who serve as the curriculum coordinators), and some I share with teachers (like disciplining children). None are left sitting around. I have found that in schools, any decision (even a bad one) is usually better than no decision at all.

I am finding that the alternative to centralized, authoritarian control is not anarchy but cooperation. Giving everyone an opportunity to make decisions affecting everyone else promotes faculty interdependence. Administrators and teachers alike often suffer from loneliness and isolation. Many tasks in schools these days — helping disturbed children, coordinating curriculum, evaluating pupils — are too big, too complex, and too frightening for any one person to deal with. If we are to address these tasks, we must collaborate. Members of a staff need not agree about all problems or solutions, but we can accept, respect, and care about one another; we can help each other work out solutions. A cartoon I once saw showed two fishermen in a sinking dory, one saying to the other, "I'm sure glad the leak's in *your* end of the boat." Leadership for me has meant trying to move the adults in the school away from that kind of detachment and indifference and toward the realization that we're all in the same boat together.

By and large, I find teachers prefer the risks and problems of independence and interdependence to those that come with isolation and patriarchal dependency. Participating in the instructional and management decisions of the school encourages teachers to take pedagogical stands and to come to terms with major educational issues. In the process, they become more conscious of their own ideals about children and learning. These beliefs pay off when translated into classroom practice. With responsibility comes active adulthood — something many never find in their work. And, perhaps most important, I have seen considerable evidence that teachers who become the agents of their own teaching can better help children become agents of their own learning. Responsibility, once shared and accepted, creates endless ripple effects within a school.

Among those ripples are personal and professional rewards for the principal. I have discovered that one can be advisor as well as supervisor; colleague as well as superordinate; supporter as well as adversary; provider as well as requirer. Acting and reacting in this way breaks down the rigid role-stereotypes that normally limit school realtionships. Indeed, I find less risk in sharing responsibility than in not sharing it, since those who participate in joint decisions care about and are willing to work for and defend the outcomes as much as I. In many respects, in fact, principals do not really posses power *until* they share it. Only by engaging teachers, counselors, and parents in the decisions to assign children to particular classes, for instance, can I have a powerful influence on the placement of children. Were I to attempt to place children by myself, the decisions would be neither thoughtful nor lasting. I think that by worrying less about control, we can often gain more real influence on a school than do those who attempt to influence by controlling.

In a school where the faculty is vitally concerned with the outcomes of decisions, where teachers work cooperatively more often than competitively, the life of a principal can even be enjoyable. I get my greatest enjoyment out of good things that happen without me, for example, when two sixth-grade teachers decide to take their classes on a field trip to Philadelphia for several days and make all the arrangements themselves. I'm intrigued by how little of me is necessary these days, not in terms of hours per week, but in terms of monitoring teachers, children, and parents. I have my share of horrendous days, but generally I'm finding things are going better and better with less and less direction from me.

Still, I don't feel superfluous. I can be a bit more thoughtful, reflective, and in control of my own behavior when I don't feel I have to control everybody else's. I can work on "orchestrating" the school. I can develop different ways of responding to different people. I can be accessible to teachers, to parents, to children. And I can identify and react quickly to situations in the school that, like the leak in the barn roof, will turn into disasters if not attended to immediately.

******

What is leadership for me? It is personal, idiosyncratic. It is not a planned way of behaving; it is different ways of responding to different people. It is risk taking, but checking the odds for success before you take the risk. It is supporting people. It is accessibility. It is the process of individualizing contacts. It is learning how to be firm and clear in expressing expectations; learning how to react quickly to situations in the school of which I disapprove or problems that will get worse if nothing is done. Leadership is learning how to share responsibility for decisions, and determining who should be included in those decisions. It's validating my perceptions with others and developing trust in their perceptions. It's being consistent in actions and statements so people realize I mean what I say. Leadership is learning that teachers hold much of the power that ultimately makes a school succeed or fail. Leadership is relinquishing control so their creative powers may be released. Leadership is trying to look freshly at every problem as it comes up and searching afresh for solutions. And finally, leadership is trying to keep your head in the clouds, your feet on the ground, and hoping like hell that it all works.

The Principal and Instructional Supervision: A Dialogue

Robert J. Krajewski, with Robert H. Anderson and Ben M. Harris

In this dialogue, Robert J. Krajewski, Alumni Associate Professor of Educational Administration at Auburn University, Auburn, Alabama, discusses the role of the principal as supervisor of instruction with Robert H. Anderson, Dean of Education at Texas Tech University, Lubbock, and Ben M. Harris, Professor of Educational Administration at the University of Texas, Austin. In the course of the dialogue, Professor Krajewski gives the results of a survey he conducted among elementary school principals and teachers in Texas and Tennessee and discusses differences in perception concerning the principal's functions. His discussion with Dean Anderson and Professor Harris centers on such issues as subjective evaluation, ways of enhancing observational and supervisory skills, the meaning of "clinical supervision," and the value of pre-service and in-service programs in upgrading both instruction and supervision. "Principals and teachers alike," says Krajewski, "should be the key for instructional improvement, but both may not accept that role in reality."

Instructional leader, personnel administrator, plant manager — role expectations are thrust on the principal from all sectors, public and private, in school and out, and each group considers its demands more important than any others. The National Elementary Principal's 1974 series on remaking the principalship and its 1977 and 1978 updates on the principalship have offered valuable insights on the elementary school principal's duties and responsibilities. Articles in those issues describe the principal's part in the improvement of instruction as crucial, yet it is by no means clear to many principals just how that role is to be played. A particularly vital question stands out: Where does instructional supervision fit into the principal's repertoire?

Challenged by Paul Houts's suggestion that practitioners themselves should help shape the multiplicity of functions that compose their role.[1] I surveyed principals and teachers in two states to find out how they viewed the principalship — both real and ideal.[2] The results of those surveys formed the springboard for the following dialogue with two leaders in the field of instructional supervision: Robert H. Anderson, dean of education at Texas Tech University in Lubbock, and Ben M. Harris, professor of educational administration at the University of Texas, Austin. Our discussion began with a general look at the elementary school principal's role and led to some specific ways that principals can best use the techniques of instructional supervision.

******

KRAJEWSKI: Is it possible to describe the typical elementary school principal?

ANDERSON: Probably not. For one thing, principals carve out their jobs in varied manners — in the ways they relate to teachers and to their communities, in the values they hold, in the priorities they set, and in the styles of leadership they use. One can find marvelous behavioral extremes even within the same city. In some schools the principals are curriculum leaders; in others their role is about the same as that of a Woolworth store manager. I suspect that it is possible, on the other hand, for us to describe the ideal principal. We all have our own definitions, but if you read the literature and listen to educators' discussions, you get the idea that above all else, the principal is ideally an instructional leader.

HARRIS: I certainly agree with that. Several other roles are becoming increasingly suspect, in particular the principal as "building manager" and the principal as "good guy." Neither of these images — and there are others, I'm sure — characterizes an instructional leader.

ANDERSON: The fact is that no principal has time in the school day to accomplish all the things people ordinarily say should be done. I constantly hear complaints from principals that role management tends to be especially time consuming — particularly so when you have to compile seemingly endless data on Title I programs and the like; when the central office makes constant demands on you; and when school bond issues and programs are threatened by back-to-basics ideas. Sometimes even the best intentioned principals and those who budget their time most carefully find that when a week is up, they have been able to devote less time than they really wanted to certain responsibilities. Thus, principals, like everyone else, have to make value judgments about their various duties. If they're not comfortable in the role of instructional leader, they can become ardent building managers; and if they're not comfortable working with teachers, they can become good pals with students, parents, or PTA leaders.

HARRIS: It's not enough simply to value instructional supervision.

Unless the principal has supervisory skills and competencies, that valuing will produce only lip service. The sad thing is that too many principals don't find the time for classroom supervision.

KRAJEWSKI. Although the delementary principal does, in fact, have certain competencies, pressures from such groups as the PTA, community, superintendents, and teachers may dictate that those competencies are not well used in the principalship. Are elementary school principals really what they think they are?

HARRIS: Yes, to a large extent they really are what they think they are. What worries me more is that they are not quite sure whether they *ought* to be what they are. Maybe that's important, that the person in the role really dictates the role to a large extent. Needs, expectations, and communities are different, but the principal's own role perception is one of the dominant elements.

KRAJEWSKI. Well, the principal sets the tone for the entire school and greatly influences the climate for improving instruction. I'm somewhat perplexed, though, about the principal's present role in instructional improvement. To get a realistic understanding of that role, I conducted a limited survey among elementary school principals and teachers in two states (Tennessee and Texas). The questionnaire listed ten role functions, and respondents were asked to rank order those functions both in terms of actual practice and in terms of the "ideal" principal. Interestingly, teachers and principals agreed on the top three and the bottom three, though their order of preference differed slightly in some cases. The chart shows the results of their rankings.

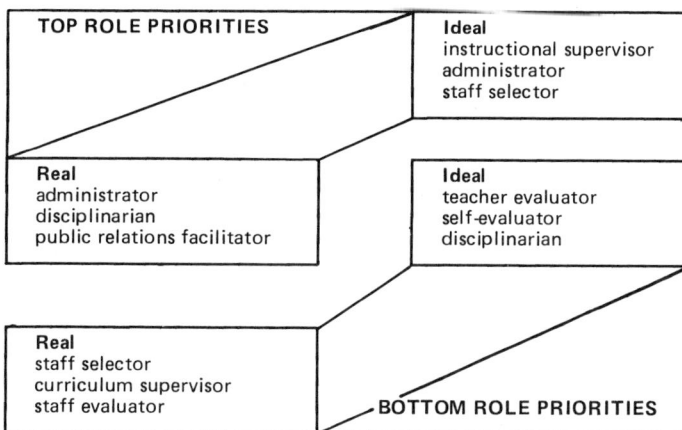

TOP ROLE PRIORITIES

Ideal
instructional supervisor
administrator
staff selector

Real
administrator
disciplinarian
public relations facilitator

Ideal
teacher evaluator
self-evaluator
disciplinarian

Real
staff selector
curriculum supervisor
staff evaluator

BOTTOM ROLE PRIORITIES

ANDERSON: From the chart, it's evident that teachers and principals both view the elementary principal as a school administrator first and foremost. Although they believe instructional supervision ought to be the principal's primary goal, administration maintains a significant top-ranking position in the ideal role.

KRAJEWSKI: In other words, teachers and principals both realize the need for adequate administration in the school.

ANDERSON: In one important aspect, then — the administrative function — the real role of today's principals matches the ideal. But what about the other functions shown in the chart that do vary greatly between the real and ideal?

HARRIS: Discipline is one. In the real role of the principal, it is ranked second, yet it is ranked last in the ideal role. More emphasis should be placed on teachers and principals working together on a collegial level, rather than on students and teachers making the principal out to be a police officer or a judge.

KRAJEWSKI: New teachers especially seem to fear the principal and try to avoid being observed in the classroom — like the student who pictures the principal's office only as a disciplinary room where punishments are meted out.

ANDERSON: Because of these fears, it's difficult for the principal to act as a supervisor trying to improve instruction in the school.

HARRIS: The same can be said of teacher evaluation, which is placed at the bottom of the ideal list. Teachers and principals are obviously sensitive about getting or giving evaluations. I don't think they realize that without some teacher evaluation, instructional supervision (their first ideal role) could not be achieved to any significant degree.

KRAJEWSKI: In the past, teachers have reacted rather negatively to evaluation, and principals realize they must use methods of evaluation that help create a climate of cooperation in their efforts to improve instruction.

ANDERSON: Self-evaluation is somewhat similar. Like teacher evaluation, it's rated among the lowest priorities of an ideal principal's role, but instructional supervision indirectly encompasses, or should encompass, both. What teachers and principals are saying by ranking teacher evaluation and self-evaluation at the bottom of the ideal role, I think, is that evaluation can be accomplished without written reports or tests, within certain defined limits. The teacher and principal should feel somewhat at ease with each other, only then can a cooperative climate be produced. Teacher evaluation and self-evaluation are important for the growth of the individual in meeting the instructional goals established by the principal or school district. But the manner in which the goals are obtained is just as important.

KRAJEWSKI: That makes sense, but school boards today will demand that the principal complete various evaluation forms and tests on each teacher. It will be difficult to break away from these traditional methods and all the paperwork they involve.

HARRIS: What is obviously lacking is the understanding that evaluation (in any form) is nothing to be feared; it's only a way to help teachers and principals reach their common goal — better communication and improved instruction for children. But better preservice and inservice programs can help by showing principals and teachers what is expected of them if they are to perform their given roles correctly. Then they will no longer see evaluation as a threat, but as a chance for improvement.

ANDERSON: That's one of our greatest problems. Training programs in supervision have been too nonparticipatory in nature, too abstract — just sitting around a table talking instead of actually getting into the classroom and supervising real people, or at least having a simulated supervision experience. Even curriculum requirements for administrators' certificates underplay the supervisory function so that principals receive too few credit hours of training in this all-important activity. That's one problem; another is that principals are former teachers themselves and have built-in negative feelings about being in the classroom and bothering the teacher — a tradition of resistance with which even the principal is somewhat sympathetic.

KRAJEWSKI. In other words, principals and teachers alike know that the principal should be the key for instructional improvement but both may not accept that role in reality.

HARRIS: It's an area where potential conflicts exist and where human relations skills become very demanding. How do I as a principal sit down eyeball-to-eyeball with teachers I respect and appreciate in many ways when, having been in their classrooms and watched them in action, I realize they have some real needs for further professional growth? The challenge is to face these teachers in a constructive manner with the fact that, as good as they are and as much merit as there is in what they're doing, there's still improvement to be made. If I evaluate them, in other words, it will be to improve instruction.

ANDERSON: It's a delicate area of supervision. No one will question the need for evaluation teachers, but there's always the danger that evaluation can damage the principal's normal role of helping teachers.

HARRIS: It's not only delicate, it's really a policy issue. Teacher evaluation is used as the basis for continuing a teacher's contract or dismissing the teacher. But it's not conceived or even designed as a vehicle for improving instruction, and as a result, principals become drustrated in their efforts to be effective supervisors.

KRAJEWSKI: That goes back to what you said before, Ben. If the principal questions going into the classroom to work with a teacher for instructional or curricular improvement, recognizing the teacher's skill but recognizing also that improvement is needed, how will the teacher see the principal's role? As evaluation or instructional improvement?

ANDERSON: Well, for one thing, if principals are in the classroom routinely, they shouldn't have to make a special visit to fill out an evaluation form.

HARRIS: Let me elaborate on that. When principals are intimately involved in instructional improvement, they are in classrooms routinely enough to be recognized and appreciated by the teacher as stimulators of professional growth. Good instructional supervision demands a kind of teacher evaluation that includes classroom observation and analysis of data, but it's quite different from the kind of evaluation we traditionally think about in terms of hiring and firing teachers.

ANDERSON: When you stop to think about it, the principal who is asked to decide whether teachers should be retained or fired without having spent much time in their classrooms must make the decision on subjective bases, such as informal conversations in the lunchroom or outside the building, social meetings, and the petty chitchat that goes on behind every teacher's back. If I were a teacher, I'd be angry at having such vital decisions made on the basis of irrelevant and inconsequential bits of information.

KRAJEWSKI: For such teachers, then, determining the principal's role is even more difficult. If the principal is to work with them for instructional improvement but the work turns into a subjective evaluation session, they naturally become suspicious.

HARRIS: Yes, given that kind of practice (and I'm afraid it's still all too common), it's understandable that the teacher feels uncomfortable in a close working relationship with the principal. But I think principals *should* — and in some schools do — work closely with teachers for instructional improvement.

ANDERSON: Which leads to an interesting question. Is it possible for a principal who spends a lot of time in classrooms to neglect anything that really matters?

HARRIS: That raises an important point. One of the complaints I hear from most groups of principals I work with — especially when I suggest the need to be systematic classroom observers and to work closely with teachers — is, "How do we find the time to do that with all the other demands on us?" I suppose all professional people have too many demands on them, but everybody has to make choices.

ANDERSON: In the university world, you and I have the same problem. In my role as dean, I engage in what I might call a kind of selective neglect. That is, there are some things I probably should be doing that I choose not to do, because I am too busy doing the things that really matter to me.

KRAJEWSKI: If you want to be an instructional supervisor, you have to budget the time for it. And that leads to another question. Suppose that principals really want to get into the classroom and work on instructional improvement but don't have the requisite skills. What kind of preservice and inservice programs are available to them?

ANDERSON: There are various ways of acquiring and enhancing skills, which include reading the professional literature, working with supervisors, and in some cases, asking the teachers themselves. You don't always have to go to a university for a course in supervision; actually working with a real teacher whose behavior is your raw material and then seeing how you react to that material and what you can do with it can be intellectually exciting. Internship is a favored method of preservice training, but it should be combined with group learning. For example, Riverside High School in California conducted a preservice internship program for teachers interested in supervision and the principalship, which consisted of fifteen evening meetings, a two-day retreat, and various other studies. The groups were led by district administrators and supervisors, and teachers were given text materials and research assignments.[3] This type of program, which included visits to other schools, is excellent preservice work for principals who want to acquire skills in instructional supervision.

HARRIS: I think we need to emphasize that the best preparation programs must begin with trainable people. In the past, we have been accused of packing our programs with unqualified people to fill the demand. Today with supply far above demand, we should look for quality, not quantity, and then build our training programs around the needs of the principal as instructional supervisor.

KRAJEWSKI: One encouraging trend in inservice training is the involvement of private organizations and professional associations at both the state and the national levels. It seems to me, too, that there is sufficient literature available.

ANDERSON: If I may say so, Ben's book on supervision is a fine contribution to the literature.[4] Principals should also look at the work of Morris Cogan, at Robert Goldhammer's marvelous book, and at two or three others.[5] The principal who really wants to learn instructional supervision skills has only to join with two or three other principals or people from the central office who have a similar need, and then they can learn together. In fact, if I were a superintendent of schools, I'd want all the members of the central staff who don't have an obvious instructional role (like the business manager) to demonstrate to me that, during the previous academic year, they had in some significant way helped principals acquire better instructional leadership skills.

HARRIS: In other words, the central office staff should see that it is as much their responsibility to help principals grow on the job as to help teachers.

KRAJEWSKI. That idea is gaining widespread acceptance. Last spring, as a member of an ASCD working group on the roles and responsibilities of instructional supervisors, I held telephone interviews with the executive directors and selected members of various educational groups, plus a number of professors of curriculum. When I asked them to specify the activities involved in instructional supervision, forty-nine of the sixty-three they proffered involved the techniques and practices of clinical supervision. The diagnosis and mediation of classroom interaction, the focus on microteaching behaviors, and the development of the counseling process for improving instruction are the bases for conducting these activities. The people I talked to were convinced that this interaction among people is central to the success of the learning process. They agreed that clinical supervision is the process through which the instructional supervisor gains insight into the quality of this interaction.

HARRIS: It occurs to me that we haven't yet defined clinical supervision. Obviously, we're not talking about the entire instructional improvement proces, because we can improve instruction in many ways. I think of clinical supervision as a very personalized process. It involves observing systematically in the classroom, sitting down with the teacher and analyzing the information that has been gathered, and then trying to help the teacher rethink what is going on and replan for something better. Is that essentially what you mean when you use the term?

ANDERSON: Yes, but I find myself wondering why we use the adjective clinical. I guess we mean much the same thing as the medical people mean when they talk of clinical practice: the work is done outside the laboratory, with real people. It's not simply theoretical or hypothetical. Real children are involved; they are being taught by a real teacher, and the supervisor in that setting is, in effect, in the clinic watching the practitioner practice.

KRAJEWSKI: Right. The relationship of the clinical supervisor and the teacher is face to face, sitting down and working together, looking at lesson objectives, observing the lesson, analyzing what took place, and then working toward improvement.

ANDERSON: Ideally, all of that happens continuously over a period of time, so that a clinical history is built up. The teacher and the clinical supervisor can refer to that history as they look at today's instruction and try to figure out what progress has been made since yesterday.

HARRIS: We should keep in mind that there are other kinds of people and resources involved in instructional improvement that are not ordinarily associated with clinical supervision but may be very important to its success. For example, it's sometimes necessary for a teacher to have new kinds of experiences not gained readily within the confines of that building, classroom, or group of students. A central office consultant (supervisor or coordinator) may be exactly the person to arrange such experiences for the teacher; for example, a demonstration the principal isn't necessarily qualified to present, a visit to another school to observe other teachers in action, or attendance at a skill-building workshop where a whole group has a common interest. So let's keep the adjective clinical, because there's much more to instructional supervision than the limited but very important elements of a clinical supervisory cycle.

ANDERSON: Now, *training* in clinical supervision ought also to be (at least to a great extent) in a real setting where real kids are being taught by real professionals. But some clinical training can be done with videotapes and other kinds of behavioral recordings. Microteaching and other training approaches are also available to us, but the payoff is when the principal who has been trained in clinical supervision is in the classroom actually using the skills to help the teacher do a better job.

KRAJEWSKI: In fact, principals can develop skills for clinical supervision by practicing microteaching at their own school. They can pick five or so students, teach them in a microteaching situation, and ask someone else to apply the techniques of clinical supervision to them as teachers. In this way the principals can learn more about the teacher's role in the observation process and later apply that knowledge effectively in supervision. It's a team effort.

ANDERSON: That's true. The more teachers acquire observation skills, the more possible it will be for them to supervise each other. But unfortunately, I seldom go into a school without feeling that the people in it have a lot more to offer, both to the kids and to each other, than they're actually giving. Most of the time, I believe that's because the principal hasn't really established the kind of open climate that inspires people to exchange criticisms and helpful comments.

HARRIS: The climate is really crucial. One important factor is the way schools are organized into watertight compartments called classrooms. With more open kinds of instructional arrangements — team teaching and the like — there's a much better basis for the principal to establish a favorable climate.

KRAJEWSKI: In an open situation, transferring the center of attention from the teacher to the students gives the students more input and lets the teacher be a sort of supervisor of what's going on in the classroom. As a result, when it comes time for peer observation, the teacher can be more objective, less defensive and not as emotionally involved.

ANDERSON: Do teachers and principals who get actively involved in clinical supervision get bruised more often than those who don't? I wonder about the penalties and the risks involved.

HARRIS: I think it's definitely worth both the risk and the price. One of the most devastating things in the lives of many teachers is never getting any real feedback on what they're doing and how they might go about doing it better. That's a big price to pay. On the other hand, I don't think we ought to underestimate the cutting edge in the clinical situation. We're always pushing and pulling and coaxing people to move out beyond where they are — otherwise there's no point in it. They are going to stumble and fall sometimes, make mistakes, and get bruised.

KRAJEWSKI: Those bruises might simply be superficial, while the bruises we suffer by not delving into clinical supervision and by not going into "what am I doing" and "why am I doing it" are internal, and they probably hurt much more. When you see the joyous looks on the faces of children when they feel they've learned something, when they come up to you and say, "Look what I've done," then you realize how important that extra effort was and it makes you feel good, too.

NOTES

1. Paul L. Houts, "The Remaking of the Principalship," *National Elementary Principal* 53 (March/April 1974): 7.

2. For more detailed reports of the findings, see Robert J. Krajewski, "Role Call for Elementary Principals," *Tennessee Association of Elementary School Principals Newsletter* 3 (May 1976): 2–3; Robert J. Krajewski, "The Real Versus the Ideal: How Elementary Principals Perceive Their Role in Texas," *TEPSA Journal* 9 (May 1977): 13; and "Role Implications of a Rank Ordering Process by Elementary Principals," *Resources in Education,* November 1977, ED140468 EA009634 (ERIC).

3. Stanley W. Williams, *New Dimensions in Supervision* (Scranton, Pa.: Intext, 1972), pp. 41–43

4. Ben M. Harris, *Supervisory Behavior in Education,* 2nd ed. (Englewood Cliffs, N.J.: Prentice-Hall, 1975), p. 90.

5. Morris L. Cogan, *Clinical Supervision* (Boston: Houghton Mifflin, 1973), Robert Goldhammer, *Clinical Supervision* (New York: Holt, Rinehart & Winston, 1969); Thomas J. Sergiovanni and Robert J. Starratt, *Emerging Patterns of Supervision: Human Perspectives* (New York: McGraw-Hill, 1971); and articles by Flanders, Graves and Craft, Harris, and Shane and Weaver, *Journal of Research and Development in Education* 9 (Winter 1976), a theme issue on clinical supervision published by the University of Georgia, Athens.

Hidden Agendas -
What Are Trustees Made Of?

Bruce McClellan

Bruce McClellan, headmaster of the Lawrenceville School, Lawrence-ville, New Jersey, describes some of the "inner fears" that private school trustees often suffer from and that affect their relationship with the head of the school, frequently leading to the latter's premature dismissal from office. He offers some remedies by which school heads and trustees can learn to live together harmoniously, stating that the latter should "not . . . find someone to blame but . . . someone to support." McClellan's analysis applies with equal validity to board members in public education.

"Hidden Agendas — What Are Trustees Made Of?" by Bruce McClellan, in *Independent School*, May 1978. Copyright 1978 by the National Association of Independent Schools. Reprinted by permission.

Last September, on the first Saturday afternoon of the new school year, I was watching the first football scrimmage and enjoying balmy temperatures and bright sunlight. Unexpectedly an old friend suddenly appeared beside me. Though I had known him well in school and college, we had barely seen each other since. Nevertheless, through correspondence and friends in common, we had remained aware of each other and I was delighted at this reunion.

Rather to my surprise, our conversation turned quickly to schools. My friend had served as president of the board of trustees of a significant independent school for 17 years. During that time, he had also been a major benefactor of that school. In a word, he had been as committed as any trustee could possibly be to independent education and to the particular school he served.

During his years of service as board president, three headmasters had come and gone. Because I had known one of them, I asked what the trouble had been. "The trouble?" exploded my friend. "The trouble was the damned trustees!"

As he shared his understanding of the circumstances that had resulted in hiring and firing three headmasters in 17 years, I began to hink about how a head evaluates trustees — the reverse of the customary view of board/head relations.

Although Lawrenceville has had only eight headmasters since 1810, and I myself am now in my eighteenth year, I share the growing concern about the casualty rate among school heads during the past few years. Is there some hidden agenda that powers the trustee tumbril?

As the 1977 NAIS Annual Conference, in Chicago, an experienced head remarked, "After 15 years of public and independent school administration — currently serving as a trustee of two independent schools and having served as a trustee of a college — I am uncertain, filled with anxiety — or is it anger? — about what I see happening to the leadership in independent schools today."

At age forty, and after five years of heading a prominent school in a large city, this schoolman is astonished to find that he has become a "senior headmaster," or rather a "surviving headmaster," because he says that he really doesn't feel "senior" or secure, and he cites his own knowledge of expected turnover in independent schools caused by forced early retirements, failure to renew contracts, summary dismissals, and discreet departures.

The evidence flutters into my office almost every week. You know what I mean — the restrained and dignified four-page 8½ x 11 leaflet with the school seal on the front and letters from the head and the president of the board facing each other in the friendliest possible way on the inside.

A 1972 NAIS study of the tenure of independent school heads showed that there had been a distinct shift in the late 1960's to shorter terms in office of heads of NAIS member schools. In 1946, 21.2 per cent of school heads had been in office 20 years or more. In 1970, that figure had dropped to 11.6 per cent.

In 1972, the average tenure of heads was 7.3 years. Since then, it has decreased by one year, to an average of 6.3 years, and there are presently very few heads who have been in office for 20 years or more in one school.

The average annual turnover from 1972 through 1977 was 103 new heads each year, or about 12 per cent of the membership. According to NAIS, 10 to 20 of these vacancies involve breakdowns of relations between the head and the board. So the problem is real.

John W. Nason, former president of Carleton College, recently spoke precisely to this question.

> *In the best interests of a school, it is essential that the relation between the trustees and the head of the school be one of mutual respect and confidence . . . . Clearly if confidence is in some sense lacking, one must either take steps to correct whatever has caused it, or get a new head of the school, or get a new board of trustees.*

Since the last of these three options is the most difficult to bring about and takes considerable time, it is less likely to be a solution, though in some cases it would be the right one.

There are, of course, good reasons why a school head should be dismissed. The initial selection process may not have come up with the right person for the particular job. Or the head may find that a responsibility that had seemed enjoyable and feasible has turned out to be something quite different from what was expected and well beyond his or her capacities.

Most school heads have little or no preparation, since there is no place one can go to learn how to be a head, except on the job. It is interesting to note that the number of school heads who have served in two or three schools has grown quite noticeably in recent years.

But what about the school head who has been chosen with care and thrives on all the new responsibility, yet something goes wrong? How is it that so many honeymoons and happy marriages wind up in a divorce court, with nothing but squabbling to be heard for miles around? How is it that perfectly sensible people who have common interests and everything to gain by working through their difficulties instead fall into wasteful quarrelsomeness and wind up at swords' points?

Changing school heads is not like changing the manager of a baseball team. Much more is involved on the part of all concerned. Emotional damage, financial loss, and diminished creative energies all follow from a change of head that takes place in the midst of a cacophony of dispute, disdain, and defensiveness.

As I talk with my fellow heads, I think that some of those 10 to 20 yearly "breakdown" separations arise from inner fears on the part of individual trustees. Such fears are seldom expressed, and perhaps even more frequently they are not recognized for what they are.

No less a person than sensible Samuel Johnson remarked in his trenchant way, in a comment about one of Shakespeare's plays, that "the greatest part of mankind have no other reason for their opinions than that they are in fashion." Fear of fashion. That may seem an unpromising beginning to my carechism of destructive fears, and indeed I do not think it is the most significant. Nevertheless, I have seen fear of fashion operate to the detriment of relations between trustees and their school head.

One conveniently neutral example I might cite has to do with the unanimous vote of the Williams College trustees to eliminate fraternities, in spite of their venerable and often positive standing on that campus. The fashion of the day mustered myriad arguments in support of fraternities. The professional judgment of the president of the college and of those closest to the actual operation of fraternities indicated that drastic surgery was in order. I shall never forget the consummate skill of the senior trustee who managed over a period of several years to understand that in that situation fashion was wrong. The trustees had to adopt a view out of phase with the expectations of many important alumni and friends.

Closely allied is fear of the future. Trustees tend to be conservators — to ride trains backwards, looking more intently at where they have been than at where they may be going. That instinct is worthwhile, solid, and natural. Why, after all, should you break up a winning combination if that happens to be the situation — or why, if there is trouble, should you introduce new troubles into a situation that is already quite difficult enough to deal with?

Fear of patrons can also create great difficulties between a head and a board. The simplest of all dilemmas arises when a powerful patron, capable not only of bringing to bear significant personal resources but also of mobilizing others of similar capacity, takes issue with the board about some particular point endorsed by the head of the school. We all know the leverage that money and good reputation can have on any institution.

Without going into detail, I would observe that of all the Ivy League institutions the one that seems to me to have been most successful since World War II is the one that has consistently paid least attention to off-campus fulcrums of power. Of course, there are times for diplomacy and persuasion, but in the last analysis being afraid of patrons makes for bad schools and for bad relations between trustees and their school heads.

Finally, and perhaps deepest of all, is fear of the young. The process of growing up inevitably results in separation from adults, who feel responsible. That separation, essential to eventual adult independence, can take peculiar turns and twists that are often perplexing, sometimes disturbing, and in a few instances downright threatening to the adult who takes his responsibility seriously.

We have passed through a decade during which the young threatened their elders more than at any other time in recent history. Things seem to have cooled a bit now. The fact remains, however, that adults have always been uneasy about children who escape their control, even though in the last analysis that is precisely what every adult should want for every young person growing up. Super-elaborate regulations, long midsummer letters expressing prohibitions, and thundering platform speeches of warning all indicate an unwillingness to let go, a kind of frantic fear of the young.

These fears exist in all of us. They create difficulties between a head and a board when their missions diverge. The head would not likely be a teacher, or, especially, a school head, if he or she did not have the emotional stability, the personal commitment, and the professional training to deal with those fears so as to be able to work intelligently in the school milieu.

Not so with trustees. Their commitment is not one of a lifetime and is not necessarily based on their own inner sense of a need for fulfillment. It is not strengthened with any kind of professional training whatever. In fact, Henry Wriston, former president of Brown University, said, in his book about college trusteeship, that being on the board of a college is "the only job where ignorance is an important qualification."

So it is that the head of a school can become the scapegoat for the fears of trustees without necessarily realizing what is happening. A board that feels concerned by its fear of some passing fashion, of what it sees in the future, or of the young themselves can easily work itself into a position of sacrificing the school head. No one likes to face the truth that ultimately "the king must die." In that case, the king is not the school head. It is the adult who is fearful of the changing world about him.

In the usual course of events, trustees are adults who themselves have children. On the strength of their parenthood, they feel themselves as qualified as the head of the school, at least in all matters not directly bearing upon academic instruction. Armed with this conviction and not really caring very much whether calculus classes are going well or not, a trustee prompted by subconscious fears can easily create a climate hostile and unprofitable for the very person whom he or she should be supporting most strenuously.

Are there remedies? Yes, and though they are obvious and simple, they are, in my experience, more honored in the breach than in observance.

First of all, established procedure saves us from friends and foes alike — as well as from ourselves. Professor John Matthews, of the Harvard Business School, has run NAIS seminars for school heads every summer for nearly 20 years. In a recent paper he remarked, "I cannot help but feel that most schools should do more in the way of making their policies, processes, and procedures . . . more formal. The act of trying to be specific will, I think, be as useful as the specificity itself." I have found that orderly decision making is often more important than the decision itself.

The forms that human beings have developed in order to accommodate one another and to draw on the wisdom of all who may be concerned about a particular issue have been distilled through ages of experience. We discard them lightly. Being civilized generally helps things along.

Thoughtful self-knowledge is another guard. It helps us to live with pressures brought by others. How do we respond to a particular situation, or need, or prospect? If we do not commit enough of our own time and energy and intelligence to know our own thinking, we are likely to be swayed by others and wind up not being able to use our own real strengths.

Not long ago, a board of trustees summarily dismissed a top-notch school head because of a divorce. I wonder whether any board in this country has ever dropped one of its own members for the same reason? Are there two standards? And if there are, do those standards reflect unwillingness on the part of trustees to accept themselves and their own responsibilities? "Do as I say but not as I do" becomes dangerous when applied to the relations between a board of trustees and its school head.

We need to have vision, to lift eyes to the horizon, beyond petty detail and frictions. Somewhere in Tennyson is the phrase "a craven fear of being great." Most of us are timid about our visions. We find it easier to deal with petty problems and the near scene, but when we get mixed up too much with trivia we tend to become trivial ourselves.

Finally, as John Matthews put it, "There must exist a high degree of trust, respect, and confidence between school heads, their chairmen, and their boards." When the tough questions come along, a trustee cannot feel free to curl up in a foxhole and snipe at the head of the school. Both parties need to understand that what's happening is sometimes unavoidable, usually has a remedy, and is always just as much a worry for the head as it is for each member of the board.

It helps a bit to have a sense of humor. If anything in our lives becomes so serious that we can't laugh at it, or at ourselves, it's really dangerous.

In *Guys and Dolls*, Miss Adelaide is in love with Nathan Detroit — she the angel, he the scoundrel; she a sweetheart, he a tough Broadway type. She sings pointedly, "If only he were different."

If only he were different. How often that kind of thinking results in an unprofitable stewpot of troubles for a school. It isn't always easy to accept the fact that a school you love and to which you have devoted time and substance is less than perfect. But less than perfect it will most surely be from time to time and in greater or lesser degree. What's important, then, is not to find someone to blame but to find someone to support.

What can trustees do to help the head who is in a bind? They can give their friendship, advice, support, and stand by because they believe in their school. It's a tough job that they've asked their school head to do. That head needs every bit of confidence they have to give.

The Role of the School Administrator

Alan K. Gaynor focuses on the role of the building principal, whom he regards as the "true target" of the current accountability movement insofar as it is directed at the evaluation of administrators. He observes that evaluation "should emphasize description and diagnosis, not ratings, rewards and sanctions." Gaynor notes that the intent of evaluation should be to help the principal understand the complexities of his school environment more clearly and to determine what changes in "task" or "style" are likely to be of help to him as he sets about improving his own performance. Alan K. Gaynor is Associate Professor of Education at Boston University.

"The role of the principal has changed rapidly — and radically — in the last two decades. Among the most important aspects of these changes are: (1) The principal's responsibilities now embrace the entire set of managerial and instructional functions, and (2) The principal is expected to cope in spite of ambiguity, conflict and diversity in expectations, power, and experience."

— Leon Lessinger (1975)

The task I have been assigned as a participant in this conference is a seemingly simple one which is straightforwardly related to the conference purposes and format. I am to speak to the role of the school administrator at a starting point for others who will then speak to the evaluation of the performance of the administrator in this role. The logic is clear and irrefutable. It is certainly useful to know what a person is expected to do before one sets about assessing how well he/she does it.

The problem for me, however, was multifold. First, there are a variety of roles in a school district which are typically classified as administrative. These include the superintendency and other central office roles as well as the principalship and assistant principalship among possible others at the building level. The specifics of these roles are quite different although plainly they also share significant common elements. A question, then, was which of these roles to speak to and how to do this in a brief and useful way.

The decision I finally came to was to choose one of these roles and define it out of a conceptual framework broad enough to relate, at least implicitly, to the other administrative roles as well. For a variety of reasons, reasons which to me were compelling, I have chosen to focus this paper upon the role of the building principal. I will make explicit my reasons for this decision further on in the paper.

A second aspect of my problem was related to the obvious fact that school principals perform roles which, although often similar in many respects, also differ significantly among school districts and even among attendance areas within school districts. It seemed important, then, even at the risk of seeming abstract or indecisive, to seek ways within the paper to speak to some of the major sources of role variation among principals.

A third aspect of my problem derived from an awareness of the multiplicity of sources of role definition for even a single school principal with her/his own school district and school attendance area. Here, too, I felt it was important to incorporate within the paper some framework which might assist the evaluation specialists in at least conceptualizing this bureaucratic and political reality.

In sum, then, and by way of introduction, it was the complexity of the problem of defining "the role of the school administrator" in some simple and unambiguous way which led me to make a series of decisions which have, ultimately, determined the format and substance of this paper. It will deal, then, with the role of the school principal and with those variables which seem to account for much of the variation and ambiguity in the principal's role over time and place.

FOCUS UPON THE PRINCIPALSHIP

The logic leading me to the school principalship as the role to focus upon as input to a conference on the evaluation of administrator performance is simple and compelling. It seems clear that the focus leading to a widening national concern for administrator evaluation, and implicitly to this conference, are those forces known collectively as the accountability movement.

Of course, school superintendents have been accountable in most localities for years. That, indeed, they have is attested to by the statistics describing superintendent turnover. The tenure of superintendents has been increasingly short in recent years as fiscal problems and community turmoil have emphasized the degree of *political* accountability inherent in this typically untenured role position.

Thus, at least at this point in time, the accountability movement is not newly directed at school superintendents. In many ways, they have always been accountable. Rather, the pressure for renewed and more systematic accountability has been directed at the school district's tenured professional personnel, those whose accountability is not so much political as it is bureaucratic. This pressure was directed first at teachers and more recently it is being directed at building principals.

The conclusion I have drawn is that the principalship is, at this stage of the accountability movement, the true target of that movement as it focuses upon the formal evaluation of school administration. Thus, it seems reasonable to assert that our energies in this conference should be directed toward explicating the role of the school principal and methods for evaluating the performance of individual school principals. Fortunately, these insights should also have payoff in addressing the evaluation of other school administrators.

ROLE AS A SOCIAL CONSTRUCT

The key starting point, it seems to me, in thinking about evaluation of personnel, is that role is a social construct, a product of the institution as a social system, and that although role *behavior* is in part idiosyncratic, the role, itself, along with the limits of variation in behavior it allows to individual roleholders, is institutionally defined. Persons who transcend the limits of behavioral variation are subject to sanction within or, ultimately, expulsion from the social system.

The importance of this understanding is that the sources of variation in the role of the principal are genetic to the society in which the individual is willing and able to conform to this role is a product of (1) the objective clarity and mutual consistency of the role expectations transmitted to the individual by diverse role senders and (2) the individual's own values, abilities, needs, and dispositions to act (Kahn, et al., 1964; Getzels, et al., 1968).

There have been several major studies in education of administrative role behavior, studies which illustrate the social definition of administrative roles in schools and the press on administrators to reconcile conflicting role expectations. Research at the University of Chicago (Getzels, et al, 1968) focused primarily upon the tension between the role expectations of the institution and the need-dispositions of individuals as roleholders in determining role behavior. In another set of studies, Gross, et al., (1958) developed and tested a theory to predict how superintendents would behave when faced with incompatible role expectations. McCarty and Ramsey (1971), consistent with the conception of role as a social construct, tested, in a third set of investigations, the impact of differences in patterns of community and school board power structure upon the role behavior of school super-intendents.

It might be noted with accuracy at this point that much of the research on administrative role behavior in education has targeted upon the superin-tendency. Some researchers, however, have focused their investigations upon the principals the Gross study of role conflict resolutions among superin-tendency. Some researchers, however, have focused their investigations upon the principalship. Sayan and Charters (1970) for example, replicated on principals the Gross study of role conflict resolutions among superintendents (Gross, et al., 1958). Foskett (1967) surveyed educators in order to describe modal patterns of task expectations for school principals and Gaynor (1975) more recently has been validating an instrument for use in analyzing dis-crepancies among members of the role set in the task expectations held for school principals. Thus, there have been some empirical studies of the role of the school principal in addition to the prescriptive offering put forth in at least fifty years of textbooks on administration and supervision.

TWO DIMENSIONS OF ROLE: TASK AND STYLE

Before moving to a discussion of the sources of their *variation,* it seems useful to identify, at least in broad outline, the model population of role expectations *typically held* for school principals. The role of the school principal, like any role, can be conceptualized in terms of two primary components. The task component of the role defines *what* the principal is expected to do. The style component of the role defines *how* the principal is expected to perform these tasks in a social contex. Evaluation designs will probably need to facilitate description and analysis of role behavior on both of these dimensions.

THE TASK DIMENSION

Findings and prescriptions describing the model tasks of school admin-istrators have been generally consistent over time. In a book on general school administration written 50 years ago, a book focusing upon the role of the superintendent, Stayer, et al., (1925), identified, among others, the following tasks of the school administrator:

Business Administration of Schools
School Publicity
Buildings and Equipment
Census and Attendance
Classification and Progress of School Children
Supervision of Instruction
Curricula and Courses of Study
Records and Reports

[1]The School Principals Task Inventory (SPTI (III)' PRELIM) is a 46 item questionnaire which scores respondents on ten tast factors and two over all dimensions of " Maintenance" and "Leadership" orientations.

Extra-curricular Activities

Personnel Management

In a similar book published 13 years ago, (Campbell et al., 1962) listed essentially the same administrative functions:

School-Community Relations

Curriculum Development

Pupil Personnel

Staff Personnel

Physical Facilities

Finance and Business Management

Organization and Structure

In a book on the principalship published just two years ago (Jacobson, et al., 1973) identified, among others, the following tasks of the school principal:

Making a School Schedule

Instructional Leadership

Educational Diagnosis

Evaluating Student Progress

Guidance

Pupil Personnel Concerns

Managing Extra-curricular Activities

Teacher Personnel Problems

Records and Reports

Supervising Non-instructional Personnel

The Principal in the Community

Although the specific phrases differ, it seems that despite 50 years difference in time and despite some shift in focus from administration at the district level to administration at the building level, the functions prescribed by the textbook writers are remarkably consistent.

My own data produced ten factors which, although different in some respects, remain generally similar to the textbook writers in their definition of the tasks of the school principal (Gaynor, 1975):

Leadership Factors

Developing and maintaining effective staff relations

Developing and maintaining effective community relations

Developing and implementing educational goals

Maintaining the principal's own professional growth

Making decisions about professional personnel

Maintenance Factors

Supervising non-professional personnel

Maintaining order and routines

Monitoring the performance of students and teachers in achieving the goals of the school

Managing the finances of the school

Monitoring and communicating student achievement data in relation to other schools

Foskett's survey instrument organized 45 task items into four broad categories which, in his research, were scored as subscales (Foskett, 1967),[2] Although less specific in their orientation from the descriptions cited above, they are broad enough to subsume many of the same tasks:

Acting Toward Teachers
Acting Toward Pupils and Parents
Acting Toward Profession
Acting Toward Community

Finally, a recent volume describing a collaborative project between the Atlanta Public Schools and the University Council for Educational Administration devotes a chapter to each of six task domains associated with the role of the school principal (Culbertson, et al., 1974). Like Foskett, Culbertson takes a broad cut at defining the task content of the principal's role, one which may prove helpful to evaluators as an alternative to more specific formulations:

Initiating and Responding to Social Change
Preparing the Organization for Effective Response
Decision-Making
Achieving Effective Human Relations and Morale
Administering and Improving the Instructional Program
Evaluating School Processes and Products

The purpose of this brief review of the literature has been to provide some broad sense of the shape of the task domain commonly associated with the role of the school principal. However, this exposition has dealt so far only with one aspect of the principal's role. It has delt with what the principal is typically expected to do. It now remains to discuss the other major aspect of the role: *How* the principal is expected to behave in performing those tasks.

THE STYLE DIMENSION

The literature on what is generally called "Leadership" or "Leadership Style" is essentially synonymous with that aspect of role which I have labelled "The Style Dimension." This literature is so extensive that several major reviews of it have appeared over the last 25 years (Stogdill, 1948; Gibb, 1954, Stogdill, 1974).

---

[2]   However, I have been able to find no description of the contruct validation procedures used by Foskett to support the empirical validity of his four subscales. Analyses done at Boston University and Bentley College on recent New Hampshire data by Murray Ingraham and Peter Graffman do not support the factor integrity of Foskett's subscales.

It is clearly not within the scope of this paper to attempt to review that literature again. However, it does seem important, first, to call this broad knowledge base to the attention of those concerned with administrator evaluation and, second, to describe several dominant themes which have characterized the thinking of theorists and researchers about leadership and leader behavior.

Much of the thinking about leadership style goes back to an early and seminal piece of research on small group dynamics by Lewin, Lippitt, and White (1939). In this study, three model types of leader behavior were posited and their effects upon group performance tested. Out of this study came concern among organizational researchers for the concepts of authoritarian, democratic and laissez-fare leadership styles and much of the research which followed has, in essence, attempted to replicate, elaborate, and refine those concepts and to understand the nature of the leader-follower interaction under a variety of conditions (Stogdill and Coons, 1957; Tannenbaum and Schmidt, 1957; Likert, 1961; Blake and Mouton, 1964; Fiedler, 1967, Reddin, 1967 and 1970; Hersey and Blanchard, 1972).

Related to the nature of the authority relationships which define the dynamics of task group operation is theory and research about the beliefs and attitudes of leaders towards other members of the task group. To what extent, for example, are those beliefs and attitudes positive and trusting, and how do differences in beliefs and attitudes toward others affect leader behavior (McGregor, 1960)?

Independent of authority relationships, conceptually if not always empirically, is the concept of leader orientation to task and/or to persons. Much research has been done to establish the social reality of these orientations and their existence, at least in the perceptions of respondents in work situations, is well documented (see Sergiovanni and Starratt, p. 88).

Several relatively simple ways of conceptualizing leader behavior have emerged from this research and become building blocks for further theory building and testing. One of these, which, derived directly from the work of Lewin, Lippitt and White (1939), deals with the nature of the authority relationship between the leader and other members of the task group. Emphasis is put upon describing the extent to which leadership is directive or non-directive, decision-making centralized or participative, and power concentrated or diffuse. (See, for example, Likert, 1967.) The most recent writing about leadership has been based upon a glowing consensus that neither leader behavior nor its effectiveness is independent of its context. There is evidence of long standing that leader behavior is affected by the group (see, for example, Merei, 1949) and that its effectiveness is contingent upon characteristics of the group (Fiedler, 1967; Hersey and Blanchard, 1972) and its environment (Lawrence and Lorsch, 1969).

The growing body of research has helped to elaborate and differentiate our understanding of the leadership act. Despite new knowledge, however, this understanding is still primitive (in fact, we probably sense better than ever before how primitive it is) and we still do not possess accurate predictive models of leadership effectiveness. What is clear is that the relationships among leaders and others in complex social situations are much more complicated than was earlier believed. The remainder of this paper focuses upon the sources of role variations for principals utilizing a known conceptual model as a framework for exposition.

SOURCES OF VARIATION IN
ROLE EXPECTATIONS FOR PRINCIPALS

I have defined role as a social construct comprised of two dimensions, task and style. The task dimension appears, at least to me, to be the more straightforward of the two, although in practice it is difficult to separate what a person does from how he/she does it. In any case, there are undoubtedly serious problems facing even those who seek to do no more than to describe what a principal actually does and how she/he does it.

Portraying accurately *role behavior*, alone, can be a demanding and time consuming mission (see, for example, Wolcott, 1973) even though the object of observation is but a single individual exhibiting a single set of behaviors. Defining role expectations and perceived role behavior, though, which involves all of the multiple persons and groups constituting the social and political reality of the principal's world, is an exponentially more complex and difficult task. And yet this is precisely the task without which the observer cannot comprehend the principal's behavior in the only way it can adequately be understood — in the context of forces, many of them conflicting, which motivate that behavior and define its success or failure *in situ*.

THE SOCIAL SYSTEMS MODEL

One of the most useful role models I know is that developed beginning about twenty years ago by Getzels, Guba and others (Getzels, et al., 1968). The "Social Systems Model" portrays the systemic interaction of individuals and institutions in shaping social behavior.

The model depicts the tension between the institution operating as an open system in its cultural environment and the individual institutional participants, replete with his/her personality and physiological characteristics, possessed of a complex of values, beliefs and attitudes deriving from a subtle overlay of personal and sub-cultural reference groups. Further refinements of the model also show groups (task groups and informal social groups within the institution) as mediators between individuals and the institution (Figure 1).

It is my view that the major sources of variation in role expectations for principals are depicted or implied in this model. Thus, it may prove helpful to those of us who are interested in developing useful systems of administrator evaluation to attend to the relationships identified in the model.

A useful way to view the Getzels-Guba paradign is as a system of major state variables impacting upon role behavior. Each variable constitutes a *general* factor which requires specification *in situ* in order for it to achieve practical utility in organizational analysis.

For example, two of the variables constituting the model are the institution and its cultural environemnt. The institution is defined by its constituent roles which, in turn, are defined by specific sets of role expectations held by influential persons or groups comprising the role set. Similarly, the cultural environment is defined by its constituent ethoses which, in turn, are defined by specific sets of attitudes, beliefs, and values.

FIGURE 1
Getzels–Guba Social Systems Model
(modified version)

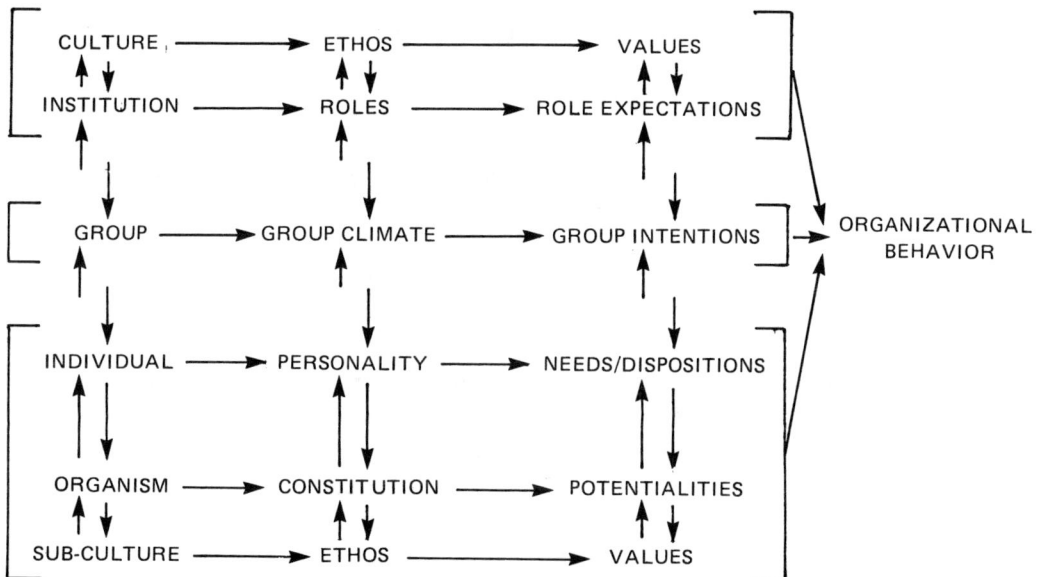

The institution can be specified at whatever level of system aggregation seems analytically useful. For example, the organization can be specified as a particular school district or as a particular school building. Once this specification is stated, system boundaries are implied and the environment becomes defined. It may sometimes even become useful to specify one set of boundaries for one level of analysis and another set of boundaries for a subsequent and different level of analysis — much as one would use maps of different scale or lenses of different orders of magnification.

WHEN IT'S SIOUX CITY IT'S NOT DETROIT

Major elements of the model with respect to the organization are its environment and the individuals and groups in the environment upon whose commitment and support the organization depends. Thus, a significant source of variation in the principal's role is place.

Community norms, sometimes homogeneous, sometimes pluralistic, provide a basis for differing and often conflicting demands upon principals. Some of these demands are for participation in decision-making; others are for allocations of staff, funds, or program resources. Still other demands are for expressions by the principal of support for one set of educational values or another, or for regulations (e.g., with respect to dress, discipline, etc.) which go beyond mere statements in the support of such values. (See Easton, 1965, and Almond and Powell, 1966.)

Community norms influence both the content of demands and the nature of action in support of demands. Communities variant in their values, beliefs, and attitudes tend to have variant expectations for what the school principal should do or even *be*. These differences among communities would seem to have significant implications for those who would evaluate the principal's performance.

WHEN IT'S THE TEACHERS IT'S NEITHER THE COMMUNITY NOR THE CENTRAL OFFICE

In understanding how she/he is expected to behave, the principal must be sensitive to the expectations not only of citizens but of teachers and upper administrators as well. Unfortunately there are many school systems in which those do not match. Often teachers are drawn from a population systematically different in values, beliefs, and attitudes from the community which the school presumes to serve. The conflicts in some cities between middle class white teachers and black or Hispanic parents and students have received national attention, for example, and can place the principal in an extremely difficult position as an administrator in the middle.

Similarly, principals often have to deal with substantial differences between the expectations of the superintendent and those of the teachers or between the conflicting expectations of teacher factions in her/his own building. It seems to me that determining the extent of the principal's awareness of these forces and the degree to which her/his responses are calculated and knowledgeable constitutes a significant domain for evaluation.

WHEN IT'S TODAY IT'S NOT YESTERDAY

Another source of variation in the principal's role is time. Time is built into the Social Systems Model implicitly. The cultural environment changes over time, in terms of the national climate for education, the legal and fiscal supports for and demands upon the school, and the composition of the community of the school district or the school attendance area. Not only do environmental factors shift over time but so, also, does the composition of the faculty in terms of the need-dispositions and cultural characteristics of new members. Sometimes these changes can be dramatic and call for a different set of priorities for the principal among tasks or even for a significantly different style of leadership.

The impact of time on the principal is to increase the pressures for personal flexibility and organizational adapriveness. The evaluation of principals should include provisions for longitudinal diagnosis. It should seek to describe the relationship between changes in the needs and expectations of community and staff and actions by the principal to alter her/his leadership style and to initiate and implement adaptations in the structures, processes and outputs of the school.

LACK OF CLARITY ABOUT CAUSAL RELATIONSHIPS

The thrust of the paper to this point is, in my judgment, consistent with the admonition of the American Association of School Administrators concerning the selection of school principals (AASA, 1967, p. 24):

> Selection of a principal requires consideration of two sets of variables: (1) Personal (How well do the aspirant's personal characteristics meet the criteria in general?) and, (2) Situational (What are the specific demands of the position that might make a difference?).

If, as I believe they are, these criteria are appropriate as a basis for selecting school principals, it can be argued effectively, I think, that they also represent sound guidelines for evaluating their administrative performance.

The major problem, however, is that despite reams of research findings on leadership, there are still not available accepted predictive equations relating specific combinations of personal and situational characteristics to administrative and organizational effectiveness. What, for example, are the key personal characteristics? Do they have the same salience in different administrative situations? What are the key variables within the situation? Do we have available a conception of situational variables (a dynamic model, for example) which is sophisticated enough to account for interactions among situational variables which alter their relative importance *in combination* with each other in different places and at different times? Is there a hierarchy of situational variables (e.g., size or complexity, degree of crisis, etc.) similar to Maslow's hierarchy of needs or are there multiple interacting hierarchies?

Only when there is some assumed knowledge about casual relationships between personal role behavior, on the one hand, and the nature of the situation in terms of known key variables, on the other, does evaluation become possible which is more than displaced evaluation (that is, evaluation of the measurable rather than the significant).

It is also important to note that organizational performance, which after all is the ultimate criterion in evaluating administrative performance, is extremely difficult to measure. This is especially so in the public schools because of vague and diffuse indicators and because of the general lack of consensus about organizational ends (Miles, 1967; Elboim-Dror, 1973). Research by Derr and Gabarro (1972) also supports this view:

> The initial studies also show that considerable difficulties arise when an attempt is made to use the [Lawrence and Lorsch] model to explain organizational performance in school systems because of the difficulty in defining system effectiveness.

CONCLUSIONS AND IMPLICATIONS FOR EVALUATORS

There are available for evaluators a variety of prescriptions and surveys defining the model tasks associated with the role of the school principal. For the most part, the lists of tasks, although written with some variation in perspective, language, and degree of comprehensiveness, exhibit enough consistency to provide a *general* basis for defining the task responsibilities of the *typical* school principal.

One problem is that there may not be sufficient typicality among school situations to enable evaluators to design standard instruments which combine ease of administration with sufficient flexibility to judge usefully the performance of principals in widely variate contexts. For example, the role of the principal in multi-unit (Pellegrin, 1970) and participative decision-making schools (Bentzen, 1974) is quite different than in traditional self-contained classroom schools. However, this thesis is ultimately an empirical one which remains to be tested.

A second problem lies in the lack of validated knowledge about casual relationships among the personal characteristics and administrative styles of school principals, situational variables, and administrative or organizational effectiveness — partly because of a knowledge base which is still inadequate to the complexities of largely counterintuitive social systems

(Forrester, 1971) and partly because of the continuing lack of consensus about the critical criteria defining effectiveness. Thus, the evaluator may often be left measuring the measurable even when those variables are neither agreed upon by a major segment of those concerned nor demonstrably predictive of operational effectiveness (for example, in terms of student achievement).

The conclusion I draw from this estimation of the current state of the art is that despite the fact that "it seems increasingly urgent that ways be found for . . . insuring that only personally effective, well-qualified people enter and remain in the principalship," (Anderson, 1973) evaluation should not seek to outstrip the knowledge base which supports it. It should emphasize description and diagnosis, not ratings, rewards and sanctions (except where causal relationships are unusually certain and where indicators of effectiveness have been mutually agreed upon).

Mainly, in my judgment, the intent of evaluation should be to help the principal to understand better the complexities of the bureaucratic, cultural-political, legal, and fiscal environment of the school and to mirror for the principal her/his behavior in relation to that environment. The prime focus should be upon helping the principal to determine what changes in task priority and administrative style are likely to work better, to help the principal to gain the knowledge and skills necessary to make those changes, and to provide formative feedback on the process over time.

The approach is probably the only one that is justified given the state of knowledge and political consensus at the present time.

REFERENCES

AASA Committee on the Selection of School Principals, *The Right Principal for the Right School.* Washington, D.C.: The American Association of School Administrators. 1967.

Almond, Gabriel A. and G. Bingham Powell, Jr., *Comparative Politics: A Developmental Approach.* Boston, MA: Little, Brown, 1966.

Anderson, Robert H., "Organizing and Staffing the School." In John I. Goodlad and Harold G. Shane eds., *The Elementary School in the United States.* The 72nd Yearbook of the National Society for the Study of Education, Chicago, IL: University of Chicago Press, 1973.

Bentzen, Mary M., Changing Schools: *The Magic Feather Principle.* New York, NY: McGraw-Hill, 1974.

Blake, Robert R. and Jane S. Mouton, *The Managerial Grid.* Houston, TX: Gulf Publishing, 1964.

Campbell, Roald F., John E. Corbally, Jr., and John A. Ramseyer, *Introduction to Educational Administration.* Second Edition. Boston, MA: Allyn and Bacon, 1962.

Culbertson, Jack A., Curtis Henson, and Ruel Morrison eds., *Performance Objectives for School Principals: Concepts and Instruments.* Berkeley, CA: McCutchan, 1974.

Derr, C. Brooklyn and John J. Gabarro, "An Organizational Contigency Theory for Education." *Educational Administration Quarterly.* Spring, 1972. 8(2).

Easton, David, *A Systems Analysis of Political Life.* New York, NY: Wiley, 1965.

Elboin-Dror, Rachel, "Organizational Characteristics of the Educational System." *Journal of Educational Administration.* May, 1973.9(1): pp. 3–21.

Fiedler, Fred E., *A Theory of Leadership Effectiveness.* New York, NY: McGraw-Hill, 1967.

Forrester, Jay W., "Counterintuitive Behavior of Social Systems." *Technology Review.* January, 1971. 73(3): pp. 1-16.

Foskett, John M., *The Normative World of the Elementary School Principal.* Eugene, OR: The Center for the Advanced Study of Educational Administration, 1967.

Gaynor, Alan K., "The Multidimensional World of the School Principal." Paper presented at the Annual Meeting of the American Educational Research Association, Washington, DC. April 3, 1975.

Getzels, Jacob W., James M. Lipham, and Ronald F. Campbell, *Educational Administration as a Social Process.* New York, NY: Harper and Row, 1968.

Gibb, Cecil, "Leadership." In the *Handbook of Social Psychology.* Gardner Lindzey ed., Cambridge, MA. Addison-Wesley, 1954. Vol. 2.

Gross, Neal, W.S. Mason, and A.W. McEachern, *Explorations in Role Analysis: Studies of the School Superintendency Role.* New York, NY: Wiley, 1958.

Hersey, Paul and Kenneth H. Blanchard, *Management of Organizational Behavior: Utilizing Human Resources.* Second Edition, Englewood Cliffs, NJ: Prentice-Hall, 1972.

Jacobson, Paul B., James D. Logsdon, and Robert R. Wiegman, *The Principalship: New Perspectives.* Englewood Cliffs, NJ: Prentice-Hall, 1973.

Kahn, Robert L., Donald M. Wolfe, Robert R. Quinn, and J. Diedrick Snoek, *Organizational Stress: Studies in the Role Conflict and Ambiguity.* New York, NY: Wiley, 1964.

Lawrence, Paul R. and Jay W. Lorsch, *Organization and Environment: Managing Differentiation and Integration.* Homewood, IL: Richard D. Irwin, 1969.

Lessinger, Leon, "Forward." In Fenwick W. English, *School Organization and Management.* Worthington, OH: Charles Jones, 1975.

Lewin, Kurt, Ronald Lippitt, and Ralph K. White, "Patterns Of Aggressive Behavior in Experimentally Created 'Social Climates'." *Journal of Social Psychology.* 1939. 10:pp. 271-299.

Likert, Rensis, *New Patterns of Management.* New York, NY: McGraw-Hill, 1961.

Likert, Rensis, *The Human Organization: Its Management and Value.* New York, NY: McGraw-Hill, 1967.

McCarty, Donald and Charles Ramsey, *The School Managers: Power and Conflict in American Public Education.* Westport, CT: Greenwich Press, 1971.

McGregor, Douglas, "The Human Side of Enterprise." In Warren G. Bennis and Edgar H. Schein, eds., *Leadership and Motivation: Essays of Douglas McGregor.* Cambridge, MA. Massachusetts Institute of Technology Press, 1966.

Merei, Ferenc, "Group Leadership and Institutionalization." *Human Relations.* 1949. 2: pp. 23-39.

Miles, Matthew, "Some Properties of Schools as Social Systems." IN Goodwin Watson, ed., *Change in School Systems.* Washington, DC: National Training Laboratories, 1967.

Pellegrin, Roland J., *Some Organizational Characteristics of Multiunit Schools.* Technical Report No. 8, Eugene, OR: The Center for the Advanced Study of Educational Administration, The University of Oregon, May, 1970.

Reddin, William J., "The 3-D Management Style Theory." *Training and Development Journal,* April, 1967, pp. 8-17.

Reddin, William J., *Managerial Effectiveness.* New York, NY: McGraw-Hill, 1970.

Sayan, Donald L. and W.W. Charters, Jr., " A Replication Among School Principals of the Gross Study of Role Conflict Resolution" *Educational Administration Quarterly,* Spring. 1970.6(2): pp. 36-45.

Stogdill, Ralph M., "Personal Factors Associated with Leadership: A Survey of the Literature." *Journal of Psychology,* 1948. 25: pp. 35-71.

Stogdill, Ralph M., *Handbook of Leadership.* New York, NY: The Free Press, 1974.

Stogdill, Ralph M. and Alvin E. Coons, eds., *Leader Behavior: In Description and Measurement.* Research Monograph No. 88, Columbus, OH: Bureau of Business Research, The Ohio State University, 1957.

Strayer, George D. and N.L. Engelhardt, *Problems in Educational Administration.* New York, NY: Bureau of Publications, Teachers College, Columbia University, 1925.

Tannenbaum, Robert and Warren H. Schmidt, "How to Choose a Leadership Pattern." *Harvard Business Review,* March-April, 1957. pp. 95-101.

Wolcott, Harry F., *The Man in the Principal's Office: An Ethnography.* New York, NY: Holt, Rinehart and Winston, 1973.

How Does Your Superintendent Measure Up?

Charles W. Fowler

In this delightful excerpt from his article, "When Superintendents Fail," Charles W. Fowler expresses some amusing thoughts about the nature of the superintendency. It is to be hoped that his measuring scale will provoke not only laughter but some empathy as well. Dr. Fowler is himself Superintendent of Schools in Fairfield, Connecticut.

HOW DOES YOUR SUPERINTENDENT MEASURE UP?

	Far Exceeds Job Requirements	Exceeds Job Requirements	Meets Job Requirements	Needs Improvement	Failing
Quality of work:	Leaps tall buildings at a single bound	Leaps tall buildings with a running start	Can leap short buildings if prodded	Bumps into buildings	Cannot recognize buildings
Promptness:	Is faster than a speeding bullet	Is as fast as a speeding bullet	Would you believe a slow bullet	Misfires frequently	Wounds self when handling guns
Initiative:	Is stronger than a locomotive	Is as strong as an elephant	Almost as strong as an elephant	Shoots elephants	Looks like an elephant
Adaptability:	Walks on water	Keeps head above water under stress	Washes with water	Drinks water	Can't find the water
Communication:	Communicates with John Dewey	Talks with the state commissioner	Talks to self	Argues with self	Loses argument with self

PART II

A Survey of Representative School Districts:

What's Going on Around the Nation

Linking Performance Improvement to Student Achievement - The School Improvement Project

Jim Sweeney

In his article, written specifically for the present book, Jim Sweeney, Associate Professor of Educational Administration at Iowa State University, explains the School Improvement Model (SIM). This is a major research project that was undertaken by Iowa State University's Research Institute for Studies in Education. The project involves school organizations in Iowa and Minnesota, with more than 50,000 students, 3,800 teachers and 300 administrators. In explaining the project, Dr. Sweeney observes that performance evaluation "requires the involvement and participation of the total school community." He stresses, too, the need for a trial period, for personnel evaluation is complex and if not implemented with care "it can cause harm and embarrassment to individuals" and to the schools. Much of the article is devoted to the Administrator Performance Evaluation system, which represents a major thrust of the SIM project. Refreshingly, the project stresses the link between administrative performance and student achievement — something that is not given due attention in most school organizations. "Schools and school administrators," says Dr. Sweeney, "can make a difference in student achievement."

Who or what makes a difference in America's schools? What is the difference between schools characterized by student achievement and those which are primarily custodial? The emergence of research linking positive student outcomes to building administrator behaviors (Brookover, 1979; Edmonds, 1979 and Rutter, 1979) is one of the significant events of the past decade. Yet, few school organizations make a valid effort to evaluate and improve administrator performance; overlooked and ignored best describes administrator performance evaluation.

A notable exception is the School Improvement Model (SIM), a major research project conducted by the Iowa State University Research Institute for Studies in Education under the aegis of the Northwest Area Foundation and a five school consortium.

The SIM Project is presently finishing year two of a four year research effort. The project is marked by four distinctive features: (1) it features an experimental design with performance evaluation as a significant independent variable, (2) the dependent variable is student achievement at the elementary and secondary level, (3) the performance evaluation system will be analyzed for cost effectiveness, and (4) the sample includes students in five school organizations differing in size, community type, pupil characteristics and funding source.

Four school organizations of Minnesota and an Iowa district are participating in the project. The four Minnesota school organizations include an urban district, Minneapolis Public Schools, two suburban districts, Edina Public Schools and Northfield Public Schools, and Breck School, a private institution. Spirit Lake Community Schools, the Iowa district, is a small (1,283) rural district. In total the project involves some 50,741 students, 3,887 teachers and 300 administrators.

The project, under the direction of national performance evaluation leader Dick Manatt, is predicated on three assumptions: (1) elevating student outcomes requires systematic performance evaluation and improvement, (2) improving student learning involves both teachers and administrators, and (3) a system which focuses on the performance needs of teacher and administrator is the ideal vehicle for boosting student achievement. The development and testing of the model requires a four-year time window which includes: 1980-1981, develop administrator performance evaluation and teacher performance evaluation systems in protypic form; 1981-1982, implement the performance evaluation systems and make them fully operational while beginning improvement interventions: 1982-1983, measure and describe the performance of administrative and teaching staffs while assessing student achievement with norm— and criterion-referenced tests, adding more intensive improvement interventions; and 1983-1984, determine the payoff by measuring, describing and analyzing all four linkages, viz., teacher behavior/student learning, administrative leadership/teacher behavior, student achievement/curriculum content and program costs/achievement outcomes. A critical phase of the endeavor was the development and implementation of an administrator performance evaluation system (APE).

Administrator Performance Evaluation (APE)

PLANNING

Effective systems flow from and are anchored by carefully thought out, sound philosophic premises. APE is tethered to an overarching belief that performance improvement is a people program—designed to do something for administrators rather then to them. While its ultimate objective is improved performance, APE also serves as a managerial tool; it provides a rational basis for making decisions related to retention, advancement, and salary improvement. Also implicit is the assumption that performance evaluation is an organizational matter, thus it requires the involvement and participation of the total school community. The planning process then, demanded a vehicle which provided school community members the opportunity for interaction and dialogue.

SIM utilized two such vehicles in each school organization: a steering committee and subcommittees. The steering committee was comprised of ten to twenty members of the school community who were chosen according to the contribution each could make to the committee. To insure broad representation, teachers from various departments or grade levels, administrators, citizens from the community, members of the board of education, and students from the secondary level were asked to serve. Their explicit objective was to provide answers to four important questions: (1) What are the criteria for administrator evaluation? (2) How high shall the standards for performance be? (3) How shall the organization monitor, measure and report performance? and (4) How will the organization plan to help the adminstrator? In addition, they also assumed responsibility for logistical and other decisions involved in developing and implementing the system.

Each steering committee had six major management tasks: they (1) created and managed the timeline; (2) informed and consulted with the chief executive officer and board; (3) informed and consulted with staff; (4) provided advice on the use of consultants; (5) determined the type of system to be developed (input-output vs. performance); and (6) selected and coordinated the efforts of the subcommittees. The subcommittees were charged with the responsibility of developing philosophy and procedures. Viable components developed by one consortium school organization were used as patterns or guideposts for the same activities in the other consortium schools, both for the obvious economy afforded and to assure comparable data. Five subcommittees in each school organization developed the system's components: (1) Philosophy and Objectives, (2) Performance Areas, Criteria, and Standards, (3) Operational Procedures, (4) Forms and Records, and (5) Test and Try.

PHILOSOPHY AND OBJECTIVES

This subcommittee set the stage for system design. Their open, candid discussion refined and articulated the organization's administrative philosophy as well as the major responsibilities of its administrators. This turned out to be a very significant activity. While the organizations typically had written administrative philosophies, the need to update and refine them becomes apparent as did the need to articulate that philosophy to all members of the organization. A written narrative helped to achieve both. Below is an excerpt froom one organization's administrative philosophy and objectives:

> "In the rapidly changing and complex world in which we live the administrator of today must be acutely aware of the needs of community, staff, and students. She/he must keep abreast of the latest developments in curriculum, instructional technology, and materials to maximize utilization of resources and talents of the school and community.
>
> "The administrator should develop and utilize managerial and human relation skills to create an environment in which staff members are challenged and encouraged to exercise responsible self-direction. Staff members should be motivated to utilize their talents and creative resources toward the accomplishment of mutually established goals."

PERFORMANCE AREAS, CRITERIA AND STANDARDS

This subcommittee was charged with the responsibility of supplying answers to three important questions: (1) What are the on-going, regular activities necessary for both the day-to-day operation of the school building or organization and the enhancement of student growth? (2) What specific criteria will be used in assessing administrator performance? and (3) What are the standards for performance?

Each organization's administrators played a key role in answering question one. For a period of a month they kept a log, recording the time spent performing daily administrative activities. These data were then compiled and a complete list of administrator activities developed. When the complete list had been developed the staff (including the administrator) discussed the activities and prioritized them. Activities which were accorded high priority were considered Critical Work Activities (CWAs), the performance areas in which to examine administrator performance. The subcommittee then involved the organization's members in identifying the humanistic, personal, and management characteristics which administrators must exhibit to successfully perform the CWAs.

Among those considered were the extent to which CWAs required social interaction and the ability to develop people as well as the commitment to work, professional ethics, and integrity necessary to perform those important tasks successfully. More traditional criteria such as the administrator's ability to plan, organize, coordinate, and evaluate organizational programs were also developed.

Finally, the subcommittee addressed the thorny question of establishing standards. Although standards were established before the position imcumbent was installed in the position, the developmental process encouraged further refinement. Each subcommittee followed three guidelines in establishing standards of performance: (1) standards were realistic within the context of the organization: (2) they were attainable; and (3) they were challenging, requiring the extra effort that separates excellence from mediocrity.

OPERATIONAL PROCEDURES

This subcommittee dealt with who, what, and how the system works. APE is based on the assumption that the process of evaluation is more important than the devices used for recording information. Each of the organization's subcommittees grappled with the difficult task of developing a nonthreatening system which focused on what administrators do to enhance school effectiveness. Each was dedicated to developing a system that provided on-going assistance and professional growth. Questions such as "Who will gather the data and how will it be used?" and "How will the evaluator and the evaluatee communicate with each other regarding the use of these data?" were answered by this subcommittee. While the APE system in the five organizations exhibited some differences in procedures, they were remarkably similar in their approach. Each utilized APE's cyclical model designed to utilize end-of-the-year data for setting goals for the following year.

Each provided multiple evaluators and built coaching and counseling into the system. Finally, each provided the administrator an opportunity for self-examination as well as for participation in developing specific, realistic, manageable, and measurable job improvement targets. The model adopted by the subcommittees is shown on the following page.

FORMS AND RECORDS

Accurate, reliable data required the development of well designed forms and records. This subcommittee, like all the subcommittees, had to be conversant with the organization's philosophy, for the forms and records had to be congruent with that philosophy. They were intent on presenting the data in a format which would enchance professional growth while de-emphasizing the judgmental aspect of evaluation. Their other specific objective was to maximize efficiency and effectiveness by streamlining paperwork.

The subcommittees adopted and modified five APE forms. The Work Activities Rating Sheet provided ratings and priorities for determining Critical Work Activities and the Critical Work Activities Rating Chart provided both the administrator and appraiser a vehicle for assessing performance in CWAs. The Summative Evaluation Report (SER) was used to gather

```
                    ┌─────────────────────────────────────────┐
                    │ EVALUATOR MONITORS EVALUATEE'S           │
                    │ PERFORMANCE:                             │
                    │                                          │
                    │     formal observation                   │
                    │     informal observation                 │
                    │     unsolicited input                    │
                    │     work samples                         │
                    │     formative conference                 │
                    └─────────────────────────────────────────┘
```

| Job Improvement Targets | Evaluator reviews and analyzes the SER | Self-evaluation |

Evaluator submits report to the Board of Education

| End-of-cycle conference | Evaluatee submits raw data and summary to evaluator (SER) |

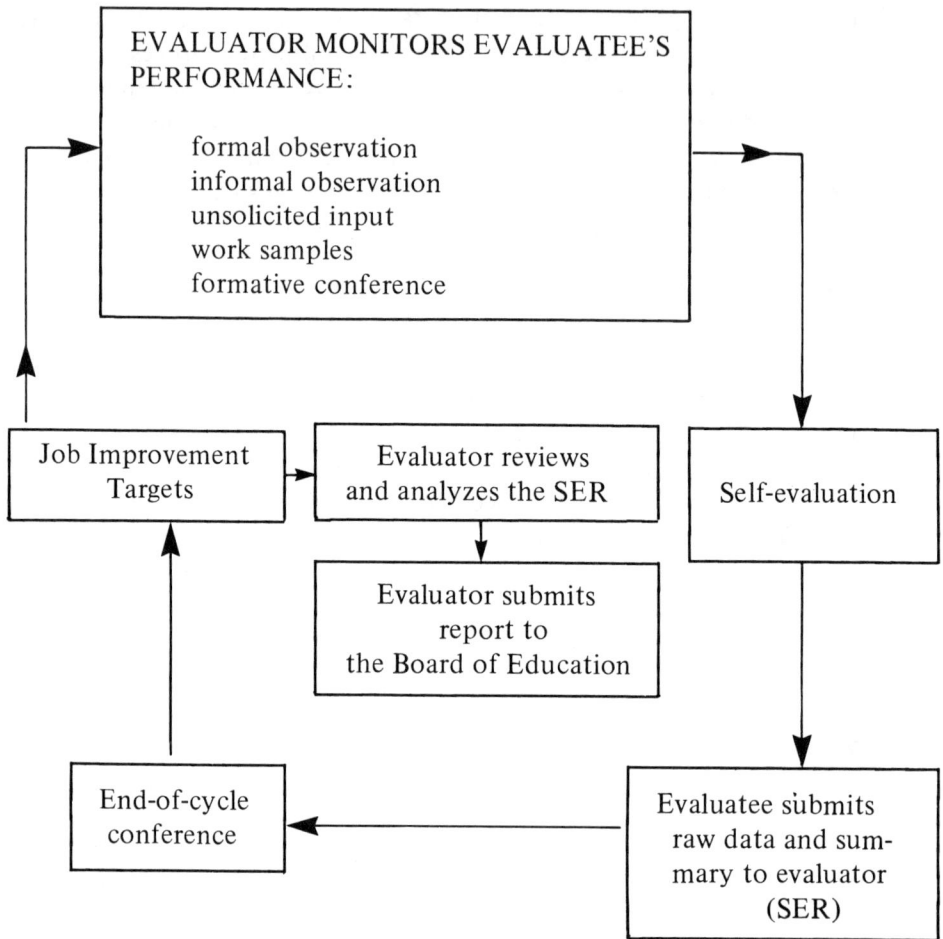

data from the administrator and his/her staff and utilizes a scale which is behaviorally anchored. The final instrument developed by the consortium organizations was the summative document, the Administrator Evaluation Report (AER), used to present the year-end evaluation. A fifth form, the Job Improvement Targets Document, provides the administrator with an opportunity to formally establish one or more goals from which job targets are written. It includes a section defining how targets will be accomplished and provisions for further explanation and comments.

TEST AND TRY

Personnel evaluation is a complex activity. Handled inappropriately, it can cause harm and embarrassment to individuals as well as to the school organization. For that reason and to work out any kinks in the system, each organization in the consortium provided nearly six months for a trial period. Each of the organizations conducted a dry run. During that six month period the subcommittee consulted with staff members in an effort to improve and refine each of the system's components; prototypic instruments were field tested and procedures were carefully examined and revised where necessary.

SUMMARY

The APE system is firmly in place in the five school organizations. What remains is an assessment of its saliency. Data have been gathered for formative evaluation purposes to assist SIM personnel to make additional revisions and improvements. Organizational climate surveys, teacher performance data, and community reactions have provided valuable insights into how the system is functioning as well as how it is perceived by the school community. But the acid test is yet to come. The researchers will examine educational outcomes by comparing fourth and eighth grade students gain scores in two learning areas — mathematics and reading. Pre- and post-testing with both norm and criterion-referenced tests were administered in 1981–1982. This testing will continue in 1982–1983 and 1983–1984 in order to measure changes in levels of achievement.

Gain scores will be compared to those students from schools with similar pupil characteristics who have agreed to serve as a control group. The results will indicate if performance evaluation makes a difference — one discernible in student achievement. The final step in the evaluation process will be to evaluate the cost effectiveness of the performance evaluation project. SIM researchers have developed a formula which will enable them to report unit costs in relation to student gains in mathematics and reading.

There are no simple answers to complex questions nor are there neat panaceas for the difficult task of educating our youth. The APE system employed in the SIM project pretends to be neither. It took the total commitment of the professional staff. Chief executive officers skillfully managed the change process; central office and other staff personnel were constantly on hand providing expertise and support, and building administrators spent long hours planning, assisting in data gathering, and participating in training. All were committed to the project because they believed in the system, had a hand in its development, and were the beneficiaries of training. It appears that they also were committed to the proposition that schools and school administrators can make a difference in student achievement — a goal that seems well worth the effort.[1]

---

[1] Further information about the School Improvement Model Project or the Administrator Performance Evaluation system may be obtained from Dr. Richard P. Manatt, Director, School Improvement Model, E005 Quadrangle, Iowa State University, Ames, Iowa 50011. (Author's note.)

REFERENCES

Brookover, W.B., and others. *School Social Systems and Student Achievement – Schools Can Make a Difference.* Brooklyn, N.Y.: Praeger Publishers, 1979.

Edmonds, R. "Effective Schools for the Urban Poor." *Educational Leadership 37* (October 1979): 15–27.

Rutter, M., and others, *Fifteen Thousand Hours.* Cambridge, Mass.: Harvard University Press, 1979.

Performance Evaluation

M. Donald Thomas

In this excerpt from his book, Performance Evaluation of Educational Personnel, *M. Donald Thomas examines systems of performance evaluation used in six school districts around the nation: Dallas, Texas; Palos Hills, Illinois; Santa Clara, California; Birmingham, Michigan; Salt Lake City, Utah; and Brown Deer, Wisconsin. Dr. Thomas is superintendent of the Salt Lake City Public Schools.*

"Performance Evaluation: Models" from *Performance Evaluation of Educational Personnel* by M. Donald Thomas. Copyright©1979 by the Phi Delta Kappa Educational Foundation. Selection reprinted by permission of the publisher.

Performance Evaluation: Models

Performance evaluation is being done well by many school districts. As a result, more and more school districts have developed more sophisticated and more effective performance evaluation programs. Pressure to develop such programs has come from state legislatures, local boards of education, and associations of school employees. All three groups have demonstrated a renewed interest in strong performance evaluation programs.

The following selection of six districts as models does not mean that these are necessarily the six best districts in the nation. Rather, they have been selected to illustrate 1) that performance evaluation is possible, and 2) that it is possible with various groups of employees (teachers, superintendents, principals, supervisors, and other central office personnel). There are hundreds of other school districts that have excellent performance evaluation programs that could have been selected as models. A list of school districts from which additional information on performance evaluation can be obtained is provided in the Appendix. However, the list is intended to be illustrative rather than exhaustive.

DALLAS INDEPENDENT SCHOOL DISTRICT
DALLAS, TEXAS

This district requires that principals evaluate the performance of teachers and indicate 1) if the teacher should or should not be re-employed for the following year and 2) if the teacher's overall performance is successful, marginal, or unsuccesful. The principal makes his decision with the aid of an instrument that evaluates the performance of teachers in 10 skill areas. The skill areas are: classroom management, pupil-teacher relationship, professional attitude and conduct, preparation and planning, knowledge of subject matter, public relations, techniques of instruction, pupil adjustment, pupil evaluation and health and appearance. Each area is evaluated as successful, marginal, or unsuccessful.

Each of the 10 areas is subdivided into competency statements. For example, under classroom management one of the competency items listed is, "Creates a room atmosphere conducive to learning." Under techniques of instruction is listed, "Provides ample opportunities for the expression of clear, accurate, complete, and pertinent ideas." In the area of pupil evaluation is listed, "Administers standardized tests in accordance with district policy." The competency items in each area range from two statements under public relations to 10 statements under techniques of instruction.

Both the official form dealing with reemployment and the evaluation instrument are filled out in triplicate. When completed by the principal, one copy of each form is given to the teacher, one copy remains with the principal, and the third copy is sent to the personnel office. Teachers who are rated successful continue in employment, those who are marginal are given opportunities to improve performance, and those who are unsuccessful are terminated from the school district.

CONSOLIDATED HIGH SCHOOL DISTRICT NO. 230
PALOS HILLS, ILLINOIS

This district has developed what it considers to be an excellent performance evaluation system for administrators in the system. The performance and effectiveness of an administrator are evaluated in these areas: 1) major areas of responsibility; 2) individual performance objectives: and 3) personal functioning.

Under the *major areas of responsibility* are included those specific duties expected of administrators by their job descriptions as well as the general functions of administration. Under *individual performance objectives* are those objectives prepared by the administrator being evaluated and mutually agreed to by the administrator and the evaluator. Usually they are related to systemwide goals and objectives, areas of responsibility, and personal growth. Under *personal functioning* the administrator is appraised in a systematic fashion, considering existing special circumstances under which he works.

In an initial conference, the appraiser and the administrator meet to agree upon performance objectives for the year. In interim conferences, progress in the achievement of performance objectives is reviewed along with a discussion of constraints and possible need for modification. Responsibilities and personal growth goals are reviewed. These conferences may be initiated by either the appraiser or the administrator. During the final conference, the administrator submits to the appraiser a self-appraisal of the achievement of performance objectives along with a brief summary of the major accomplishments for the year. Supportive material may be provided. At this conference, the appraiser and administrator review overall performance for the year.

The appraiser prepares a written summary, evaluating the performance and effectiveness in the three areas. Copies of the report are provided to the administrator, to the superintendent, and to the school board. The superintendent utilizes the reports to develop an evaluation designation for each administrator as either unsatisfactory, competent, or highly effective. The designations are established by school district policy and are defined as follows:

Unsatisfactory Performance

> This designation will be used when the superintendent determines after reviews of the appraisal, that the overall performance has been unsatisfactory for the time period. The major job functions have not been maintained, or the individual performance objectives have not been attained, or the personal functioning has not been satisfactory. The superintendent will convey his determinations to the appraiser, whose responsibility it shall be to inform the appraisee which specific job functions have not been attained, and how the personal functioning has not been satisfactory....
>
> The superintendent shall be given for his approval a set of performance objectives for the ensuing year. These shall be developed by the appraiser and the appraisee and shall be aimed at upgrading those areas in need of attention. During this year, an intensive appraisal will be conducted.

Competence Performance

> This designation will be used when the superintendent determines, after review of the appraisal, that the overall performance has been acceptable for the time period. The major job functions have been maintained, individual performance objectives have been attained, and the personal functioning has been satisfactory.

Highly Effective Performance

This designation will be used when the superintendent determines, after review of the appraisal, that the overall performance has been highly effective for the time period.

Responsibility for Appraisal

One person will be responsible for the appraisal of an individual, but he may have the assistance of others in the process. The superintendent will be responsible for the appraisal of the deputy superintendent, the assistant superintendent, and all building principals. The building principals, in turn, will be responsible for the appraisal of their assistant principals and other administrators who are assigned to the building. The deputy superintendent (curriculum) will be responsible for the appraisal of the director of career and vocational education and for all district coordinators.

SANTA CLARA UNIFIED SCHOOL DISTRICT
SANTA CLARA, CALIFORNIA

This district has developed a sophisticated performance evaluation system for the superintendent, administrators, and teaching staff. Under the supervision of Nick Gervase, assistant superintendent for personnel services, it has implemented a "certificated employees uniform evaluation system." The program is a management by objectives approach modified for the school setting. Intensive evaluation is conducted for all certificated staff, including the superintendent of schools, Rudy Gatti.

The performance evaluation program is based on district objectives, board of education policies, administrative procedures, and classifications of certificated employees. Performance standards are established for each certificated employee each year. Employees are rated either outstanding, effective, improvement needed, or remediation required. The same classifications are used for both teachers and administrators. In addition, some central office administrators are evaluated on specific responsibilities. Persons who are evaluated as needing improvement are given specific ways to improve. Those who are evaluated as needing remediation are provided remediation services. If remediation is not successful, termination follows.

Of particular interest is the process used to evaluate the superintendent. In the early fall the board of education establishes district goals to be achieved by the superintendent. Such goals are formally adopted by the board of eduation. Once the goals have been established, the superintendent develops specific plans for achieving them. Throughout the year, progress reports are presented to the board of education related to the goals. In December, the board of education meets with the superintendent to evaluate his performance in achieving the board of education goals. The discussion also includes areas of interest to the board or to the superintendent. Following the December meeting, the superintendent is given a "letter of evaluation." It discusses what areas are satisfactorily being achieved and what areas may need more aggressive attention. The letter may also make additional suggestions to the superintendent and/or compliment him for his work.

In the spring, the superintendent reports to the board the degree to which the objectives have been achieved and steps that are being taken if a particular goal will not be achieved. The process requires the superintendent to identify corrective action if such action is needed. A formal report on district objectives is accepted by the board at the end of the school year.

The following August or September the process begins again: goals are established; conferences are held to assess progress; validation of achievement is made; and the superintendent's performance is evaluated. The system provides frequent opportunity for the board to visit with the superintendent and to let him know its feelings about what is happening in the school district. Frequent evaluation and progress conferences build trust between the superintendent and the board of education.

The evaluation of other employees is done in much the same way as the evaluation of the superintendent. Objectives are established, progress is assessed, and conferences are held. If help is needed, assistance is provided. If an employee needs remediation, such services are put into operation. Both the attainment of objectives and human qualities are evaluated. The system appears to work extremely well in the Santa Clara Unified School District.

BIRMINGHAM PUBLIC SCHOOLS
BIRMINGHAM, MICHIGAN

This district has developed what is called "The Evaluation of Teacher Personnel for the Improvement of Instruction." The plan is reviewed annually by a committee of teachers and administrators. It includes five sections: introduction, purpose for evaluation, goals for performance, procedures for evaluation, and an evaluation instrument. The plan is compatible with the requirements of the *Michigan Teacher Tenure Act.*

What is unique about this plan is its great amount of detail. Each of the performance goals contains a statement of competency and the "sample evidence" to support competency. There are 10 performance goals to be achieved and evaluated. They are:

1. The teacher is competent in the subject area(s) and level(s) of instruction or area of service to which he is assigned.

2. The teacher focuses attention on the learner, his learning, and his growth.

3. The teacher makes effective use of instructional methods and materials.

4. The teacher demonstrates competency in management and control in the classroom or area of service.

5. The teacher maintains written evidence of adequate planning and organization.

6. The teacher evaluates students. He uses information gained to inform appropriate staff members, students, parents, and supervisors regarding pupils' progress.

7. The teacher relates positively and communicates effectively with students, parents, members of the community, and other staff members.

8. The teacher maintains acceptable qualities that serve as models for students.

9. The teacher supports students, staff, and community and observes professional ethics in his relationships with students and community.

10. The teacher shows an interest in student activities and willingly shares and participates in the activities of the school.

Each area is given one of five ratings: acceptable, needs strengthening, not acceptable, does not apply, or not observed. In addition to the evaluation of these 10 items, a general evaluation is provided. The evaluator may write in comments. Both the evaluator and the teacher sign the instrument. Separate instruments are used for tenured and nontenured (probationary) teachers.

SALT LAKE CITY SCHOOL DISTRICT
SALT LAKE CITY, UTAH

This district's performance evaluation program requires that each certified employee shall be evaluated each year. It is the policy of the school district that "persons not suited to the educational setting should not be employed by the school district." Performance evaluation is directly related to board of education objectives. Each certified employee completes a new accountability plan each year. The plan includes performance standards to be achieved and methods for validating that such standards have been attained.

To achieve board of education goals, the superintendent establishes performance standards for himself and his immediate staff and directs the interests, energies, and talents of the staff to support the board's goals.

Principals meet with supervisors for administrative services to establish building unit performance standards. Each principal supports board of education objectives, establishes additional building objectives, and accepts a personal growth objective.

Once the principal establishes unit performance standards, he meets with each teacher to establish individual performance standards. Standards support board of education goals, but each teacher may also establish additional personal goals. Principals may also suggest goals for specific teachers in areas that need improvement. Principals supervise the achievement of teacher performance standards and report achievement to the supervisors for administrative services.

In September, each teacher develops an accountability program in conference with the principal. This contains each teacher's contribution to the attainment of board of education objectives. Once the standards of performance are agreed to, the teacher has freedom to achieve the objectives as long as he operates within the framework of school policy, law, professional ethics, and the prescribed budget. Principals and teachers periodically discuss progress being made to achieve objectives. If help is needed, both principal and teacher may receive additional help from central office personnel. Each teacher reports to the principal in May to validate the attainment of the objectives agreed to in September. Validation may be by test scores, teacher judgment, documents, observation, performance of students, or other mutually accepted methods.

A key factor in the Salt Lake City School District plan is the work of the staff coordinator. He is the one that integrates the various accountability and evaluation functions. The staff coordinator has three major functions: 1) to work closely with the board of education, 2) to monitor the district's accountability program, and 3) to assign schools to administrators for supervising services. He accounts for all reports, deadlines, and conference schedules. In developing priorities, the coordinator gives emphasis to board of education goals. He validates that the following steps have been taken to incorporate the district goals into an accountability process:

1. Development of specific performance objectives for every certificated employee.

2. Planning and implementation of programs to carry out objectives in each unit.

3. Identification of budget support for each objective.

4. Identification of the kind of evidence needed to assess attainment of objectives.

5. Determination of the manner in which attainment of objectives will be reported.

6. Implementation of inservice training needed to achieve objectives.

7. Review of programs, goals, or objectives by the staff and by the board of education as needed.

8. Implementation of programs to properly inform the board of education, employees, patrons, and the public.

Of particular interest in the Salt Lake City School District performance evaluation programs are two items: remediation programs for teachers and administrators and performance payments for administrators.

Remediation Process. Employees who are not making a satisfactory contribution to the district goals are placed on remediation. When remediation is needed, it begins with a 30-day period of informal remediation. This applies to both administrators and teachers. If remediation is not accomplished after 30 days, a formal remediation team is established. For teachers, the team consists of a learning specialist, the principal, and two teacher colleagues. For administrators, the team consists of the superintendent and two administrators who are members of the professional rights and responsibilities committee.

Teams work with the persons on remediation for a five-month period. At the end of five months a recommendation is made to terminate or to destroy all records (if remediation has been successfully achieved). During the remediation period, reports are made to the individual on remediation and to the superintendent. Due process rights of individuals on remediation are protected and massive help is provided by the team. If remediation is not satisfactorily achieved after five months, the superintendent holds a termination conference with the person to be terminated. If remediation is succesful, the employee is congratulated and all records are destroyed.

Performance Payment. The Salt Lake City School District performance evaluation program provides a 2% (of salary) performance payment for all administrators (including the superintendent) if all board of education objectives have been achieved. In administering the 2% performance payment the following criteria are used:

1. Ability to understand and effectively implement board policy.
2. Ability to achieve performance standards as designated by the superintendent of schools.
3. Ability to administer the accountability program and achieve district and local objectives.
4. Ability to operate within budgetary limits.
5. Ability to operate within the limits of education law.
6. Ability to operate in accordance with principles of shared governance.
7. Ability to keep current, to continue learning, and to be aware of education development.

The judgment to award the performance payment is made by the superintendent or by an administrator who supervises another administrator. The award is made in June of each school year. Those who do not receive the payment are provided with a plan to remediate the area of deficiency that caused them to lose the award. The plan has worked succesfully for five years.

SCHOOL DISTRICT NO. 1
BROWN DEER, WISCONSIN

This district has a comprehensive performance evaluation plan for both teachers and administrators. Based on a management by objectives approach, it was first implemented in 1974. The program is divided into 1) management by objectives and merit pay for administrators, and 2) professional staff improvement and evaluation of teachers.

Administrator Evaluation. The administrator evaluation system consists of a management contract, a management by objectives plan, an evaluation process, and a merit pay scale of 1% to 5%. Merit pay is determined after a rigorous evaluation of each individual performance. Here is how the system works.

Early in September, meetings are held with each principal to establish objectives to be achieved for the school year. Three or four major objectives are established and written into the "Administrator MBO Contract." The contract contains: the rationale, objectives to be realized, the expected results, strategies to be followed, a definition of responsibilities, resources needed, evaluation process, and evaluation dates. Each contract is an agreement between administrator and a supervisor.

Once the objectives for each administrator are established, three or four reveiw conferences are held during the school year to evaluate progress and to identify ways to improve performance. These sessions provide an opportunity to check progress, to discuss problems, and to discuss concerns not related to the MBO contract. Frequent informal discussions augment the formal evaluation conferences.

Each June meetings are held to evaluate administrative performance and the achievement of objectives. Strengths and weaknesses of each administrator are discussed and performance is rated to establish merit pay. Merit pay is granted to the extent that performance has been above satisfactory.

In late June, a three-day retreat is held with administrators to review the accomplishments of the district (including individual schools) and to establish priorities for the following year. The priorities serve as a basis for establishing objectives to be written into MBO contracts for the next school year. In September the process begins again with individual meetings with each administrator.

The unusual part of the Brown Deer administrator evaluation plan is the merit pay provision of 1% to 5% of salary. Merit pay is earned by the accumulation of points obtained in the performance of job responsibilities and the achievement of district objectives. Performance can be evaluated as exemplary, well done, satisfactory, and less than satisfactory. The more points one receives, the higher the merit pay.

Teacher Evaluation. The teacher evaluation system is similar to that used for administrators. Teachers are expected to develop objectives for the school year and to establish methods for validating their achievement. Conferences are held early in the year with each teacher to establish the basis for evaluation. However, teachers' attainment of objectives is not tied to merit pay.

During the year, principals meet with teachers to assess progress toward the achievement of objectives. Such meetings are held after formal classroom observations. At the end of the school year in May, a final formal evaluation conference is held with each teacher. The items discussed in these conferences are detailed in the "Professional Staff Improvement and Evaluation System" for teachers.

Administrator Merit Pay - Theory Into Practice

Larry G. Ruttan

Larry G. Ruttan describes how California's Rialto Unified School District instituted the Management Evaluation and Development Program, whose purpose was to judge and improve managerial performance and to make merit pay decisions accordingly. Commenting that the ultimate goal of the entire process was to enable the students "to acquire a quality education through improved evaluation," he is one of the few practitioners of evaluation actually to express that all-important goal. Ruttan discusses how the process operates in Rialto, how the district's in-service program for the managerial team fits into the evaluation system and plays a role in merit pay, and how its merit pay plan works. Despite initial resistance to the plan by the staff, Ruttan believes it is now accepted because it brings certain advantages to the evaluatees that were not apparent before the plan was implemented. Larry G. Ruttan is Superintendent of the Palm Springs Unified School District, California.

In recent years there has been frequent debate regarding the desirability of merit pay for school administrators. For numerous reasons there have been very few districts actually trying merit pay. This article explains how one district does it.

In 1977 the Board of Education of the Rialto Unified School District and the superintendent began to refine a "Management Evaluation and Development Program." The purposes of this program were: (1) to judge performance levels of managers, (2) to improve performance and/or maintain it at the highest possible level; (3) to encourage retention of effective managers; (4) to identify needs of managers and to provide assistance for those needs; and (5) to identify outstanding performance which would result in merit pay.

This program was designed to support Rialto's goal of providing students with the opportunity to acquire a quality education through improved evaluation. It was also designed to be a positive continuing process that involves management in examining and discussing how each individual is performing. During the two years this program has been in effect, there have been several changes in the procedure, each one an attempt to answer a problem raised or to improve the existing process.

In looking at other merit pay programs, it was felt that the reasons why they had failed were that the plans had been concerned with merit pay alone and had ignored the importance of the evaluation process and the necessity of an inservice training program. This in turn caused managers to resist merit pay, as they were apprehensive that, without an evaluation criterion, placement on the merit pay salary schedule would be arbitrary and that, without an inservice program, there would be no opportunity for them to improve their specific skills. All three of these points are incorporated into the Rialto program.

The Rialto Board was committed to developing quality educational leadership designed to increase both personal and professional effectiveness on the part of all 50 members of the management team. It was believed that a personal increase of effectiveness would in turn make an increase in organizational effectiveness. To see how the entire process really works, let's bring the evaluation process into focus.

The district's management team has adopted a list of over 40 criteria called the "Performance Criteria for Managers." This list defines a manager's major areas of responsibility and provides a foundation for rating managers. The purpose of the evaluation program is aimed at the improvement of job performance. Fundamental to this program is the belief that communication, trust, respect, encouragement and assistance (with a mutual sense of involvement by both the evaluator and evaluatee) can stimulate individual satisfaction, internal motivation, professional renewal and increased effectiveness. It is also recognized that evaluation must give adequate attention to the total environment, the unique variables that affect one's ability to perform, the many acceptable varieties of methods and personalities, and a tolerance for diversity.

All management personnel are evaluated annually. Prime evaluators are assigned at the beginning of each school year by the superintendent. By October first of each year managers meet with their evaluator to complete a Pre-Evaluation Agreement. First the evaluator and evaluatee review the list of "Performance Criteria for Managers" and add or delete criteria as appropriate. Next, they review the evaluatee's 10 written objectives. These objectives must be congruent with (but not limited to) the goals of the board of education and incorporate any specific directions from the superintendent. Both the objectives and the means of achieving them must be discussed and agreed upon by the evaluator and the evaluatee. The purpose of writing these objectives is to improve the manager's total performance in relation to the performance criteria and to establish his priorities for the coming year.

It is essential to understand that even if a manager accomplishes one hundred percent of his/her objectives, he/she might not receive merit pay, as this is only a portion of overall performance. It is also conceivable that a manager might be deterred by changing circumstances from accomplishing specific objectives and still receive merit pay based on overall performance.

During the school year the evaluator begins gathering information about the evaluatee from a number of sources. The most important is from making frequent personal observations during visits to the evaluatee's school or work location, and a series of regular conferences. Communications with members of the cabinet, other managers, staff and community provide additional input and are discussed with the evaluatee.

By February first of each year, the manager and his/her evaluator hold an interim evaluation conference and a written "Evaluator's Interim Report for Managers" is completed. Suggestions for improvement figure strongly in this evaluation. Final evaluation and the final evaluation conference are held prior to May first of each year. In a written evaluation that follows this conference, each manager receives a rating for each of the Performance Criteria categories and for each objective. Also taken into consideration at this time is the element of personal growth. All members of the management team are expected to improve their skills through participation in both the scheduled district management inservice programs and through an individual plan for personal growth. The prime evaluator then makes an overall recommendation regarding the total performance of the evaluatee for the year. This recommendation is either. marginal performance; above average to excellent performance; or outstanding performance.

Final evaluation forms are then submitted to the superintendent. Each of these evaluations is reviewed by the superintendent's executive cabinet, consisting of the superintendent and the assistant superintendents. The final determination of performance ratings is then made by the superintendent, based upon the recommendations of the prime evaluator and the members of the executive cabinet.

Implicit in this evaluation plan is the understanding that, concomitant with the more objective portions of the evaluation, subjective judgment is used by the evaluator, the superintendent and the executive cabinet as to how well the evaluatee has performed.

An Evaluation Review Committee will hear any concerns related to the process of evaluation or placement on the management salary schedule. The Review Committee will consist of the superintendent, an assistant superintendent, and a member of the management team. After hearing any concerns related to the evaluation process, this Review Committee will make a recommendation to the superintendent. The superintendent's decision, however, will be final. At the beginning of each year, any evaluatee may request the superintendent to assign a new evaluator.

Now let's look at the Rialto inservice program to see how it fits into the total process and why it plays such an integral part of the merit pay plan.

The board recognized the importance of inservice education for all members of the management team because, as in the business world, managerial obsolescence can be one of the greatest handicaps a district can face. The board recognized that it had the responsibility to invest both time and money in a planned, systematic and continuous effort to keep its management staff abreast of current knowledge and technology and to assist administrators to become more effective educational leaders.

The district inservice program is divided into two areas: those district inservice programs planned for the entire management team and those conferences, workshops or programs available from other sources that can be taken to meet the individual manager's needs.

The number and variety of inservice activities attended by members of the management team would provide an article in itself. However, a general overview is necessary to show the importance that the board and the administration place on the necessity of good inservice programs and to indicate the connection of inservice and our merit pay plan.

The district management inservice program was planned to meet the needs of the entire management team and involved a number of areas. During the past year, two full-day inservice programs were held before the opening of school. During the school year the management team met for regular two-hour workshops every other Thursday. Four administrators participated in ACSA's Project Leadership activities. All elementary and instructional administrators completed a 10-day instructional program conducted by the Upland Professional Development Center. This was in preparation for developing a series of workshops to be provided by our principals for our entire elementary teaching staff during the coming school year.

A Friday evening and Saturday morning workshop was held with the entire management team including board members. This workshop was a needs assessment activity designed to clarify the district's internal problems. A task force will now be appointed to work on solving the problem for each area identified. One outgrowth of the numerous inservice activities carried on by members of the management team has been an upsurge in inservice programs planned by the administrators for their own staffs.

In addition to district inservice programs, managers have attended numerous conferences, workshops, etc., all over the state. These activities were chosen either to meet a district need or some special need of the individual manager.

Now let's look at the merit pay plan itself. The management salary schedule is computed from a study of the salary schedules of 25 selected unified school districts in Southern California. This study establishes a "benchmark" position at the per diem rate of Range II for the elementary school principal. This benchmark is equal to the median of the maximum salary of the districts surveyed. All other management positions are on a fixed ratio to the benchmark position. (Ratios vary from .5121 to 1.14 of the benchmark position.) All salaries are computed on the daily rate due to the various number of days in the work year for the various positions. The salary schedule is then divided into three ranges for each position: Range 1 − Marginal Performance; Range II − Above Average to Excellent Performance, and Range III − Merit Performance. Range II reflects the position's ratio to the benchmark position. Range I is five dollars per diem less than Range II, and Range II is five dollars per diem more. Any new manager is placed at a fixed rate below Range II for the initial year of employment.

Any manager evaluated at Marginal Performance is paid at Range I of the appropriate salary schedule for the coming school year. If no substantial improvement is made by February of the second school year, that manager will receive a written notice of reassignment by March first.

Salary placement is for one year only, and placement for subsequent years is dependent upon the previous year's evaluation. By June first of each year, all members of the management team are notified in writing of their placement on the salary schedule for the coming school year.

The granting of merit pay is not limited to any fixed percentage of managers, rather, it is granted to all managers who in the judgment of the superintendent are performing at an outstanding level. During the first year this merit pay program was in existence, it resulted in one administrator being reassigned to classroom duties and seven managers being recommended for outstanding performance resulting in merit pay. The second year of the program saw no manager evaluated at below merit and 14 evaluated at merit performance.

It must be admitted that the merit pay plan has not been without its problems. There was an original reluctance on the part of most managers and some very vocal resistance at its implementation. As the process became better defined and more easily understood, resistance diminished. As indicated previously, numerous changes have been made in the process to improve the procedure and to respond to some of the valid issues raised by members of the management team as the plan was implemented. As these changes were made, acceptance became more general.

We believe the merit pay plan is accepted because: the evaluation process is considered to be fair, it gives evaluatees a stated criterion by which they will be evaluated; they have the opportunity to select areas of need for inservice education that lets them grow professionally; and the inservice education program may enable them to have a better chance to receive merit pay in future years.

Another factor leading to acceptance is that most managers have found that agreeing on objectives with their evaluator means a commitment on the part of the district to provide finances and support to the manager in carrying out their objectives. This means that the individual can, in large part, determine his or her own destiny.

R.E.A.S.O.N.S.

The Newark, Ohio, City School District has developed a system — Responsive, Evaluative, Accountability System Operating Newark Schools — whose felicitous acronym is R.E.A.S.O.N.S. and whose purpose is to evaluate the district's educational leadership. The following are two excerpts from the R.E.A.S.O.N.S. manual: "Linking Performance with Compensation" and a demonstration form. The latter is a useful checklist of tasks performed by administrators — in this case the junior high school principal. The comments on merit pay should prove of interest to those districts contemplating the establishment of similar links between compensation and performance.

LINKING PERFORMANCE WITH COMPENSATION

THE PERFORMANCE MODEL

Effective leadership in today's public schools requires a variety of specific management skills and competencies. Correlating instruction, activities, budget, and services into an effective educational program for students requires talented and forward-looking leadership. The role of the educational leader continues to become more important and more complex with recent state and federal legislative mandates, the retention of a larger percentage of the school population in school, and the general demands of the public.

The R.E.A.S.O.N.S. system of the Newark City Schools is performance and competency based. There are certain previously cited management skills and competencies that are expected and required from Administrative Team members. Each administrator's performance is evaluated and rated in terms of System Developmental Objective related to district-wide annual objectives for which an administrator has responsibility as a key mover or as a support person, Unit Developmental Objectives related to building or supervision assignments, Personal Growth Objectives related to individual administrative leadership development, and Operational Objectives related to daily job performance.

COMPENSATION PROVISIONS

The public has a right to expect a high degree of administrative competency from the educational leaders responsible for managing their community's schools. The community expects and needs to be able to see efficient and effective leadership for its tax dollars. Conversely, competent administrators should be adequately rewarded for their performance. Historically, this has not been possible in school systems utilizing an administrative salary schedule tied to training and experience, or to teacher salaries. Likewise, administrative salary schedules based upon factors such as building size and number of staff supervised do not take leadership effectiveness into consideration. Such practices may even reduce effective leadership and might be a deterrent to accountability. It is possible in such systems for two administrators with equal experience, training, and other factors to be making the same salary with their actual job performance and competencies being quite different in terms of quality and quantity. Therefore, the R.E.A.S.O.N.S. system of the Newark City Schools incorporates a program of incentives that link performance with compensation.

SALARY ADJUSTMENTS

Annual salary adjustments for individual administrators, after initial employment, shall be based upon two areas, a merit pay adjustment and a cost of living adjustment. Such adjustments will commence after August 1 of the following year.

MERIT PAY ADJUSTMENT

The merit pay adjustment shall be based upon an evaluation of the following:
  (a) achievement of System Developmental Objectives (20% — 40%)
  (b) achievement of Unit Developmental Objectives (20% — 40%)
  (c) achievement of Personal Growth Objectives (05% — 15%)
  (d) achievement of Operational Objectives (20% — 40%)

                    Total   100%

Achievement of System Developmental Objectives is defined as progress toward the completion of district level concerns as evaluated by a committee of three peer evaluators. The Superintendent of Schools shall, by the fifth of May each year, appoint committees of peer evaluators consisting of (1) the administrator's immediate supervisor, who serves as the chairperson of the evaluation team, (2) an administrator at a comparable administrative position (i.e., elementary principal, secondary principal, supervisor, director, or assistant superintendent), and (3) another administrator from a different administrative position.

Achievement of Unit Developmental Objectives is defined as progress toward the completion of specific concerns at the building, administrative, or supervisory level as evaluated by the immediate administrative supervisor.

Achievement of Personal Growth Objectives is defined as progress toward the completion of personal professional developmental concerns (i.e., through course work, workshops, participation in professional organizations, individual reading, professional conferences, research, visitation, professional committees, etc.) of the administrator as evaluated by the immediate administrative supervisor.

Achievement of Operational Objectives is defined as progress toward the completion of daily job performance tasks (i.e., as is defined in the job description) as evaluated by the immediate administrative supervisor.

For each of the above areas of evaluation, self-assessment is a major consideration utilized in the evaluation program. The timelines shall be followed in initiating, implementing, and evaluating these objectives.

Each of the above stated areas of evaluation shall be given a final rating from a range of 0 to 10. On the determined percentage basis, as indicated above, an average shall be made of these ratings. The percentage of salary adjustment to the administrator's then current salary shall be determined by placing the average rating on the salary adjustment scale below.

Rating	Salary Admustment
10.0	9%
9.0 – 9.9	8%
8.0 – 8.9	7%
7.0 – 7.9	6%
6.0 – 6.9	5%
5.0 – 5.9	4%
4.0 – 4.9	3%
3.0 – 3.9	2%
2.0 – 2.9	1%
0.0 – 1.9	0%

For example, if an administrator having only one objective in each of the four performance areas, received a rating of 7 on System Development Objectives, a rating of 8 on Unit Developmental Objectives, a rating of 4 on Personal Growth Objectives, and a rating of 9 on Operational Objectives, he/she would have an average rating of 7.6. This figure was calculated as follows.

Objective	Rating	Percent of Final Rating	Product
System Developmental	7	30%	2.10
Unit Developmental	8	30%	2.40
Personal Growth	4	10%	.40
Operational	9	30%	2.70
			7.60

Since receiving an average rating of 7.6, this administrator would receive a 6% salary adjustment as determined from the rating scale above.

If the average administrative merit pay salary calculation is 5.0% or greater, the superintendent or Board of Education may limit the administrative merit pay salary adjustments to a sum equal to a 5.0% total increase (excluding the cost of living adjustment described below), or to a figure between 5.0% and the total average merit pay adjustment based upon the previously cited scale. If this procedure is utilized, the merit pay portion of salaries will be calculated based upon the following formula:

1. A ratio between (a) of the above stated limitation on administrative merit salary increases and (b) the amount determined as necessary for full implementation of merit slaary increases as determined by the evaluation from the R.E.A.S.O.N.S. system shall be established, using the formula a/b = % of dollars available.

2. The above percentage shall be applied to each administrator's merit salary adjustment for the following year.

3. An example might be:
   Administrator A's base salary = $22,500
   Evaluation rating = 5% increase or $1125 for the following year.
   Amount available for salary increases for that year based on the limiting factor cited above: $35,000
   Amount needed to implement full administrative increases: $50,000
   Formula application: $\dfrac{a}{b} = \dfrac{\$35,000}{50,000} = 70.0\%$

   Thus, 70% of $1125.00 = $787.50, or amount available for Administrator A's increase for the next contract year.

DEMONSTRATION FORM
Operational Task Management Objectives Evaluation Form
Junior High Principal

Administrator: _____ Fiscal Year 19 ___ 19 ___
Directions: Place circles on Profile Chart around appropriate Evaluation Scale 1 — 10
numbers and connect circles to show profile. En- (10 most positive) Points=
circle the appropriate numbers on the Evaluation Evaluation x % assigned)
Scale. Use N/A for sections that are Not Applicable. (3 x 10% = 30 points)

% ASSIGNED FOR YEAR	OPERATIONAL TASK AREA		EVALUATION	POINTS

(%) I. **INSTRUCTION**   1 2 3 4 5 6 7 8 9 10 ☐
  A. Maintains appropriate knowledge   Comments: _____
    of curriculum   1 2 3 4 5 6 7 8 9 10   _____
  B. Encourages use of Instructional
    aids and equipment   1 2 3 4 5 6 7 8 9 10   _____
  C. Evaluates instructional programs   1 2 3 4 5 6 7 8 9 10   _____
  D. Plans and implements instruc-
    tional programs   1 2 3 4 5 6 7 8 9 10   _____
  E. Administers volunteer, aide, stu-
    dent teaching programs   1 2 3 4 5 6 7 8 9 10   _____
  _____   1 2 3 4 5 6 7 8 9 10   _____
  _____   1 2 3 4 5 6 7 8 9 10   _____
  _____   1 2 3 4 5 6 7 8 9 10   _____

(%) II. **STAFF PERSONNEL**   1 2 3 4 5 6 7 8 9 10 ☐
  A. Assigns teachers and schedules   Comments: _____
    classes   1 2 3 4 5 6 7 8 9 10   _____
  B. Administers a program of in-
    service training   1 2 3 4 5 6 7 8 9 10   _____
  C. Administers a program of pro-
    fessional growth   1 2 3 4 5 6 7 8 9 10   _____
  D. Supervises and evaluates teachers
    effectively   1 2 3 4 5 6 7 8 9 10   _____
  E. Supervises and evaluates other
    employees effectively   1 2 3 4 5 6 7 8 9 10   _____
  F. Recommends persons for em-
    ployment/dismissal   1 2 3 4 5 6 7 8 9 10   _____
  G. Promotes harmonious staff rela-
    tions   1 2 3 4 6 6 7 8 9 10   _____
  H. Utilizes teacher potential   1 2 3 4 5 6 7 8 9 10
  I. Utilizes other employees'
    potential   1 2 3 4 5 6 7 8 9 10   _____
  J. Manages conflict effectively   1 2 3 4 5 6 7 8 9 10   _____
  K. Delegates authority and responsi-
    bility   1 2 3 4 5 6 7 8 9 10   _____
  _____   1 2 3 4 5 6 7 8 9 10   _____
  _____   1 2 3 4 5 6 7 8 9 10   _____

(%) III. **STUDENT SERVICES**   1 2 3 4 5 6 7 8 9 10 ☐
  A. Provides a program of guidance   Comments: _____
    services   1 2 3 4 5 6 7 8 9 10   _____
  B. Effectively manages office func-
    tions   1 2 3 4 5 6 7 8 9 10   _____
  C. Coordinates program of special
    education services   1 2 3 4 5 6 7 8 9 10   _____
  D. Coordinates school health serv-
    ices program   1 2 3 4 5 6 7 8 9 10   _____
  E. Coordinates program for student
    safety   1 2 3 4 5 6 7 8 9 10   _____
  F. Provides services for attendance/
    accounting   1 2 3 4 5 6 7 8 9 10   _____
  G. Provides services for student
    discipline   1 2 3 4 5 6 7 8 9 10   _____
  H. Provides program for student
    activities   1 2 3 4 5 6 7 8 9 10   _____
  I. Reviews student handbook
    annually   1 2 3 4 5 6 7 8 9 10   _____
  _____   1 2 3 4 5 6 7 8 9 10   _____
  _____   1 2 3 4 5 6 7 8 9 10   _____

(%) IV. MANAGEMENT FUNCTION   1 2 3 4 5 6 7 8 9 10 ☐

    A. Manages school facilities and   Comments: _____

       equipment   1 2 3 4 5 6 7 8 9 10 _____

    B. Effectively manages office

       functions   1 2 3 4 5 6 7 8 9 10 _____

    C. Effectively manages fiscal affairs 1 2 3 4 5 6 7 8 9 10 _____

    D. Effectively manages time   1 2 3 4 5 6 7 8 9 10 _____

    E. Approves all requisitions   1 2 3 4 5 6 7 8 9 10 _____

    F. Coordinates development of

       building budget   1 2 3 4 5 6 7 8 9 10 _____

    G. Completes tasks on time   1 2 3 4 5 6 7 8 9 10 _____

    H. Completes state department

       reports appropriately   1 2 3 4 5 6 7 8 9 10 _____

    I. Manages state/federal programs 1 2 3 4 5 6 7 8 9 10 _____

    _____ 1 2 3 4 5 6 7 8 9 10 _____

    _____ 1 2 3 4 5 6 7 8 9 10 _____

(%) V. SCHOOL COMMUNITY RELATIONS 1 2 3 4 5 6 7 8 9 10 ☐

    A. Encourages employee/parent   Comments: _____

       participation   1 2 3 4 5 6 7 8 9 10 _____

    B. Develops effective lines of com-

       munication   1 2 3 4 5 6 7 8 9 10 _____

    C. Encourages positive public rela-

       tions   1 2 3 4 5 6 7 8 9 10 _____

    D. Encourages student involvement

       in community affairs   1 2 3 4 5 6 7 8 9 10 _____

    E. Serves as admin. liaison with

       school, community   1 2 3 4 5 6 7 8 9 10 _____

    F. Effectively manages conflict   1 2 3 4 5 6 7 8 9 10 _____

    G. Publishes newsletter regularly   1 2 3 4 5 6 7 8 9 10 _____

    _____ 1 2 3 4 5 6 7 8 9 10 _____

    _____ 1 2 3 4 5 6 7 8 9 10 _____

(%) VI. ADMINISTRATIVE DEVELOPMENT 1 2 3 4 5 6 7 8 9 10 ☐

    A. Displays effective educational   Comments: _____

       leadership   1 2 3 4 5 6 7 8 9 10 _____

    B. Participates in professional

       growth activities   1 2 3 4 5 6 7 8 9 10 _____

    C. Practices effective communication

       skills   1 2 3 4 5 6 7 8 9 10 _____

    D. Demonstrates appropriate deci-

       sion-making strategies   1 2 3 4 5 6 7 8 9 10 _____

    E. Participates in professional

       associations   1 2 3 4 5 6 7 8 9 10 _____

    _____ 1 2 3 4 5 6 7 8 9 10 _____

    _____ 1 2 3 4 5 6 7 8 9 10 _____

    _____ 1 2 3 4 5 6 7 8 9 10 _____

    _____ 1 2 3 4 5 6 7 8 9 10 _____

(%) VII. RESEARCH AND DEVELOPMENT 1 2 3 4 5 6 7 8 9 10 ☐

    A. Promotes planned exploration/   Comments: _____

       experimentation   1 2 3 4 5 6 7 8 9 10 _____

    B. Encourages and supports innova-

       tion   1 2 3 4 5 6 7 8 9 10 _____

    C. Keeps current with pertinent

       research, literature, and practices 1 2 3 4 5 6 7 8 9 10 _____

    D. Coordinates teacher grant activi-

       ties   1 2 3 4 5 6 7 8 9 10 _____

    _____ 1 2 3 4 5 6 7 8 9 10 _____

    _____ 1 2 3 4 5 6 7 8 9 10 _____

    _____ 1 2 3 4 5 6 7 8 9 10 _____

    _____ 1 2 3 4 5 6 7 8 9 10 _____

```
% ASSIGNED
FOR YEAR      OPERATIONAL TASK AREA                              EVALUATION    POINTS
```

(%) VIII.	**DISTRICT TEAM RELATIONS**	1 2 3 4 5 6 7 8 9 10 ☐
		Comments: _____
	A. Supports district goals and objectives	1 2 3 4 5 6 7 8 9 10
	B. Supports and cooperates with other employees	1 2 3 4 5 6 7 8 9 10
	C. Cooperates with other organizations of the school district to meet identified goals and functions	1 2 3 4 5 6 7 8 9 10
	D. Promotes general welfare of the district	1 2 3 4 5 6 7 8 9 10
	E. Participates on district-wide committees	1 2 3 4 5 6 7 8 9 10
	F. Accepts assigned responsibilities	1 2 3 4 5 6 7 8 9 10
	G. Accepts suggestions/constructive criticism	1 2 3 4 5 6 7 8 9 10
	H. Demonstrates active interest in administrative council	1 2 3 4 5 6 7 8 9 10
	_____	1 2 3 4 5 6 7 8 9 10
	_____	1 2 3 4 5 6 7 8 9 10
	_____	1 2 3 4 5 6 7 8 9 10
	_____	1 2 3 4 5 6 7 8 9 10
(%) IX.	**OTHER RELATED ASSIGNMENTS**	1 2 3 4 5 6 7 8 9 10 ☐
		Comments: _____
	A. Performs such other duties as the Superintendent may assign	1 2 3 4 5 6 7 8 9 10
	_____	1 2 3 4 5 6 7 8 9 10
	_____	1 2 3 4 5 6 7 8 9 10
	_____	1 2 3 4 5 6 7 8 9 10
	_____	1 2 3 4 5 6 7 8 9 10
	_____	1 2 3 4 5 6 7 8 9 10
	_____	1 2 3 4 5 6 7 8 9 10

Comments: TOTAL POINTS   ☐

This evaluation was completed on _____

_____
Signature/Evaluator

I have read this evaluation.

_____
Signature/Evaluatee

_____
Date

Indicators of Administrative Effectiveness

Highland, Indiana, Public Schools

The Highland, Indiana, Public Schools have developed a manual for administrator evaluation entitled "Educational Leadership by Objectives." In the following excerpt, a number of what are termed "indicators of administrator effectiveness" are described. These relate to such areas as curriculum and instruction, finance, and school-community relations. The rationale given for listing these indicators is "to let the administrator know how he is expected to perform his responsibilities" and "to enable the individual to judge how well he is performing." After the administrator has developed a role description based both on his formal job description and on the indicators, he can than proceed to develop the objectives by which a judgment will be made about the effectiveness of his performance. The descriptions of the indicators are sufficiently detailed to give prospective evaluators a good "handle" on the complexity of the tasks administrators are generally expected to perform.

This section of the Highland Superintendency Team Assessment Plan describes Indicators of Administrative Effectiveness in eight task areas. The categories of tasks are:

A. Curriculum and instruction
B. Staff Personnel
C. Pupil Personnel
D. Finance and Business Management
E. School Buildings and Equipment
F. School-Community Relations
G. Professional Growth
H. Supporting Services

Beneath the heading for each task category are descriptions of administrative performance which are required to effectively perform the task. Few of these descriptions will be appropriate for all administrators, some will not; the descriptions of performance cover all levels of administration in the Highland school system.

To determine which descriptions of effective administrative performance are appropriate for him, the individual administrator must:

A. Become familiar with his formal job description.

B. Review carefully the descriptions of desirable administrative performance within each of the eight task areas.

C. Compare his formal job description with the Indicators of Effectiveness for each of the eight task areas.

D. Develop a role description of his specific responsibilities as he sees them.

The administrator can then select specific areas in which he wishes to improve his administrative skills or knowledge, and develop a self-assessment plan for achieving the desired performance and effectiveness in each of the areas selected for improvement.

To develop an effective plan the educational administrator must try to describe the specific terminal performance which would bring about the desired improvement. The educational administrator should then identify the particular activities which will enable him to reach the described terminal performance. Finally, the educational administrator should develop a system for measuring his progress toward his desired terminal performance, i.e., how he will know when he has achieved his objective. After the administrator has completed this process for each of his selected areas for improvement he will be ready to develop his professional improvement plan with his appraisal team.

A. Curriculum and Instruction

1. The effective educational administrator coordinates his efforts with the efforts of others for cooperative development of the instructional program.

   a. Initiates, administers, and facilitates systematic development of a school system philosophy specifying instructional and curricular objectives.

   b. Assumes leadership in developing school, departmental, or area philosophy consistent with school system philosophy.

   c. Contributes to the development of system-wide curricular structure consistent with school system philosophy.

   d. Develops administrative structure and defines administrator responsibilities in the area of curriculum and instruction.

   e. Develops comprehensive goals and related sequences of performance objectives for particular curriculum areas. Analyzes results and revises goals and sequences accordingly.

   f. Cooperatively develops instructional guidelines and resources, and makes provisions for their use and refinement.

   g. Develops and administers assessment program and in-service programs for staff members.

    h.   Establishes and maintains a professional library for staff use.

    i.   Develops programs of student activities consistent with school system philosophy.

    j.   Organizes and administers supplemental programs, such as adult education and summer school, based on identified needs of those served by the programs.

2.   In cooperation with other staff members, the effective educational administrator consistently seeks improvement of instruction and of the total instructional program.

    a.   Accepts responsibility for becoming informed about significant new developments in curriculum and instruction.

    b.   Stimulates and assists staff members in investigating and evaluating promising new developments.

    c.   Implements instructional changes under way in the Highland Schools and secures staff support for them.

    d.   Works with staff in his area of responsibility so as to support and strengthen Instructional Staff Assessment:

        (1)   Communicates philosophy effectively.

        (2)   Secures staff cooperation and support.

        (3)   Assists staff members in selecting appropriate and significant objectives for professional growth.

        (4)   Assists in development and execution of professional growth plans, including means of measurement.

        (5)   Completes required general evaluations as outlined in Teacher Assessment Program.

    e.   Conducts research projects related to curriculum and instruction in Highland.

    f.   Obtains and disseminates information and initiates proposals relative to supplemental funding of curriculum and instruction projects.

    g.   In cooperation with staff, evaluates and makes recommendations concerning materials and texts for use in Highland Schools.

    h.   Works for curriculum development and improvement of instruction through a program of regular meetings with staff.

    i.   Prepares annual report of status, accomplishments, needs, and unresolved issues in area of responsibility.

    j.   Effectively resolves conflicts within area of responsibility.

    k.   Follows systematic plan for involving students in curricular and instructional planning.

    l.   Contributes to overall efforts by accepting responsibility for special assignments.

B.   Staff Personnel

    1.   Recruitment and Selection.

The effective educational administrator responsible for recruitment and selection:

a. Cooperatively and appropriately participates in the employment cycle of the school system.

b. Actively participates in the development and implementation of recruitment programs for certificated personnel.

c. Exhibits professional behavior and personal characteristics which will attract capable and desirable personnel to the school system.

d. Devises a systematic means of collecting data whereby judgements can be made about prospective candidates for vacancies.

e. Makes a positive contribution in the school system visitation phase of the recruitment and selection process for certificated personnel.

f. Recommends to the appropriate person in the school system which candidate is best qualified for each vacancy.

g. Develops recruitment materials and works with other educational administrators in recruiting and employment of non-certificated personnel.

h. Attempts to correlate the effectiveness of selection procedures with teaching performance.

i. Develops a plan for analyzing causes of employee turnover and retention.

j. Provides information and suggestions for upgrading the effectiveness of the substitute teacher program.

k. Encourages capable high school students to participate in cadet teaching programs designed to encourage consideration of teaching as a career.

l. Encourages capable student teachers in the school system to seek a teaching career in Highland.

2. Assignment, Load and Transfer

The effective educational administrator responsible for assignment, load and transfer:

a. Implements school board policies pertinent to these areas.

b. Consults with other administrators regarding assignment procedures and enlists their cooperation in making the process as effective as possible.

c. Makes work assignments based on the strengths of the individual in relation to the description of his job.

d. Makes assignments on the basis of the individual's qualifications and consideration of his desire for the assignment.

e. Makes instructional and service loads equitable and fair for each employee.

f. Cooperates with other administrators in determining assignment, load and transfer requirements for the school system.

3. Orienting the School Employee

The effective educational administrator responsible for orienting the new school employee:

a. Develops orientation programs to introduce new personnel to the school system and the community throughout their first year of service in the school system.

b. Designs orientation programs which naturally lead into the in-service training programs of the school system during the second and succeeding years of employment.

c. Demonstrates that an employee's professional development and commitment is largely dependent upon his active participation in the improvement of the school system.

d. Develops programs and procedures which provide the opportunity for experienced staff personnel to assist new employees.

4. Staff Management Role

The effective educational administrator responsible for fostering the staff management role:

a. Develops a cooperative and positive relationship with other school personnel to achieve the goals of the school system.

b. Stimulates staff morale, promotes organizational purpose and readiness to change, and pursues traditional goals of efficiency and economy.

c. Exhibits rational administrative behavior in job-relevant situations which encourages other school personnel to trust and respect his leadership.

d. Prevents his personal satisfactions from standing in the way of meeting organizational needs and goals.

e. Seeks a balance between concern for organizational needs and personal satisfaction.

f. Represents management at the various levels (as appropriate) of the grievance procedure.

5. Development of Personnel

The effective educational administrator responsible for developing staff personnel:

a. Cooperates in developing comprehensive in-service education programs which are well-organized and well-planned.

b. Communicates with all members of the school system the nature of the professional development program and how its objectives relate to their areas of concern.

c. Provides opportunities for selected professional development experiences for school employees under his supervision.

d. Utilizes a wide variety of in-service techniques and tools in implementing the program in order to meet the needs and interests of the whole staff, i.e., workshops, brainstorming, buzz sessions, demonstrations, group discussions and role playing.

e. Supports in-service training programs on a systemwide basis by his words, actions and attitudes.

f. Serves as a model of professional growth to his subordinates.

6. Personnel Administration and Employee Organizations

The effective educational administrator responsible for establishing positive relationships with employee organizations:

a. Operates within his appropriate role in the organizational plan of the school system.

b. Encourages informal organizations within the framework of the formal school organization to support the goals of the formal organization, support its activities, and assist in securing public participation in improving its services.

c. Cooperates in establishing a communication procedure whereby problem situations or concerns can be discussed in terms of the goals and objectives of the school system.

d. Develops relationships with employee organizations which will encourage such organization to assist in the attainment of the further development of each employee in meeting the school system's goals and objectives.

C. Pupil Personnel

1. The effective educational administrator devises and maintains efficient records systems to meet student and organizational needs:

a. Provides for efficient and systematic maintenance of necessary and desirable individual records.

b. Provides for maintenance and use of special purpose short-term records.

c. Formulates and consistently follows clear policies regarding confidentiality of student records.

2. Plans, develops, and expands general guidance functions in the Highland Schools.

(In this context, guidance functions are not specialized service, but constructive courses of action for meeting individual needs throughout the school setting. Teaching strategies, adapting instruction to individuals, and methods for resolving student problems, as well as special program features, are thus guidance activities. Guidance and instruction are viewed as inseparable.)

a. Plans, develops, and refines group and individual guidance activities.

(1) Involves staff members in the study of student needs and

development of appropriate policies, strategies, and classroom activities emphasizing developmental and preventive guidance.

    (2) Conducts in-service programs directed to initiating, maintaining, evaluating, and refining school guidance functions.

    (3) Basic decisions for changes on evaluations of proposed and existing guidance activities for suitability and effect on students.

  b. Applies principles of effective guidance to handling of student problems and conflict situations.

    (1) Deals with causes as well as symptoms of student problems.

    (2) Conducts systematic, constructive followups to crisis encounters with students.

    (3) Develops case studies of persistent or severe student problems.

    (4) Acts to influence future behavior by securing teacher or student commitments to positive courses of action.

    (5) Uses many sources of data for making major decisions affecting students.

    (6) Consults with and makes referrals to specialists in seeking to resolve persistent or severe student problems.

    (7) Defines and pursues courses of action which emphasize enabling as well as controlling functions.

3. Cooperatively develops and implements changes of viewpoint, teaching strategies, and school program to serve varying needs of students.

  a. Works cooperatively with staff members to increase flexibility in instruction.

  b. Works with staff in development and application of teaching strategies which place students in active roles. (e.g. − student-teacher planning)

  c. Develops programs of voluntary activities based on students' interests.

  d. Identifies and uses special abilities of staff members and students in particular activities.

  e. Provides for systematic review, evaluation, and refinement of methods for meeting individual differences.

  f. Develops and refines methods of reporting pupil progress which are satisfying to parents and which are consistent with instructional objectives for individual students.

D. Finance and Business Management

1. The effective educational administrator responsible for general

business procedures and management:

    a.   Cooperates with all other concerned personnel in the overall management of financial and business affairs relating to the operation of the school system.

    b.   Follows federal, state and local laws, rules and regulations relating to school finance and funding as they apply to his particular assignment.

    c.   Provides his superiors with information relating to the funding under his supervision.

    d.   Provides information to his staff as to the current financial developments and situations as they may apply to his position or assignment and to the staff.

    e.   Develops an insurance program for appropriate coverage of facilities, equipment and personnel. The program to provide property, liability and crime protection.

2.   The effective educational administrator responsible for budget preparation:

    a.   Secures the cooperation and involvement of all affected personnel in preparing budgetary needs and recommendations. (Teachers, department heads, non-certificated employees and others are involved in recommending needs and priorities to implement the educational program.)

    b.   Prepares a realistic budget that considers the educational program, the expenditures necessary to support the program, and the anticipated available revenues.

    c.   Develops cost estimates of proposals that would change the number of professional and/or non-certificated staff members or their compensation.

    d.   Allocates budget funds in accordance with expressed needs and budget limitations.

    e.   Arranges for public meeting to inform the general public as to educational needs, the proposed budget to meet these needs, and the financial problems relating thereto.

3.   The effective educational administrator responsible for managing requisitions and purchases:

    a.   Informs personnel who are responsible for the management of budget funds as to the amounts of funds available.

    b.   Provides for systematic and efficient purchasing procedures and expenditure of funds under his jurisdiction and for the instruction of the staff in these procedures.

    c.   Arranges for storage and equitable distribution of materials and supplies and reports to the proper school officials.

    d.   Checks carefully the receipt of equipment, materials and supplies and reports to the proper school officials.

        e.   Arranges for efficient purchasing through proper bidding procedures.

    4.   The effective educational administrator responsible for managing expenditures of funds:

        a.   Secures established procedural approval before obligating the expenditure of budget funds.

        b.   Consults with his superiors before obligating any funds when the expenditure might be controversial. Example: Equipment which might be dangerous, require building alteration, etc.

        c.   Establishes an accurate and efficient system of controlling the expenditure of funds (budget, extra-curricular) within the framework of all federal, state and local rules and regulations and of reporting the status of all accounts .

    5.   The effective educational administrator responsible for funding (securing of finances).

        a.   Is informed as to the availability of federal, state and local sources of revenue.

        b.   Secures all possible funds from available sources that are necessary for the efficient implementation of the total school program.

        c.   Manages funds so as to have sufficient funds available to meet obligations in an acceptable business manner, to properly invest idle funds and accurately account for funds.

    6.   The effective educational administrator responsible for business affairs relating to personnel:

        a.   Organizes and operates a system of accurate personnel accounting and reporting relating to such items as sick leave, personal business days, loss of time, etc.

        b.   Develops cooperatively with the Board of School Trustees and school personnel salary schedules and fringe benefit programs that will attract capable personnel to the system.

E.   School Buildings and Equipment

    1.   The effective educational administrator responsible for school building plans:

        a.   Keeps informed as to advances in educational programming, building design, equipment and materials development through reading, attendance at conferences, workshops and exhibits, contacts with architects, contractors and suppliers.

        b.   Causes surveys to be made to determine the adequacy of existing facilities to provide for the system's educational program.

        c.   Analyzes results of surveys and other predictors of enrollment projection and educational program needs in developing an overall plan for meeting facility needs.

      d.   Provides an opportunity for staff (certificated and non-certificated) and the community to become involved in the planning construction (new or remodeling) of facilities to house the educational program.

      e.   Keeps informed as to all rules and regulations concerning building construction and causes proper forms and procedure to be completed and followed.

  2. The effective educational administrator responsible for management of physical facilities:

      a.   Provides and organizes a staff for the effective and equitable utilization of buildings, grounds and equipment.

      b.   Cooperates with all personnel in organizing and conducting an effective maintenance program for buildings, grounds and equipment.

      c.   Submits to the proper staff members, requests for repairs, alterations and improvements.

      d.   Provides for care and for respect of physical facilities in their usage.

  3. The effective educational administrator responsible for buildings and equipment:

      a.   Provides for sufficient equipment, materials and supplies, for the operation and maintenance of the physical facilities and equipment.

      b.   Plans for and supervises the effective and economical use of materials and supplies in building maintenance.

      c.   Follows stated procedural practices in the requisition, storage distribution and inventory of materials, supplies and equipment.

      d.   Develops a program for the selection, training, assignment and supervision of the custodial and maintenance staff.

      e.   Develops a long-range maintenance program which provides for emergency maintenance, preventive maintenance, recurring and periodic maintenance and deferred maintenance. Such program is to include the development of a maintenance records system.

F. School-Community Relations

  1. Establishing a School-Community Relations Program

      To develop an effective school-community program, the educational administrator:

      a.   Contributes to the development and implementation of a system-wide school-community relations program.

      b.   Identifies the publics with which the school-community relations program interacts, such as (1) the students, (2) the faculty, (3) the parents, (4) the taxpayers, (5) the non-taxpayers and (6) organized service and social agencies in the community.

c. Interprets the policies, rules and regulations, objectives, conditions, and needs of the school system to the various publics in the school system and the community.

d. Is consistent in the administration of policies and rules and regulations within the framework of the school system.

e. Creates a climate and provides opportunities which strengthen the lines of communication between the home and the school, i.e. parent-teacher conferences, home visitation, "open house," school visitation, etc.

f. Utilizes the various media of public communications available to the school (radio, newspaper, speaker's bureau, staff newsletter).

g. Informs patrons and the community of the school program, calendar, policies, and innovations through the use of a school handbook, newsletter, school newspaper, and bulletins.

h. Prepares and distributes annually a brochure listing topics and certificated and non-certificated personnel who participate in the systemwide Speaker's Bureau.

i. Studies and develops programs to involve pupils who are the primary agent for establishing an effective school-home relationship.

j. Makes check lists or develops assessment instruments to see if patrons in the community understand educational programs of the school system and to collect data for the purpose of future program development.

2. Community Relations

To develop the proper attitude for a successful school-community relations program, the effective educational administrator:

a. Identifies the needs and concerns of various constituencies in the school system and provides this input for an effective system-wide school-community relations program.

b. Devises means and programs which enable the school to aid in the cultural, recreational, and educational interests of facilities, equipment and instructional materials.

c. Involves parent organizations in the utilization of school facilities, equipment and instructional materials.

d. Provides for home-school conferences on a systematic basis.

e. Provides a training program for teachers before they begin home visitations.

f. Uses special weeks and special educational programs to show the citizenry what pupils are accomplishing in the school system.

g. Prepares mailings to be sent to taxpayers who would not normally receive items or materials from children enrolled in the school or school system.

h. Develops and maintains an up-to-date listing of organizations and clubs, service or social, who can be valuable sources of support for school programs.

3. Utilization of Community Resources

The effective educational administrator endeavors to encourage utilization of community-wide resources:

a. Prepares a community file of parents and others willing to share their specialized knowledge.

b. Cultivates leaders in industry, business, labor and community organizations who can communicate vocational opportunities to school system personnel.

c. Develops citizens committees to aid as resource agencies or as study groups to serve as two-way communicators for school and community.

d. Organizes parent groups to aid on tours, field trips and parties.

4. Utilization of School Personnel Talents

Since the school system has a rich pool of talented personnel, the utilization of these individuals enriches the educational administrator who:

a. Consults with school personnel in the planning, production, and presentation of specific communications.

b. Assists in coordinating work with civic and other groups which contribute to the advancement of the school system.

c. Provides assistance to staff members in preparing and submitting articles to be printed in periodicals, or used with other forms of media.

d. Provides staff members with assistance and materials for exhibition at educational conventions, workshops, and seminar meetings locally and in preparation of materials for community and staff distribution (handbooks, recruiting booklets, etc.)

e. Guides those responsible for developing publications in formulating a consistent style.

f. Assists in coordination of the publication of manuals which would be subject to periodic up-dating and revision.

g. Encourages and instructs school personnel in the use of school-community relations techniques and informs them of the activities of the school system.

5. Program Evaluation
    The effective educational administrator:
    a. Conducts systematic evaluation of communications and reports utilized in the total school-community relations program.
    b. Plans interaction with community leaders to determine the reaction to education programs in operation and also to obtain reactions to proposed programs.
    c. Develops methods for assessing feedback from internal and external audiences to modify communications operation or initiate action to establish new objectives.
    d. Evaluates relative effectiveness of various communication media and channels.
G. Professional Growth
    1. The effective educational administrator is an active participant in group activities for professional growth of administrators:
        a. Helps to identify and select desirable professional growth projects to be undertaken cooperatively by the Superintendency Team.
        b. Participates actively in group undertakings for professional growth of administrators, such as —
            (1) Workshops and conferences
            (2) Study groups
            (3) Planning and research projects
            (4) Pilot programs
            (5) Appraisal and evaluation activities
    2. The effective educational administrator assumes responsibility for a continuing personal program of professional improvement:
        a. Identifies and assigns priorities to significant professional growth areas directly related to his particular administrative responsibilities.
        b. Follows a systematic plan for attainment of personal professional growth objectives through such activities as —
            (1) Planned programs of independent reading and study
            (2) Selected university courses
            (3) Selected professional meetings
            (4) On-the-job role development
    3. The effective educational administrator uses new understandings and skills to improve his on-the-job performance:
        (a) Changes or enlarges his activities to reflect changed concept of his role.
        (b) Changes management of time to reflect revised priorities.
        (c) Provides impetus and direction for change.

d.   Adopts new leadership techniques.

H.   Supporting Services

The effective educational administrator:

1.   Organizes and administers *guidance* and *counseling* services to meet the anticipated and expressed needs of students, teachers, and administrators through:

   a.   Assessing vocational trends, communicating educational implications of new vocational developments to professional staff and students, providing resources and activities which encourage student exploration of occupational and professional alternatives; providing assistance in job placement for enrolled and graduating students.

   b.   Providing educational counseling services by systematically identifying appropriate educational agencies for a wide range of vocational interests, by providing accurate and current financial assistance information to both parents and students, and by providing resources and activities which promote student exploration of post-high school educational opportunities.

   c.   Providing educational counseling services on a confidential and individual and/or group basis for Highland secondary (grades 7-12) students.

   d.   Providing in-service programs to enable instructional staff to develop skills in assisting students to develop positive attitudes toward self and the school environment.

   e.   Identifying supplemental and supporting community service agencies which can be utilized to help students with special physical and psychological needs.

   f.   Designing and administering in-service programs for the professional development of guidance and counseling personnel.

   g.   Systematically examining the effectiveness of the guidance and counseling program by obtaining evaluation from parents, graduates, administrators, teachers and parents; modifies program on basis of evaluation obtained.

   h.   Designing and administering a testing program which provides a sound basis for the vocational and educational counseling of secondary students and which provides a basis for curriculum and instructional decision-making by administrative and instructional personnel.

   i.   Assisting in initiating and completing research studies related to graduates, students, and dropouts.

   j.   Providing annual reports to appropriate administrators relative to the status of Highland guidance and counseling services.

2. Organizes and administers *library* resources and services to meet the needs of Highland students, teachers, and administrators by:
   a. Supervising the selection and ordering of library materials for all instructional materials centers.
   b. Supervising the collection of recommendations for additional library materials from teachers and administrators.
   c. Training librarians and clerk-librarians to administer library services in the various buildings.
   d. Providing up-to-date catalogues of library resources and services to all instructional personnel.
   e. Providing assistance to all instructional personnel in the identification, selection, and ordering of all types of commercial A-V materials.
   f. Ensuring that appropriate instruction in the proper use of library facilities and materials is provided for staff and students.
3. Organizes and administers Audio-Visual services to meet the anticipated and expressed needs of teachers and administrators by:
   a. Maintaining an inventory of all A-V equipment in the school system on a school by school basis.
   b. Providing in-service workshops for instructional personnel in the use of A-V equipment and the construction of A-V materials.
   c. Assessing the A-V equipment needs of each school annually; budgets for necessary equipment.
   d. Assisting administrators and teachers in the evaluation and selection of A-V equipment.
   e. Supervising the circulation and maintenance of the school system film library.
   f. Selecting, training, and supervising student audio-visual assistants.
4. Directs the operation of efficient *food services* for schools in accordance with state and local laws and health regulations and in compliance with state and local laws and health regulations and in compliance with directives of the School Lunch Division of the State Department of Public Instruction by:
   a. Selecting of capable personnel and assignment to appropriate duties.
   b. Efficient budgeting and economical purchasing procedures for equipment, supplies, and food.
   c. Maintenance of high standards of food quality and sanitation.
   d. Providing (within limits of cost) food and service attractive to those using the lunchroom.
5. Provides, organizes, and directs an adequate, safe and efficient

transportation service for the students that is in compliance with all local policies and state laws regulating school buses and drivers by:

    a.   Determining transportation needs through the use of spot maps indicating the resident location of all pupils.

    b.   Providing adequate physical equipment and personnel to meet the transportation requirement needs.

    c.   Developing a transportation plan of routes and schedules.

    d.   Determining that all physical equipment meets all local and state laws and regulations concerning to construction, design and safety.

    e.   Providing a system for selection of personnel (drivers) that will ensure legally qualified drivers, in good physical condition and of high moral character.

    f.   Providing for an efficient operational and maintenance program that will ensure the availability of the buses.

6.   Provides for essential social services directly affecting students' school experience, in close cooperation with other school services and community agencies by:

    a.   Supplying essential information about available social services to teachers, nurses, guidance personnel, and administrators.

    b.   Coordinating efforts of Social Services and Guidance in areas and matters of mutual concern and responsibility.

    c.   Developing orderly procedures for referrals to Social Services and for providing follow-up reports on referrals.

    d.   Evaluating services and establishing work priorities through systematic efforts to identify social services yielding greatest student benefits.

    e.   Developing and maintaining close working relationships with community agencies.

7.   Organizes and administers *data processing* services to meet the anticipated and expressed needs of Highland administrators by:

    a.   Assisting in the selection, training and assessment of data-processing personnel.

    b.   Sharing the responsibility for cooperatively planning and organizing data-processing instruction for Highland students.

    c.   Systematically identifying educational recording and service functions which can be facilitated by utilizing data-processing services.

    d.   Annually submitting to the superintendent a report concerning the status of the data-processing department.

8.   Contributes to maintenance and development of necessary and beneficial *Health Services* by:

    a.   Participating in cooperative planning for the organization and administration of School Health Services.

    b.   Maintaining records and reports of Health Service activities, including those to meet State requirements for periodic vision, hearing, and tuberculin tests.

    c.   Using Health Services as a resource for aid in diagnosis of student problems and identification of handicapped children.

    d.   Developing programs of health and hygiene for students through consultation between Health Service personnel and the general staff.

    e.   Providing for in-service activities for professional growth of Health Services personnel and improvement of services.

    f.   Providing, in cooperation with Health Services personnel, recommendations and information related to dealing with students with special physical or health problems. (e.g., epileptics, diabetics).

    g.   Coordination of Health Services with other school and community agencies serving students.

    h.   Participation in regular evaluation of the operation of Health Services.

10. Works with therapists to organize *Speech and Hearing* services for maximum effectiveness in overcoming student disabilities.

    a.   Preparing a written description of the program, including objectives, criteria for kinds and degrees of disability to be served, and methods of screening and referral of students.

    b.   Providing for systematic communication between therapists and classroom teachers and between therapists and parents arents when essential.

    c.   Establishing case loads and schedules for therapists.

    d.   Providing for case records to include therapy provided and progress made.

    e.   Preparing an annual report summarizing therapists' activities, results, and recommendations.

11. Maintains, supports, and develops an effective program of *Special Education* by:

    a.   Disseminating information about services of Special Education, types of disabilities served, and methods of referral.

    b.   Following systematic procedures for identifying students in need of Special Education services and for placement in Special Education.

    c.   Formulating and following specific procedures for incorporating Special Education into the total school program and for including Special Education students in the total program of school activities.

     d.   Working with other personnel to enrich the instructional program for Special Education.

     e.   Providing in-service activities for school personnel to enable them to recognize and meet needs of exceptional children.

12. Works with special reading teachers to secure maximum benefits for students needing *Remedial Reading* services.

     a.   Developing written description of the program of services, including statement of objectives, screening and referral methods, services to teachers, criteria for including students in the program, and means of measuring improvement.

     b.   Establishing procedures for coordinating efforts of special reading teachers and classroom teachers.

     c.   Providing for individual case records showing disabilities, instruction received, and progress made.

     d   Preparing an annual report summarizing services, results, and recommendations.

Work Plan and Evaluation System

Frederick County, Maryland, Public Schools

This procedure is, in the words of its organizers, "an approach to planning, controlling, and evaluating organizational operations which places emphasis on clearly defined objectives and performance standards against which organizational results may be measured." Throughout the succinct document, emphasis is placed on written definitions of objectives and on the method by which the objectives may be obtained. The authors begin by discussing the purposes of the process, then outline the benefits to be expected from it, the elements composing the work plan, the process by which the plan is to be implemented, and procedures and schedules for a specific year — 1978. (The excerpt does not include a number of forms to be utilized in the course of the evaluative process.)

The Work Plan and Evaluation procedure described here is an approach to planning, controlling, and evaluating organizational operations which places emphasis on clearly defined objectives and performance standards against which organizational results may be measured. Sometimes called management by objectives, this method of management usually involves at least (1) identification in writing of performance objectives by superiors and subordinates and (2) identification of how and by what time objectives should be reached.

In the Frederick County public schools, we will be introducing such a system in a limited way. As we gain experience, we will add to, subtract from, or revise our procedures.

The rest of this communication describes the Work Plan and Evaluation System by reference to:

1. Purposes
2. Expected Benefits
3. Elements and Processes
4. FY-78 Installation Procedures
5. FY-78 Installation Schedule
6. Plans for the Future

PURPOSES

Since the administrative structure of the Frederick County schools has been reorganized, and because the Board of Education has established clear directions for the school system, it is crucial that we systematically focus our energies on those priorities. The Work Plan and Evaluation System is intended to address the need to organize our work around these priorities. The specific purposes of the Frederick County system are:

1. Communication of system priorities to all personnel
2. Establishment of clear objectives for all administrative personnel consistent with system priorities and in concert with functional responsibilities represented in the reorganized system
3. Establishment of fair and objective procedures for evaluating administrative personnel and for appraising the work of the system

EXPECTED BENEFITS

The major expected benefit to be derived from the installation of the Work Plan and Evaluation System is more effective accomplishment of objectives. Other possible benefits include:

1. Better understood work expectations
2. Improved communications because objectives provide a common framework within which plans, progress, and performance may be discussed
3. Increased feedback on performance through review of performance progress
4. Facilitation of teamwork through indentification of common objectives
5. Development of alternative ways of achieving objectives
6. Increased participation in decision making
7. Production of more precise and useful information for planning
8. Increased emphasis on results

ELEMENTS AND PROCESSES OF THE FREDERICK COUNTY WORK PLAN AND EVALUATION SYSTEM

The Frederick County Work Plan and Evaluation System revolves around the use of four documents. Those documents are: (1) System Priorities, (2) Position Description, (3) Administrative Work Plan, and (4) Administrative Performance Evaluation.

SYSTEM PRIORITIES

System priorities reflecting the goals of the Board of Education will be distributed by the Superintendent as the first step in the process. The priorities describe, in general terms, the most important work of the organization for the fiscal year.

POSITION DESCRIPTION

For each administrative position in the system, a position description has been, or will be, developed. The position description outlines the role and duties of each administrative job. These duties provide the framework for determining the objectives and the kinds of activities to support objectives which administrative personnel may select.

ADMINISTRATIVE WORK PLAN

The Administrative Work Plan is a form listing the system priorities addressed by an individual and the objectives designed to satisfy those priorities. Also included are major activities supporting the objectives, completion dates, and performance standards against which work on objectives may be measured.

Originally completed by the individual administrator, the Administration Work Plan is then shared in a conference with the employee's immediate supervisor. In that conference the immediate supervisor assesses the plan in relation to (1) internal consistency, (2) relevance to system priorities, (3) feasibility, (4) relationship to objectives submitted by other subordinates, (5) consistency with the employee's position description, and (6) consistency with Board of Education policies and procedures. The immediate supervisor may wish to add, subtract, or revise objectives and activities.

Having reached agreement on the plan, the immediate supervisor then passes his subordinate's plans on to his supervisor. The process continues in that way until all plans reach the Superintendent. If irreconcilable differences should arise over the plan, those differences would also be taken to the next level and, if necessary, on to the Superintendent.

The Superintendent reviews the plans in mcuh the same way described for each immediate supervisor. Once the Superintendent approves the plans, that approval is communicated and work on the listed objectives begins.

ADMINISTRATIVE PERFORMANCE EVALUATION

The Administrative Performance Evaluation form is directly related to the Administrative Work Plan and will replace previously used administrative evaluation instruments. It lists the immediate supervisor's appraisal of the subordinate on the following points: (1) performance plan objectives achieved, (2) performance plan objectives not achieved, (3) performance on position description functions not included in the performance plan, and (4) management style. Also recorded are plans for the improvement of job related competencies, resources needed to improve competencies, suggestions for system changes to improve performance, a general performance rating, recommended personnel actions, and employee reaction to the evaluation.

Although the performance evaluation is not completed until the end of the fiscal year, it is preceded by at least two progress reviews between the subordinate and his immediate supervisor. In those reviews, the subordinate reports on progress, explains discrepancies between actual and proposed completion dates, outlines problems and reports needs for additional resources. The Administrative Performance Evaluation report, then, reflects any revisions agreed upon in the progress reviews and takes into account problems revealed in the progress review sessions over which the employee could not exercise control.

Once the report is signed by both the employee and the immediate supervisor, it is passed through the organization until it reaches the Superintendent's Office. The results of the Administrative Performance Evaluation may then be used for staff development planning and for establishing priorities in the ensuing fiscal year.

FY-78 INSTALLATION PROCEDURES

During FY-78 a limited Work Plan and Evaluation System will be initiated. The process will apply to the work of all persons paid on the administrative and supervisory scale.

Each employee will be asked to develop *three* objectives. At least one objective should be developed in response to system priorities. Owing to the nature of their position descriptions, some employees may only be working on one objective related to system priorities, while all three objectives of other personnel may reflect system goals. Other responsibilities which are reflected in routine, maintenance, or reactive functions, and which comprise a considerable portion of the workload, will not be listed on the Administrative Performance Evaluation, although they will be part of the evaluation process.

It is expected that as personnel become comfortable with the process, the system may be expanded. Once the process is clearly understood, it will become apparent that the Work Plan and Evaluation System is a tool which can effectively organize and serve to actually reduce administrative workload.

FY-78 INSTALLATION SCHEDULE

Action	Person(s) Responsible	Date(s) of Completion
1. Distribution of System Performance Priorities and Explanation of Work Plan and Evaluation System	Superintendent	September 23, 1977
2. In-Service on Plan for Those Affected	Superintendent and Area Directors	October 7, 1977
3. Completion of Individual Performance Plans	A&S Personnel	October 14, 1977
4. Review, Decision, Acceptance of Administrative Work Plans of Subordinates by Superordinates	A&S Personnel	October 28, 1977
5. Administrative Work Plans Received by the Superintendent	Superordinates	October 31, 1977
6. Administrative Work Plans returned by Superintendent	Superintendent Assistant for Planning and Evaluation	November 8, 1977
7. Progress Reviews of Administrative Work Plans (2)	Superordinates Review with Subordinates	January 31, 1978 March 31, 1978
8. Completion of Administrative Performance Evaluation Reports	Superordinates	June 30, 1978
9. Administrative Performance Evaluation Reports Received by the Superintendent	Superordinates	July 7, 1978

PLANS FOR THE FUTURE

Experience gained in FY-78 and information received on FY-78 Administrative Performance Evaluation reports will provide data on the need for changes in the system. In addition, a management information center, operating out of the Office of Planning and Evaluation, will be established during FY-78. That center will collect in one central location data important to needs assessment for system priorities. The Work Plan and Evaluation System process for FY-79, then, would begin with a more systematic needs assessment, followed by a schedule similar to the one described for FY-78.

SYSTEM PRIORITIES FOR FISCAL YEAR 1978
BOARD OF EDUCATION OF FREDERICK COUNTY

The most important work before us as we go through this school year is the effective implementation of the approved task force recommendations which were made last spring and over this summer. With the addition of only a few other items, I see this year as one in which we implement and improve upon those recommendations. The priorities listed below reflect the need to consolidate our gains.

CONTINUATION PRIORITIES

1. Complete implementation of the task force recommendations for improvement in instruction in the basic skills.
    a. Complete the development of marked deficiency evaluation and curriculum.
    b. Monitor and evaluate the system for quarterly recording and reporting of student progress.
    c. Complete implementation of the language arts curriculum K-12, develop the methods to assess its effectiveness, and report on its impact and on suggestions for improvement.
    d. Complete implementation of the mathematics curriculum K-8, develop the methods to assess its effectiveness, and report on its impact and on suggestions for improvement.
    e. Complete implementation of the integration of basic skills instruction with other subject matter areas and report on its impact and on suggestions for improvement.
    f. Complete implementation of the developmental skills program, assess its effectiveness, and report on its impact and on suggestions for improvement.

2. Consistently apply the discipline and attendance policies and procedure

which appear in the Policies and Procedures Handbook, assess their effectiveness, and report on their impact and on suggestions for improvement.

3. Provide additional alternatives for disruptive youth.
4. Implement, assess, and improve the effectiveness of procedures to increase parental involvement in the schools and to improve school-community relationships.
5. Implement, assess, and improve the effectiveness of the reorganization plan.
6. Implement, assess, and improve the effectiveness of plans to increase participation in school food service menu planning.
7. Monitor, assess, and improve the effectiveness of the plan of administrative reorganization.
8. Implement, assess, and improve the effectiveness of the Work Plan and Evaluation System.

NEW INITIATIVES

1. Evaluate and make recommendations regarding revision of the family life curriculum.
2. Design and begin a training program to improve the personnel evaluation skills of school principals.
3. Develop a clear and consistent homework policy.
4. Develop a clear and consistent promotion policy.
5. Refine and expand educational opportunities for exceptional children.
6. Develop a systematic procedure for determining on a continuing basis the cost effectiveness of programs, policies, and procedures.
7. Design and begin a continuing training program to improve the skills of support personnel.

MANAGING THE REPONSE TO SYSTEM PRIORITIES

Although the list of priorities may seem imposing, the framework for working with continuation priorities has already been developed through the action plans which were designed last year. Four of the seven new initiatives are essentially extensions of task force action plans.

The management method by which these priorities will be addressed is described in the document, *Work Plan and Evaluation System.* Each member of the administrative and supervisory staff will develop and be responsible for the achievement of at least one objective related to these priorities. Some members of the administrative and supervisory staff, according to their position descriptions, will be spending most of their time on objectives directly responsive to the priorities. Others, however, because of the nature of their jobs, will continue to spend most of their time on maintenance, reactive, or routine fuctions.

ADMINISTRATIVE WORK PLAN / BOARD OF EDUCATION OF FREDERICK COUNTY

Name of Employee:	Title:	Date of Preparation:	
Approval/Acceptance Signature: Employee		Date:	Date:
Superintendent:		Date:	Immediate Supervisor
System Priority Objectives: Specific key results stated in measurable terms.	Activities: Major action steps to achieve objectives.	Completion Date	Performance Standards: Criteria for accomplishment.
Priority: Objective 1.0	1.1		

ADMINISTRATIVE WORK PLAN
BOARD OF EDUCATION OF FREDERICK COUNTY
CONTINUATION
PAGE _____

System Priority Objectives: Specific key results stated in measurable terms.	Activities: Major action steps to achieve objectives.	Completion Date	Performance Standards: Criteria for accomplishment.

ADMINISTRATIVE PERFORMANCE EVALUATION
BOARD OF EDUCATION OF FREDERICK COUNTY

Name of Employee: Title:
Name of Evaluator: Title:
Date of Report:

Performance Plan Objectives Achieved/Comments:

Performance Plan Objectives Not Achieved/Comments:

Assessment of Performance on Position Description Functions Not Included
in the Performance Plan:

Assessment of Management Style (e.g., decision making, staff and community relationships, problem solving, delegation):

Plan of Action for Improvement of Job Related Competencies.
Competencies:

Resources Needed:

Suggestions for System Changes to Improve Performance (e.g., workload distribution, staffing, position description):

Performance Rating (Check one):
Superior —
Satisfactory (meets requirements of position) —
Needs Improvement (to meet requirements of position) —
Unsatisfactory —

Recommended Personnel Action:

Employee Reaction (Check one):   Agree —   Disagree — (Attach comments)

_____   _____   _____   _____
Employee Signature   Date   Evaluator Signature   Date

BOARD OF EDUCATION OF FREDERICK COUNTY
OFFICE OF PLANNING AND EVALUATION
REVIEW OF ADMINISTRATIVE PERFORMANCE PLANS

Employee _____ Date of Review_____

Location _____

	Rating		Dimension
	Satisfactory	Unsatisfactory	
1.	_____	_____	Objectives stated in measurable terms
2.	_____	_____	Activities related to objectives
3.	_____	_____	Completion dates realistic
4.	_____	_____	Performances standards measurable, realistic and related to objectives and activities.
5.	_____	_____	At least one objective related to system priorities
6.	_____	_____	Objectives and activities consistent with one another
7.	_____	_____	Plans are feasible
8.	_____	_____	Plans are consistent with position description
9.	_____	_____	Plans are consistent with Board of Education policies and procedures

Suggested Revisions:

Suggested Linkages:

Comments:

PRIORITY _____

Objectives	Employee	Location

Understanding and Using
the Georgia Principal Assessment System

Chad D. Ellett

Chad D. Ellett describes a system — developed over a period of years in Georgia — whose purpose is to assess the performance of school principals. The system was field-tested in well over 100 schools throughout the state, involving literally thousands of people in the process. In his article, Ellett explains how the system developed as part of Project R.O.M.E. (Results Oriented Management in Education) at the College of Education, University of Georgia. He describes the instruments used in the system, details how the Principal Performance Description Survey was utilized, and suggests how the various instruments that comprise GPAS can best be used for evaluation. A number of general considerations are addressed at the end of the article through a series of questions and answers. Dr. Ellett is Vice-President of Performance Systems, Inc., of Athens, Georgia.

The *Georgia Principal Assessment System* (GPAS) is a set of practically administered instruments and procedures for assessing performances (behaviors) of school principals. The instruments and procedures were developed over a four-year period of Project R.O.M.E. (Results Oriented Management in Education) assessment staff within the College of Education at the University of Georgia. The GPAS has been field tested in 120 elementary and secondary schools in the State of Georgia to establish the useability of the instruments in meeting local school assessment and evaluation needs, and in order to select instrument items having known relationships to other school characteristics of educational importance. The field testing and development work involved the cooperation of, and contributions from, approximately 18,000 students, 4,500 teachers, 500 principals and school administrators, 20 to 25 school systems, numerous central office personnel, the individuals at the Georgia State Department of Education, the University of Georgia, the Valdosta State College. Descriptions of the developmental work that went into designing and field testing the GPAS instruments comprise some 1,200 pages to date, and are only briefly reviewed here.

The effort to produce the GPAS was fostered by the Georgia State Department of Education's Division of Program and Staff Development and the Thomas County, Georgia, Board of Education's interest in making a critical examination of principals' behaviors in the school setting, and in developing simple but useful measures of these. The procedures used in developing the GPAS instruments included a maximum input from practicing school administrators who both helped develop and made critical judgments about the importance of the instrument items (performance statements) for the effective operation of a school.

This document provides a brief description of the GPAS and its developmental history, its administration and scoring procedures, and potential school uses of the instruments. It is non-technical in nature, and those desiring more detailed information about characteristics of the various instruments are referred to the separate technical manuals available for each instrument, and the 11 R.O.M.E. assessment reports and various research papers produced to date.

OVERVIEW OF INSTRUMENT DEVELOPMENT ACTIVITIES AND THE GEORGIA PRINCIPAL ASSESSMENT SYSTEM (GPAS)

The *Georgia Principal Assessment System* (GPAS) began in 1974 with an initial identification and development of competency statements for school principals from several sources: reviews of the professional literature in educational administration, objectives-based workshops with principals themselves, on-the-job observations of principals' performances in real school settings, and a task for operationalizing critical educational goals for Georgia. These efforts identified approximately 3,500 to 4,000 statements of principals' various duties, roles, responsibilities, functions, and competencies. This large number of job-related descriptions was reduced to a more manageable and inclusive set of performance statements (306) that reflected input from the variety of sources used in their identification and development.

A classification system was developed for the 306 competency statements that reflected seven traditional *Functional Areas of Administrative Responsibility* associated with the principalship (Curriculum and Instruction, Staff Personnel, Pupil Personnel, Support Management, School-Community Interface, Fiscal Management, and System-wide Policies and Operations), and six *Administrative Operations* (Collecting Information, Planning, Communicating, Decision-Making, Implementing, and Evaluating), all processes in the traditional school management cycle. Each of the 306 performance statements for principals was classified by both the Administrative Operation and Functional Area reflected in each statement. An example of a principal performance statement reflecting the *Functional Area* of Curriculum and Instruction and the *Administrative Operation* of Evaluating is given below:

"PERIODICALLY ASSESSES THE EFFECTIVENESS OF TEACHING METHODS"

A statewide *content verification* survey was undertaken in the State of Georgia during 1974 using practicing school principals, competency-based education experts, and state department of education and central office personnel to reduce the 306 performance statements to a more manageable, high-priority set. One hundred and fifty-five participants in the survey made judgments about the 306 statements and selected those most "frequently important" for the effective operation of a successful school. This process reduced the 306 statements to a high-priority set of 80 competencies for principals judged to be frequently important for the effective operation of a school.

A second step in developing the GPAS was the generation of performance indicators for each of the 80 verified competency statements. In a workshop setting 30 to 35 principals developed performance indicators for each of the 80 competencies by simply stating what they would *do* in carrying out the competencies in a successful (ideal) school. R.O.M.E. assessment staff at the University of Georgia developed additional indicators for the 80 competencies which, when added to those developed by principals themselves, produced 885 indicators for the 80 competencies.

In order to develop and field test assessment instruments, this large number of indicators (885) had to be reduced. Therefore, a second statewide *verification* survey was undertaken during 1974-1975 with approximately 300 principals in the state. These participants were asked to identify which indicators were *essential for the effective operation of a school.* Using the results of this survey, R.O.M.E. staff selected 338 performance indicators for developing first forms of the *Georgia Principal Assessment System* (GPAS). The indicators were assigned to appropriate data sources for assessment purposes, and a field test and validation model was designed.

After the 338 items had been classified according to the appropriate assessment source, several forms of the *Principal Performance Description Survey* (PPDS) instruments emerged. These instruments were field tested in 45 schools (10 secondary and 35 elementary) in the State of Georgia during the Spring of 1975 to provide data for the *validation* of the competencies and for instruments revision.

As the R.O.M.E. project continued during 1976, a second set of 273 competency indicators was assigned to appropriate instruments and field tested in an additional 60 schools (1976-1977). To date, forms of the various instruments have been field-tested in approximately 120 public schools in the State of Georgia, and have been used to provide information, and to evaluate a field-based training program for principals administered through Valdosta State College.

Having conducted two major field tests of the various PPDS instruments, final items were selected during 1977 for each of the PPDS instruments using three basic considerations. First, items were selected that were demonstrated through past R.O.M.E. research to be related to other factors of importance in the school setting (e.g., teacher morale factors, students' perceptions of school climate/learning environment characteristics, school achievement, and school attendance). Secondly, items were selected that had meaningful content for the operation of a school and the purposes for which the instruments were designed. Thirdly, consideration was given to the original items deemed essential for effective school operation by principals themselves, and to the practicality of final instrument length. The most important of these considerations was selecting valid items . . . items having known relationships to other meaningful factors in the educational setting. Thus, each of the various PPDS instruments contains statements of principal performance (competencies) that have been *validated* through large-scale research in the State of Georgia, a unique and important assessment instrument characteristic.

BRIEF DESCRIPTION OF THE PRINCIPAL PERFORMANCE DESCRIPTION SURVEY (PPDS) INSTRUMENTS

In developing rating scales for the various instruments comprising the *Principal Performance Description Survey* (PPDS), two dimensions of a principal's performance were selected. The first of these was the *frequency* dimension, or "how often" a principal is viewed as performing a certain activity in the school. The second dimension was effectiveness of performance, or "how well" a principal is viewed as performing activities in the school. Research with the R.O.M.E. field test data has demonstrated that both of these rating dimensions are valid for assessing principals' performance reflected on the various PPDS instruments. As mentioned in later sections of this manual, however, the meaning of particular ratings for any principal should be considered in view of both local system and school expectations, and the variety of job requirements of the principalship. The sections that follow provide a brief description of the various PPDS instruments and their administration, scoring and response formats. A more detailed description can be found in the separate technical manuals for each instrument.

1. **The Principal Performance Description Survey (PPDS) - Principal Form**

    The *PPDS - Principal Form* instrument consists of 100 statements of principal performance (behaviors) to be responded to by principals themselves. Scores on the instrument represent a principal's self-perception of "how often" and "how well" he/she performs selected job-related tasks. Two ratings are provided for each instrument item: *Frequency With Which I Perform Task* . . . from 1 — NEVER to 5 — VERY OFTEN, and *Effectiveness With Which I Perform Task* . . . from 1 — INEFFECTIVE to 5 — VERY EFFECTIVE. The instrument has a separate answer and scoring sheet, and requires approximately 30 minutes to complete.

The instrument yields scores in five Functional Areas of Administrative Responsibility: Curriculum and Instruction, Staff Personnel, Pupil Personnel, Fiscal Management, and System-wide Policies and Operations. The first 64 items on the instrument yield scores that can be compared to teachers' assessments of their principal's performance The next 36 items yield scores to be compared to assessments by an external observer/interviewer. Or, the entire 100 items can be combined for a global self-assessment to be compared to normative data for the instrument. Instrument instructions allow principals to build and plot their own performance profiles for each of the instrument subscores and for each part of the instrument. These profiles can be compared to other principals' self-assessments, assessments by teachers, normative profiles, or assessments by an external observer, all part of the larger GPAS.

2. **The Principal Performance Description Survey (PPDS) - Teacher Form**

   The PPDS - Teacher Form instrument consists of 64 statements of principals' performance deemed appropriate for assessment by teachers. The instrument can be administered to all teachers within a school, or on a sampling basis. Like the *PPDS — Principal Form,* teachers provide two ratings for each instrument item: *Frequency With Which Principal Performs Task* . . . from 1 — NEVER to 5 — VERY OFTEN, and *Effectiveness With Which Principal Performs Task* . . . from 1 — INEFFECTIVE to 5 - VERY EFFECTIVE. The instrument is designed to assess teacher opinions of how often and how well their principal performs selected school-related activities.

   Scores are provided in four Functional Areas of Administrative Responsibility: Curriculum and Instruction, Staff Personnel, Pupil Personnel, and System-wide Policies and Operations. A separate answer sheet is provided, and teachers can take and score the complete instrument in approximately 30 minutes.

Scores for all teachers in a school are summarized by a school data collector and given to the principal on an anonymous basis to be used in building a performance profile. This teacher profile can be compared to a normative or self-assessment profile by the school principal. Of all instruments comprising the GPAS, the *PPDS - Teacher Form* instrument scores have been demonstrated through field testing to be the most valid.

3.   **The Principal Performance Description Survey - External Observer Form**

The *PPDS - External Observer (EO) Form* instrument consists of 36 statements of principal performance which are assessed through a structured interview with the principal by a trained observer/ interviewer. The scoring system for the instrument is based on the idea that performances (behaviors) in the school produce certain kinds of tangible, observable "evidence" by which the quality of performance can be assessed. The *PPDS - EO instrument requires the use of a trained assessor,* but does have a training manual that makes it still useful for local school assessment. Administration and scoring procedures and limitations concerning the nature of the instrument are included in the separate training materials and manual. Items on the *PPDS - EO* instrument are scored on a four-point scale ranging from O — NOT APPLICABLE to 4 — PRO-DUCT. The Instrument yields subscale scores for five Functional Areas of Administrative Responsibility: Curriculum and Instruction, Staff Personnel, Pupil Personnel, Fiscal Management, and System-wide Policies and Operations. Scores are plotted by the principal to build a performance profile to be compared to a normative plot, and to his/her own self-assessments.

4.   **The PPDS — Superintendent Form**

The *PPDS - Superintendent Form* is a series of 42 performance dimensions rated with a 6-point scale from 1 — EXTREMELY INEFFECTIVE to 6 — EXTREMELY EFFECTIVE. It is completed by the local system superintendent or other members of the central office staff having knowledge of the particular performances reflected in the performance dimensions to be rated. The performance dimensions are based on 7 Functional Areas and 6 Administrative Operations classifications, and ratings are provided for each *Administrative Operation by Functional Area of Administrative Responsibility.* For example, in the Functional Area of *Curriculum and Instruction*, one rating is supplied for how effectively the principal Collects Information, Plans, Communicates, Makes Decisions, Implements, and Evaluates. These same ratings are applied to the other six Functional

Area performance categories. The instrument is hand-scored and yields subscores for each of seven Functional Areas and six Administrative Operations. Performance profiles can be built from the assessment scores to be compared to system and R.O.M.E. norms. Special uses and limitations of the *PPDS - Superintendent Form* are specified in the instrument's technical manual.

The GPAS thus consists of 4 different forms of the *Principal Performance* Description Survey (PPDS) instruments, completed by four different assessment sources: principals themselves, teachers, an external observer, and the superintendent or other central office personnel. Ideally all instruments in the GPAS should be administered to collect as much information about principals' performances as possible from a variety of assessment sources. However, separate instruments in the GPAS can be selected to meet individual school and system needs. Some suggestions for instruments in the GPAS to fit school assessment needs are discussed more fully in the sections that follow.

SUGGESTED USES OF INSTRUMENTS IN THE
GEORGIA PRINCIPAL ASSESSMENT SYSTEM (GPAS)*

The various instruments comprising the GPAS can be used to fulfill a variety of school assessment needs and programs. *The emphasis* in conducting an assessment with the instruments *is on the performance of building level principals,* and in certain cases, pre-service administrators. Since the items selected for the instruments have been demonstrated to have adequate validity (i.e., have known relationships to teacher morale factors, students' assessments of characteristics of the school climate/learning environment, and school achievement and attendance), assessment information yielded by the instruments is suggestive of areas in which principals might improve their performance to more likely have an impact on school outcomes. At both the in-service and pre-service levels, assessment with particular GPAS instruments can be useful in pointing out performance deficits around which training goals can be structured to hopefully lead to skill and performance improvement. Users should keep in mind that the GPAS instruments were designed to provide an *assessment* of selected principal performances by a variety of sources. They were *not designed* to render any final "evaluation" of how well principals do their job. Nor were they designed to distinguish between "good," "bad," and "mediocre" principals. As with other school personnel, a comprehensive "evaluation" of principals requires many different kinds of information from many different sources before these judgments

---

*A separate assessment document is in preparation that shows how performance profiles from the separate PPDS instruments are compared and how assessment information can be translated into "action plans" for school principals. (Author's note)

can be made. The sections that follow in this document provide some general suggestions concerning possible uses of assessment information yielded by the various instruments in the GPAS, as well as some general cautions concerning different aspects of performance assessment.

General Performance Appraisal

Instruments in the GPAS can be used for the general performance appraisal of principals on-the-job. As with other types of assessment instruments available, any data yielded by the various PPDS instruments is limited by the instrument items themselves. For example, if a principal attains a given score in the Functional Area of Curriculum and Instruction on the *PPDS - Teacher Form*, one needs to keep in mind that the score is based solely on those items making up that particular subscale. Since the items on the PPDS instruments represent only a *sample of possible performance*s in any given Functional Area, users should be cautious in making "evaluative" judgments about the quality of a principal's work. The scores can be, however, suggestive of performance areas needing improvement when compared to both the system and the larger R.O.M.E. norms. Assessment discrepancies apparent when principals compare their self-assessments to those by their teachers are another primary source of performance appraisal information.

When administering the PPDS instruments for general performance appraisal purposes, systems and schools might best proceed by first considering which informational source about the principal's performance is of most importance. That is, if one is most interested in the perceptions of teachers, then administration of the *PPDS - Teacher Form* would probably become a priority. If potential users are most interested in the formality with which principals perform on the job, then administration of the *PPDS - External Observer (EO) Form* might be in order. Ideally, all PPDS instruments should be administered to obtain the maximum amount of information from a variety of assessment sources.

One suggested strategy for performance appraisal is to administer the GPAS at the beginning of the school year to identify performance goals for individual principals or all principals in a particular system. If, for example, a Fall assessment shows that principals achieve their lowest scores in the Functional Area of Staff Personnel, then the Staff Personnel items can be reviewed, and work in this area might become a system-wide priority. Data from follow-up assessments during the school year can then be compared to previous assessments to measure performance improvement. If personnel in a given system agree that particular performance areas assessed by the various PPDS instruments reasonably fit their conception of the principal's job responsibilities, then performance standards might be set using the instruments from one year to the next. A performance priority for a system might be, for example, to have all principals in the system attain at least 50% of the maximum possible score in selected Functional Areas deemed important by the system, and to maintain this performance level from one year to the next.

Needs Assessment and Staff Development

Past experience with the Georgia Principal Assessment System indicates that it can be a useful addition to school system plans for staff development activities based on needs assessment information. Since one of the State Department of Education requirements for approved staff development plans is evidence of evaluation activities and effectiveness/ success, instrumentation in the GPAS can be used to identify performance needs and monitor inprovement activities implemented for school principals during the course of staff development activities.

Most school needs assessments are based on accumulating information from a variety of sources (e.g., students, teachers, community, etc.) to set system priorities and educational goals. A variety of needs assessment methods are available, but most results of needs assessments represent summary opinions of "what the schools should be doing or working toward." They frequently do not get more directly at an examination of on-the-job performance as a basis for the identification of school needs, and thus are one step removed from the school setting where actual performance occurs. Administration of the various PPDS instruments can be considered an on-the-job assessment of principals' performances that generates information pointing out performance "needs" in a variety of areas, and from a variety of sources. For systems developing comprehensive needs assessment/staff development plans, the GPAS can be effectively used to identify performance needs and in-service training objectives for principals, at both the system and building level.

It is suggested that data summaries based on a GPAS assessment can be totaled for all principals in a particular system to identify system-level performance priorities from which training goals can be developed. In addition, each individual principal could select particular performance areas for improvement based on the data from his individual school assessment. This can be easily done by comparing scores within or between the different PPDS instruments, or by comparing individual scores for individual principals to system norms produced by a system-wide assessment.

The place of the GPAS in staff development plans is best viewed as a means of identifying critical performance areas needing improvement, and of structuring specific staff development (training) goals based on the assessment information. Such staff development plans with principals have obvious advantages over the many attempts to identify what school principals need through the "armchair opinion" approach. Among these is the collection of information about valid job-related performances from a variety of different sources . . . a true data-based approach to planning staff development activities for administrators.

Once an assessment has occurred with all or some of the instruments in the GPAS, "action plans" can be constructed by looking at individual and system assessment scores. Individual performance statements on which these scores are based can be examined and interpreted within the context of the broader goals of the school system. Action plans (training goals and procedures) can then be derived from the performance statements themselves.

For example, suppose an individual principal's assessment in the Fall demonstrated that he was rated as *infrequently* and *ineffectively* carrying out the following performance in the *Staff Personnel* Functional Area: *Participates in professional improvement activities with teachers.* Working with staff development leaders, the individual principal could operationalize the meaning of the performance in his school and begin to structure activities in which he will participate during the year to improve his performance in *professional improvement activities with teachers.* He/she might, for example, decide on methods of communicating professional association information to teachers, on making certain to announce and discuss this information at all faculty meetings, on scheduling visitations with selected teachers to other schools running exemplary programs in different curriculum areas, etc. These efforts would become part of the individual principal's "action plan" to improve his performance in the Area of Staff Personnel. Similarly, actions plans could be written based on assessment information for *all* principals in the system combined, in any general performance area viewed by the system as less than optimal.

Individual schools and school systems will need to be innovative in their approaches to using information based on an assessment with the PPDS instruments, since no standardized procedures in using the instruments to meet local school staff development objectives are available. The absence of structured "action plans" to fit different PPDS assessments is probably a good feature in the sense that local schools can interpret assessment information in view of their own system needs and staff development objectives. A small, rural school system, for example, having principals scoring low in the area of staff personnel, might decide to develop specific performance improvement activities that would be vastly different from those developed for a large urban school system because of the way the principalship with its variety of duties and responsibilities is viewed.

Pre-Service Applications

Individual items (performance statements) on the various PPDS instruments were developed using a maximum of input from practicing school principals. Principals themselves provided judgments about the importance of the various items for the effective operation of a school program at several stages in the larger R.O.M.E. project. Thus, the items logically have the most utility for principals in service. However, certain PPDS instruments might be used with "pre-service" principals in developing educational objectives and in evaluating educational progress.

One suggested approach to using the PPDS instruments at the pre-service level is to allow students entering educational programs in administration to conduct a "self-assessment" with the instruments to identify areas in which they feel their performance needs to be improved. An individual student, for example, could take items on the *PPDS - Principal* or *PPDS - Teacher Forms* and rate the extent to which he/she feels they possess the requisite knowledge, skills, and abilities to carry out the performances in a real school setting. This self-assessment could then be used as an aid in selecting specific courses and training programs during the pre-service educational experience more likely to improve performance skills on the job. The student, having completed a self-assessment with the PDS instrument might discuss the results with a faculty advisor in planning his educational program and course sequence leading to a higher degree or certification level. This approach to pre-service use of the GPAS instruments serves as a student's "needs" assessment on a set of performances that practicing school principals have judged as important and job-related — and that research has demonstrated to be related to important school outcomes.

At various points in a pre-service educational program, student advisors (faculty members) might use the PPDS instruments to assess students' progress. For example, one could review the various PPDS instrument items and make professional judgments concerning whether the student has mastered the knowledges and skills necessary to implement all, or some set of, performances once employed in a school setting. If the judgment is a negative one, then specific remedial experiences might be discussed with, and designed for, the pre-service student to raise his performance level and to fulfill his perceived needs.

Another strategy for pre-service use of the instruments would be to compare supervisors' (faculty members) ratings and students' ratings. Students' self-assessments in various Functional Areas (e.g., Curriculum and Instruction skills) could be compared to those of their supervisors (faculty members) at various points in the pre-service training experience and discussed. Hopefully greater agreement between advisor and student would be seen as the student progressed through the pre-service program. Again, pre-service use of the PPDS instruments requires considerable innovation on the part of those using them, since no exact methods have yet been designed. However, their use at the pre-service level seems reasonable, since the items on the instruments have been judged as job-related and important for the effective operation of a school by a large sample of practicing school principals.

GENERAL CONSIDERATIONS IN ADMINISTERING THE GEORGIA
PRINCIPAL ASSESSMENT SYSTEM (GPAS)

This section of the manual provides the reader with several general considerations to be kept in mind when administering the variety of instruments in the GPAS. The most important of these is the basic purpose for which the instruments were designed and the philosophy on which an "assessment" is based. As mentioned in other parts of this manual, the GPAS instruments were designed to be practically administered and scored, and to validly and reliably measure sets of performances of school principals known to be related to other important facts in the school. Critical to the development of the items on the instruments were judgment about their *importance* by practicing school principals. Any individual principal undergoing an assessment with the BPAS is thus being assessed on sets of performances seen as important for effective school operation by his/her peers. The GPAS was not developed to "evaluate" whether a principal is doing a "good" or "bad" job, a judgment that requires many different perspectives and many kinds of information, and it should not be used in making such judgments. However, the GPAS provides important and useable information from which school improvement and self improvement activities can be developed and monitored. Any information yielded by an assessment with the instruments should be interpreted and used only in view of the general goals, needs, educational philosophy, etc., within a given school and/or school system. Since the definition of the principalship and the job roles of principals change considerably from one system to the next, this point is important to remember.

How Should The Decision For Assessment Be Made?

During the three year field test of the GPAS in some 120 elementary and secondary schools in the State of Georgia, much has been learned about the "evaluation apprehension" that principals sometimes feel when assessment is discussed. School systems can best alleviate this apprehension by being certain that the purpose of administering the GPAS is to provide information for *performance improvement,* not for *performance evaluation.* This has been successfully done at many system level meetings attended by both key central office personnel and principals themselves. The decision to be assessed is best made by *principals themselves,* once they have enough information about what the assessment is for, and how the information will be used. Our experience has been that principals will view the assessment as both meaningful and useful if they know the assessment information is to be used in "non-evaluative" ways by system level personnel. The best approach has been to explain to any principal being assessed that information derived from his school belong to him, and is to be shared with others in the system only at his/her discretion. When assessment guidelines are followed, principals can provide system level personnel with assessment information to be combined to establish system norms, *and still remain anonymous.* General instructions for the various PPDS instruments explain for the principal how this is accomplished.

Can Teacher Anonymity be Maintained?

Administration instructions for the *PPDS - Teacher Form* instrument are designed to protect the anonymity of individual teachers in a given school. Since the interest in a school is on teachers' collective responses as a group, it is not necessary to identify individuals providing assessment information about a principal's performance. Teachers are instructed when taking the *PPDS - Teacher Form* instrument how to score their responses. These, in turn, are given to a designated school data collector on an anonymous basis to be summarized for the school principal. A short document for school data collectors explains how to maintain teacher anonymity and to score response to the *PPDS - Teacher Form* instrument.

How Are Teachers Selected To Participate In The Assessment?

Since an assessment with instruments in the GPAS seeks to maximize information about principals' performances from a variety of perspectives, it is suggested that *all* teachers in a school participate. Like soliciting the cooperation of principals in the assessment, maxmum teacher participation probably comes about when teachers are asked to participate *on a voluntary basis,* and when they understand that the purpose of the assessment is *performance improvement* — not *evaluation.* They should be assured by the school principal and system that their anonymity will be maintained at all times. Specific instructions on the *PPDS — Teacher Form* describe how teachers are to respond to the instrument, and how the instrument is to be scored. In addition, teachers are asked to turn in their answer sheets to a "neutral" person in the school or system (e.g., the school librarian) so that data for all teachers in a school can be combined for the principal's use.

How Are The Instruments Scored?

Each of the *Principal Performance Description Survey* (PPDS) instruments in the *Georgia Principal Assessment System* (GPAS) can be easily scored by hand by individuals responding to the instrument. The PPDS instrument for the principal and for teachers are simply scored by adding *frequency* and *effectiveness* ratings for instrument items coded by *Functional Area of Administrative Responsibility* (i.e., Curriculum and instruction, Staff Personnel, etc.). These scores are then plotted on performance profile sheets in order to pictorially display what a principal's assessment "looks like." These graphs can then be compared to both system norms and the larger R.O.M.E. norm derived from the Georgia statewide field test of the instruments.

The *PPDS - Superintendent Form* is also hand scored by the appropriate central office personnel completing it, and a profile for each principal is plotted that allows for a comparison of Functional Areas of Administrative Responsibility and the Administrative Operations subscores. Instructions for this instrument also show how system norms are to be compared and displayed.

Connecticut's Teacher Evaluation Law-
Teacher Evaluation in Connecticut

The two items that follow are closely related. The first is an excerpt from Connecticut's Teacher Evaluation Law, a publication of the Connecticut State Department of Education. It gives an overview of the law enacted by the state legislature in 1974, making Connecticut one of the relatively few states mandating systematic teacher evaluation. (As the law states it, "teacher" here means anyone below the rank of superintendent; hence the term encompasses administrators as well.) The second item is taken from Teacher Evaluation in Connecticut, *also published by the Connecticut State Education Department. Consisting of a number of forms used in evaluating teachers and administrators, it seems eminently adaptable to educational systems anywhere.*

Connecticut's Teacher Evaluation Law - An Overview is reprinted by permission of the State Department of Education, Hartford, Connecticut. *Teacher Evaluation in Connecticut* is reprinted with the permission of the Bureau of Research, Planning and Evaluation, State Department of Education, Hartford, Connecticut.

Connecticut is one of only a handful of states having a comprehensive and positive law concerning the evaluation of teachers. Adopted by the legislature on July 1, 1974, the Teacher Evaluation Law (Section 10-151b of the Connecticut General Statutes) has demonstrated that a cooperative effort of elected officials, local and state educators, and numerous parents and other citizens serving on local and state committees can have an impact on improving the educational opportunities for Connecticut's children. The law states that:

    (a)   The Superintendent of each district shall, in accordance with guidelines established by the state board of education for the development of evaluation programs and such other guidelines as may be established by mutual agreement between the town or regional board of education and the teacher's representative chosen pursuant to section 10-153b of the general statutes, continuously evaluate or cause to be evaluated each teacher. The superintendent shall report the status of such evaluations to the town or regional board of education on or before June 1 of each year. For purposes of this section, the term "teacher" shall include each employee of a board of education below the rank of superintendent, who holds a certificate or permit issued by the state board of education.

(b) On or before January 1 of each year, each town or regional school district shall submit, in writing, to the state board of education a report on the development and implementation of teacher evaluation programs consistent with guidelines established by the state board of education.

As a direct result of this law the following "guiding principles" were established by the State Board of Education to serve as a framework for assisting Connecticut school districts in the development and adaptation of their programs for evaluating professional staff.

I.   The primary purpose of teacher evaluation is the improvement of the student learning experience.

II. The local school district establishes its own educational goals. Such goals form the basis of the teacher evaluation program.

III. Ample time is provided for this goal oriented approach to to teacher evaluation.

IV. A fiscal support system is established for the purpose of assisting school districts to prepare for and conduct evaluations.

Each of these principles is designed to provide a school environment in which teachers may develop the art and science of teaching to their maximum potential.

These principles promote the following:

• For teachers — improved professional performance
• For students — improved learning experiences
• For Connecticut LEA's — meaningful educational goals and programs

The primary purpose of teacher evaluation was established by the State Board of Education, with the assistance of the Teacher Evaluation Advisory Committee, as the "improvement of the student learning experience." While recognizing that local districts may have secondary purposes for their evaluation programs, the SBE further directed each district to cooperatively develop an evaluation program that would adhere to the following eleven State Board of Education Guidelines for Teacher Evaluation:

I.   Each professional shall cooperatively determine with the evaluator(s) the objectives upon which his or her evaluation shall be based.

II. The evaluation program is cooperatively planned, carried out and evaluated by all levels of the staff.

III. The purposes of the evaluation program are clearly stated in writing and are well known to the evaluators and those who are to be evaluated.

IV. The general responsibilities and specific tasks of the teacher's position should be comprehensively defined and this definition should serve as the frame of reference for evaluation.

V. The accountability relationship of each position should be clearly determined. The teacher should know and understand the means by which he or she will be evaluated in relation to that position.

VI. Evaluations are more diagnostic than judgmental. The process should help analyze the teaching and learning to plan how to improve.

VII. Evaluation should take into account influences on the learning environment such as material and professional resources.

VIII. Self-evaluation is an essential aspect of the program. Teachers are given the opportunity to evaluate themselves in positive and constructive ways.

IX. The self-image and self-respect of teachers should be maintained and enhanced. Positive self-concepts can be fostered by an effective evaluation plan.

X. The nature of the evaluations is such that it encourages teacher creativity and experimentation in planning and guiding the teacher-learning experiences provided children.

XI. The program makes ample provision for clear, personalized, constructive feedback.

Teacher evaluation as defined by this law will have a beneficial impact on the student learning experience for the following reasons:

- Comprehensive job descriptions will be developed for each position to serve as a reference for evaluation.
- The school system and individual school goals will serve as a reference for individual teachers in determining their own classroom goals.
- Teachers will be involved in self-evaluation activities.
- Teachers and evaluators will agree on specific teaching goals and how they will be achieved and evaluated.
- Evaluations of teachers will focus on identifying strengths and weaknesses and developing plans for continually improving the student learning experience.
- Teacher creativity will be encouraged.
- Clear and concise forms will be used to insure that constructive and useful feedback will be understood.

- Levels of support resources (materials, facilities, specialists, etc.) affecting the achievement of objectives will be considered as part of the evaluation process.

July 1, 1978 was the beginning of the fifth year allowed for the development of local evaluation programs that conform to the law and guidelines. The previous four years involved considerable activity on the part of local districts toward understanding the law and guidelines, forming committees, exploring alternative models, and trial testing various components of a teacher evaluation program. All of these activities are necessary for fulfilling the mandate to implement an evaluation program consistent with the law and its guidelines.

Throughout this period of time the Connecticut State Department of Education has provided leadership and assistance through informational materials, inservice events, and consultant services. The CSDE has also monitored local implementation progress through the examination of annual reports submitted each January and through continuing on-site visitations.

Funds to support the implementation of this law have come from the Connecticut General Assembly which has appropriated $173,000 for this purpose for the five-year period from the law's inception in 1974. However, the greatest effort has been made by local school districts. The State Board of Education Teacher Advisory Committee has estimated that $250,000 was expended by local school districts during the first three years of this legislation and $500,000 contributed in in-kind services during this period.

The level of involvement and activity toward complying with this law has been a credit to the state and local officials and educators who have embraced the concepts and recognized the value of teacher evaluation toward improving the student learning experience.

THE PROCESS

The Teacher Evaluation Law and guidelines prescribe a complex evaluation process that generally was not in use in Connecticut public schools that generally was not in use in Connecticut public schools prior to the law. The teacher and evaluator form a partnership under this new system to enhance teaching competencies and the student learning experience. Evaluation becomes a method for communication and cooperation to achieve this goal. The focus is on sound cooperative planning and on implementing these plans during the course of the year. This contrasts with previous evaluation procedures which involved visitations by an evaluator to a classroom for a checklist appraisal of the conditions at that specific time.

The new teacher evaluation process begins with the school district setting direction for the educational program by establishing system-wide goals and objectives which express the learning expected of most students. A classroom teacher reflects on these goals and objectives in relation to his or her own job description and responsibilities and identifies areas for growth. The next step is for the teacher to prepare several personal performance objectives, that, when successfully implemented, will improve the student learning experience. Most often these performance objectives include a statement of what the teacher will do to improve the learning program in his or her classroom, resources that will be needed to carry this out, a timeline, and a method to determine how successful the teacher's actions were. The evaluator and teacher meet to discuss the performance objectives and if necessary, modify them. After agreement is reached by the teacher and evaluator on the performance objectives, several additional meetings and classroom observations are scheduled. These insure that the activities agreed to are being carried out and are having the desired effect. Revisions or adjustments to the plans can be made to take into account any new information learned during the process. It is also a responsibility of the evaluator to assist the teacher by bringing in appropriate resources and providing instructional leadership.

The evaluator and teacher meet at the completion of the indicated span to determine how successful the activities were in improving the student learning experience. Generally the teacher evaluates him or herself in preparation for this discussion with the evaluator.

It is clear that such a process as described requires considerable planning by the school district as well as training for the staff. The process is new and different, and personnel involved need to learn new evaluation skills. Several studies investigating the types of training required to fulfill this mandate have identified writing and implementing performance objectives, supervisory skills, observation skills, and conferencing skills as integral to the process. These studies were conducted independently by the State Department of Education, the Connecticut Association for the Advancement of School Administration, the Connecticut Educational Service Centers, the University of Connecticut, and the Connecticut Association of Secondary School Principals.

Connecticut State Board of Education

Progress Report to State Board of Education

by

_____ School District

Due January 1, 1979

The following reporting forms ask for information on your school system's progress in implementing the 1974 Teacher Evaluation Law (Section 10-151b). Please include all activities, including completed ones, that reflect an observance of state guidelines. The term "teacher" as used in the law refers to every certified person under the rank of Superintendent.

The reporting forms are the same as those used in previous years and ask for supporting evidence. It WILL BE necessary to include evidence previously submitted, in addition to any documentation not included in past years' reports. In future years a shorter form will be available for use by those districts whose documents are scored as being in accordance with the guidelines.

Also enclosed please find a copy of your district's Teacher Evaluation Status Report, which you received last spring. Your response on this year's reporting forms should speak directly to that prior status as well as present conditions and future plans. Even if your program has been judged to be in partial or total accordance with the guidelines, we ask that you describe any changes that have occurred since last year.

We hope that the forms will serve as planning as well as reporting documents. Form A contains a list of possible planning activities. Please add any other activities you feel are important within your school system. You should also keep in mind that the criteria listed under each guideline in Form B are SUGGESTIONS and that any additional criteria that you have developed should be attached and described.

The glossary of terms does not pretend to be exhaustive, but we hope that it will clarify some of the questions most frequently raised.

Your program under each guideline will be coded by the State Department of Education as follows:

1 = Substantial Achievement
2 = Activities Initiated
3 = Activities Planned
4 = No Evidence Provided

FORM A

If you have a written statement of your teacher evaluation plan, please attach it to this form. ("Plan" refers to a document that specifies major tasks that must be accomplished to develop a teacher evaluation program and indicates the timetable and personnel responsible for completion of the tasks.)

If you do not have a documented plan, please complete the following form which lists some major planning components.

Please check the appropriate Rating Criteria for each component.

	Rating Criteria*			
Major Program Components	1	2	3	4
1. Establishment of Steering Committee.	____	____	____	____
2. Identification of school systems goals and objectives.	____	____	____	____
3. Development of a clear statement of evaluation program philosophy and purpose.	____	____	____	____
4. Identification and definition of general job responsibilities.	____	____	____	____
5. Identification and definition of specific task responsibilities.	____	____	____	____
6. Written statement of teacher evaluation program.	____	____	____	____
7. Development of a process for evaluating and improving the evaluation program.	____	____	____	____

*RATING CRITERIA
1. Substantial completion of component.
2. Activities have been initiated.
3. Component is in planning stages.
4. No evidence of progress.

GUIDELINE I

"Each professional shall cooperatively determine with the evaluator(s) the objectives upon which his or her evaluation shall be based."

What things are you now doing, or do you plan to do, to see that this guideline is met?
(If the space allotted is insufficient, please attach additional pages.)

Criteria	Activities	Evi-dence*	Start-ing Date	Comple-tion Date
Written objectives for the evaluatee are developed.				
Objectives are stated in operational (observable) terms.				
Teachers and administrators work together in developing objectives.				
Objectives are jointly approved.				
Additional criteria developed within your school system.				

*Please note whether evidence is attached or was submitted last year. If evidence is attached, please label as specifically as possible (e.g., page number and activity to which it relates).

On the scale below please check how far you believe you have progressed toward meeting this guideline.

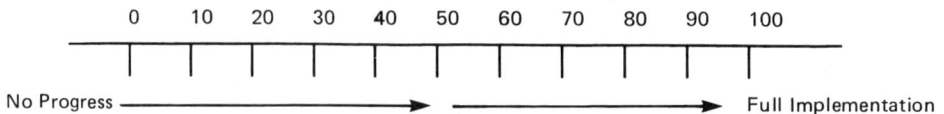

```
        0   10  20  30  40  50  60  70  80  90  100
        |  |  |  |  |  |  |  |  |  |  |  |
No Progress ─────────────────────►  ─────────────────────►  Full Implementation
```

— 140 —

"The evaluation program is cooperatively planned, carried out and evaluated by all levels of the staff."

What things are you now doing, or do you plan to do, to see that this guideline is met?
(If the space allotted is insufficient, please attach additional pages.)

Criteria	Activities	Evi-dence*	Start-ing Date	Comple-tion Date
There is input from all reference groups.				
There is substantial approval of program by all groups.				
Active roles for each group are specified.				
There is a procedure to provide feedback from all groups concerning the evaluation program.				
Additional criteria developed within your school system.				

*Please note whether evidence is attached or was submitted last year. If evidence is attached, please label as specifically as possible (e.g., page number and activity to which it relates).

On the scale below please check how far you believe you have progressed toward meeting this guideline.

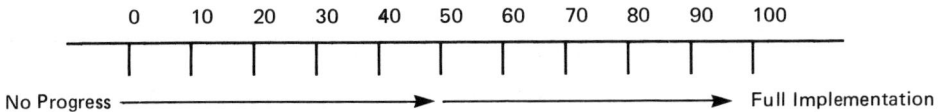

```
        0   10  20  30  40  50  60  70  80  90  100
```

No Progress ——————————————————————→ ——————————————————————→ Full Implementation

"The purposes of the evaluation program are clearly stated in writing and are well known to the evaluators and those who are to be evaluated."

What things are you now doing, or do you plan to do, to see that this guideline is met?
(If the space allotted is insufficient, please attach additional pages.)

Criteria	Activities	Evi-dence*	Start-ing Date	Comple-tion Date
There is a clear written statement of the purposes of the evalua-tion program.				
Statement of purposes is widely dis-tributed to evaluators.				
Statement of purposes is widely dis-tributed to those to be evaluated.				
Statement of purposes is explained and discussed with and by all levels of the staff.				
Additional criteria de-veloped within your school system.				

*Please note whether evidence is attached or was submitted last year. If evidence is attached, please label as specifically as possible (e.g., page number and activity to which it relates).

On the scale below please check how far you believe you have progressed toward meeting this guideline.

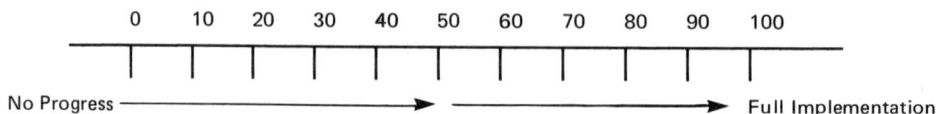

0 10 20 30 40 50 60 70 80 90 100

No Progress ⟶ ⟶ Full Implementation

GUIDELINE IV

"The general responsibilities and specific tasks of the teacher's position should be comprehensively defined and this definition should serve as the frame of reference for evaluation."

What things are you now doing, or do you plan to do, to see that this guideline is met? (If the space allotted is insufficient, please attach additional pages.)

Criteria	Activities	Evi-dence*	Start-ing Date	Comple-tion Date
General responsibilities of each professional position are defined in writing.				
Tasks for each individual are specified.				
Above procedures serve as a refer-ence for evalua-tions.				
Additional criteria de-veloped within your school system.				

*Please note whether evidence is attached or was submitted last year. If evidence is attached, please label as specifically as possible (e.g., page number and activity to which it relates).

On the scale below please check how far you believe you have progressed toward meeting this guideline.

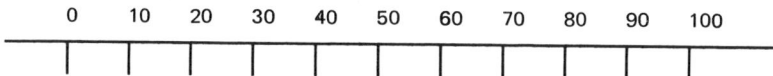

0   10   20   30   40   50   60   70   80   90   100

No Progress ⟶ ⟶ Full Implementation

— 143 —

GUIDELINE V

"The accountability relationship of each position should be clearly determined. The teacher should know and understand the means by which he or she will be evaluated in relation to that position."

What things are you now doing, or do you plan to do, to see that this guideline is met?
(If the space allotted is insufficient, please attach additional pages.)

Criteria	Activities	Evi-dence*	Start-ing Date	Comple-tion Date
The evaluation process clearly states the responsibility of the evaluator to the evalua-tee.				
The evaluation process clearly states to whom and for whom each person is responsible in the evaluation process.				
The evaluation process clearly states how (methods/procedures) the evaluation is to be carried out.				
Additional criteria developed within your school system.				

*Please note whether evidence is attached or was submitted last year. If evidence is attached, please label as specifically as possible (e.g., page number and activity to which it relates).

On the scale below please check how far you believe you have progressed toward meeting this guideline.

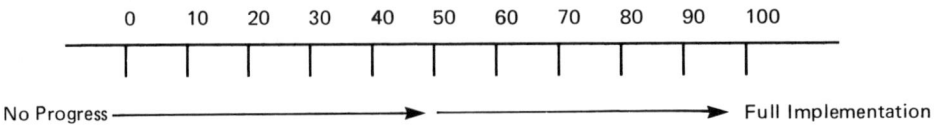

0 10 20 30 40 50 60 70 80 90 100

No Progress ⸻⸻⸻⸻⟶ ⸻⸻⸻⸻⟶ Full Implementation

"Evaluations are more diagnostic than judgmental. The process should help analyze the teaching and learning to plan how to improve."

What things are you now doing, or do you plan to do, to see that this guideline is met?
(If the space allotted is insufficient, please attach additional pages.)

Criteria	Activities	Evi-dence*	Start-ing Date	Comple-tion Date
Evaluation procedures utilized deal with identification of strengths and weaknesses of the teaching-learning process.				
Outcomes of the evaluation process is a plan or prescription for improving the teaching-learning process.				
Additional criteria developed within your school system.				

*Please note whether evidence is attached or was submitted last year. If evidence is attached, please label as specifically as possible (e.g., page number and activity to which it relates).

On the scale below please check how far you believe you have progressed toward meeting this guideline.

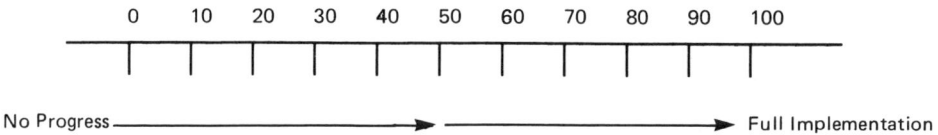

```
     0    10   20   30   40   50   60   70   80   90   100
  |   |    |    |    |    |    |    |    |    |    |    |

No Progress ———————————————————►  —————————————————————►  Full Implementation
```

GUIDELINE VII

"Evaluation should take into account influences on the learning environment such as material and professional resources."

What things are you now doing, or do you plan to do, to see that this guideline is met?
(If the space allotted is insufficient, please attach additional pages.)

Criteria	Activities	Evi-dence*	Start-ing Date	Comple-tion Date
The evalua-tion process takes into con-sideration the level of support resources and other influences affecting the achievement of objectives.				
Additional criteria de-veloped within your school system.				

*Please note whether evidence is attached or was submitted last year. If evidence is attached, please label as specifically as possible (e.g., page number and activity to which it relates).

On the scale below please check how far you believe you have progressed toward meeting this guideline.

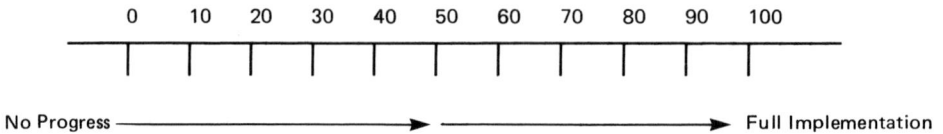

```
        0   10  20  30  40  50  60  70  80  90  100
        |   |   |   |   |   |   |   |   |   |   |
```

No Progress ⟶   ⟶ Full Implementation

— 146 —

"Self-evaluation is an essential aspect of the program. Teachers are given the opportunity to evaluate themselves in positive and constructive ways."

What things are you now doing, or do you plan to do to see that this guideline is met?
(If the space allotted is insufficient, please attach additional pages.)

Criteria	Activities	Evi-dence*	Start-ing Date	Comple-tion Date
Opportunities are provided to each profes-sional staff member to conduct a self-evaluation.				
Individuals are given the op-portunity to include self-evaluation re-ports as part of the total evaluation re-port.				
Additional criteria de-veloped with-in your school system.				

*Please note whether evidence is attached or was submitted last year. If evidence is attached, please label as specifically as possible (e.g., page number and activity to which it relates).

On the scale below please check how far you believe you have progressed toward meeting this guideline.

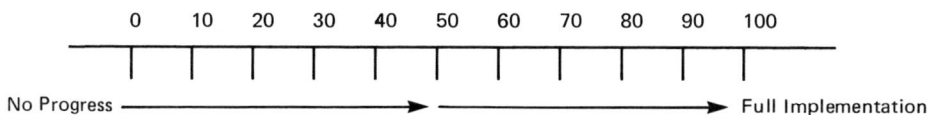

```
       0    10   20   30   40   50   60   70   80   90   100
       |    |    |    |    |    |    |    |    |    |    |
No Progress ──────────────────────▶ ──────────────────▶ Full Implementation
```

GUIDELINE IX

"The self-image and self-respect of teachers should be maintained and enhanced. Positive self-concepts can be fostered by an effective evaluation plan."

What things are you now doing, or do you plan to do, to see that this guideline is met?
(If the space allotted is insufficient, please attach additional pages.)

Criteria	Activities	Evi-dence*	Start-ing Date	Comple-tion Date
The evaluation plan focuses on strength of professional staff members, not just weaknesses.				
There is a clear statement of responsibility for maintaining and enhancing the self-image and self-respect of all professional staff throughout the evaluation process.				
Additional criteria developed within your school system.				

*Please note whether evidence is attached or was submitted last year. If evidence is attached, please label as specifically as possible (e.g., page number and activity to which it relates).

On the scale below please check how far you believe you have progressed toward meeting this guideline.

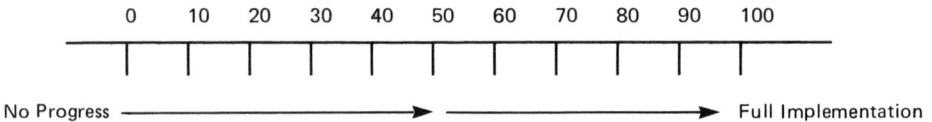

```
    0   10  20  30  40  50  60  70  80  90  100
    |   |   |   |   |   |   |   |   |   |   |
```

No Progress ————————→ ————————→ Full Implementation

"The nature of the evaluations is such that it encourages teacher creativity and experimentation in planning and guiding the teacher-learning experience provided children."

What things are you now doing, or do you plan to do, to see that this guideline is met?
(If the space allotted is insufficient, please attach additional pages.)

Criteria	Activities	Evi-dence*	Start-ing Date	Comple-tion Date
The evaluation program clearly states encouragement of teacher creativity and experimentation in planning and guiding the teaching-learning experience provided children.				
The evaluation program makes provision for teacher creativity and experimentation in planning and guiding the teaching-learning experience provided children.				
Additional criteria developed within your school system.				

*Please note whether evidence is attached or was submitted last year. If evidence is attached, please label as specifically as possible (e.g., page number and activity to which it relates).

On the scale below please check how far you believe you have progressed toward meeting this guideline.

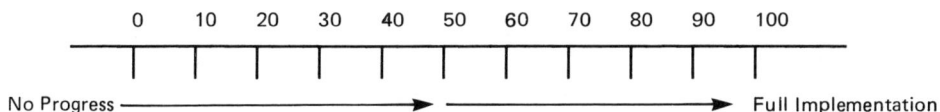

```
         0    10   20   30   40   50   60   70   80   90   100
    ┬────┬────┬────┬────┬────┬────┬────┬────┬────┬────┬────┬───
No Progress ───────────────────►  ─────────────────────►  Full Implementation
```

GUIDELINE XI

"The program makes ample provision for clear, personalized, constructive feedback."

What things are you now doing, or do you plan to do, to see that this guideline is met?
(If the space allotted is insufficient, please attach additional pages.)

Criteria	Activities	Evi-dence*	Start-ing Date	Comple-tion Date
A procedure (conference or written report) for review of the evaluation is provided.				
Feedback is given on an individual basis.				
Feedback is based on diagnosis of the teaching learning process and includes positive suggestions for improvement.				
Additional criteria developed within your school system.				

*Please note whether evidence is attached or was submitted last year. If evidence is attached, please label as specifically as possible (e.g., page number and activity to which it relates).

On the scale below please check how far you believe you have progressed toward meeting this guideline.

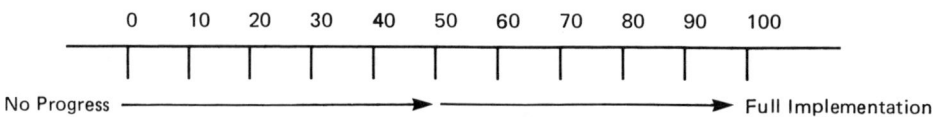

```
        0    10   20   30   40   50   60   70   80   90   100
        |    |    |    |    |    |    |    |    |    |    |

No Progress  ──────────────────────►  ──────────────────────►  Full Implementation
```

An Application of the Assessment Center in Education

Edward Deluzain and Barry M. Cohen

Deluzain and Cohen argue that school districts can improve their approach to management selection and development by applying assessment center techniques that have been successful in business, industry, and government. They report on how a group of nine school districts in the Florida panhandle region undertook a pilot assessment center program, funded by provisions of a state "leadership training" act. Reactions to the program were enthusiastic. The authors present would-be users of such centers with some thoughtful caveats, but conclude that the centers can "increase objectivity and add relevancy to manpower planning and selection." Edward Deluzain is Director of Special Services in the Bay County Public Schools, Panama City, Florida; Barry M. Cohen is Associate Professor of Management Psychology at the University of West Florida, Pensacola.

Increased demands for public accountability in education and pressures by teacher unions, State agencies and others are forcing school principals to assume new and more responsible roles in such administrative areas as fiscal control, planning and budgeting, program development and evaluation, employee relations and special services. The school principal today must be an able manager and organization expert; his direction, guidance and support are all important in getting results.

In response to the need for management results, local school boards might follow the lead of business, industry and government by planning their manpower needs and carefully selecting principals with validated, systematic assessment methods. The schools, of course, are the organization testing grounds and candidates must demonstrate their capabilities there. However, the important point is that better assessment methods could be used to identify high potential candidates at lower management levels. The school board would be in a better position to select the best candidates in this way.

One approach to management selection and development that is widely used and accepted in business, industry and government is the assessment center, which, with some modifications, can be applied successfully in education. The assessment center process consists of having participants engage in a set of management exercises, administrative discussions, interviews, writing assignments and personnel situations that are specifically designed to highlight the presence or absence of certain behaviors that have been determined to be necessary for successful leadership. Each assessment activity occurs under different circumstances, so that the management dimensions can be observed several times. While the participants are performing in the exercises, they are carefully observed by a team of assessors who are thoroughly familiar with the demands of the job to which the participants aspire and who have been trained in the observation of behavior. Generally, the term of assessors is made up of three people, and each assessor observes two of six participants per exercise. Groups of more than six participants can take part in the assessment center, as long as a ratio of about three assessors to six participants is maintained. The assessors rotate and concentrate on different participants in each exercise, so that the overall assessment never depends on the exclusive observations of a single person.

In most cases participants engage in exercises for two full days and then return to their jobs, but the assessors stay on at the assessment center after the participants have left for panel discussions about each participant. A panel discussion for a single participant lasts from two to three hours. The discussion is guided by an assessment center administrator and centers on observable behavior and not on judgments made by the assessors. Each assessor then writes assessment reports about two participants. The reports always include examples of behaviors, the consensus of the panel regarding management strengths and weaknesses and recommendations for personal development. Feedback on how a person performed in the assessment center is generally given orally to the individual himself and in writing to the superior.

SOME APPLICATIONS OF THE ASSESSMENT CENTER IN INDUSTRY

The assessment center model can take many forms and can be expanded to assess a few or many management dimensions. The basic model grew out of efforts of German psychologists to establish a systematic way of identifying potential officers during World War I, and the model was later used by psychologists to select candidates for promotion in the British Civil Service System. The first large scale use of the assessment center model came about in the middle 1950's when American Telephone and Telegraph personnel officials undertook a long range study of the career progress of young managers in six telephone companies.[1] In order to establish the validity of the assessment center process as a predictor of promotability, AT&T employed a team of outside assessors to assess candidates and to rate them as to the extent of their management potential. The results of the assessments were withheld from both participants and company management for 8–10 years in order to prevent any bias to the study, and at the end of the period it was determined that the assessment center process was highly effective in predicting success in management positions. For example, 64% of the participants predicted to enter middle management had done so by the eighth year after assessment, while only 32% of those participants predicted not to achieve middle management had done so. A number of other research studies of varying sophistication have born out the AT&T results. The assessment center process has been used with over 100,000 AT&T employees and has been adopted by hundreds of companies and agencies, such as J.C. Penney, the Internal Revenue Service, General Electric, Standard Oil (Ohio), U.S. Department of Agriculture and the Civil Service Commission of Wisconsin.[2]

AN APPLICATION OF THE ASSESSMENT CENTER IN EDUCATION

The Panhandle Area Educational Cooperative (P.A.E.C.), which is a shared services consortium of nine school districts in the predominately rural northwest Florida panhandle, undertook a pilot assessment center program to apply the model to the early identification of potential school principals and assistant principals. The PAEC pilot program was funded with monies authorized by the Florida Educational Leadership Training Act.

The first step in establishing the pilot assessment center program was to compile a list of behavioral dimensions that were considered highly desirable for effective school leaders in the Panhandle counties. Most of the professional literature in the area of "competencies" required of school principals consists of lists of behaviors that are either so specific (e.g., effectively controls the flow of student traffic in hallways) or so general (e.g., creates an effective learning environment in the school) that it was impossible to use them as dimensions for assessment within the framework of the assessment center model. In order to establish dimensions that were "assessable" and that described the characteristics of an effective principal, dimensions that described the behavior of effective managers were chosen from several lists of various organizations that have implemented the assessment center technique. The selected dimensions and their definitions were submitted to superintendents of schools, school board members, principals and selected teachers, who were asked to select those dimensions essential for an effective principal. The survey resulted in a list of 16 dimensions including some redefined dimensions (see Table 1).

TABLE 1

THE DIMENSIONS CHOSEN FOR
THE ASSESSMENT CENTER PROGRAM

Dimensions	Definitions
1. Impact	To what extent does this individual make an early impression on others?
2. Energy	To what extent can this individual maintain a continuous high level of work activity?
3. Oral Communication Skill	Effectiveness of expression in individual or group situations?
4. Written Communication Skill	To what extent can this individual effectively express ideas in writing?
5. Range of Interest	To what extent is this individual interested in the world around him?
6. Stress Tolerance	To what extent will this individual's work performance stand up in the face of unusual pressure?
7. Work Standards	To what extent will this individual want to do a good job, even if he could get by with doing a less acceptable job?
8. Career Ambition	To what extent will this individual need to be promoted significantly earlier than his or her peers?
9. Leadership	To what extent does this individual get people to perform a task effectively without arousing hostility?
10. Sensitivity	To what extent does this individual perceive subtle cues in the behavior of others toward him?
11. Flexibility	To what extent can this individual, when motivated, modify his own behavior to reach a goal?

TABLE 1 (continued)

Dimensions	Definitions
12. Independence	Action based on his own convictions, rather than a desire to please others.
13. Planning and organizing	To what extent can this individual effectively organize and plan his work and the work of others?
14. Decisiveness	To what extent is this individual able to make decisions when required?
15. Decision Making	To what extent can this individual make decisions of high quality?
16. Self-Objectivity	To what extent does this individual realize his own asset and liabilities?

Exercises were then selected or developed to be used in the assessment center that brought out the behaviors relevant to the dimensions. One such exercise is a *City Council Group Discussion* in which roles are assigned (city council members responsible for a department of city government) but in which no leader is appointed. The participants in this exercise are told that the city has received a special federal grant for one million dollars that must be allocated to city projects in a staff conference with other councilmen. Each participant is given detailed information about the needs of his department and general background information about the city.

In two other exercises that are related to each other, *The Writing Exercise and Writing Group Discussion*, the participants write a position paper. Then each participant makes a brief presentation to the others summarizing his key points and his thinking, and lastly the participants are again asked to work together to develop a written outline of a position paper that represents the concensus and best thinking of the group on the same subject. The topic that was used concerned collective bargaining in the school systems (the subject is timely in the State of Florida because by court order all public employees now must be represented). The participants were given the assignment of preparing a position on the role of the school principal and assistant principal in the professional negotiations of teachers and in carrying out a negotiated contract in the schools. During the group discussion, the assessment center administrator interrupted the discussion at times to either ask about the thinking of the participants or to present some other school related matters to the conference group. In this way, the flexibility and responsiveness of the participants were more readily observed.

Sometime during the assessment each participant is interviewed in depth by an assessor who has been furnished background information in advance. The *Background Interview* is unlike both the employment interview and counseling interview. It focuses on the participant's own perception of his school experiences, administrative goals and developmental needs. The interview may last more than two hours, and it is carefully planned in advance by the assessor. The focus of the interview is based on the assumption that an effective school principal must be reality centered and adaptive.

Another challenging exercise is the *In-Basket*. Each participant is asked to assume the role of a personnel director in a hypothetical organization. The participant is put directly into the personnel director's shoes. The former director was suddenly forced into early retirement for health reasons. The participant accepted the job while in New York and before flying to the West Coast to prepare to move East, he decided to stop by the office on a Saturday morning and handle the items that have piled up in his predecessor's in-basket. The items are detailed and interrelated, and it is very difficult to handle all the items in the three hours given. The participant also must carefully study various organization charts, policy manuals and so forth that are needed to respond to the items. The participant works alone, delegating work, making administrative decisions, planning conferences and responding to employee complaints. All responses must be in writing, including ideas and notes the participant wishes to make to himself for follow-up at a later time. An assessor carefully studies the in-basket responses, and the participant's reactions. The reaction forms are used to get each participant's explanation for the actions he took, the items he handled, the organization plan he used in approaching the items and his attitude toward the work and the role of the manager.

Each assessment exercise is carefully designed to bring out some of the management dimensions that were chosen for the PAEC program.

The most significant aspect of the assessment center process is the people who take part in it both as participants and assessors. In the PAEC program, participants were required to have attained a master's degree, to have state teacher certification in educational administration and supervision and to have taught for at least five years. The participants were given sufficient information about the program to ease any anxiety they might have about participating. They were told that they and their school superintendents would be the only people informed of the results, and were given the option of not participating if they had any reservations about the program.

The people chosen to serve as assessors were selected on the basis of their experience in a variety of administrative positions and their proven leadership abilities in their school districts and in regional and state education organizations and activities. The assessors were trained in the use of the assessment exercises, in behavioral observation techniques and in recognizing behaviors associated with each dimension. Care was taken so that the assessors were never assigned to observe participants from their home school districts. Thus, there would be little or no chance of the assessors having formed opinions about the participants' abilities or performance in settings other than the assessment center.

Probably the most important aspect of the assessor's role occurs during the panel discussions. Here each assessor presents his behavior observations to the other assessors. The assessors, with the aid of an administrator, strive toward objectivity. That is, the panel discussions focus on the performance of the participants and must be quite detailed. The final assessment report is written by an assessor only after the assessment panel has reached consensus first on the behaviors observed in the relation to the dimensions; secondly, on the competencies, and thirdly, on developmental recommendations.

As part of a small scale research study, data were collected from six assessors, twelve participants and three superintendents of schools who had personnel participate in the pilot program.[3] The reactions of all three groups were overwhelmingly favorable and enthusiastic. The research results can be summarized as follows:

ASSESSORS:
> The assessors felt that their participation in the assessor training and the assessment center program sharpened their observational skills and increased their awareness of behaviors relevant to the dimensions of the program.

PARTICIPANTS:
> The participants felt that their work with the exercises gave them insight into the demands of school administration and taught them how to better handle their group assignments and other work. They also felt that the final assessment reports were very accurate pictures of their potential and that the recommendations for self-development were relevant to their needs.

SUPERINTENDENTS:
> The superintendents of schools felt that the assessment reports were more accurate than their own observations and that they would be most helpful in providing staff development opportunities and in screening job applicants. The superintendents were very willing to send more subordinates to the assessment center.

FUTURE APPLICATIONS IN EDUCATION

Although the assessment center process is well validated in related fields of management, additional research is needed to determine the advantages of the process to manpower needs in educational leadership. The first question concerns the *utility* of the program. The important points here include:

1) The accuracy of the assessment center reports as measured by the correlation between the reports, and later performance of the participants as assistant principals and principals, 2) the impact of the assessment center program as a stimulus to participants to begin self-development, and as a management tool in planning in-service training programs for educational administrators, 3) the receptivity of school superintendents to use the assessment center reports as an aid in actual selection decisions and 4) the training impact from the experience of participating in an assessment center or serving as an assessor. There are various ways of conducting the research, although these efforts must all include some reasonable time frame for the participants and others in the schools to make use of the assessment center reports.

The second important question about the assessment center is its *practicality*. The important points here include: 1) the costs of the program in both dollars and man hours, 2) the availability of assessors for the program and a consultant to help implement the programs and train the staff and 3) the size and number of school districts that will implement the assessment center.

Assessment center activity is likely to grow in school systems because there is a need to identify high potential school administrators. It is important, however, to conduct such activities with careful planning and implementation procedures. Simply purchasing assessment materials beginning without, for example, a thorough analysis of management dimensions in the schools is fraught with many dangers. Improper applications will lead to invalid results, and could cause more harm than good.

The assessment center process can be successfully implemented in the schools with positive acceptance by the participants. The assessment reports in the PAEC program were favorably received, and included suggested plans for development activities. More assessment center activity in education is needed. The assessment center is a performance based approach, and is designed to increase objectivity and add relevacy to man-power planning and selection.

Endnotes

1. Douglas W. Bray and Donald Grant, The Assessment Center in Measurement of Potential for Business Management, *Psychological Monographs*, 1966, 80, 1110-17.
2. William C. Byham, Assessment Centers for Spotting Future Managers, *Harvard Business Review*, 1970, 48, 150-60, plus appendix.
3. Edward H. Deluzain, Evaluation Report: *School Leadership Assessment Program*, Panhandle Area Educational Cooperative, Chipley, Florida, 1974.

The School Principal: Recommendations for Effective Leadership

Assembly Education Committee - California State Legislature

This handbook was pepared in 1978 by the Task Force for the Improvement of Pre- and In-Service Training for Public School Administrators under the chairmanship of Dennis Mangers. In the portion we have reprinted, the current system of evaluation used in California is discussed, including problems that the system has generated and their effects on educational programs. A plea is made for an effective evaluation procedure and an outline for such a procedure is then laid out. In the final portion of this excerpt, general criteria for evaluating principals are listed — with the wise parenthetical note: "Exemplary only." The state legislature's interest in the question of evaluation administrative performance is an encouraging sign that its importance is being recognized at the highest levels of government.

Excerpts from *The School Principal: Recommendations for Effective Leadership* by Task Force of the Assembly Education Committee, 1978. Reprinted by permission of the Assembly, California State Legislature, Sacramento.

EVALUATION OF SCHOOL PRINCIPALS

THE CURRENT SYSTEM

Since 1972 every school district in California has been required by law to evaluate administrators on a regular basis. In many school districts evaluation of administrators has followed the same pattern as that for teachers. Principals, like teachers, are expected to write objectives for their work, have these objectives approved by their supervisor, and be evaluated regularly consistent with these identifed objectives.

PROBLEMS WITH THE CURRENT SYSTEM

The evaluation of principals, as described by principals, is inadequate in many districts. Some principals report: (1) little knowledge of criteria used by supervisors to evaluate them, (2) infrequent evaluations, (3) judgments by supervisors which are seldom based on direct observation, (4) little involvement of those to whom their work was most visible — teachers, students, parents and other administrators, (5) primary attention is given to minor objectives, such as "accuracy and punctuality in submitting reports" and maintaining an attractive school.[1] Thus, in some districts the effectiveness of school principals is too often measured by their ability to "keep the lid on" and serve the needs of the school district bureaucracy. "When there are no problems, there are no questions," explained one principal. "We usually only hear about our mistakes."[2]

AN EFFECTIVE EVALUATION SYSTEM

A set of criteria is needed which can be used to evaluate the principal's ability to provide leadership to the school.

Such criteria should themselves have certain characteristics:

1. They should be clearly set forth and commonly understood by the the Board of Education, district administration, school site council, teachers and other staff members, students and the principal. The principal should play a major role in their formulation.

2. They should be based on performance, that is, the criteria should deal specifically with how the principal performs his or her leadership role at the school and not what the principal says, for example, at district meetings.

3. They should provide for regular, visible review responsive to local needs and school clients. Student populations vary; educational needs and wants differ from community to community. Therefore, specific criteria and procedures should be developed by each principal within a districtwide evaluation framework applicable to all principals.

4. They should provide that those to whom the administrator's work is most visible, such as peers, teachers, students and parents, are involved in the evaluation process.

5. They should be fair, equitable and should speak to obtainable goals for each individual principal. Peter Drucker in his book, *The Effective Executive,* points out that no industry or institution has a cadre of "super-leaders."[3] Rather, there are human beings, well meaning but often fallible, who occupy leadership positions. Evaluation of principals, like evaluation of teachers and students, should be viewed as assisting the principal to be more effective. Thus, performance evaluation is a formative process which includes comments from the person evaluated.

6. Evaluation criteria, themselves, should be formative; that is, as conditions change, criteria of effectiveness should change also. Principals should be involved in assessing the need to change the criteria.

While there is no exclusive set of criteria for the evaluation of all school principals, there are general areas of school leadership which can be used in the design of general criteria for the evaluation of all principals. Such areas are derived from Appendix A of this report, "Skills and Competencies Needed for the School Principal" and presented in Appendix B. They are meant to be exemplary only and to be used as individual principals and localities determine they are appropriate.

RECOMMENDATIONS FOR THE IMPROVEMENT OF PRINCIPAL EVALUATION

1. We recommend that all school districts establish policies regarding the evaluation of school principals which meet the criteria established in Section VII. We recommend that the California School Boards Association lend their support and encouragement to this effort. We recommend that the Legislature request the Legislative Analyst to monitor the implementation of this recommendation over a three-year period, and, if necessary, develop legislation to ensure timely implementation following the three-year review.

2. We recommend that the State Department of Education establish a base of information regarding the substance of, and procedures for, the evaluation of school personnel, including school principals. We recommend that the resource base be developed with the assistance of county offices of education, school districts, colleges and universities and organizations of administrators and school board members.

3. We recommend that county officers of education, school districts, colleges and universities, and administrator and school board associations design and conduct staff development for central district administrators and others in the evaluation of school administrators based on the criteria established in Section V.

4. We recommend that the Legislature, the State Department of Education and colleges and universities support research regarding the effectiveness of school principals which will lead to the refinement of the criteria established in Section VII.

GENERAL CRITERIA FOR THE EVALUATION OF PRINCIPALS (Exemplary Only)

1. INSTRUCTIONAL SKILLS

1.1 The principal will demonstrate an ability to monitor instruction by:

    a. evaluating with teachers their performance using criteria derived from sound principles of learning (e.g. knowledge of objectives, appropriate practice, knowledge of results, appropriateness of content and materials).

    b. assisting teachers in planning improved instructional

1.2 The principal will demonstrate an ability to provide curriculum leadership at the school level by:
   a.   establishing a process for defining goals for the school.
   b.   establishing a process through which learning opportunities (e.g., courses or instructional programs) are selected and organized to meet the goals of the school.
   c.   establishing an ongoing process of evaluation which allows for continual improvement of the school's instructional programs.
1.3 The principal will demonstrate an ability to bring to the classroom and school the human and material resources necessary for improvement of instruction at the school.

2.   MANAGEMENT SKILLS

2.1 The principal will demonstrate an ability to set and attain work objectives.
2.2 The principal will demonstrate management skills through the successful use in the school of such procedures as:
   a.   needs assessment and goal setting;
   b.   problem identification and solving;
   c.   unit budgeting;
   d.   monitor and review procedures.

3.   HUMAN RELATIONS ABILITIES

3.1 The principal will demonstrate human relations abilities through the development and implementation of plans which:
   a.   involve parents, teachers, students and others in school based decisionmaking;
   b.   provide for open, honest and ongoing communications within the school and between the school and community;
   c.   create an atmosphere of trust at the school;
   d.   motivate students and staff to perform to their capacity at the school.
3.2 The principal will periodically involve staff and community in the assessment of the school work environment, decisionmaking structures and communication between the school and community.

4.   POLITICAL AND CULTURAL AWARENESS

4.1 The principal will develop ongoing communication between the school and community.

4.2 The principal will be able to assess the constituencies and power blocks within the school community and will see that they are involved in school level decision-making.

4.3 The principal will demonstrate an ability to resolve conflict as it arises within the school or between the school and community.

4.4 The principal will see that the needs of all clients of the school are met by the school program. (See also 1.1 and 3.2 above.)

5. LEADERSHIP SKILLS

5.1 The principal will demonstrate a willingness to keep abreast of current developments in the field through a stated plan of self-development which includes reading, participation in in-service activities, conference attendance, visitations and/or other professional development activities.

5.2 The principal will demonstrate leadership skills through a willingness to share new ideas with the school staff, other principals, district personnel, parents and the public.

6. SELF-UNDERSTANDING

6.1 The principal will periodically involve staff and community in the assessment of his or her leadership abilities.

6.2 The principal will develop a plan for self-improvement. (See also 2.1.)

FOOTNOTES

1. T. E. Deal, S.M. Dornbusch, and R. A Crawford, *Evaluating Principals – Applying A Theory of Evaluation* (Cambridge: Harvard University, 1976).

2. *Ibid.*, p. 11.

3. P. F. Drucker, *The Effective Executive* (New York: Harper and Row, and Row, 1967) p. 18.

Basic Policies

Salt Lake City School District

The Salt Lake City School District has drawn up a "Basic Policies" statement which contains, among other things, a number of statements on procedures as well as philosophies on accountability and evaluation, some of which are reprinted here. Though they speak for themselves, it should be pointed out that they place a heavy emphasis upon performance objectives. As the readings elsewhere in this book demonstrate, this emphasis is typical of current evaluation and is a trend that can be expected to continue in the foreseeable future.

Basic Policies of the Salt Lake City School District (1981-82). Reprinted by permision.

MANAGEMENT GOALS
1981–1982

1. Continue efforts to revise curricula to reflect important contributions of women and minority groups.
2. Continue efforts to attain high average daily attendance and support absent students with homework assignments.
3. Continue efforts to involve superintendent in local school activities: visits, goverance councils, PTA activities and school functions.

Educational excellence in the Salt Lake City School District begins with the adoption of goals by the Board of Education. These goals, once adopted, give purpose and direction to the district. They are the bases for allocating resources, for establishing accountability, and for evaluating personnel.

All administrative personnel are expected to demonstrate the following abilities:

a. Ability to understand and effectively implement board policy.
b. Ability to achieve performance standards as designated by the Superintendent of Schools.
c. Ability to administer the accountability program and achieve district and local objectives.

d.   Ability to operate within budgetary limits.
e.   Ability to operate within the limits of education law.
f.   Ability to operate in accordance with principles of shared governance.
g.   Ability to keep current, to continue learning, and to be aware of educational development.

SUPERINTENDENT'S ACCOUNTABILITY PROGRAM

To support Board of Education goals the Superintendent establishes performance standards for himself and his immediate staff. Such standards are aimed at achieving board goals. The standards direct the interests, energies, and talents of the staff toward Board of Education goals. They serve as criteria for Superintendent and staff evaluation.

PRINCIPALS' ACCOUNTABILITY PROGRAM

Principals meet with supervisors for administrative services to establish unit performance standards. Each principal supports Board of Education objectives, establishes additional unit objectives, and accepts a personal growth objective.

Once the principal establishes unit performance standards, he/she meets with each individual teacher to establish performance standards for each teacher. Standards support Board of Education goals. Each teacher may establish personal goals. Principals may also suggest goals for specific teachers in areas which need improvement.

Principals supervise the achievement of teacher performance standards and report achievement to the supervisors for administrative services.

PRINCIPALS' PERSONAL GROWTH OBJECTIVE

In addition to performance standards related to Board of Education goals principals identify a personal growth goal. For the 1981-1982 school year all principals will work in the area of curriculum. Their personal growth goal is to become fully informed about the contributions of various ethnic groups and minorities. (Performance standards will be established by October 1, 1981.)

The principals in the district have achieved a high standard of keeping themselves informed by utilizing a variety of methods and strategies. They will continue to keep themselves informed in a combination of ways listed below.

1.   Attendance at meetings of the Board of Education.
2.   Reading reports of Board of Education meetings.

3. Visits with the Superintendent of Schools or members of the Superintendent's staff.
4. Attendance at meetings of the Superintendent's staff.
5. Informal calls to the Superintendent.
6. Attendance at weekly briefing meetings with the Superintendent.
7. Invitations to central office personnel to visit schools.
8. Sharing information in collegial teams with member of Superintendent's staff.
9. Participation in decision-making committees and councils.
10. Personal contacts to identified group to disseminate information.
11. Participation in collegial teams.
12. Other methods chosen by principals.

TEACHERS' ACCOUNTABILITY PROGRAM

In September of each year, each teacher develops an accountability program in conference with the principal. The accountability program contains each teacher's contribution to the attainment of Board of Education objectives.

Once the standards of performance are agreed to, the teacher has the freedom to achieve the objective within the framework of policy, law, ethics, and budget. Principals and teachers periodically discuss progress being made to achieve objectives. If help is needed, both principal and teacher may receive additional help from central office personnel.

Each teacher reports to the principal in May to validate the attainment of the standards agreed to in September. Validation may be by test scores, teacher judgment, documents, observation, performance of students, or other mutually accepted method.

ROLE OF THE STAFF COORDINATOR

The staff coordinator has three major responsibilities: (1) to work closely with the Board of Education, (2) to monitor the district's accountability program and (3) to assign schools to administrators for supervisory services.

The staff coordinator coordinates the work of the Board of Education, the staff, and the principals. She keeps the board informed of district activities and plans the Board of Education agenda.

The staff coordinator monitors the work of the superintendent, the staff, and the principals. She accounts for all reports, deadlines, and conference schedules. In developing her priorities she gives emphasis to Board of Education goals. She validates that the following steps have been taken to incorporate the district goals into an accountability process.

1. Development of specific performance objectives for every certificated employee.
2. Planning and implementing programs to carry out objectives in each unit.
3. Identification of budget support for each objective.
4. Identification of the kind of evidence needed to assess attainment of objectives.
5. Determination of the manner in which attainment of objectives will be reported.
6. Implementation of inservice training needed to achieve objectives.
7. Review of programs, goals or objectives by the staff and by the Board of Education as needed.
8. Implementation of programs to properly inform the Board of Education, employees, patrons, and the public.

SUPERVISORS FOR ADMINISTRATIVE SERVICES

Supervisors for Administrative Services supervise a group of principals. In addition, they have other supervisory and administrative responsibilities. Their responsibilities as supervisors for administrative services are these:
1. Formulate unit standards of performance.
2. Provide support services to the schools each one supervises.
3. Act as information sources for principals.
4. Assist principals to obtain services from central office personnel.
5. Monitor the achievement of Board goals in the schools each one supervises.
6. Make periodic reports to the superintendent.
7. Hold periodic conferences with principals.
8. Collect necessary documents to validate achievement of goals.
9. Compile materials for staff coordinator.
10. Validate performance payment.

EVALUATION STRATEGIES

Remediation Program. Employees who are not making a satisfactory contribution to the district are placed on remediation. When remediation is needed, there is first a period of informal remediation. If that is not successful, formal remediation is implemented.

The remediation process is to help the employee correct weaknesses or initiate improvements in services. In most cases remediation is successful. In some cases however, remediation is not successful and the employee terminates his association with the district. Persons on remediation are not advanced on the salary schedule until remediation is successful.

Review of Services Process. If a person believes that the district has violated an agreement or has committed an unfair or unjust action, a Review of Services process is initiated. Any individual may request a review of services of an employee or a school program.

Review of services is an orderly and fair process for evaluating decisions made by employees or for reviewing programs. It requires that individuals who wish to review first try to adjudicate the situation in an informal manner. If that is not successful an appeal may be made to the superintendent and then to the Board of Education.

Audit Procedure. When there is a concern that a particular class is not achieving at a proper level, the district may conduct an educational audit. The audit is used to assist the teacher to find out if additional help is needed in certain areas or for certain students.

The audit may be initiated by the teacher, the superintendent, or by the principal. Information obtained by an audit should be discussed with the teacher. The audit is a method of evaluating if proper achievement is being made and if any corrective measures should be initiated.

Progress Conferences. Progress toward the achievement of Board of Education goals can be determined through periodic conferences. The superintendent visits with principals and supervisor. Principals visit with teachers. All certificated staff periodically assess the degree of progress being made so that adjustment can be made if needed.

Progress conference should examine progress being made, help needed, adjustments to be made, and validation information. Adequate progress evaluation prevents surprises from occurring later in the school year.

Shared Governance. Each school in the Salt Lake City School District has a School Community Council which serves as a sounding board for local school ideas, problems and plans. Both community and staff members serve together to benefit the students and the school.

The purpose of the council is to provide a cooperative means fo improving educational programs and conditions within the school. The council meets at least monthly — more often if needed — and minutes of all meetings are kept and distributed to all members of the council.

Under the philosophy of shared governance of the Salt Lake City School District each School Community Council participates actively in the decision-making process for the school rather than in an advisory capacity. The council, like all other governance or administration units of the district, operates within the guidelines of:
1. Board of Education policy
2. School District budget
3. Ethical practices
4. Education law.

Shared governance operates on the principal of parity — equal position of the parties. In this case there are two parties: 1) the parents and 2) the employees of the Salt Lake City School District. Voting should be a last resort, and then each party has one vote. The best process under parity relationship is to work for consensus.

The principal, the PTA president, and the PTA first vice president serve as members and each of these nominates one community representative to serve as members. Each of the three nominated members then nominates one additional member, providing a total community membership of nine people. Members of the School Improvement Council — from faculty and staff of the school — are members of the School Community Council.

The council operates within the following guidelines:

1. Representatives from minority groups and all geographic areas of the school shall be considered in the selection of membership.
2. *Ad hoc* committees may be appointed by each individual council. The findings of such committees shall be reported to the council.
3. Additional participation or representation on the council shall be determined by the council as needs arise.
4. The chairman shall be elected by the council and operating procedures of the council shall be determined by the council.
5. Items beyond the scope of the School Community Council shall be referred in writing to the Superintendent of Schools.

Schools operate best when there is close cooperation between home and school. Shared governance is a method for establishing that cooperation. A strong partnership between home and school results in benefits for students and creates a positive climate in the schools. It also provides parents and teachers opportunities to develop excellence in all that is done.

The School Community Council extends local decision-making to each local school unit. It is there that decisions can best be made concerning those items that augment Board of Education policies. It is at the local level that what is best for the school can be decided. Working in harmony with the Board of Education, each school can decide local issues which support the values and desires of the school patrons and teachers.

The councils are charged with important responsibilities. Their decisions affect the lives and education of many children. It is their obligation to decide fairly, to adjudicate for justice, and to create relationships which support cooperation and orderly processes. Recognizing board policies, abiding by state and federal regulations, staying within budget limits, and promoting ethical practices, the School Community Councils are a tremendous asset to the Salt Lake City School District and make a significant contribution to the operation of our schools.

Visitations. Visitations to schools and to classrooms are used to obtain general impressions. Visitations cannot establish if goals are being achieved, but they can indicate the climate of the school, the general learning atmosphere, and the attitudes of people toward the school.

Visitations are also helpful in understanding concerns which principals and teachers may have. They assist supervisors to understand the problems which may inhibit goal achievement.

Visitations also help to clarify communications and to demonstrate support for the work of principals and teachers. Principals are urged to invite staff personnel to visit the school at least three times each year.

VALIDATION PROGRAM

Achievement of goals may be validated in various ways. Here are a few methods used in the Salt Lake City School District.

Periodic Reports. Employees make periodic reports to the superintendent and to the staff coordinator to validate achievement of goals. These reports indicate the status of progress being made and the areas of weakness that need to be improved. Such reports make it possible for supervisors to take corrective action if needed.

Periodic progress reports are presented to the Board of Education to keep them informed of what is happening to achieve its goals. Such reports are also made available to the public and to the media.

Testing Program. Under the supervision of the educational auditor, a testing program is conducted to measure pupil achievement. Test results indicate progress being made and also identify areas where additional help is needed.

Testing is concentrated at these grade levels: first, third, fifth, seventh, and ninth. Longitudinal studies are prepared and given to the Board of Education, teachers, staff and administrators.

Teacher Judgment. In the final analysis, teacher judgment plays an important part in validating achievement. The human judgment is usually more accurate than test data, observation reports, and other forms of validation. Each teacher must validate achievement in the basic skills by considering all data and making a judgment.

Validation Conferences. In May or June of each year conferences are held to validate that the Board of Education goals have been achieved. These conferences are held between principals and teachers and between supervisors and principals. The superintendent also meets with staff members to validate that performance standards have been attained. All conferences are validated by the staff coordinator, who also accumulates all documents needed by the school district. These conferences are held with each certified employee.

End of Year Reports. At the end of each school year each certificated staff member prepares an end-of-the-year report. The superintendent prepares a district report for the Board of Education. Each principal submits the following documents to the supervisor for administrative services.

1. Certification of Satisfactory Service
2. Teacher Goal Achievement statements

3. Principal's Success Review Form
4. Report to the Board of Education
5. Validation of performance payment for assistant administrators
6. Validation documents related to district goals

These reports and others prepared by central office personnel serve to validate that the Board of Education goals have been achieved. The reports also verify that satisfactory service has been provided or that certain individuals have been placed on remediation. The documents also serve as a basis for awarding a performance payment to all administrative staff who have provided satisfactory service.

PART III

Setting Up an Evaluation System

Administrator Evaluation: Concerns for the Practitioner

Lloyd E. McCleary

Written specifically for the present book, Professor McCleary's article points out that while progress is being made in developing sound evaluative procedures, much of the knowledge base for evaluating personnel is new "and is in a relatively untested and primitive stage." In a fine analysis of problems currently besetting the state of the art, McCleary notes that current evaluative practice can all too often be characterized as "informal, subjective, judgmental and covert." Part of what must be done to create valid and usable procedures is to develop systems that will carry such labels as "formal, objective, rationally judgmental and overt." Discussing work by Sarason, Raup, Alley and others, as well as procedures advocated by such organizations as the National Association of Secondary School Principals, he assesses current strategies and offers a number of important caveats. He is Professor of Educational Administration at the University of Utah, Salt Lake City. (See also Professor McCleary's related article elsewhere in this section.)

School administrators face problems and dilemmas in conducting personnel evaluations but these occur in much greater proportion as administrators establish formal procedures and undergo evaluation themselves. This is so for a variety of reasons but primarily because of pressures for formal evaluation, lead time required by the profession to conduct needed R & D work, political and human values which impact evaluation and difficulties entailed in the installation of a defensible system. Included in the term "installation" are the system accommodations and adjustments needed to put formal evaluation procedures in place in a given district.

Evaluation as applied to personnel encompasses the entire process of determining performance requirements, establishing criteria, adapting and validating instruments, collection and treatment of data, reporting, making decisions about performance and determining review procedures. Assessment, on the other hand, includes only the first four stages of the process. Most who are considered as evaluation specialists deal only with assessment. This distinction between evaluation and assessment becomes important later in this treatment, and it is particularly relevant because school districts frequently attempt merely to adopt procedures and instruments without regard to the conditions of a particular district.

From the simplistic logic of those who make policy for education, such as memebers of school boards and even top level administrators, personnel evaluation should be a normal, even natural function. After all, evaluation is not new to education. Student performance has always been evaluated. Program and institutional evaluation has a shorter history, but the conceptual and technical foundations of program and institutional evelution are rooted in a fairly clearly formulated knowledge base which spans more than five decades. The knowledge base for personnel evaluation is new and is in a relatively untested and primitive stage. Without a well codified knowledge base even the purely technical aspects of assessment present difficulties. A characterization of current practice in personnel evaluation, whether for teachers or administrators, would have to include such labels as informal, subjective, judgmental and covert. It is hoped that current efforts might lead to a characterization which would include such labels as formal, objective, rationally judgmental and overt.

The above observations are offered as a commentary on personnel evaluation not as an assessment of the "state of the art" which is a primary contribution of this entire volume. Hopefully, they indicate to the reader that difficulties with, even reticence about, formal evaluation of administrators has some foundation in terms of the science itself. Additional aspects of the science of evaluation as applied to personnel evaluation are treated which might serve to explain why we are in the present knowledge dilemma and what administrators should concern themselves with in examining an evaluation system. The treatment then turns to organizational conditions which impact administrator evaluation and to the personal-professional conditions which must be treated if administrator evaluation is to contribute to organizational health and productivity.

ADMINISTRATOR EVALUATION AND THE SCIENCE OF EVALUATION

As a field of study educational administration, as well as evaluation, has adopted the mystique of a science such that the modes of inquiry, assumptions about problem resolution and values attendant to science are applied, almost unconsciously, to practical problems. There is a predisposition to believe that evaluation of personnel can be made "scientific", that answers to problems of evaluation have definitive solutions and that the exercise of judgment can be reduced to objective decisions. There are three conditions which mitigate against the acceptance of scientific doctrine as a basis for establishing evaluation systems for administrators.

The first condition is that most of the problems attendant to the creation of an evaluation system for administrators are not amenable to a scientific mode of inquiry. They are not researchable problems. Sarason (1971), among others, has pointed out that the questions which are fundamental to decision making, evaluation and change in schools are at base value questions: what should be done, what is the best or the right thing to do at this time, who is to be included or excluded in a decision, what can one expect others in the school to do and feel as a result of actions taken. The enormous situation specificity found in each school and school district makes the answers to these questions highly judgmental and highly lacking in predictability of consequences. In a much earlier work by Raup, and others, (1943) the authors examine in detail what they term the art of practical intelligence. They argue that values clarification and consensus building are the heart of the administrator's job not the technical-managerial, or even purely educational, aspects of the job. The matter of how judgment enters into administrator evaluation and the problem of values in that process are critical to whether formal personnel evaluation is productive to educational effort. The point here is that scientific methodologies are not amenable to many important aspects of personnel evaluation.

The second condition is that the current conditions of research and inquiry in education generally are not up to the task of producing a codified knowledge base even of the assessment phases of personnel evaluation. David Krathwohl (1979) in a verbal report to a U.S. Office of Education Research Policy Committee noted what he characterized as hard "facts" about research in education. He reported that: 1) the effort is very small in relation to other fields, such as agriculture and medicine, 2) much of the effort is used up in justifiying basic social values, 3) the products of research are scattered, not incremental, and therefore not very useful, 4) research in education over-promises on results and creates unrealistic expectations, and 5) pressing needs in schools will continue to produce fads and frills rather than sound, long term development. To the extent that Krathwohl is correct there is a serious need to codify what is known, this volume being one effort in that direction. However, practitioners need to become aware of the knowledge base from which they might work with confidence.

The third condition relative to administrator evaluation and the science of evaluation stems from the second condition, noted above. There is a need for sound, developmental work from the field such that studies can be undertaken and a base of knowledge and a record of practice becomes available. There are those districts which do resist, or mitigate, the pressures which produce fads and frills, and it is to these districts that the burden and satisfaction of moing the field ahead will accrue. However, just as there exists only a very small effort in research and development, there apparently exist a small number of districts that are engaging in sound, developmental efforts related to administrator evaluation. At least this is true if a recent study of Indiana school districts is representative. Reene Ann Alley (1981) completed a study with the following findings: 1) the majority of Indiana school districts have no policy or procedure for evaluation of the performance of the high school principal; 2) most practices used in the evaluation of the high school principal were not developed for use in a particular district but were adopted from previously prepared documents; 3) informal assessment of the principal's performance occurred frequently and was influenced by community standards and values, and 4) evaluation was influenced by such factors as the individual's personality and understanding of his/her role, type of procedure used, principal's relationship with the evaluators, and the school board's understanding of, and desires for, the principal's role in a particular community.

ORGANIZATIONAL CONDITIONS AND ADMINISTRATOR EVALUATION

School systems are univerally organizationed in terms of implicit assumptions which derive from classic bureaucratic models. Efforts to decentralize, to engage in school-based management, to operate under management by objectives (MBO) procedures, and the like only confirm this assertion because these are means to either more fully implement or modify the effects of bureaucratic models. In addition to the well known characteristics of bureaucratic organization two implicit assumptions are significant as far as administrator evaluation is concerned. First is that organizational (school) goals are unambiguous, reasonably stable over time and agreed upon by staff, administrators and publics. Second is that the means and procedures for achieving goals are standardized, specific and equally applicable across schools. In point of fact, the many occurences and situationally specific conditions which exist in schools are not easily accountable as being rational and efficient; often they are treated as pathological.

Schools seem to be better understood as loosely-coupled organizations (Weick, 1976) in which goals are relatively unclear and changing: participation is fluid in terms of publics, higher authority, and internal staff; and technologies, particularly in teaching and learning, are highly varied. Schools are held together and function more from shared understandings, low level and easily adaptable procedures and commitments to basic beliefs about schooling: (Mayer and Rowan, 1977). Schools are not held together primarily on the basis of prescribed procedures, inspection and administrative controls.

In the matter of formal evaluation of administrators there is the need to attend to, and note with care, those commitments and understandings about administrator performance which are shared and *not* shared. In this author's experience with evaluation of administrators three primary concerns seem always to surface from those being evaluated. First is the concern that those judging performance do not perceive the role in the same way; there is role ambiguity, even role conflict. Second is the concern about situational specificity; that instruments and criteria used to judge performance in one school are not valid in another. Finally, there is concern that forces influencing the role are not accounted for: the administrator, particularly the school principal, is not in control of how time and effort are expended.

The National Association of Secondary School Principals (NASSP, 1977) has made a considerable effort over the past seven years to develop what they refer to as an Assessment Center. Studies of school principals show that twelve areas of competence seem to be generic to judgments about effectiveness regardless of level (elementary, middle or secondary) as well as to situation. Instruments for measuring performance in the twelve areas have been validated; however, the measurement of performance on test instruments and performance on the job has not been established. The twelve areas of competence and the NASSP definitions of them are as follows.

1. Problem Analysis. Ability to seek out relevant data and analyze complex information to determine the important elements of a problem situation; searching for information with a purpose.

2. Judgment. Skill in identifying educational needs and setting priorities, ability to reach logical conclusions and make high-quality decisions based on available information; ability to critically evaluate written communications.

3. Organizational Ability. Ability to plan, schedule, and control the work of others; skill in using resources in an optimal fashion; ability to deal with a volume of paper work and heavy demands on one's time.

4. Decisiveness. Ability to recognize when a decision is required and to act quickly. (Without an assessment of the quality of the decision).

5. Leadership. Ability to recognize when a group required direction, to set others involved in solving problems, to effectively interact with a group, to guide them to the accomplishment of a task.

6. Sensitivity. Ability to perceive the needs, concerns, and personal problems of others; tact in dealing with persons from different backgrounds, skill in resolving conflicts; ability to deal effectively with people concerning emotional issues; knowing what information to communicate and to whom.

7. Range of Interests. Competence to discuss a variety of subjects (educational, political, economic, etc.), desire to actively participate in events.

8. Personal Motivation. Showing that work is important to personal satisfaction; a need to achieve in all activities attempted; ability to be self-policing.
9. Educational Values. Possession of well-reasoned education philosophy; receptiveness to change and new ideas.
10. Stress Tolerance. Ability to perform under pressure and opposition, ability to think on one's feet.
11. Oral Communication Skill. Ability to make a clear oral presentation of ideas and facts.
12. Written Communication Skill. Ability to express ideas clearly in writing; to write appropriately for different audiences-students, teachers, parents, other administrators.

The list provides an indication of the elements of administration performance to be assessed. If the assessment center concept proves to be valid, it will offer a means of conducting a formal assessment of competencies known to be generic. It will not establish that other competencies, perhaps equally important, do not exist. It will also not remove the judgment functions which must occur in the complete evaluation cycle, but it should offer some means to control the judgment functions required in the assessment phase of evaluation.

The argument for formal evaluation on the organization side is largely based upon bureaucratic premises: that administration should be accountable, that organizational goals and priorities require controls and that evidence of performance is necessary to sound planning and decision making. There are other reasons for accepting, even advocating, formal evaluation. Those being evaluated should know the procedures to be employed, the elements of performance to be assessed, the standard (expectations) for performance upon which judgments are to be mad and the organization assistance to be provided in meeting standards. Only through formal evaluation can these be made known and applied in a fair consistent fashion.

Apart from evaluation itself, organization has an obligation to its members to insure that satisfying and productive careeers are possible. In education, both satisfaction and productivity are becoming more difficult to attain. Successful careers in teaching and administration are in danger. The danger increases when political considerations enter into personnel decisions, when the demarcation between public and professional domains become blurred, when priorities are unclear and when standards by which success is measure remain implicit. The danger will only increase as resources become more of a problem and the margin of tolerance for deviation, even creative and experimental activity, is reduced.

PERSONAL-PROFESSIONAL CONCERNS IN
ADMINISTRATOR EVALUATION

Many administrator concerns have already been noted. In addition to the difficulty of specifying the critical elements in an administrative role, there is a heavy political component. Individual and organizational policies, particularly in schools, are never congruent and, therefore, the performance of the administrator will never be viewed with satisfaction by all those who will have input to evaluation. This leads to the concern for who is to be involved and for the standards to be employed. The NASSP Assessment Center represents one example in which trained assessors are employed and in which standards are external. Other approaches which attempt to alleviate these concerns employ an annual plan, either for the school and including administrator responsibilities in the plan or a self developed performance plan. The latter is an adaptation of MBO and a standard instrument, SPAR (1978), is available in which the administrator makes a plan, identifies goals to be accomplished and the activities to be accomplished. This plan is monitored, usually by peers as well as superiors, and a formal evaluation prepared in terms of it.

The administrator should be aware of the type of standards to be employed in an evaluation, regardless of the procedures used. Basically there are three kinds of standards, two are relative and one is absolute. Relative standards can be set in terms of past performance of the administrator being evaluated, or they can be set in terms of performance of others with whom the administrator can be compared. Absolute standards are those which are, more or less, arbitrarily set in terms of perceived organizational goals. In so called "turn around" schools absolute standards have been employed, with the initiation or participation of the administrator, indicating what is expected of the principal and what assistance is to be made available. For obvious reasons the administrator should be aware of the standards, understand which type(s) are being used and how they are to be employed in the evaluation.

Perhaps the most difficult aspect of administrator evaluation from the aspect of procedural matters is the separation of data collection from application of standards and judging performance from decision making about actions to be taken. Administrators, sometimes with apparent justification, report that judgments are made as data is being collected or that decisions about administrator competence are made before judgments about the data collected are adequately considered. Questioning of procedural matters is as important to valid outcome as is the content of evaluation itself.

The adoption and implementation of a formal system of evaluation can provide personal-professional problems in addition to the technical problems involved. Formal systems reduce assessment of specifics which somehow do not carry the vividness of actual experience or the insight into real experience. The experienced administrator, who is undergoing formal evaluation for the first time or who is contemplating it, can have many misgivings of a personal kind. There is every reason to begin slowly, to proceed incrementally adding areas and procedures as experience is gained. With proper preparation and due caution much can be gained through formal evaluation, some of the important considerations, hopefully, have been communicated in this treatment.

Notes

1. Seymour Sarason, *The Culture of the School and the Problem of Change* (Boston: Allyn & Bacon, 1971).

2. R. Bruce Raup, et al, *The Improvement of Practical Intelligence: the Central Task of Education* (New York, Harper & Brothers, 1943) pp 48-60.

3. David Krathwohl, from the author's notes, 1979.

4. Reene Ann Alley, *Evaluating Role Performance of High School Principals: School District Policies and Procedures and Their Impact On Those Evaluated* (Bloomington, Ind.: Unpublished Doctoral dissertation, 1981).

5. Karl Weick, "Educational Organizations as Loosely Coupled Systems," *Administrative Science Quarterly,* 21 (March 1976) pp 1-19.

6. John W. Mayer and Brian Rowan, "Formal Structure of Organizations as Myth and Ceremony", *American Journal of Sociology,* 83 (September 1977) pp 340-363.

7. NASSP, *Bulletin,* 61:40 (September 1977) pp 81-82.

8. CADRE, Self Performance Achievement Record (SPAR) (Tulsa: CADRE Publication Center of the University of Tulsa, 1978).

Current Issues in Evaluation

Robert B. Howsam

"Never in the history of education," says Dr. Howsam, "has there been so much external demand for evaluation." In this article, Howsam's comments are directed to the general question of the role and value of evaluation in the educational setting. His perceptive observations — psychological, sociological, philosophical — are valuable as an introduction to the study of specific evaluative methods. Robert B. Howsam is Dean of the College of Education at the University of Texas, Houston.

Whenever there are human beings, there will be evaluation. Man is a valuing and goal-seeking being. Even if he were to decide not to evaluate, he would end up evaluating how well he had succeeded in giving up evaluating.

So the issue is not whether there will be evaluation; rather it must involve questions such as what, how, by whom, for what purpose, and with what consequence. This in no way obscures the fact, however, that questions of evaluation continue to be among the most thorny that education faces.

Adequate evaluation has been a central concern of educators and researchers for many years. It remains so even though much progress, particularly in measurement, has been made. A reasonable prediction would be that ongoing instructional developments of a rather radical nature will cause a continuation of the pressure. In addition, many more issues will emerge.

Never in the history of education in the country has there been so much external demand for evaluation. Rising costs, troubles within schools, loud voices of criticism, the specific attention of the federal government, and the widespread emphasis on accountability are all factors contributing to the heightened interest. It would appear that responding to these pressures will be a major task of education for some time to come.

EVALUATION AS JUDGMENT

Evaluation is a procedure that involves judgment. If the reader keeps the connotation of judgment clearly in mind, the issues in connection with evaluation will be sharper.

Evaluation of an object (person, performance, item, behavior, and so forth) can be accomplished only if there is an idea of what the object should be like. Hagen and Thorndike[1] indicate that evaluation is a three-phase process that involves selecting the atributes desired in the object, describing the objects in terms of the attributes, and arriving at a judgment as to the merit or worth of the object. This insight is useful since it provides a straightforward basis for differentiating between measurement and assessment on the one hand and arriving at judgments on the other.

Tests and other forms of measurement and assessment are not evaluation — they are means of collecting descriptive data needed in the evaluative and decision-making processes.

FORMATIVE AND SUMMATIVE EVALUATION

In education, as elsewhere, two major and very different kinds of evaluation are used — *formative* and *summative* evaluation — and some of the major issues in evaluation are related to the degree of emphasis on each.

Formative evaluation refers to the use of data to make a process or operation effective as it goes along. By being able to redirect the process as it progresses, the goal seeker has a greater chance of reaching his goal. If the objectives will not be met, corrections can be made. On a space shot, for example, there is a goal or target and a precise design of the path (attributes) that must be followed if the target is to be reached. The process of the flight is monitored, and the data (descriptions) are studied constantly. When a discrepancy between the intended path and the actual path is found, the discrepancy is studied and corrective action taken. This kind of evaluation is termed formative since its purpose is to continually fashion and refashion behavior in such a way as to achieve objectives. Another word commonly used to mean the same is "feedback," a term widely used in systems theory and applications. Formative evaluation is critical in the teaching-learning relationship, in the supervisor-supervisee relationship, and in all planning and management processes.

Summative evaluation occurs at the conclusion of an act or process; it is terminal. Summative evaluations have a characteristic of finality. These evaluations are entered into records and are used as the bases of decisions. Teachers retain or lose their positions on the basis of summative evaluations. Student summative evaluations become grades, appear on transcripts and report cards, and affect decisions that others make about them.

Probably no set of issues is more important than the use of formative and summative evaluation in educational practice. In general, teachers overuse the summative and underuse the formative evaluation processes. Sound education is formative in intent. Its evaluation processes should emphasize the formative and attempt to ensure that the necessary summative processes interfere as little as possible with the formative.

THE APPROVAL-DISAPPROVAL TENDENCY

Evaluation is a process that involves making judgments on the basis of evidence regarding the attainment of previously determined conditions or objectives. At its best it is a rational, objective process. The data speak for themselves. Approval or disapproval is not implied.

In our culture, however, there is a deep-seated tendency to mix data and judgment with approval or disapproval and to be punitive; this kind of behavior is referred to as judgmental. The tendency appears most markedly in the primary institutions of home, school, and church, and hence becomes part of us. Teachers have long been observed to share abundantly in this characteristic. Granting or withholding approval is a major mechanism of pupil control, it is also believed to be an effective means of motivating behavior. It should be noted here that the assumption underlying this kind of behavior, whether stated or unstated, is that the constant use of summative evaluation is formative in its effect. There is ample evidence, however, that judgmental and punitive behavior interferes with motivation and with formative processes such as teaching and learning. It tends to inhibit the capacity to receive feedback and to redirect behavior on the basis of the evidence. Sound education proceeds from clearly established objectives, which both teacher and pupil understand. When the learner knows what is expected, feedback data on performance permit him to redirect his energies. Criticism and punishment highten tension and anxiety and so interfere with the needed helping relationship between teacher and pupil. The role of the teacher is more effectively played if the instructional process itself yields the data while the teacher supports the pupil as a person in a positive way.

This issue of being formative and supportive as against being punitive and judgmental lies close to the heart of the problem of using evaluation effectively. The former characterizes the professional approach, while the latter derives from the conventional wisdom of the society. Developing a science of evaluation will add little to educational practice unless the tools of evaluation can be properly used.

GOALS AND OBJECTIVES

One can evaluate "being," or he can evaluate "doing," or he can evaluate the "consequences" of being or doing. For example, he can evaluate a teacher for what he is, or for what he does, or for what he achieves. Clearly the intent is to evaluate his effectiveness as a teacher, which means the consequence of what he is or does. This could not be done unless there were goals or objectives for the act or process of teaching. The achievement of goals — broad expectations or purposes — or the achievement of objectives — more limited in scope and leading toward more specific goals — is the ultimate object of all evaluation. Some of the most important issues facing our schools and our profession arise directly from differences of opinion over goals and objectives and even over how desirable it is to have precise objectives. In the absence of substantial agreement on purpose, agreement on evaluation is impossible.

When goals and objectives are vague and imprecise, evaluation of outcomes is virtually impossible. The tendency is to settle on other criteria that can be inferred to be related to outcomes. It is this imprecision in education objectives that has led to efforts to evaluate what the teacher is and what the teacher, or the pupil, does. For many years researchers have sought to identify the characteristics of the effective teacher, more recently, attention has turned to analysis of teacher behaviors. None of these efforts should obscure the fact that pupil learning and behavior are the purpose of the school and, therefore, must be the ultimate objects of evaluation.

But the imprecision of evaluation has had another unfortunate effect: it has led to widespread criticism of schools and more recently, it has brought demands for "accountability" and even suggestions for "deschooling America."

It is probably fortunate that the years of this decade are likely to see the greatest attention to the objectives of education that our schools have ever known. Education can go either forward or backward with this thrust. The impetus for emphasizing objectives comes from a variety of sources. Some wish objectives for accountability purposes; others see them as necessary for effective teaching and learning. On the other hand, some see the movement as a dehumanizing threat and resist it. What the emphasis finally means will depend in large measure on what professional educators make of the opportunity it presents.

GOALS AND OBJECTIVES CAN CHANGE

One of the problems confronting the education profession in this country is that society has experienced changes that make some of the traditional roles of the school no longer proper or possible to achieve. Changes in one or more elements of a system inevitably require changes in the other parts. The rapid pace of technological developments has induced the need for massive changes in the social institutions that serve the society. But there is a great reluctance to change our primary institutions — traditionally the custodians of the values, beliefs, and ways of life of a culture. The school, which in this society is very close to the people and the community, is not permitted the rapid adaptation necessary to keep up with changing conditions. Thus its goals tend to become increasingly unrealistic. There is little point in evaluating the outcomes of the processes of education if evaluation of the hoped for outcomes reveals that they themselves are not proper or possible to attain. I believe that this is indeed the case at this time.

Every society is concerned with the enculturation of its children. The role of bringing up children, of forming them according to the image of the society is assigned to one or more institutions. In less complex societies, the primary institutions of home, school, and church are assigned this function, with villages and communities supporting their efforts. Invariably these institutions operate within closely defined limits, doing only what the community permits. In effect they limit the experiences a child can have. Thus he is taught what to value, believe, think and do. Societies all have this characteristic to some degree. As in the case with all school systems, the school in the American society started out as an instrument of enculturation. It continues so. But therein lies the source of many of its problems.

Societies dominated by primary institutions can be relatively closed. Their school programs include only those subjects that have social approval. The pupils accept whatever is taught, particularly if the other primary institutions seems to concur. This pattern succeeds only as long as the boundaries of the culture-village-community can be preserved. Clearly, this condition no longer exists in this country. The opposite has become true.

As our society developed and became more complex it established, or permitted to be established, institutions that promoted change that in turn upset the culture and its primary institutions. This situation is not confined to our country, but it probably is most true in a society that values individual initiative and free enterprise. Our society long ago removed the functions of production, distribution of goods and services, communication, travel, and entertainment from the primary institutions. These activities were turned over to secondary institutions with a very high degree of autonomy and a low level of social accountability. The success of these secondary institutions has been phenomenal, but so has the impact.

Primary institutions seek to maintain and preserve; secondary institutions seek to develop and change. Invention and promotion, within a part of a century, took us from the horse and buggy to space travel, from weekly newspapers with scant coverage of events to instant observation of the events of the whole world via satellite, from church socials and family gatherings to television and Hollywood, from place boundedness to world travel and high mobility; and from expanded family and community groups to minute social stratification based on a multiplicity of factors such as age and interests. Literally, in the pursuit of progress and profit, the secondary institutions have transformed our world. And the process, which has accelerated greatly, appears scarcely to have begun.

The world has become one in terms of accessibility. In this setting the traditional closure-enculturation role of the primary institution becomes anomalous. At best the home, school, church and community fight losing rearguard actions if the maintenance of closure is their stance. Unless they can adapt and take on new and relevant roles, they can only hope to prolong an agonizing demise.

Though it could not be successfully contended that schools have not changed, it is widely recognized that they have experienced no fundamental alteration over generations of time. Neither have they shown a capacity to adapt. They still emphasize the knowledge and values transmission role, even though much of the common knowledge is acquired from mass communication and recreation. Schools are still enclaves in which children can be safe from heresy, immorality, and danger — despite the fact that the majority of the child's hours are spent away from school. In this technological society, the schools are almost void of technical applications to learning and teaching. Most serious of all, they avoid the controversial in a world of controversy and confrontation.

Meanwhile we are charged with being one of the most lawless societies on earth; increasingly schools as well as streets are full of crime. The drug culture flourishes despite legal and social opposition. Home and family life deteriorate, the breakup rate of families quickens, the work ethic erodes; and the generation gap widens. Legislative bodies strive to replace the lost stabilizing influence of the primary institutions with misdemeanor laws with which neither law enforcement nor courts or justice can cope. More and more the whole system is questioned.

Certainly now is the time to radically rethink the role and function of the school. This will have to be a renegotiation process within the society, which present conditions might make possible. It is hard to escape the conclusion that we are already engaged in a searching examination of the institutions of education in our society and their capacity to meet the educational demands of our times. The continuance of schools as we know them is at issue. The outcome may depend on how insightful, creative and forceful professional leadership proves to be.

THE MASTERY ASSUMPTION

Of critical importance for evaluation are the assumptions that are made about learning and teaching. For many years it was assumed that the capacity to learn was normally distributed among the population of learners. Thus some could be expected to achieve while others could not. In recent years a counter hypothesis has been proposed and widely accepted. The mastery learning theory[2] holds that a high proportion of the children can reach a mastery level of learning if given the time needed. Research in support of this contention has grown. Given precise objectives, formative evaluation, and adequate time, 75 percent of the learners have reached mastery levels equal to that of the highest 25 percent under conventional instruction and assumptions.

The mastery approach holds the learning expectation constant while time is a variable. Traditional approaches have held time constant (for example, grade, year and timed tests) while learning was accepted and expected as a variable. Evaluations differ accordingly. The traditional approach emphasized summative evaluation, giving grades of A, B, C, D, or F according to where the learner fell in the distribution of grades. Mastery approaches emphasize formative evaluation and deemphasize the summative; time to learn with frequent feedback and a passing or completed "grade" at the end for those who meet the expectations are allowed. Competition, particularly as it relates to time, is deemphasized. Central to the approach are precise objectives with express performance objectives and criteria.

From this approach and its antecedents have sprung new instructional systems that are promising for education and threatening to long established beliefs and practices. Educators have little choice but to address the issues involved in the confrontation between the two approaches.

EMPHASIS ON OBJECTIVES

Mastery learning and performance based instruction (PBI) both emphasize instructional objectives. In each case the objectives are precisely stated in behavioral terms. A criterion level of mastery or performance is established, and the method of assessing performance is determined. Both learner and teacher are aware of these conditions. The learner is neither rewarded nor penalized for quicker or slower performance — unless he makes more or less rapid progress, in which case he can do more or less in a given block of time.

Critics of the approach point to the danger that only the more obvious objectives of instruction will be identified and that these may not be the most important ones. Proponents respond that it is not possible to teach that which cannot be identified, that if it can be identified the performance approach can encompass it. They see the vague and ill-defined "take it on faith" objectives as illusory and even fraudulent.

Critics also express fear that the precise objectives approach has an inherent tendency to move toward mechanistic approaches to instruction and toward dehumanization. Proponents respond that many of the features of traditional education are in themselves dehumanizing — dependence on the teacher, not knowing what is expected, being graded on a curve or other grade distribution system, or having low expectations of pupil capacity, are some examples. They also maintain that the human values are a goal of the school, and if what they mean behaviorally can be identified, then objectives can be stated and learning opportunities provided. Above all else, they claim that the positive assumptions of mastery learning and the approaches used result in accomplishment and in positive self-images.

These newer approaches have addressed the issue of imprecision in the goals and objectives of the school and have proposed solutions. The performance and objectives orientation is consistent with other significant social movements, such as accountability and management by objectives.

CRITERION OR
NORM REFERENCED EVALUATION

Much has been made of the difference between the traditional and mastery approaches in the use of norms in evaluation. This is particularly true of the literature on performance or competency based instruction. It is claimed that performance based instruction is criterion referenced; the inference often is that norms are disregarded. In truth, however, the distinction is in the respective use made of each. In PBI, criteria of performance and the means to be used to determine whether the criteria are met are decided in advance and made known to the learner. As in mastery learning, there is only one acceptable level: one meets the criteria or he doesn't. Clearly no norm is used directly in the assessment of the adequacy of the individual performance.

Norms are used, however, in deciding on the criterion level of performance. They are needed to determine the reasonable level to expect. Also, they are used in evaluating the performance of the instructional system itself.

The issue relates to the mastery assumption. If mastery or competence or a criterion level of performance is the objective, the only "yes" or "no" evaluations are available. If "do as well as you can in relation to your competitors" is the objective, then the normal distribution concept has validity. Evaluation can accommodate either position; it follows rather than leads the assumptions about learning.

It is true, however, that the normative approach has been dominated in education for a long time and is securely entrenched. Newer approaches to instruction have had to accommodate to the existing system. Permitting sufficient leeway for the development of systems compatible with the approaches is necessary if a true test of alternative assumptions and systems are to be made.

CULTURAL DIFFERENCES AND EVALUATION

Educators and other citizens alike have long been aware that the commitment to equal access to education opportunity is much easier to state than it is to achieve. Awareness of discrimination, whether intended, or inadvertent, has risen. Progress has been made, but there is widespread belief and strong evidence that schools still contain bias in favor of children whose backgrounds correspond to that of the elusive but functionally real "ideal" student.

From the culturally biased test of intelligence to the self-image depressed by repeated failure, schools continue to frustrate large segments of the population. Evaluation continues as a major contribution to this situation. The instruments used for summative evaluation fail to take into account factors that impeded adequate assessment. Language, sophistication in test taking, background and elements on which the bias might be in favor of the majority child. The relative absence of formative evaluation deprives the already deprived of the very assistance they need in learning to cope with their learning problems. To a great extent evaluation, including testing, serves to turn the child off or away rather than bring him in or along.

The concepts and practices of mastery learning and performance based instruction tend to bring about a more equitable opportunity for all, since the task itself is the basis for assessment. Problems remain, however, in determining tasks, in setting objectives and criterion levels, in the instructional delivery system, and in the human aspects of feedback and supportive relationships.

At issue for the foreseeable future will be the question of whether evaluation is at least neutral, if not deliberately biased in a compensatory direction.

WHAT ABOUT US?

The growing obsolescence of education and the need for change have been suggested throughout the preceding sections. The central role of evaluation both in the present conditions and in the reconstruction process has been emphasized. Perhaps not too clearly stated but implicit throughout, is the position that the attitudes, beliefs, and behaviors of professional educators will have to be markedly altered if new approaches to education are to be achieved.

It is one thing to devise an education system that is formative for our children. It is quite another to fashion and gain acceptance of a development program for those on whom instruction depends. If progress is to be made, educators have no choice but to develop process by which we redefine our own professional goals, identify our objectives, proceed toward them, and put into operation an evaluation system that is strongly formative in its effect.

No challenge to evaluation could be greater.

Notes

1. Hagen, Elizabeth P., and Thorndike, Robert L. *Evaluation. Encyclopedia of Educational Research.* (Edited by Chester W. Harris.) Third edition. New York: Macmillan Co., 1960. p. 482.

2. Block, James H., editor, *Mastery Learning: Theory and Practice.* New York: Holt, Rinehart and Winston, 1971.

Villains as Victims: Evaluating Principals

Terrence E. Deal, Sanford M. Dornbusch and Robert A. Crawford

Though often portrayed as "villains or pawns . . . principals may be victims as well." Such is the belief of the authors after a study of thirty-four principals in three Northern California school districts. Many of those questioned felt they were being evaluated in ways that seemed quixotic, subjective, unsystematic, with the obvious inference that such systems are of little value. Having discussed the manner in which evaluations are carried out in these districts, the authors offer suggestions for improving evaluation there — and everywhere. Among their suggestions: increase the frequency of evaluation, develop specific evaluative criteria, improve methods of data-gathering, and develop a system of peer evaluation. Terrence E. Deal, who also contributed the foreword to the present book, is Associate Professor of Education at Harvard University; Sanford M. Dornbusch is Professor of Sociology at Stanford University; Robert A. Crawford is Superintendent of Schools of the Carlsbad Unified School District in California.

As evaluators of teacher, principals are often portrayed as villains or pawns. Because they too are evaluated, however, principals may be victims as well.

Responses from 34 principals in three school districts of northern California describe processes used in evaluating their administrative performance and suggest that the process of evaluating principals has some major limitations. Half of the principals were unaware of the criteria used in evaluating them; half did not know what information was used in the evaluations. Gossip and hearsay were important sources of information; evaluations were infrequent and informal.

Our earlier studies have shown that principals are even more dissatisfied with the system of teacher evaluation than are the teachers themselves. But evaluations may be more important to principals than to teachers, because the role of principal is less well defined; and principals can be fired, transferred, or reassigned more easily.

The 34 principals were interviewed (primarily on criteria used to evaluate principals), and 31 completed questionnaires. All had completed one year or more at the current schools. Although diverse in many respects, the sample was limited geographically and did not represent schools with students of low educational background. Thus the findings may not apply in all situations, but they do provide interesting insights into current evaluation practices.

To help the principals identify the criteria used in evaluating their performances, we divided the principal's role into four main tasks: 1) curriculum development — the introduction and development of new courses and techniques; 2) supervision of personnel — the selection, supervision, and evaluation of employees; 3) school management — the keeping of financial records, maintenance and improvement of plant and facilities, and other administrative duties; and 4) community relations — meeting with parents, working with the PTA, and meeting with community groups.

For each of the tasks, we first asked the principals whether they knew of any criteria used to judge how well or poorly they were performing. Seventeen reported that they did not know even one criterion. Fifteen listed criteria used to evaluate them, but the criteria were usually vague, and methods of acquiring information were mixed in with the criteria.

In the area of curriculum development, criteria focused most often on the successful implementation of new courses or on educational outcomes — comparing results on achievement tests inside and outside the district. Among specific criteria, principals listed teacher morale, community satisfaction, and innovativeness. These administrators are evidently being judged primarily on their innovativeness and on their abilitiy to keep teachers and parents happy.

Two criteria were listed in the category of supervision of personnel: the quality of forms evaluating teachers' classroom performance and principals' ability to keep teacher morale high and personnel disruptions low. The main criterion for the task of school management was accuracy and punctuality of reports. Appearance and condition of the school as observed by the district staff appeared to be a secondary criterion for evaluating principals.

The most important criterion for the task of community relations was the satisfaction of parents as evidenced by parent calls or comments. Hearsay, gossip, and "making too many waves" were also frequently listed by administrators as criteria. Of lesser importance were criteria that stressed parent participation and involvement.

Asked what personal characteristics were used as evaluation criteria, the principals listed 89. Attitudes were most frequently cited, followed by appearance and education. Sex, race, age, personality, and ability to relate to others were also frequently mentioned, as well as religion, community standing, and health. The principals felt that their personality has as much potential impact on evaluation as does the quality of their performance.

Besides being influenced by evaluation criteria, principals' administrative performances are influenced by their superiors' process of gathering information on which to base evaluations. Each principal was asked how often he learned the superintendent or assistant supperintendent's evaluation of his performance and whether he knew what information is selected to judge how well or poorly each task is performed.

Only 28% of the principals reported that they were evaluated frequently or very frequently. Seventeen were ignorant of the kinds of information collected to provide a basis for the evaluation. Those who reported knowing what information was collected said the information was informal, nonsystematic, and seldom based on direct observation.

For the task of curriculum development, principals reported most often that evaluation information derives from their interaction with superiors, participation on district committees, and achievement scores of their students, but also from hearsay and gossip, phone calls and complaints, and initial impressions after short visits to the school. Information for determining how well or poorly principals are supervising personnel was based heavily on the adequacy of evaluation reports assessing classroom teachers, but such information was also obtained from teachers and from district superiors.

Information for evaluating a principal's school management was thought to be based on inadequate data. According to principals, "When there are no problems, there are no questions." The adequacy of the school management fuction was determined primarily by gossip and comments by teachers and parents, the attendance clerk's view of the punctuality of reports, and the appearance of the school plant on chance visits from central office staff. How well a principal handles community relations was sometimes determined through polls showing the principal's participation in community affairs and tax elections, most often, however, the evaluation was based on comments from parents.

Evaluations are used to improve performance; they are also used as a basis for distributing organizational rewards and penalties. Principals may be rewarded by a better assignment or a higher salary or sanctioned by being transferred, fired, or reassigned as classroom teachers. To determine the relative influence of various groups in influencing principals' rewards and penalties, we asked principals to assign ratings to the school board, superintendent or assistant superintendent, fellow principals, teachers in the school, parents, and students. The principals perceived the superintendent and teachers as the most influential evaluators, but principals are obviously squeezed between several other influential evaluators.

According to our theory of evaluation, evaluators are considered important in direct proportion to their degree of influence on penalties and rewards. Because superintendents and teachers were labeled the most influential evaluators, they were also viewed as most important. Fellow principals were perceived as least influential and also as least important.

Overall, principals reported high levels of job satisfaction and emphasized the personal rewards they derive from their role. Principals are greatly displeased, however, with the current system of evaluation and are even more unhappy with their evaluations than are teachers with theirs.

In order to improve the evaluation procedure, several steps might be taken. First, principals should be evaluated more frequently. Most often suggested by principals, this recommendation is also supported by our research, which shows that greater frequency of evaluation is related to greater principal satisfaction with both criteria and sampling. Visits to the school are not the final stage in evaluation but should be followed with a continuing discussion of strengths and weaknesses.

Second, specific evaluation criteria, which should reflect a balance between performance and outcome measures, should be developed and made known before evaluations are conducted. Such criteria are difficult to generate, and one principal suggested that teachers, parents, students, and district office personnel be included in the process of developing criteria. Other suggestions were that principals should generate the criteria or that the principal and superintendent together should establish a job description from which criteria could be developed.

Third, sampling procedures for gathering information should be improved. Because the relationship between an administrator's activities and educational results is highly complex, educational outcomes as a criterion must be augmented by direct observations by clients, teachers, or superiors. One principal suggested that a team including other principals and district office staff should observe the principal in action. Other principals suggested that information be collected from various sources and that different weights be assigned to each source.

A fourth strategy for improving the evaluation of principals would be to have them evaluate one another. This approach emphasizes professional or collegial relationships among principals as a vehicle for self-improvement. In this collegial process, principals would jointly develop criteria, observe each other in action, gather information from self-appraisals, and rely on periodic conferences to mutually appraise performance and to distill appraisals and information into concrete plans for improvement.

The role of the principal is still evolving, and contradictory pressures are increasing. As ambiguity and pressures increase, so does the necessity of providing principals with sound evaluations of their work in order to structure a more systematic basis for promotions, transfers, and terminations, to assure that administrators are rewarded for performing tasks that move the organization toward its goals; and to protect principals from contradictory role expectations. Above all, evaluations are needed as a basis for professional improvement and development. Current emphasis on inservice training for principals ignores the importance of a sound evaluation system that encourages improved performance after training. Finally, the evaluation system itself can be used to change the relative emphasis principals place on various tasks and how their time and energy are spent.

How to Evaluate Administrative and Supervisory Personnel

H. Robert Olds

In this excerpt from a handbook developed for the American Association of School Administrators, H. Robert Olds observes that good performance evaluation programs appear to have "no visible ending." Although they proceed continuously in the organization that uses them, they cannot be aimless wanderers. Olds stresses that evaluation is sometimes made more complicated than necessary by confusing it with compensation or rating efforts. His system involves the drawing up of preliminary questions about evaluation that must be answered before evaluation can begin; proper drafting of a job description; adoption of a code of behavior for all administrators; selection of improvement of objectives; gathering data and using them properly; and a variety of other procedures that must be addressed and problems that must be confronted in the course of the evaluation. "The effort to determine strategies and steps for improvement. . ." when performance results are in, "holds extreme significance for school districts desiring to assure administrative-supervisory job satisfaction." H. Robert Olds is an educational consultant in Santa Barbara, California, and is editor of the newsletter, "Successful School Management."

One disconcerting characteristic of a good performance evaluation program is that it has no visible ending. Like life, it proceeds continuously, actively involving administrative personnel while they are associated with the organization. But there can be no aimless wandering.

As in a baseball game, for example, there are important bases which must be recognized and fully understood — and must be touched in the proper order and without fail during every cycle.

Some evaluation programs limp along and never mature. Components may be missing or are misused. This has been the case in many work organizations. Some of the components, historically, have not been used widely or have been minimized in their importance.

Performance evaluation is not complicated, although some attempts to mix evaluation with rating or compensation efforts have yielded marvelous creations of complicated formulas, checklists and point systems.

BUILDING A SECOND FOUNDATION

Five questions constitute the foundation of a good performance evaluation program:
- What are we trying to do here?
- What shall we attempt in order to improve our performance levels?
- How will we know we are making progress?
- How will we recognize success?
- How can we take advantage of what we have learned?

The simplicity of this approach to evaluation is somewhat deceptive. Determination of the answeres to these questions in advance of performance action requires an effort which ordinarily is not formally applied to work planning.

Work in virtually every organization is neither planned solely by an individual nor carried out in such a fashion. In many educational organizations, where there is a physical decentralization of work places, a lack of clear goals, many specialized work assignments and a laissez faire tradition of supervision, those in the organization tend to see themselves functioning on separate tracks. Interdependence is not recognized.

The organization on paper may contrast sharply with the real life organization to a degree which may occasionally offer embarrassing management surprises.

There may be the old superintendent the school board wanted to fire but did not dare to buy up his contract. He now appears on the organization chart as a "research director," but he actually is planning the cutbacks which will be necessary because of declining enrollments. His office is next to that of a public relations director, whose job description labels him as adult education director.

The administrative assistant, who was hired to write proposals and to get government and foundation grants, is spending most of his/her time as affirmative action officer, managing details of the affirmative action program mandated by the federal government.

The personnel director is similarly situated. The time he formerly spent in recruiting has been reduced to almost nothing. For six months he has been working on an added assignment to developing an accountability plan which has been set up by the state board of education.

Most of the job information which has been described above does not appear in the job descriptions, which have never been updated or contain deliberate omissions.

The development of a performance evaluation plan, which clearly sets forth its goals, objectives, and procedural steps, may still offer little promise for success unless it is undergirded by a genuine understanding of the work being performed by administrative and supervisory personnel.

Improvement on the job is doubtful, and genuine supervision is impos-- sible, if there is faulty information about who is doing what. Any thoughts about improving job performance must necessarily be preceded by know- ledge of the actualities of existing job performance.

Improvement also requires some legitimate base to move from if the effort is to have validity. Such a base has been called by several different terms in various evaluation plans. Some of these are "performance stan- dards," "yardsticks," "benchmarks," "standards of excellence," etc.

In some plans, there is the inference that the standards should be statements of perfection. Such statements may be so far from reality as to destroy belief in the objectives of the evaluation plan.

A good job description, which actually describes the work to be per- formed by a fully competent person in that position, can serve as a state- ment of standards for a given position. The quality of job description in a good many districts, as had been indicated, leaves much to be desired. In some instances, the description has been skewed so that it fits only the incumbent. Another typical shortcoming is the management pretense that all jobs having the same general title also possess the same job require- ments.

A single job description for all secondary school principals, for ex- ample, may be more fictional than descriptive of any single position with that title.

THE JOB DESCRIPTION MUST ACTUALLY DESCRIBE

If job descriptions are to be used as the standards base in adminis- trative evaluation, they must be reviewed carefully. Evaluator and evalu- atee must be in mutual agreement that the position statement describes the job involved when it is well-performed.

A problem frequently bothersome to those developing evaluation plans is that the job description may lack any reference to personal qual- ities. Despite all of the cautions about attempting to evaluate personality traits, the belief that these must be judged is strong in many educational organizations. This preoccupation sometimes exists because of the absence of "hard" performance results content in previous rating systems.

Thus, there is concern that there should be spaces on the evaluation instrument for the specific grading of honesty, loyalty, sense of humor, thoughtfulness, etc., of administrators and supervisors. Although newer plans in school districts do tend to show an absence of personality rating, many systems apparently cannot bear to relieve the evaluator of such a God-playing responsibility.

A BEHAVIORAL CODE FOR ALL

One relatively simple solution to the problem of advising all administrators and supervisors that good job performance also calls for high standards of personal behavior is to draw up a code describing proper behavior for members of the administrative-supervisory staff. It serves in effect as a job description of personal attributes and behavior minimums which apply to anyone serving in an administrative or supervisory capacity.

Under this kind of an arrangement, personality traits have no place in evaluation except as they may relate directly to the achievement of a performance objective and can be supported by performance data. Otherwise, the fault must be regarded as an alleged violation of the administrator-supervisory code to which all persons in that group subscribe.

GOALS POINT TO DESIRED STANDARDS

In addition to job descriptions, individual administrators and supervisors may look increasingly to school district formal goals, adopted by school boards, as sources of standards.

A goal points to major directions of intent and desired general achievement which ordinarily has no specific time frame or blueprint of operational specifics. In effect, it is the school board's formal statement of where the shcool district should be at a future time as stated in qualitative terms. It represents desired standards to be achieved.

Districts using management by objectives and program budgeting systems are supposed to operate on the basis of organizational goals which are implemented by specific action objectives adopted at institution, division, unit and individual levels.

Some standards, increasingly, are being set for the school district by bodies which themselves have no direct accountability to the school district and are only indirectly accountable to the public. Congress, federal agencies, state legislatures and agencies, and the courts, are mandating that school districts achieve specific conditions and adhere to or abandon certain practices, policies and programs.

Employee unions and organizations, even less accountable to the public, can have great impact through collective bargaining upon the nature of work in school organizations and this, too, must be recognized as a source of standards.

Thus, there can be a close relationship between goals and standards when it has been determined that the achievement of certain standards is a desirable or necessary goal. Goals, of course, may be adopted by school boards which are not necessarily related to specific existing standards.

OBJECTIVE DESIGN: THE MOST IMPORTANT STEP

All of these sources afford the basis for selecting improvement objectives in a performance evaluation program. Unlike a goal, an objective is a planned accomplishment which, under specified conditions and in a given time period, can be attained in accordance with predetermined evidences of accomplishment to help fulfill a related goal.

While an objective ordinarily is linked directly to organizational achievement, it can sometimes concern itself with personal competence which will benefit the organization.

This contrasts sharply with the sabbatical leave type of personal improvement which often is regarded by boards and staff members to be a type of personal "reward" opportunity and, by taxpayers, as an otrageous ripoff.

The big breakthrough in designing performance objectives has taken place largely during the past decade. Prior to that time, it was believed generally that the evaluator should provide the evaluatee with objectives which had been devised solely by the evaluator. This still is the practice (and, possibly, a major weakness) in quite a few industry-developed models, like some MBO operations which have been carried over into education.

The idea of the evaluatee, not the evaluator, serving as chief designer of his proposed objectives, clashes sharply with the "boss knows best" approach. Similary, it is in opposition to the thesis that the job is the place for performance and not necessarily personal growth.

Nevertheless, the trend toward ever-deeper involvement by the evaluatee in performance evaluation has continued at a rapid pace. This trend acknowledges many realities of higher skilled jobs, particularly those which involve technical skills, and those who perform them. In many, many organizations the person doing the work unquestionably does know the job better than anyone else. When invited to study thoughtfully and propose personally how an aspect of the job might be improved, chances are that the organization may have received from the incumbent its most competent advice for improvement.

THEN CAME THE OBVIOUS

Let the evaluatee develop the proposed performance improvement objective and present it to the evaluator for review, comparisons with alternatives, and modifications, if necessary. Out of the review and joint planning may come confirmation that two heads are better than one.

A few years ago one of the major problems in teacher performance evaluation planning was getting participants to understand the essentials of a good performance objective. The situation has changed markedly with the advent of pupil behavioral objectives individually prescribed instruction, learning contracts, and other systems which require clear statements of objective expectancies, conditions and evidences of achievement.

If large numbers of teachers are now able to construct sound behavioral objectives for students, it is very likely that administrators will be capable of making their transition to a performance-based kind of evaluation.

Objective design is an exercise which improves with practice — by both evaluatees and evaluators.

Not all objectives will necessarily be of the performance improvement variety. Some normally will fall into the "process" category and may involve carrying out a procedure which has a high priority like closing out a school, installing a major new student code, setting up a new accounting system, and the like. As was pointed out earlier, one of the hazards of using process objectives for improvement evaluation is that they can be abused and misrepresent routine regular performance.

The superintendent who claims his objective for improvement of community relations merely is continuing to attend civic club luncheons is helping no one understand what is meant by developmental performance evaluation.

FROM OBJECTIVES TO PERFORMANCE

The amplification of a one or two-sentence formal statement of a performance objective may frequently require a more detailed supplementary statement which describes the undertaking in greater detail, including the specifications of conditions, assistance required, other persons who may be involved, and the specifics of performance data to be used to determine progress and success.

This detailed program, which in part may be a verbal sharing between evaluatee and evaluator, represents a more precise specification of what will be attempted. The development of the program may be completed after the initial planning session between evaluator and evaluatee and the adoption of the formal statement of objectives.

The involvement of the evaluatee in the work to be carried out, to this extent, offers personal job satisfaction values in addition to increasing the likelihood that there will be better job understanding and improvement.

SPECIAL PROBLEMS IN A BUREAUCRACY

In a bureaucracy, the enthusiasm and drive of the very able administrative and supervisory employees may be stifled as they perform duties which afford little evidence of achievement. This is true, particularly, when the work involves intangibles and few obvious evidences that the effort personally has been wothwhile.

Performance evaluation, in a sense, opens the door to a quality of entrepreneurship in planning, job execution and recognition, in league with a partner-counselor-coach, which the large organization, until now, has been unable to provide. Thus, it may be possible to nurture and develop job enthusiasm, skills and career potential to a greater degree than ever before, rather than blunting or extinguishing them in the deadening routine of bureaucracy.

MONITORING THE OLD-NEW DIMENSION

The monitoring of performance data, next to breathing, comes about as naturally as anything. Yet it apparently is difficult for many to understand its function in evaluation.

Kids do it. Adults do it. The activity becomes almost a reflex action.

If an automobile trip is taken for the first time to Centerburg, the driver keeps an eagle eye upon the highway direction signs. They feed back to him progress data. He must have them in order to avoid getting lost. In the airliner overhead, pilot and co-pilot are preoccupied with scores of dials and pointers which feed back comprehensive information on performance — how well the plan is performing, and progress being made toward the chosen destination.

Golfers check their efforts against par for each hole on the course. The girl waiting on a date notes the appearance of her hair and makeup in a mirror. The cook consults the oven time and temperature controls. The carpenter uses a steel measuring tape and a level to make certain that specifications are being followed.

The data checking, in every instance, is regarded to be both very normal and essential behavior. In each instance, when the data indicates a condition where things are not going according to plan, there is immediate concern. It is time for an examination, consultation perhaps, and the possible taking of corrective action. Success is known to hinge upon the proper regard for and use of performance information.

WHY THE BLIND SPOT

Why does this whole business of data and feedback constitute such a blind spot in many evaluation plans, particularly those involving executive personnel in positions where convenient sales or production records do not apply?

Operational improvement in many evaluation plans is abandoned at this point. This fault has caused many plans to yield minimal benefits.

In most discussions about evaluation plans, a great deal of attention is given to proper execution of the basic organization plan and the mechanics of designing objectives and handling the evaluation conference. But the whole area of data and its use is likely to be given a minimum review. The gap may be easy to come by because there are no standardized kinds of paperwork involved. Nor are there time elements or conditions which mandate specific responses by either evaluator or evaluatee.

THE 'GOTCHA' HANDICAP

There may be underlying reasons and traditions in education which have hampered the data concept as it applies in performance evaluation. One of these possibilities is the "gotcha" complex. In rating systems there seems to be a secret compulsion by the evaluator to use the data for punitive purposes. While the evaluator may pay little or no attention to success data regarding the work being performed, he is very much motivated to discover negative tidbits about the evaluatee and the performance. These are squirreled away by the evaluator until "the day of reckoning" when the evaluator and evaluatee have a confrontation at the close of the evaluation period. As one superintendent has described the scene, the evaluator pulls out his negative notes, and to the evaluatee, he says gleefully: "Gotcha!"

Such administrative behavior, of course, is ludicrous if the objective is to improve performance. This kind of treatment virtually assures a lack of success. The evaluator, rather than the evaluatee, must bear much of the responsibility for the evaluatee's inability to succeed.

The entire concept of data, as used in an evaluation program seeking to bring about improved performance, bears no relationship whatsoever to the collection of data in rating.

RESULTS ANALYSIS HAS HAD LITTLE APPEAL

Data is construed to be "evidence" when rating is used in a judgmental sense. This viewpoint stems undoubtedly from the traditional report card judgments which teachers make. The letter grade scarcely offers any basis for results analysis. State legislatures, too, tend to support a narrow interpretation for the use of performance data where statutes mandate regular evaluations of teachers and administrators. Significantly, the sections of the laws dealing with evaluation usually are to be found adjacent to legal sections about the dismissal of personnel.

The use of performance data for operational improvement and personal development does not necessarily rule out the legitimate use of performance data in making personnel decisions. In fact, when data is used in the analytical sense called for by developmental performance evaluation and follow through, it holds far greater validity for all concerned in any resulting

206 —

personnel decision.

PERFORMANCE INFORMATION'S NEW PURPOSE

For developmental purposes and sound operational use, performance information should be thought of in an entirely new light, one which could be construed as blasphemy by traditionalists in evaluation.

When there is a partnership relationship between evaluator and evaluatee regarding improvement needs and the setting of performance objectives, obviously the interest in performance information is something also to be shared.

Traditionally, performance data in American work organizations has been thought to be of primary value for top management. All formal reports dealing with organizational performance and output have been transmitted to the top of the organization first. Those performing the work have not been regarded to be priority users of the data. They may receive some data eventually in "trickle down" management communications. The classic use of data is understandable because performance objectives have been set in the "front office" and were handed down to lower levels for implementation.

SHOULD THE LAST BE FIRST?

In a sound performance evaluation program, evaluatee and evaluator are most immediately interested in the nature of performance data and provisions for its feedback to the evaluator and evaluatee. They have primary responsibility for carrying out the work. They have set the performance objectives. They have the most immediate need for access to the performance information.

The feedback of performance information is vital where corrective action must be taken. If they obtain the data, "tor" and "tee" are in the best possible position to bring about early corrections. If a performance objective must be modified in order to achieve success, an immediate response is possible. This is true also when the data indicate an objective should be abandoned.

Periodically, there are news accounts of management bungles in both public and private sectors which occurred simply because performance information was either not obtained or failed to reach those who might have been able to make operational changes and save the situation.

The evaluatee and evaluator, as prime users of the performance data, also have an enlarged responsibility to plan the nature of performance data and its delivery when they design the performance objectives. As the initiator in the design of objectives, the evaluatee must also shoulder a counterpart role as designer of performance data and monitoring sources for use by both evaluator and evaluatee.

Too often evaluatee has complained that performance data has been so inadequate as to be unfair to the evaluatee. When the evaluator becomes a designer of objectives in the positive evaluation program, the evaluatee is obligated to play an action role in the design of the performance indicators which will be required for use by evaluation and evaluator.

INFORMATION NO LONGER IS NIGGARDLY

In the successful program, performance information will more likely be bountiful than scarce. The evaluatee and evaluator will be seeking new and improved sources of data which they can share in checking progress made toward objectives.

This approach to performance data indentification runs counter to the cliche uses which have long existed in education. Some teachers, for example, have traditionally declined to provide any information which might be used in the evaluation of a fellow teacher. This was considered to be "tattling" and "unethical." In the absence of evaluatee-planned objectives, this claim might have more merit.

If it should become general practice for evaluatees to be seeking the help of collegues in collecting performance information, it is likely that this would contribute greatly to a profound change in staff attitudes toward evaluation. The handicap of "Gotcha" rating psychology, however, surely will retard educator understanding of the development and improvement values of evaluation.

Even in districts where there is a desire to have assistance in expanding the horizons of performance evaluation data feedback, it is not unlikely that the data collectors are to be identified improperly as "co-evaluators."

The prompt feedback of performance data to those who do the performing has been the subject of a number of fascinating studies in other management areas. The self-correcting results in performance have been spectacular.

THE ULTIMATE PATTERN

Some speculate that the ultimate in developmental performance evaluation will be a type of collegial evaluation within a framework of goals and objectives. It is obvious that success in such a venture will depend as much upon the feedback and use of performance evaluation data as any other factor.

Several large and well known corporations have very recently established experimental factories in which the hierarchical work structure has been replaced by work groups having no conventional "boss." One of the imperatives in making these work groups function successfully is the feedback of performance information so that members can be informed immediately of the results of their work and positively affect performance.

Another national company which has made extensive use of results information feedback has experienced an extremely beneficial impact upon operations. It began by asking employees periodically to monitor their performance against standards which they had set and assumed they were achieving. The self-knowledge of acquiring the data (which revealed that the assumed performance was actually 20 to 50 per cent below standards) was, in itself, sufficient to be fully self-correcting within 48 hours from the time the employees became informed about the results of their own data monitoring!

FEEDBACK MAKES PERMANENT PERFORMANCE CHANGES

Continuation of the periodic self-monitoring showed that the performance correction was not a temporary phenomenon but had resulted in permanently improved performance. Some years later a new top executive took charge of one of the company divisions which had been employing self-monitoring and feedback. He felt that the practice was unnecessary and ordered it discontinued. Performance began to sag. After a few months, he was persuaded to permit one more round of monitoring and feedback. The involvement of those doing the work in monitoring their own performance results was again enough to hike performance to the level where it met standards.

One rather sad and revealing characteristic of numerous evaluation programs in education is a ground rule which compels the evaluator and evaluatee to hold some specified number of interim conferences during the work period being evaluated. In the case of teacher evaluation, the evaluator is required to make a specified number of classroom observations each lasting a minimum number of minutes.

GOING THROUGH THE MOTIONS

This infers a mechanical and procedural relationship, even one tinged with suspicion, rather than any kind of mutal "partnership" interest in performance progress toward the winning of individualized objectives.

Some plans, similarly, specify the holding of a certain number of "progress conferences" between evaluator and evaluatee, These, of course, are quite necessary. It is only unfortunate that program specifications appear to be needed to assure that the sessions will be held.

Some of the more realistic plans provide that either the evaluatee or evaluator can request a progress conference whenever one is desired. If performance data or other special circumstances have a bearing upon one or more of the objectives, immediate attention can be given to the problem rather than being forced to delay action until the arrival of an inflexible date specified by an impersonal plan.

THE NEW SOPHISTICATION

The entire accountability movement in education signals a new level of sophistication about performance information, its quality and use, and its communication to those having direct and indirect involvement in the educational operation.

This is reflected not only in the complaints of the public and legislators that educators must be able to justify their claims and programs in terms of results, but also in educator criticism of standardized tests, and the soaring classroom interest in instructional performance objectives, criterion-referenced testing, and other evidences of systematic planning and instructional accountability.

The compartmentalization of educational management, due to geographic, bureaucratic and traditional constraints, and the fact that it is a public enterprise, has resulted in unusually high requirements for performance information and feedback to a wide spectrum of participants.

These requirements are far more elaborate than can be satisfied by acquiring a computer and developing a conventional management information system.

Much of the trouble in which educational organizations find themselves today can be traced to inadequate performance information, inadequately communicated and used by those in the organization.

The foundation for corrective action lies in a sound performance evaluation program which first embraces the management personnel.

THE SLOW EVALUATION EVOLUTION

The making of an evaluation used to be a one-sided affair. The evaluation was something to be made by the evaluator. The evaluatee sometimes was given a chance to see the evaluation in the presence of the evaluator and was expected to sign it. This was merely for the purpose of documenting the fact that it had been viewed. If the evaluatee had any questions or objections, such intrusions were not regarded to be germane.

But that's the way it still is today in many school districts!

Under circumstances like these, evaluations have been something to be dreaded by both evaluator and evaluatee. In most instances, the evaluator has not been in a position to acquire genuine performance information, except for personal "observation."

There might be in the files a collection of complaint reports of unknown validity. The evaluator has his or her impressions about the evaluatee. They may or may not be valid. In the absence of target objectives as well as performance information, the evaluator really has very little to do unless he wants to brave the risks of personality evaluation. What the evaluator is most likely to do is to first select something for flattery in the belief that this could pass for motivation. The evaluator might find a safe "flaw" to comment about in order to justify "room for improvement."

In the end, the evaluator has realized nothing but rather a pointless conversation. The evaluatee has sustained frazzled nerves worrying about unknown skeletons which might be extracted from a closet and largely uninformed comments about job performance.

The organization has gained nothing in terms of individual or organization betterment. This has been the fruitless history of much of the evaluation effort in public education. Plans have been used largely to fulfill legal attempts to force a very minimum level of supervision. Despite the claims that these evaluation practices typically are used for educational improvement, there has been no valid documentation of the claims.

How do evaluations differ under a plan of positive performance evaluation?

TWO EVALUATIONS – OR MORE

First of all, there are usually two evaluations. Under some conditions there may be more than two. Ordinarily the evaluatee and evaluator make separate evaluations, following review of the performance information which the two have been collecting during the work portion of the cycle.

An evaluation summary statement is prepared by each party. Comments are made regarding the nature of progress, or lack of it, for each of the performance objectives which has been agreed to at the start of the performance cycle. Most attention is devoted to performance results which were unique and unanticipated. This would include instances of tremendous success as well as difficulties.

In certain evaluations, a co-evaluator may be involved. In some unusual job situations where objectives selected are so specialized the performance data may be highly technical, a co-evaluator may be called upon to assist in the evaluation. Such a decision should not be one taken by the evaluator in secrecy. Rather, it should be a determination, probably one which has been discussed with the evaluater, made at the time of considering the target objectives.

This specialized role of co-evaluator is one which must be differentiated from those persons who assist an evaluator-evaluatee duo by simply gathering and feedback of certain performance data. The co-evaluator analyzes and interprets performance data in light of objectives, a supplier of data is not so involved.

Co-evaluators are recognized in some programs where there may be a supervisory ratio which is poor because there are large numbers of evaluatees per evaluator.

TOP LEVEL EVALUATION IS DESIRED

It is only natural for most persons in an administrative group, especially those having responsibilites for departments, divisions and building units, to want to be evaluated by the top administrators rather than to be buried several layers deep in the hierarchy.

The top administrator also may want to keep as closely in touch with as many individual administrators as possible in order to maintain the personal touch of coach, communicator and counselor. Some type of direct relationship also is needed if the chief executive hopes to build and maintain a strong management team.

This opportunity exists under a positive performance evaluation program.

One or more assistants to the top executive may fill the role of surrogate evaluators and carry out all of the evaluator's responsibilities in relationships with the evaluatee. However, the top executive serves as a reviewer of the evaluation. This would include a review of the performance objectives selected by the evaluatee and evaluator.

THE TOP BOSS CAN TAKE PART

Thus, the evaluatee is assured that his work plans and results will be seen and reviewed by the top boss. The assistant also is aware that his contribution as evaluator will not go unrecognized (Note: Too often the evaluator's special efforts and skills at helping the evaluatee *do* go unknown, unrecognized and unrewarded).

One additional value, perhaps as important as the reviewing of the evaluations by top management, is the opportunity thus afforded to gain a far better understanding of the workings of the organization than has before been possible.

It is not easy in staff meetings or informal conversations to acquire the high quality operational information of plans and results which are revealed in a good performance evaluation program.

EVALUATING THE EVALUATOR

Obviously, a review of evaluations also affords great insight into the qualities of administrative team member skills as evaluators, In at least one instance, the review of evaluations made by an evaluator has served, in part, as the evaluation of the evaluator by his superior.

The evaluation reviewer plays an extremely sensitive part. If he abuses his role by intruding and, as an unannounced third party, brashly substituting his own judgment for the considered efforts by the evaluator and evaluatee, he most certainly has destroyed the evaluation program and probably more. On the other hand, if he defaults on his role, he also risks destruction of an important vehicle which his colleagues may value highly.

Co-evaluators and evaluation reviewers both represent departures from the classic evaluation formula. Decisions to incorporate either feature into an administrative evaluation plan designed for performance improvement of the individual administrators should be made with considerable caution.

THE EVALUATION CONFERENCE

For trauma, suspense and strain upon the evaluator and evaluatee, there is nothing like the conventional evaluation conference where the outcome of a personality rating will be discussed.

On the other hand, were it not for the deep personal involvement of both evaluatee and evaluator in a positive performance evaluation program, the meeting most certainly would be dull.

There are likely to be no surprises at the latter. Both parties have had a hand in deciding upon the performance objectives. They have rounded up and shared performance information, and have discussed problems and progress all during the work cycle. They have observed the effort from the viewpoint of partners.

What is there to talk about? Any differences in the two evaluations would be a starting point. Most of the discussion probably would not deal with what had happened because both would know. The evaluation conference is more a setting for analysis than for an exchange of facts which both have shared previously.

THE SIGNIFICANCE OF DISCOVERY

There always are mysteries about why certain ventures were unusually successful, while others may have been disasters. In either case, finding the answers and messages can be tremendously important. In some cases, the entire organization and other districts across the country may benefit eventually from such discoveries.

The analysis of the significance of performance results should be the main burden of the evaluation conference. In the case of most objectives, assuming they were properly designed and performance information specified and received, the conference should be one of expressing mutual satisfaction and congratulations.

Evaluator and evaluatee in developmental performance evaluation are professional explorers who seek pathways to improved future performance.

This type of evaluation conference, of course, clashes sharply with traditions. The evaluation conference in performance evaluation is future-oriented. Evaluation conferences based upon ratings are anchored to the past.

THE VITAL FOLLOW-UP STEP

Part of the agenda of the performance evaluation conference between evaluatee and evaluator is a determination of what is to be done with the new knowledge which has emerged from the evaluation cycle and has been identified by the partners. How can the results of the long effort be used to capitalize performance improvement efforts?

Most evaluation programs, unfortunately, come to a grinding halt following the consideration of the evaluations. The cliche outcome of many teacher evaluation programs at this point has been to determine whether the teacher should be sentenced to "inservice."

Obviously, few developmental benefits are going to be derived by the school system which holds to such "canned" ideas about staff growth.

Since a good performance evaluation program permits and insists upon individualized analyses of growth requirements, it is not very realistic to think that every need can be matched by a course, workshop or seminar.

A review of administrative staff evaluations and follow-up sessions can, however, produce valuable information about specific developmental needs of the administrator-supervisory staff. In effect, an unusual developmental needs survey is a built-in product of the developmental performance evaluation program. Common needs can be identified where they exist.

INDIVIDUALIZED AND INNOVATIVE

Follow-up planning, under a good evaluation plan, is very likely to be individualized and innovative. Perhaps the conditions existing in some of the previous performance objectives will be altered because of newly-discovered conditions. Or a previous objective may be abandoned because it has been found to be unrealistic in terms of future school district operations.

The study of performance results may suggest to either evaluatee or evaluator a completely new approach to a particular kind of job challenge.

This joint effort to determine strategies and steps for improvement, potentially, holds extreme significance for school districts desiring to assure administrative-supervisory job satisfaction.

Evaluation of
Administrative Performance

Richard L. Featherstone and Louis Romano

The authors believe that boards of education are moving towards the development and use of "rational and intelligent means" of administrator evaluation. Though the path from the current emotional and subjective methods of appraisal towards more rational procedures is an arduous one, they applaud the move away from the "haphazard approach" that characterizes so many school systems. In concise terms, the authors deal with questions of why evaluation is needed, who should set evaluative criteria, and what assumptions must be made if administrative productivity is to be judged rationally. Both Drs. Featherstone and Romano are on the faculty of Michigan State University at East Lansing; the former is Professor of Administration and Higher Education and of Elementary and Special Education; the latter is Professor of Administration and Higher Education.

Administrative performance is constantly appraised. Judgments stem from every public touched by the actions of the educational administrator, and there are many groups affected by the administrator's decisions. The board of education, other administrators, teachers, secretaries, students and the public at large appraise the behavior of the administrator. When examined from a literal viewpoint, appraisals of worth are largely based on the emotional response of the evaluator to some perceived behavior of the administrator. These judgments are often made without understanding that complex organizations have long lines of communication that depend upon fallible human communicators to carry and interpret information. With biased (favorable or unfavorable) human interpretors, accurate judgments are not likely to occur. For example, students may appraise the behavior of a superintendent using information available to them through peer gossip, accurate or inaccurate newspaper reporting, a limited television clip, or parental reactions and conversation at the dinner table. Thus, the students may make their appraisal of the worth of the superintendent through vague and haphazard data gathering coupled with teenage emotions.

Citizens supporting the educational system who have no vested interest or personal contact (citizens without children or retirees) tend to have weaker lines of communication than those available to students; yet they engage in judging the worth of the educational administrator. With the continued growth of educational systems, there is little hope of improving markedly the quality of data used by some publics in appraising administrative performance. However, there is no excuse for the same type of emotional, haphazard approach to evaluating the performance of educational administrators by individuals or groups charged with assessing performance. Thoughtful administrators and responsible boards of education are developing rational and intelligent means to evaluate the performance of the administrators serving their systems. These groups are moving from a pattern of emotional appraisal toward a matrix of performance evaluation. The path from the present rather weak methods of appraisal toward a rational evaluation procedure based upon intelligent criteria is difficult, but for a myriad of reasons, it must be followed.

WHY FORMAL EVALUATION OF ADMINISTRATIVE PERFORMANCE?

The evaluation of administrative performance may be used as a basis for promotion, compensation and other personnel services. Certainly, accountability, or the reporting on performance progress to one's superiors, requires evaluation. Barro indicates that accountability measures can be used to improve personnel selections and assignments and provide "personnel incentives and compensation."[1] Barro uses the phrase "accountability measures" as relating to measurements of performance. It would be hard to refute the position that a rational and intelligent evaluation of performance can contribute to improved personnel decisions.

Are there other reasons for committing time and energies to the admittedly difficult task of developing a systematic process and well-defined criteria for evaluating administrative performance? The authors believe that a major reason is that the outcome will contribute positively to the mental-health of the administrators. Actually, the appraisor and the appraisee should benefit from a rational and intelligent evaluation of performance. It is possible that the most significant contribution that will be made by the development and use of modern appraisal of performance techniques for administrators will be in the realm of emotional well-being. Too many times, the educational administrator says or hears such comments as "What did I do wrong?" "Why does he value ------'s work above mine?", "The action of board was a shock — a complete surprise," and "I don't know what was wrong — I thought my performance was acceptable." In practically every comment, one senses a degree of trauma. The appraisee has had an emotional shock. He did not understand the basis for approval or disapproval of his performance. The mental anguish in such cases can be deep and debilitating. The usual "emotional" appraisal can have long-term negative effects on the behavior and performance of the appraisee. Efforts on the part of administrators and boards of education to develop a rational evaluation procedure, coupled with intelligently conceived criteria to measure performance, would tend to remove much of the potential trauma that now exists. Who should contribute to the development of procedures and criteria that should be used in the performance evaluation matrix?

INVOLVEMENT IN THE DEVELOPMENT OF PROCEDURE AND CRITERIA FOR THE EVALUATION OF PERFORMANCE

Those responsible for the development of procedures and criteria for evaluating administrative performance may or may not be designated as those actually involved in the evaluation process. In fact, it is much easier to designate categories or groups that should have voice in the developmental phase than it is to decide the degree of involvement and importance of the input from each group during the evaluation process.

In general, those persons or representatives of groups that should have involvement in the developmental phase include.

- those who have a legal responsibility to appraise, i.e., the board of education and administrative superiors;
- those who will be appraised and have knowledge of the competencies needed to perform the tasks of administration, i.e., administrators serving in line and staff positions; and
- those who are affected by leadership and management and are in the position to appraise, i.e., teachers, students, and non-academic employees.

Representatives from these three groups should develop the procedures for the evaluation process and have the opportunity to contribute toward defining the criteria used to measure performance.

Most administrators agree that representatives from the first group, i.e., those who have a legal responsibility to appraise, should be involved. In addition, administrators tend to accept the need for the involvement of individuals to whom they are accountable for their performance. The second group, those who will be appraised, are generally accepted as important contributors to process and criteria. The third category is more controversial. Those affected by leadership and management may provide a threat to administration. Administrators in states where teacher unionism is defined by law and practice may be particularly concerned. Further, it is possible that some teachers and non-academic employees and many students will not wish to accept responsibility for contributing to process and criteria. The authors believe, however, that an effort should be made to include representatives from this category in the hopes that the procedures and criteria they develop will foster a degree of responsibility and reasoned judgment on their part.

In addition, the authors are of the opinion that administrators who reject the use of teachers, non-academic employees and students in the appraisal process will acknowledge the possibility that those affected by management and leadership may be in a better position to evaluate the results of behavior than those who supervise performance.

GUIDELINES FOR DEVELOPING PROCEDURES AND CRITERIA

The developmental phase will be long, tedious and difficult; but consulting certain guidelines may alleviate some of the agony. Redfern believes that administrative productivity can be evaluated if several assumptions are accepted:

Can the administrative team's productivity be evaluated? The answer is YES. This response is predicated upon several assumptions.

- Each member of the administrative team should understand what is expected of him and should know how to work with his colleagues.
- Responsibilities should be stated in written form. If this is not the case, oral understandings should be clear and comprehensively delineated.
- Each member of the team should know to whom to look for directions and supervision and understand that accountability involves evaluation.
- Standards of excellence should be designed and used against which individual and team performance may be measured.
- Performance objectives, related to the standards of excellence, should be formulated. Action should be designed to achieve the objectives, and results should be evaluated.
- Good working relationships with peers, subordinates and superiors should be highly prized, carefully cultivated, and deliberately safeguarded.
- Among all members of the administrative team the key person is the leader — the superintendent. It is his duty to help his team members do better what they are already doing, and enlarge the scope and substance of performance.

These prerequisites may or may not exist in a school system or educational organization. If not, it is exceedingly important that steps be taken to bring them into being.[2]

In addition to Redfern's assumptions, the authors suggest that individuals who develop the procedures and criteria should consider:

1. Adopting a part of the procedural design, acknowledging that the development must be a continuing process and providing for a period of implementation and use and a date for review;
2. Providing in the design for receipt and storage of suggestions for improvements of procedure and modification of criteria; and
3. Requiring that no procedure or criteria for evaluating performance be developed or adopted until job descriptions for administrators contain information which
    — delineates the leadership and managerial functions for which the administrator has responsibility;
    — identifies the authority the administrator has for leadership and managerial functions; and
    — establishes lines of accountability.

The words "authority," "responsibility," and "accountability" are used throughout with the following meanings:

Authority is the mandate to act.

Responsibility is legal obligation for specific and ancillary functions.

Accountability is the channel of communication (to whom one reports for a specific or ancillary function).

Thus an individual (or group) within an organization may have the authority to make decisions and to indicate actions to carry out the decisions relating to functions for which he is responsible, and to report (be accountable) to the individual(s) delegating or authorizing his authority to act.

The first two suggestions are classic in that they call for a continuous examination of an operational procedure in order to eliminate negative actions and add steps which will improve the procedure.

The third suggestion is, in reality, a requirement. The authors believe that no procedure or criteria should be developed or adopted without first dealing with administrative responsibility, authority, and accountability. Directly or indirectly, all performances criteria will relate to administrative authority and responsibility and all communication procedures will relate to administrative accountability. Thus, the first task of the developers is to make sure that each administrator knows his field of responsibility, the limits of his authority, and those to whom he is accountable. The guidelines cited above will provide a structure from which the procedure and criteria may be developed.

DEVELOPING CRITERIA TO BE USED IN
EVALUATING ADMINISTRATIVE PERFORMANCE

If an educational institution chooses to respect performance rather than chronological age to aid in making decisions relating to promotion, compensation, and other personnel matters, it must assume that observable performance can be identified and appraised. In fact, the procedure can be operationalized only to the extent that performance can be isolated, understood, and internalized. Identifying performance is not easy, and performance is often not easily evaluated. In addition administrative performance, once identified as having worth, must also be described in such a fashion that the appraiser is in a position to observe the demonstrable outcomes of the performance.

Notes

1. Stephen M. Barro, "An Approach to Developing Accountability Measures for the Public Schools," *Phi Delta Kappan* (December 1970): 205.

2. George Redfern, "Evaluating Administrative Productivity: Can It Be Done?,"*The School Administrator* (July 1971): 15.

The What, How, and When of Professional Improvement

John N. Mangieri and David R. McWilliams

Mangieri and McWilliams talk about the advantages of their "Collaborative Instructional Improvement Process." They believe that the process can be of real significance in facilitating planning among administrators and in opening dialogue among them. As an ancillary benefit, the system has a built-in evaluative function. It also can serve as what the authors call a "documentor of accomplishments." John N. Mangieri is Professor of Education at the University of South Carolina at Columbia, S.C. David R. McWilliams is an Administrative Assistant in Charge of Elementary and Special Education in the Switzerland of Ohio Local School District, Woodsfield, Ohio.

John N. Mangieri and David R. McWilliams. "The What, How, and When of Professional Improvement." EDUCATIONAL LEADERSHIP 38(17): 535-7; April 1981. Reprinted with permission of the Association for Supervision and Curriculum Development and John N. Mangieri and David R. McWilliams. Copyright © 1981 by the Association for Supervision and Curriculum Development. All rights reserved.

"In my job, I associate constantly with uncooperative faculty members and indifferent principals."

Sound familiar? This statement, made by a district science supervisor, represents the frustration of supervisors from every educational level.

Since the roles supervisors, and principals play are so critically important, we might expect them to possess a natural allegiance to each other. Unfortunately, in many instances they are adversaries. One principal, commenting on the district reading specialist assigned to his school, said, "I don't know what she really does. When she's in my school, nothing happens."

Regardless of the specific complaints a supervisor and a principal, teacher, or a fellow supervisor may have about each other, the heart of the problem is invariably a breakdown in communication. Each may assume the other is carrying out certain responsibilities and imitating certain actions.

When they finally get together, they find their assumptions were quite wrong.

This negative relationship, of course, is not universal or irreversible. When supervisors and professional personnel do make efforts to enhance their relationship, improved instruction usually is the end result.

For the past three years, we have been involved in developing and using a process that removes much of the guesswork from the supervisor/professional relationship. We call it the Collaborative Instructional Improvement Process. It is a communication-facilitating process that enables the supervisor and a colleague to sit down together, identify problems, delineate action strategies and responsibilities, specify time constraints, and establish an evaluation design.

Five basic steps constitute the process:

1. The supervisor and the other professional should *individually* list behaviors, factors, variables, and so on, that they feel are creating the immediate problem.

2. They should list and compare their individually perceived needs and then *together* identify the major needs they have determined by consensus. This list represents *what* is to be accomplished.

3. When the consensus list is completed, they should then develop an action strategy and list of responsibilities to meet the demands of the problem. These strategies and responsibilities need to be carefully delineated so that each party will know *how* the other will perform the collaboratively established tasks.

4. Next, for each *how* strategy or responsibility listed, the two parties should establish a corresponding timeline. Actual dates should be stated to determine *when* activities will occur or be completed.

5. Finally, they should schedule regular meetings throughout the problem-resolution sequence. Progress should be assessed in terms of the previously delineated *how* and *when* items, which can be altered as the goal warrants.

Changes in the consensus list (*what*) are not recommended during these progress check sessions. Discerning the consensus needs is critical to the entire sequence; the individuals involved should have taken adequate evaluative measures to affirm the accuracy of the *what* phase of the sequence. If, during the process, both parties agree that the identified consensus needs are in error or need to be rectified, the original sequence should be discarded and a new one initiated.

AN APPLICATION

Let's consider an actual application of the process, as used by an assistant superintendent for instruction and a reading supervisor. The general problem area was to determine how the supervisor's time and expertise could be used most effectively in designated schools.

Figure 1. Reading Supervisor's How and When

Strategies and Responsibilities	Timeline
Visit every designated school and discuss role with all teachers.	by October 1st
Visit with the principal of every designated school, outline supervisor's role, and seek support in performing duties.	by September 15th
Publish and distribute a monthly reading idea sheet for personnel in designated buildings.	Ongoing, by last school day of each month
Chair reading committee to encourage inter- and intra-school activities in the designated schools.	Ongoing; monthly
Review status in buildings with principal at least twice per semester.	October, December, February, and April
Work with assistant superintendent for instruction to develop general visitation schedule.	Prior to September 1st

Figure 2. Assistant Superintendent's How and When

Strategies and Responsibilities	Timeline
Meet with principals of designated schools to review job description and role of reading supervisor.	August principals' meeting
Utilize reading supervisor for testing and/or consultation with teachers from designated schools who request or need technical assistance.	Ongoing
Arrange for reading supervisor to have a leadership role in districtwide staff development endeavors.	As per date
Assess the effectiveness with which the time and expertise of reading supervisor is being used by principals and teachers.	November, January, March, and May
Meet with reading supervisor every two weeks.	First and third Thursday of each month

In step one, the assistant superintendent and the supervisor each identified the reasons creating the general problem. The assistant superintendent cited the following: (1) teachers were unsure of the precise nature of the supervisor's role particularly due to district and federal policies about developmental reading and Title I reading; (2) the supervisor needed to use the time better, and (3) most of the principals the supervisor served had limited awareness and knowledge of reading; as a result, some principals didn't know precise services to request of the supervisor. The reading supervisor's perceived problems were: (1) too many buildings located over too large a geographical area, (2) lack of significant referrals from principals, (3) lack of time for follow-up work with teachers, and (4) teachers' reluctance to ask for help.

After the supervisor and the assistant superintendent compared and discussed these factors, they collaboatively agreed on the *what* of the process. The consensus needs they identified were: (1) to increase the visibility of the reading supervisor in the designated schools; (2) to clarify the role of the reading supervisor as it relates to developmental and Title I reading efforts, (3) to establish an effective scheduling sequence for the reading supervisor, and (4) to create a follow-up process to reinforce the efforts of the reading supervisor and facilitate effective feedback.

Figure 1 shows steps three and four, the *how* and *when*, as they relate to the reading supervisor's involvement in the process.

Figure 2 conveys the *how* and the *when* of the assistant superintendent in relation to the consensus needs.

The two parties agreed to meet on the first and third Thursday of each month in order to discuss problems and issues pertinent to the reading supervisor's duties. A significant portion of each meeting was to be devoted to the process' final step, the progress check.

IMPLICATIONS

The Collaborative Instructional Improvement Process is effective because it can serve so many crucial purposes. First, it can be the vehicle for meaningful dialogue between two professionals, helping each individual develop a better understanding of the other's position, educational beliefs, and expectations.

Second, the process is excellent for facilitating initial planning. Using the process, two professionals can lay out a cooperative action plan for a particular problem. This mutual effort will establish what is to be accomplished, the responsibilities of both individuals, and the manner in which they will judge their effectiveness.

Third, as it is implemented, the process can be the focal point of discussions between the two participants. In these meetings, as contrasted with the meaningless exchanges that frequently take place, substantive educational issues are discussed and action strategies identified and agreed upon. Both people know the terms of the process, and their discussions can focus on their progress in implementing it. Past activities are described, future ones are planned, and problems and successes are shared.

Fourth, in these days of accountability, evaluation is always a significant issue. The very nature of the process makes evaluation a relatively simple matter. Both professionals know the priorities, and as the *when* portion is being implemented, they can determine the degree of progress. After this evaluation is completed, the professionals can analyze what has occurred, what "needs" remain, and determine the emphasis of future planning sessions.

Finally, the process can serve as a "documentor" of accomplishments. Using such a written record, the professional can quickly and comprehensively show not only his or her activities but also the positive changes in which he or she has played a part.

CONCLUSION

The Collaborative Instructional Improvement Process is a practitioner's tool. It has been effectively used in school districts of varying size, affluence, and location by individuals with different levels of educational training and professional experience. Their areas of expertise have spanned the total range of educational disciplines, and their positions of authority and power have represented an equally broad spectrum.

Despite the differences among the users of the process, it has proven successful in virtually every instance. The process will work if two persons strive to make it work.

Assessing Administrative Performance

George J. Rentsch

Dr. Rentsch, Professor of Educational Administration at the State University College, Brockport, New York, states the intent of his article as an attempt "to present a framework around which an administrative assessment program can be developed." Stressing the need for clarity of purpose and procedure, he suggests a number of steps that can be taken towards the implementation of an effective administrative assessment program. He concludes that staff evaluation is necessary, though difficult, for only systematic assessment will help ascertain that the administrator's performance is indeed contributing to the realization of the organization's goals.

Accountability is a current catchword of educational institutions. Cries for cost effectiveness, for increased productivity, and for greater student achievement are heard on all sides. The school administrator, as the person most directly responsible for making resource allocation decisions, is the person usually considered to be most accountable for the quality and quantity of teaching and learning taking place in his unit. For this reason, one would expect that the assessment of administrative effectiveness would be an area in which great progress has been made.

However, if current literature is an accurate indicator, scant attention has been focused on this area. The questions — in what way, to what extent, and how systematically should administrative assessment be organized — have so far gone unanswered.

CLARIFYING THE PURPOSE —
PROGRAM OR PERSON?

The intent of this article is to present a framework around which an administrative assessment program can be developed. Attention is first given to the need for clarity in purpose, in procedure, and in what is observed, recorded, and discussed. Following this, a series of steps to effect an administrative assessment program is suggested.

Both personal and program assessment are important, but one should not be confused with the other. Program assessment considers the objectives, materials, approaches, procedures, and attainment measures of that program. While it considers the role of persons in the implementation of the program, it is not concerned with evaluating the person *per se*. Personal assessment, on the other hand, is designed to identify areas of strength and weakness in a particular person. It is concerned with bringing about increased effectiveness on the part of that person. As such it has an effect on program but it is not concerned with improving the program *per se*.

Because the administrator bears considerable program responsibility, it is easy to confuse the two assessment purposes when considering the need for an administrative assessment program. While both kinds of assessment should be conducted in an organized fashion in all school districts, this article is concerned only with personal administrative assessment procedures.

The term "accountability" has an air of finality about it. It seems to stress end product measurement that can then lead to statements about work accomplished or work not accomplished. Before establishing any assessment program, it is essential that consideration be given to the relative importance and implications of formative and summative assessment.

Formative assessment is supervisory in nature. As such, it is process oriented. It is neutral in value orientation, supportive of the person, and designed to help the person's observed performance fall more in line with expected performance.

Summative assessment, on the other hand, is administrative in nature. It is product oriented, designed to provide a terminal measure of the person's performance. It is, therefore, judgmental and often value laden. Since it serves as a final record of performance, it influences decisions on appointment, promotion, tenure, and retention.

Both formative and summative assessment are important. Man might never have landed on the moon if scientists believed only in summative assessment procedures. It is extremely important to track the progress of the ship toward the moon (formative assessment), to relate actual position and speed to expected position and speed; and, *most important*, to take corrective action during the course of travel. It is also important to complete a summative assessment of the entire operation (How much did it cost? How close to the anticipated touchdown spot did it land? What malfunctioned and why?), but this would be senseless without having engaged in formative assessment. In fact, it is likely that a moon probe without formative assessment would miss the moon entirely, let alone the anticipated point of touchdown.

DETERMINING WHAT TO EVALUATE

There are three areas within which an administrator can be assessed: what he is, what he does, and what he accomplishes. Dean Speicher (1971) refers to essentially the same three areas when he identifies a "Characteristic of Traits Approach," a "Process-Behavior Approach," and an "Administrative Outcomes Approach."

A person is being assessed for what he is when he is classified as "single-minded," "emotionally dependent," "ideologically committed," "intelligent," "tall," and/or "handsome." No evidence exists to indicate that certain traits or characteristics are common to effective administrators.

A person is being assessed for what he does when he is measured against such job functions as "supervises clerical workers," "prepares budget documents," "develops policies for student safety," and "recruits and selects qualified staff." Unfortunately such assessments seldom lead to little more than "Yes, he does" or "No, he doesn't" responses.

A person is being assessed for what he accomplishes when he is held responsible for a certain level of production, or for a particular outcome. Since the ultimate purpose of the school is to develop knowledgeable citizens, the effectiveness of a school administrator-supervisor would most logically be measured against the level or amount of student learning. Unfortunately, finding a direct correlation between teaching and learning is difficult enough. Just thinking about a possible direct link between administrative acts and student learning is almost mind-boggling!

DETERMINING WHAT TO RECORD

Three categories of information are recorded as part of a personal assessment procedure — raw data, quantitative judgment, and qualitative judgment.

Raw data are recorded to describe specific behavior when no one who has observed the behavior would disagree with the accuracy of the recorded information. Overspending or underspending budget allocations, timeliness of submitting reports, hours spent in the school or office, number and kind of grievances submitted, or frequency and number of professional conferences attended might serve as some of the raw data for a personal administrative assessment program. Such data are of little use when simply collected, recorded, and filed. They require analysis and interpretation to be of any value.

Quantitative judgment is required to reduce the raw data to a summary statement. "Frequently ill," "seldom late," "often conducts long meetings," "seldom spends entire budget allocation," "always submits reports on time," "has many grievances submitted protesting his decisions," or "frequently attends conferences and professional meetings" are examples of quantitative judgments. Unlike raw data, where no one who observed the behavior would doubt the accuracy of the data, quantitative judgments might be challenged. Since, however, it is assumed that any quantitative judgment would represent a challenge to the professional competence of the person submitting the statements. Quantitative judgments, especially when coupled with the raw data that have produced them, can serve as points of departure in superior-subordinate conferences. As such they become more useful than the raw data alone.

Qualitative judgment is recorded when a belief is expressed about the value of the reality of the raw data. Qualitative judgments result in such statements as "is a poor organizer," "is a good speaker," "conducts effective meetings," "makes poor decisions," "ignores his work to attend conferences." Unlike raw data and quantitative judgments, qualitative judgments lend themselves to varied interpretations. Further, these varied interpretations are often based on deeply held values that are not easily changed, that are sometimes not recognized and that are seldom expressed. Qualitative judgments, therefore, can easily lead to disagreements that will not be resolved through the simple presentation and analysis of raw data.

A COMPOSITE MATRIX

Plotting the three evaluative areas against the three recording areas

	IS	DOES	ACCOMPLISHES
Raw Data	1	2	3
Quantitative Judgment	4	5	6
Qualitative Judgment	7	8	9

results in a nine-celled matrix. Cells 1, 4 and 7 should be eliminated from any assessment program since the evidence suggests the futility of trying to identify desirable traits of administrators and supervisors. Further, even if such traits could be identified, changing physical traits that are an accident of birth is probably impossible, and changing those mental, emotional, and social traits firmly established over a long period of time may be equally impossible.

Cells 7, 8, and 9 should also be eliminated from assessment programs to the extent that this is possible. There will always be a fine line between quantitative judgment and qualitative judgment but since value-laden qualitative assessment comments do little to facilitate communication they should be discouraged if not eliminated.

Through this process of elimination, a four-celled matrix is left. This, it is proposed, should serve as the basis for an administrative assessment program.

To assess what a person does, it is necessary to observe that person doing something. To be certain that what a person does is important to the organization, it is essential to set forth a series of expectations. Such expectations need to go beyond the simple litany of a job description. High priority items must be identified — whether these be the stated goals of the district, major areas of responsibility for the administrator, or high priority but quite specific job responsibilities.

Through observation and discussion, major areas of personal and organizational need can then be identified. These needs can be translated into major goals and/or specific objectives to be accomplished over a period of time. Further, specific steps leading to the accomplishment of the goal could be listed.

For example, an instructional supervisor for a school district might be aware that providing for greater student awareness of the metric system is a district need. This supervisor might, therefore, design a program similar to the following:

GOAL AREA: CURRICULUM — METRIC SYSTEM

1. By Sept. 15, students in grades K-3 will engage in the equivalent of at least _____hours of study/activity in the metric system.

2. By June 25, X percent of the students in Grade 3 will attain a score of at least _____on the XYZ standardized test of metric knowledge.

Steps to attain objectives:

1. By Oct. 1, inform teachers and principals of the need for increased attention to metric awareness.
2. By Oct. 15, appoint committee to develop suggested class activities for use in grades K-3 and to select appropriate instructional materials.
3. By Nov. 1, obtain sample published and/or manufactured materials appropriate for use in classes.
4. By Dec. 1, order recommended instructional materials.
5. By March 1, conduct orientation workshops for K-3 teachers.

Obviously, additional steps will be necessary (and should, therefore, be listed) in order to accomplish the stated objectives.

As a result of this process the supervisor would know that what he is doing is in keeping with the priorities of the district. Further, he would know and his superior would also know what specific steps will be taken to accomplish the goal. Monitoring progress is then simply a case of periodic verbal or written repots indicating the degree of progress being made. Of great importance in this process is the opportunity that is present for the supervisor and his superior to discuss what each can do to facilitate progress toward the goal, to speed up the schedule,to get back on the schedule, or to revise the schedule in light of new evidence.

Assessing what a person does in this process is then a matter of analyzing the relationship between anticipated progress and actual progress. Raw data for matrix cell 2 is collected in terms of activities undertaken and events scheduled and completed, and feedback obtained from program participants is collected. These data are then used in making cooperative quantitative judgments that form the basis for cell 5. In this way a formative evaluation process is conducted.

Assessing what a person accomplishes is also possible through this process. Such accomplishments would not be identifiable as specific pupil learning. Instead, the accomplishment would be described as goals attained or, at least, as progress being made toward the attainment of the goals. Measurement of the progress toward the goals (the raw data of cell 3) would be part of the formative evaluation process since both subordinate and superordinate would be primarily interested in taking the necessary steps to assure the attainment of the goal.

Summative evaluation (cell 6) would occur only after progress toward the goal has been terminated. The primary questions asked would be: "Has the goal been attained?" "If not, why not?" "If so, have new problem areas or issues been identified — can these serve as bases for setting new goals?" A complete record — from the establishment of goals, to the identification of steps to attain the goals, to the documentation of conferences held by the subordinate and the superordinate, to an analysis of goals attained – would serve as the primary source from which to make and document quantitative statements about a person's accomplishments. This, in turn, would form the basis for summative evaluation of the work of an administrator.

SUMMARY

Staff evaluation, although difficult, is necessary. Administrators who assess others cannot be immune from personal assessment. While administrators are constantly being assessed informally, systematic assessment procedures are necessary to be certain that the administrator's efforts will contribute to the attainment of organizational goals.

References

Boston, Robert E. "Management by Objectives: A Management System for Education," *Educational Technology,* May 1972.

Castetter, William B. and Richard Heisler. *Appraising and Improving the Performance of School Administrative Personnel.* Philadelphia: University of Pennsylvania Graduate School of Education, 1971.

DeVaughn, J. Everette. *A Manual for Developing Reasonable, Objective, Non-Discriminatory Standards for Evaluating Administrative Performance.* State College, Miss.: Mississippi State University, 1971.

Educational Research Service, American Association of School Administrators and National Education Research Division. *Evaluating Administrative/Supervisory Performance.* E. R. S. Circular No. 6 Washington,, D.C.: The Service, 1971.

Nyguard, Debra. *Evaluating Administrative Performance: An E.R.S. Report.* Washington, D. C.: Educational Research Service, 1974.

Speicher, Dean. "Evaluating Administrative and Supervisory Personnel," *Personnel News,* March 1971.

A Six-Point Plan For Evaluating Your Superintendent

Robert J. Roelle and Robert L. Monks

This article gives a broad overview of the process involved in evaluating the superintendent. Stressing that there is no "sacrosanct method" for doing so, and that a "personalized approach" is necessary in each individual school district, the authors proceed to list some general criteria that should be kept in mind as an evaluation system is devised. Their work is based on a study of superintendents and board presidents in a suburban Chicago area. Robert J. Roelle is Director of Student Services in Bay Shore, New York; Robert L. Monks is an Associate Professor of Administration and Supervision at Loyola University, Chicago.

Understand from the start that there's no sacrosanct method for evaluating the performance of your superintendent. Understand also that you can't arbitrarily appropriate another school district's evaluation method and expect it to work smoothly in your own. What's needed — you guessed it — is a personalized approach. The superintendent and board of education must cooperate on devising an evaluation framework.

Here are some guidelines for developing or revising criteria to evaluate a superintendent of schools. They are based on a study of school superintendents and board presidents in Lake County, Illinois (in suburban Chicago):

1.   Agree that a formal evaluation of the superintendent is needed. Assuming everyone accedes to a formal evaluation, the burden then is on the board to encourage the superintendent to provide members with inservice help on how to conduct one. If necessary, resources such as university faculty, state school board associations, and other consultants should be called in.

2.   Determine the purpose of the evaluation. The purpose sets the

stage for development and implementation of the formal evaluation system. Evaluations are conducted in entirely different ways, depending upon the purpose behind the evaluation. Clearly, the superintendent and the board must be in accord on the purpose, basing their agreement on two major considerations: to determine whether district goals have been attained; to improve board/superintendent relations. Research shows that in addition to the two purposes just mentioned (goals and relations), there *can be* at least four other purposes behind the board's evaluation of a superintendent: dismissal, compensation, professional growth, placation of teacher unions. When asked to weigh the importance of the purposes, participants in the Lake County study were in close agreement that all purposes *except for dismissal and placation of unions* were legitimate reasons for evaluating a superintendent's performance.

3.   Choose an evaluation system. There are four major categories, which often overlap, of superintendent evaluation systems: Management By Objectives (M.B.O.), checklists; rating scales; essay or blank narratives.

M.B.O. is useful for evaluation purposes when the superintendent and board are goal oriented; it involves the setting of specific objectives, the completion of which becomes the main scope of the superintendent's performance evaluation.

The checklist system, as the name suggests, consists of an inventory of tasks that the board thinks the superintendent should complete. If board members are satisfied that the assignments have been accomplished, the items are checked off the list.

The rating scale is a list of high priority items identified by the school board. Each board member rates the superintendent (usually on a scale ranging from a low of one to a high of seven) on how he has performed on each high-priority item. These numerical evaluations are compiled and a mean rating for each item is presented as the total evaluation of the superintendent.

The essay or blank narrative is an open-ended summary, which has board members collaborating on a report that describes the superintendent's strengths and weaknesses together with suggestions for improvement.

(One informal method of superintendent evaluation holds that the superintendent is under continuous appraisal by the board — and often by the public — and that an appropriate summary of the superintendent's performance is made during salary and contract renewal discussions.)

4.   Recognize that goal attainment does not necessarily result in board satisfaction. Boards and superintendents should understand that, aside from achievement of goals, the superintendent must perform some standard administrative functions. Thus, the extent to which the board is satisfied with the superintendent's performance of administrative functions, coupled with the successful completion of goals, should constitute the board's evaluation of the superintendent.

When putting the functions to paper, it helps to review what the authorities have to say. Specified functions can serve as concrete measurements for the board when it judges the effectiveness of the superintendent's performance in working toward goals. Writing the functions for the record also permits the board to devise a rating scale. Such a scale furnishes a mechanical means for recording the board's observations of the superintendent's expertise in performing administrative functions.

5. Select information sources for reviewing performance. The board's own observations and perceptions of the superintendent represent the main body of information for reviewing performance. Depending upon the specific goals that have been established, it must be decided when — as a committee of the whole — the board will review performance and when that review will be done by select committee.

Another source of information used by some boards is a monthly progress report prepared by the superintendent. The report pertains to the achievement of goals, it should be discussed and reviewed by the board, with a notation of the review included in official board minutes. In addition, the superintendent should provide an annual self-appraisal that describes the progress toward completion of goals, as well as specific emphasis on competencies in various administrative functions.

6. Develop the process. Soon after new board members have been elected, the superintendent should organize an inservice program that explains the evaluation process. The superintendent furnishes the board with an assessment of the current condition of the school district, this is done at the first board meeting following the start of the fiscal year. The report contains the superintendent's recommended goals and objectives for the new school year. At the board meeting that follows the superintendent's presentation, the board and superintendent carefully review the goals and objectives and reach an agreement concerning which of the targets are to be pursued aggressively.

At subsequent board meetings, the superintendent follows up with progress reports on how goals are being met. As objectives are achieved throughout the year, the superintendent analyzes them and notes specifically what has been attained. Progress reports, particularly those that concern goal achievement, ought to be recorded in the official board minutes.

Formal evaluations should be scheduled scrupulously, which is to say that they should occur *before* the election of new board members so that those members who have worked with the superintendent are included. During the meeting that precedes the formal evaluation session, the superintendent and board president summarize the evaluation process for the board. At the same time, the president distributes the evaluation instrument. Also at this meeting the superintendent passes out copies of his self-appraisal containing the narration mentioned earlier.

Finally, the evaluation is conducted in executive session. During the session, the board examines the responses to the instrument. After that, a composite evaluation is prepared. And after that, the superintendent is called into executive session during which the evaluation is presented to him. To ensure that everything is on the up-and-up, the board president submits the summary in open session so that it can be recorded in the official minutes.

Occasionally, the uncomfortable question arises as to whether the board (never mind the superintendent) has made demonstrable progress toward achieving objectives and goals. Mostly, as we know, the answer is given at the polls — where the evaluation is terse and without provision for appeals.

Yearly Evaluation -
A Key in Assessing Superintendent

Joseph M. Appel

In this brief but informative article, Joseph M. Appel says that superintendents should be evaluated annually and that the evaluation should include concrete information and data that delineate "his effectiveness in attaining . . . the goals and objectives" previously established. These goals should be related to the superintendent's responsibilities in several important areas: curriculum development, educational management, school/community relations, and fiscal responsibility. The process of evaluation should be four-phased: a pre-evaluation conference with the board at which district priorities are outlined; identification of goals and objectives in the areas listed above; a progress report to the board; and a final evaluation conference. Joseph M. Appel is Deputy Superintendent for Curriculum and Instruction in the Mountain View-Los Altos Union High School District in California.

To insure educational excellence, the assessment of the superintendent should include two important dimensions: (1) identification of priority goals and objectives in curriculum improvement, educational management, school and community relations, and fiscal responsibility; and (2) completion of a yearly evaluation, including concrete information and data delineating the effectiveness of the superintendent in attaining the identified goals and objectives.

Curriculum improvement is the foundation of a district's educational program and the *sine qua non* of a superintendent's evaluation. Indicators of effectiveness include student achievement, growth of the professional staff qualifications, and learning environment, and effective utilization of the many available resources — personnel, facilities, equipment — in the community. All of these measures should be considered in assessing the superintendent's competence in curriculum management.

To effect curriculum improvement the superintendent must exercise sound educational management. Managerial skill is evidenced in the superintendent's ability to formulate and articulate the priority goals and objectives of the district, to select a highly qualified administrative staff, to work harmoniously with school and community personnel, to anticipate the needs of the district, to communicate clearly and effectively with individuals and groups, and to make decisions which reflect personal integrity and a commitment to public education. Sources for determining effectiveness in these areas include formal and informal measures, ranging from written reports to observations of the interactions of the superintendent with the board, community and school personnel, and the district administrative staff.

In the management of the district, the superintendent must maintain a close relationship with the school community. This relationship includes involvement in community affairs, participation in community organizations, communication with the media and public leaders, and integration of school and community resources. The measurement of the superintendent's effectiveness is both qualitative and quantitative. Qualitatively the board will be able, based on input from the public, to determine the perceptions of the community in their relations with the superintendent; quantitatively the superintendent can verify participation and involvement with community leaders, organizations, and advisory groups. A synthesis of these qualitative and quantitative elements will be necessary to reach an accurate assessment of the superintendent's community relation skills.

It is important to the connunity that the superintendent establish a budget that provides a sound financial structure for the school district. The criteria for assessing the superintendent's effectiveness in fiscal responsibility should include procedural and substantive elements. Procedurally the superintendent must establish a process which provides regular reports of tne district's financial status, periodic auditing of major accounts, and monitoring of actual and budgeted expenditures. Substantively the superintendent must insure that the budget is based on priority goals and objectives, that district programs are cost-effective, and that adequate reserves and contigency funds are available for unanticipated expenditures. Most important, the superintendent must insure that the board and the public are provided with financial reports that are clear.

The assessment of these elements — curriculum, educational management, school and community relations, and fiscal responsibility — should provide a framework for evaluating the superintendent. Operationally the process should involve four phases: a pre-evaluation conference with the board to discuss district priorities, the identification of the superintendent's specific goals and objectives in the four major areas; a progress report to the board; and a final evaluation conference. This assessment process should provide an objective and constructive means for evaluating the superintendent.

Superintendent Evaluation

Dallas P. Dickinson

Dallas P. Dickinson, Vice President of Hoverman and Associates, Inc., a Fort Worth, Texas, management consulting firm, says that "casual, unspecified evaluations of a superintendent don't work." Superintendents want their boards to tell them how they're doing, but when the response is a simple, "You're doing fine" or "You're doing lousy," says Dickinson, misunderstandings can multiply and "the effective conversion of board policy into school system practice" is hindered. The response that is needed is an evaluation process characterized by formality, specificity and structure and one that adheres to a predetermined time-table. Boards that have utilized the system discussed here, says Dickinson, report improvement in superintendent morale and performance.

"Superintendent Evaluation Requires a Step-by-Step Plan Like The One You'll Find Right Here" by Dallas P. Dickinson. Reprinted, with permission, from *The American School Board Journal*, June, 1980. Copyright 1980, The National School Boards Association. All rights reserved.

The president of the board received a telephone call from someone with a heavily disguised voice, asking whether the superintendent's position was open. The president replied that it had been filled nine months ago. The person on the telephone then asked, "Is your new superintendent fulfilling your expectations for him? Has he provided the board the leadership it needs? Has he been an effective administrator? Has he represented the district well to its internal and external public? Has he shown initiative, accomplished results, and gotten along well with people?" The president responded in the affirmative to all questions, but was so impressed by them that he told the caller of a superintendency open in a neighboring district and then asked if the man was interested in that job. "No thanks," responded the caller. "I already have the job as your superintendent and was just calling to find out how I'm doing."

How am I doing? That's the question New York City Mayor Edward

Koch asks every constituent he meets, and it's the question that superintendents want their boards to answer. The problem in too many school districts, however, is the boards answer the question just as the New Yorker might answer Mayor Koch during a chance encounter on Fifth Avenue: "You're doing fine." (Or: "You're doing lousy and you won't get my support next time.")

Casual, unspecified evaluations of a superintendent don't work. They won't head off misunderstandings that develop between a board and its chief executive officer and they don't facilitate the efficient conversion of board policy into school system practice. What you need is an evaluation process that's formal, specific, and structured — and one that follows a set timetable. Before I get into a suggested timetable, here are hints for ensuring that the evaluation process is as effective as possible.

1.   The board should start by identifying and listing all of a superintendent's responsibilities including, of course, all those spelled out in state law, school district policy, and the superintendent's own contract. One effective way of stating the superintendent's responsibility areas is to do so in terms of constituencies, as shown in the following examples. For the board of education constituency, the superintendent's responsibility area is to provide leadership as an education professional and as the chief executive officer. For the taxpayer constituency, the superintendent's responsibility area is to manage effectively the district's resources. The board should list other constituencies (and corresponding responsibility areas), which might well include students, the broader community, the state and nation (superintendent's responsibility: administer the schools in full compliance with all laws, regulations, and guidelines), and school district employees.

2.   The board should weigh each area of responsibility to ensure that the superintendent's overall evaluation isn't excessively influenced by performance in any one area — or isn't unduly influenced by especially vocal critics or supporters. The weight or priority of each responsibility area can be designated in percentage shares: "In the coming year, 30 percent of the superintendent's evaluation will be determined by his success in reorganizing the schools' curriculum programs, especially in the areas of elementary school reading and secondary school mathematics (college preparatory program)."

3.   The board should identify the degree of the superintendent's responsibility and control over any area in which the superintendent is being evaluated. For example: Reorganization of the central office staff to make it more responsive and cooperative toward principals might be something for which the superintendent has a high degree of responsibility and control, the failure of this reorganization would be heavily against the superintendent. The failure of an art appreciation program, on the other hand, might not be counted so heavily against the superintendent if that program was initiated at the request of some outside group that promised — but did not

deliver — personnel, materials, and some funding. What this means is that a superintendent can't simply be graded on a "did well, did poorly" basis; each evaluation "grade" must contain an explanation: "Policy on art appreciation activities not carried out because of lack of promised support from area council on the arts."

4.   Evaluation comments should be specific and carry with them suggestions for improvement. Don't say: "The superintendent did an inadequate job of informing the board about employee concerns." Rather, point to specific incidents when the board wasn't informed and then make your evaluation comments read something like this: "The superintendent failed on the aforementioned two occasions to inform the board accurately about likely teacher and teacher association reaction to new board policy initiatives. In the coming year, the superintendent's recommendations on all policy matters should include discussions of likely reaction from teachers and their associations."

5.   The evaluation process should follow a formal, annual cycle as suggested by the following timetable:

This summer, your board has hired a new superintendent with a contract that begins in September and expires on August 31 of the following year. The board and superintendent have agreed to establish a formal procedure for evaluating job performance. The board has appointed a three-person subcommittee to work with the new superintendent to design the procedure.

Early June: *Superintendent and evaluation committee meet to consider their charge, establish the purposes of evaluation, and agree on the major responsibility areas of the superintendent.*

The new superintendent and the evaluation committee have been charged with presenting to the full board, at its regularly scheduled September meeting, a fully developed evaluation process. The first meeting of the committee and superintendent takes place in early June, and at that meeting they:

a.   agree to a plan proposed by the superintendent which calls for (1) the committee chairman to report progress briefly at the next meeting of the full board, (2) the superintendent to develop for discussion at the next committee meeting a list of "evaluation elements" for each responsibility area, and (3) each committee member to be prepared at the next meeting to reach agreement on priorities among the several responsibility areas for the coming year (the next meeting should be scheduled for two weeks later);

b.   agree that their primary purpose in establishing a formal job performance evaluation process for the superintendent is to provide for rational, structured communications between the board and superintendent to encourage more constructive and effective working relationships;

c.   agree that the evaluation will also serve as the basis of contact and compensation decisions,

d.   agree on the major responsibility areas of the superintendent, which will serve as the structural skeleton of the evaluation process and instrument.

Late June: *The committee meets to agree on priorities among responsibility areas and evaluation elements.*

The committee's second meeting is a long one, but does result in agreement on:

a.   *Priorities:* Of six major responsibility areas that have been identified, the committee agrees that the needs of the district require that above average attention be given to one — improving relationships with the community. (Recent bond issues have been defeated; criticism of school programs has been vocal at board meetings and in letters to the editor.) Twenty-five percent of the superintendent's evaluation for the coming year will depend on his success in this area; fifteen percent is assigned to each of the other five areas.

b.   *Evaluation elements:* The superintendent's proposed listing is discussed in depth and modified, and agreement is reached on two to four evaluation elements in each responsibility area. For example, it is agreed to evaluate the superintendent's performance in the area of leadership to the board of education based on (1) providing training in boardmanship, (2) helping the board organize itself to be more effective and efficient, (3) providing effective leadership to the board, and (4) maintaining constructive working relationships with board members.

At the conclusion of this second meeting, the superintendent is charged with developing one or more criteria to be used to measure success in each of the evaluation elements in the coming year. The next meeting is scheduled for late July.

Late July: *Agreement is reached on criteria.*

The month has been a demanding one for the new superintendent. After hours of studying the district's long-range plans and other formal documents (including minutes of past board meetings) and conducting lengthy discussions with each board member, the superintendent brings his proposed list of evaluation criteria to the next committee meeting. After discussion and some revision, the list is accepted.

In my previous example about the responsibility area of "leadership to the board," four evaluation elements were mentioned. Here are the performance criteria the superintendent developed for each of the evaluation elements:

Evaluation element: Provides training in boardmanship. *Performance criteria:* Develop an information packet for new board members; design a one-day orientation program for new board members, identify external training opportunities (conventions, workshops, seminars) for all board members.

Evaluation element: Helps the board organize itself to be more effective and efficient. *Performance criteria:* Study and recommend improvements in the board's committee structure; develop an improved agenda that minimizes the rush of important business at the end of meetings, develop an annual calendar for the board.

Evaluation element: Provides effective professional leadership to the board. *Performance criteria:* Include in regular superintendent's report a summary of emerging trends/issues likely to affect the district; streamline the format and content of periodic program reports to the board.

Evaluation element: Maintains constructive working relationships with board members. *Performance criteria:* Provide more opportunities to meet with individual board members informally; attend all board committee meetings as a resource person; work with members of the board to develop and carry out strategies for improved communication between the district and its minority populations, work with the board's evaluation committee to develop improved understanding of board member/superintendent roles and relationships.

Mid-August: *Agreement is reached on the format of the evaluation instrument and the steps and timetable in the evaluation process.*

During the fourth meeting of the evaluation committee, the committee agrees on the specifics of the process of evaluation. The format of the written evaluation instrument is agreed to, and will include:

a. Section I, in which each board member will rate the superintendent's performance against each criterion on a forced-response scale of 1 to 5 (5 being the best possible performance). Section I also will encourage board members to give brief written comments for each criterion (". . . did a particularly commendable job in this area," or ", . . the superintendent cannot put this off any longer").

b. Section II, in which each board member is invited to summarize in a brief statement his perceptions of the superintendent's key personal and professional strengths and weaknesses, and the superintendent's development needs for the upcoming evaluation period. This section allows for less task-oriented, concrete reactions, and gets at questions of the superintendent's "style."

c. Section III, in which each board member rates the superintendent's performance overall, both as a forced response scale of 1 to 5 and in a brief narrative. In this section, school board members also are asked to recommend future contract and salary actions for the superintendent.

In the mid-August meeting, the committee also agrees on the several steps in the evaluation cycle and a timetable for the upcoming (1980-81) year:

September: Approval by the full board of the evaluation process and timetable as well as the responsibility areas, priorities, evaluation elements and performance criteria.

January: Meeting of the superintendent with the evaluation committee to discuss progress and problems to date, and to agree on any modifications in process, priorities, criteria, and the like.

Early June: Preparation (by the superintendent) and distribution (to each board member) of (1) the evaluation instrument, and (2) the superintendent's written summary of his perceptions of performance, progress, and problems.

Late June: Completion of the evaluation instruments and return to the chairman of the evaluation committee, who tallies them and prepares a preliminary narrative evaluation.

Mid-July: Meeting of the superintendent with the evaluation committee (and other board members who care to attend) to discuss the tally and preliminary narrative evaluation. This session should be characterized by honesty and openness, and should focus on the whys of past performance in a constructive way. This meeting also should address changes and improvements in the evaluation process for the upcoming year as well as modifications in responsibility areas, priorities, evaluation elements, and performance criteria.

Late July: The chairman of the evaluation committee circulates the following items to other committee members and the superintendent for comment: a revised draft of the narrative evaluation, to reflect the comments made in the early July meeting; a draft of proposed procedures for evauation and responsibility areas, priorities, evaluation elements, and criteria to be used in the coming year's evaluation; and recommended contract and salary actions.

If committee members have no objections, these materials will become the basis of the committee's September report to the full board.

September: In executive session, the full board receives the report of its evaluation committee, including recommended contract and salary actions. After discussion, agreement should be reached on three main points: (1) the superintendent's performance in the past year; (2) the evaluation process for the coming year, and (3) any appropriate contract and salary actions.

At this point the entire evaluation process has come full circle and begins another round.

Boards that have implemented this type of evaluation process for their chief executive officers report that it has greatly improved the rationality, objectivity, and constructiveness of superintendent evaluations, and that it has improved the job performance of superintendents. But, even more important, board members report that the process has improved their effectiveness by forcing them (1) to understand the superintendent's roles and responsibilities better, which helps them to understand more fully their own roles and responsibilities, and (2) to think more concretely about the needs of their district and plan better to meet those needs, because in setting priorities, goals, and performance criteria for the superintendent, they also are setting priorities, goals, and performance criteria for themselves.

By carefully and completely answering the superintendent's *How am I doing?* question, the board also poses — and answers - the *How are we doing?* question for the entire school system.

Evaluation of Principals

"The evaluation process," says Professor McCleary, "is the heart of the appraisal system." The various levels of evaluation that should occur in any school system, e.g., institutional, program, administrative performance, staff performance, and student achievement, are all interrelated and require careful coordination if each is to be effective. He discusses several approaches to evaluation and a number of processes and instruments in current use. Lloyd E. McCleary is Professor of Educational Administration at the University of Utah, Salt Lake City. (See also a related article by Professor McCleary elsewhere in this section.)

Evaluation of educational personnel, particularly school principals, is receiving increasing attention due to such immediate influences as pressures for improved administrative performance, need for schools to demonstrate problem solving capability, the performance-based and management-by-objectives movements, and demands for accountability. In addition, two conditions, largely developing during the past ten to fifteen years, underlie the immediate influences noted. The first of these is the increased complexity of the school unit brought about by consolidation and increases in school size, the addition of special programs and technologies, and the impact of social problems. The second condition is due to the gains made in knowledge about the relationship of human needs and organizational effectiveness, about management control systems which employ planning methods to relate personnel performance requirements to goals and to development activities, and about measurement and evaluation as applied to performance assessment.

The need for sound, systematic evaluation of administrative performance as a general principle hardly needs treatment, and, if the literature is accurate, is accepted by school administrators as desirable. However, evaluation of the principal in his job is intensely emotional and personal. The evaluation process includes subjective judgments regardless of how objective data collected about his performance might appear. Many underlying assumptions and beliefs need to be made explicit and examined in an atmosphere that is emotionally and psychologically satisfactory, professionally enhancing, and clearly relevant to plans and understandings about personal and organizational needs. Without these conditions an evaluation system, no matter how sound, is likely to have limited if not adverse effects. What appears to be needed is to clarify present knowledge and practice, to examine evaluation processes that take into account the limitations of current capability, and to propose defensible evaluation procedures.

PERSPECTIVE FOR EVALUATION
OF PRINCIPALS

Evaluation in a school is necessary at five levels: institutional, program, administrative performance, staff performance, and student performance. Each is related to the other, and thus, in best practice, each is related in terms of a unified, coherent appraisal *system*. Each, however, has its own discrete methods and purposes, an evaluation *process*. In practice each often is undertaken in an isolated fashion, and interrelationships occur only in implicit, informal, sometimes covert, ways. Even in the evaluation literature personnel evaluation is treated quite separately and usually in terms of compensation and collective negotiations. Finally, the system and the specific process need to be part of explicit, overall administrative functions usually referred to as *planning* and *controlling*.

Current theory holds that the primary purpose of evaluation is to establish a basis for change of individual behaviour such that both personal satisfaction and organizational effectiveness is improved. Factual information collected through explicit procedures is obtained about performance in relation to specified objectives. Expectations for performance resulting from evaluation is determined both by the individual whose performance is being evaluated and by the superior(s). Performance strengths and weaknesses are identified and plans made in terms of them in relation to changes, improvements, and revised expectations for the future. Decisions about compensation, promotion or transfer, dismissal, and progress are related to the evaluation results and communicated to the individual evaluated.

Several important premises form the basis for the theory. The evaluation process is the heart of the appraisal system. For this reason performance evaluation as a process is examined in some detail in a later section. Administrative performance, of which the principal is key, requires regular examination in terms of both operational effectiveness to the principalship itself and in terms of its contribution to the purposes of the school.

Because of this premise the five levels of evaluation — institutional, program, administrative performance, staff performance, and student performance — were said to be interrelated, and evaluation of each needs careful coordination. The administrative function through which planning is related to actual achievement of organizational goals has been referred to as controlling. Evaluation, particularly performance evaluation, contributes to the controlling fuction because the controlling function represents attempts to close the gap between the desired and actual organizational achievement. The controlling function comprises the administrative means to determine the extent and nature of deviation between plans and performance and the actions necessary to aid the organization and its personnel to achieve goals.

Additional premises stem from belief systems relative to the concept of the individual and his participation in formal organization. McGregor's (1960) Theory X and Theory Y are well known as a formulation about such belief systems. The two theories are depicted as extremes of a continuum. The X belief system assumes the individual to be passive, inherently lazy, resistant to change, and unresponsive to the organization. The Y belief system assumes the individual to be capable and desirous of self direction and initiative, willing to participate to achieve organizational goals, and ready for growth. Theory X assumes lose, direct control of individuals, while Theory Y assumes that management needs to provide an environment where individuals are able and motivated to pursue organizational ends. Thus, one can assume that the evaluation system reflects the belief system of its designers, and that an evaluation system will be quite different if based upon the beliefs embodied in one theory rather than another.

To extend the premises which derive from basic belief systems relative to the individual in formal organization, two premises represent significant departures from the traditional. Evaluation is now seen as a meaningful process for intergrating individual and organizational interests. Evaluation can be a means of openly examining individual needs and expectations in terms of those of the organization — adjustment of grievances, security and recognition, self development, fair treatment, and strong leadership frequently are in conflict with authority relationships, rules and procedure and other organizational expectations. Sound evaluation procedures offer the possibility of identifying and ameliorating such differences. A final premise is that evaluation should have self development of the principal as a primary focus. The shift toward management by results changes the focus of evaluation to facilitating on-the-job performance and the conditions necessary to it.

APPROACHES TO EVALUATION

Three approaches to evaluation are recognized by specialists of that field. They represent distinct types and the explanations given here may be treated as definitions. They are decision-making matrices, goal-free evaluation, and discrepancy evaluation. Each represents a well-recognized approach, and each has been employed in performance evaluation.

Decision-making matrix approaches may be thought of as the specification of a process of selecting, obtaining, and organizing information necessary to decision making. Often this approach is employed in isolation as a means of arriving at retention, promotion, transfer, selection of personnel for specific training, and the like. Stufflebeam, *et al.* (1971) provides a complete explanation, although Erlandson (1974) has developed and illustrated the decision matrix as integral to evaluation.

The second approach to evaluation can best be thought of as an assessment of effects. Scriven's (1973) goal-free evaluation is the most incisive statement descriptive of this type. His basic argument is that to measure performance only in terms of objectives or intended results is fallacious and that unintended outcomes and unanticipated results are always present and are frequently critical factors in success or failure.

The third approach is that of an assessment of the discrepancy or gap between expected or needed performance and actual performance. Referred to as discrepancy analysis, Tyler's classical model is an exemplar of this type as is Provus (1971) and the Stake Countenance Model (1967). One can see that this approach is basic to any need assessment. Measures of desired or ideal conditions are projected, and measures of actual conditions determine the needs or targets for improvement. This type is most frequently employed in personnel assessment of the more objective types.

The focus of each approach is respectively upon decisions, effects, and objectives. Seen as definitions, the selected approach to evaluation conditions the kinds of purposes to be pursued, the kinds of data collected, and the kinds of outcomes to be reached. Therefore it is highly important to give consideration to the approach to be taken, as that decision alone may predetermine the nature and uses of any evaluation process adopted.

Each of the three approaches described provdies a framework for structuring an evaluation process. Although each approach differs, four basic elements comprise each approach. They are: 1) specifically what is to be evaluated, 2) how are measures to be made, 3) what standards are to be employed, 4) who is to employ the standards to do the judging. Surrounding these four phases of the process several important considerations occur, and each approach,as indicated, is directed toward a different treatment of each phase. Obviously the first two phases are descriptive; that is, a faithful report is to be made of what is expected, and valid measures are to be made of what is actually done. The latter two phases are more troublesome. Most performance evaluation is based upon implicit or subjective standards — benchmarks of performance are simply not available in terms of norms, while locally developed criteria are difficult to develop and validate, and they change rapidly.

Differences between the approaches, in terms of the four phases, are relatively easy to distinguish. The decision-making approach to evaluation is summative in character. Here the evaluator must arrive at a decision about merit. He must be as explicit as possible about standards and either reach a judgment about adequacy from the descriptive data in terms of measures of past performance of the individual evaluated or in terms of some specified, or expected, norms. Goal-free evaluation may be either formative or summative but rests upon descriptions of both intended and unintended results arriving at a "cost benefit" balance sheet of whether the steps taken by a principal produced a net return worthy of the effort made. Discrepancy analysis is usually more complex, but it seems to provide the most developmental, self-validating approach in terms of use with personnel. This latter approach is illustrated with the use of the quadrant assessment model (QAM) in the next section.

EVALUATION PROCESSES AND INSTRUMENTS
FOR EVALUATION OF THE PRINCIPAL

Five evaluation processes for the performance evaluation of the principal which are sufficiently discrete to merit description as identifiable types are in use in American school today. These are: the informal annual evaluation, rating form, performance contract, quadrant assessment model (QAM), and the standardized instrument. In addition to these evaluation processes, the National Association of Secondary School Principals (NASSP) has established an Assessment Center to work with local districts to create rational assessment procedures. The assessment Center activities are described at the conclusion of this section.

Informal Rating. The informal rating takes a number of forms. Perhaps the most valid stems from an annual school plan in which priorities, types of activities, allocation of resources, and expected results are specified (Plath, 1977). Periodic meetings, three or four times a year, indicate administrative steps taken and results being obtained and expected. Near the conclusion of the school year a conference and a written description of the principal's work and reactions to it are prepared and shared with the principal. Usually these reports are submitted as a report to the board. The quality of planning and the character of the evaluation process itself determine whether the process is effective in providing the results intended. Treated as a formative evaluation and integrated with the other kinds of evaluation noted at the beginning of this article, informal evaluation can be a useful goal-free approach to evaluation in that both intended and unintended administrative actions can be examined and the focus is upon results obtained rather than upon specified predetermined criteria for performance.

Rating Forms. Rating forms, usually employed by superiors and subordinates, provide composite measures of how the principal's performance is viewed by teachers and by the central office. Often such forms are made up of items relating to what are viewed to be important behaviors: the principal is open to suggestions and proposals to change routine procedures; the principal consults with those involved before making decisions; the principal prepares for meetings in advance with agenda, prepared reports and materials, etc., necessary to intelligent participation. As noted in the foregoing section, the interpretation and use of such information is the critical factor. If responses are treated as "absolute" descriptions rather than as indicators of sentiment, and if they are unrelated to conditions in the school and directions of needed improvement, they are of little value. However, some school districts have specified categories of behaviors tied to program, staff and students relations, etc., and have school and district improvement targets tied to activities in which such ratings are useful indicators of performance. In some cases ratings are related to compensation schedules.

Performance Contracts. Performance contracts are often tied directly to an annual school plan as described in the informal rating description above. It is basically a personal growth plan that is usually tied to an institutional evaluation and to a plan for school improvement. The origin of performance contracts stems from a management-by-objectives approach to accountability. Based upon a set of district and individual school goals, priorities are chosen and specific action projects are programmed, usually using a PERT or system analysis process. Administrator performance needs are thus identified, and the principal's performance objectives and self-improvement plan are specified. Perhaps the most comprehensive planning device of this type is the Self Performance Achievement Record (SPAR) especially designed for school principals. SPAR is a planning guide which relates an individual administrator's activities to school improvement through a process of identifying goals and specific objectives, activities and time lines, check points, and evaluation procedures. Many less formal performance contract approaches are in use in the public schools, often as a mean of decentralizing administrative authority and permitting more autonomy at the school unit.

Quadrant Assessment Model. The quadrant assessment model (QAM) is illustrative of an open-ended evaluation process which is adaptable to a given school, district, or region. The QAM is a process by which "ideal" profiles of the principal's role may be generated and related to "actual" profiles of a given principal or group of principals. Items which make up the profile are usually generated by task forces of principals and checked across other administrative roles for continuity and for face validity. These items then are each given a rating scale, usually a five-point, Likert-type scale. Items are rated in terms of the "ideal" principal, and the numerical ratings permit the items to be identified as "high ideal" and "low ideal." The same items then are used in an instrument to obtain "actual" ratings of performance, It is recommended that self, subordinate, and superior ratings be obtained and a correlation of concordance used to obtain the extent of agreement among raters. In this way role conflict or role ambiguity items can be identified and removed from the evaluation for treatment in a role clarification procedure. The remaining items are used to construct the actual profile showing "high actual" and "low actual" items. The ideal and actual profiles are then compared.

The comparison of high ideal to high actual items is indicative of important competencies that are judged to be performed well. Low ideal, high actual items are indicative of competencies of lesser importance being performed well — many such items may be interpreted as being given too much emphasis by the principal. High ideal, low actual items are indicative of competencies judged to be important and not being done well. Low ideal, low actual items may or may not be in need of attention depending upon priorities of particular principals.

The QAM is a sound example of the type of evaluation described as discrepancy analysis. The discrepancy between ideal and actual ratings is a means of arriving at a need assessment for performance, which may result in restraining, transfer, or dismissal. The QAM provides a means of validating statements of competency, of identifying role ambiguity or role conflict, and controls for situation specific conditions. Situation specific items, those behaviors required in a particular school, are identified by the ratings acquired for the ideal profile since a profile is produced for each school. The clarification of tasks, establishment of expectations, identification of conflict, and feedback data which the QAM provides are all important to the improvement of performance and should be the outcome of sound evaluation procedures (McCleary and Miller, 1977).

Standardized Instruments. The only carefully constructed and validated standardized instruments available for the evaluation of school principals that are on the market today are a set of four instruments which comprise the Georgia Principal Assessment System (GPAS). GPAS (Ellett, 1978) consists of four different forms of the *Principal Performance Description Survey* instruments. These are completed by four different assessment sources: principals themselves, teachers, an external observer, and the superintendent or central office personnel.

Each instrument yields scores in a specified set of functional areas of administration and in specified administrative operations depending upon the rater. Groups of items may be used to yield sub-scores that can be compared across raters, or the entire set of items in the principal's self-rating may be compared to normative data for the instrument. Instrument construction allows principals to build and plot their own performance profiles for each of the instrument subscores and for each part of the instrument. These profiles can be compared to other principals' self assessments, assessments by teachers, normative profiles, or the assessments of an external observer.

The various instruments comprising the GPAS can be used to fulfill a variety of school assessment needs. The emphasis in conducting assessments with the GPAS is on the performance of building-level principals. The items have been demonstrated to have validity; information has been demonstrated to be effective in targeting areas for improvement, and performance defects have been identified and corrected using these instruments. GPAS is a product of four years of development work by the Results Oriented Management in Education project (ROME) of the University of Georgia. A bibliography of documents and research papers is available from Project ROME as are the instruments (1977).

NASSP's *Assessment Center.* In 1975 the NASSP (Hersey *et al.,* 1977) established a center in cooperation with the American Psychological Association's Division of Industrial and Organizational Psychology. The assessment center is viewed as a psychometric tool for predicting administrative performance. Its main function is to train assessors in an evaluation process adaptable to a given district, yet operate in a standardized fashion. The center is an event rather than a place in that a group is observed as individuals in a group setting, performing a series of exercises that simulate tasks involved in the role of principal. A written report is prepared by the assessors concerning strengths and weaknesses. This report is reviewed in a feedback session with the participant, and it provides the district with an objective assessment of the administrator evaluated.

CONCLUDING STATEMENT

Evaluation of the performance of principals is a developing field in which several approaches are being genuinely and ably pursued. A review of the state of knowledge would suggest that any effort at the school district level should be: 1) incremental in nature; that is, those aspects about which information is available should be done first with other areas developed later, 2) conducted in cycles so that a thorough job can be done relating to those areas in which reliable information is available; 3) separated in terms of descriptive and judgmental phases so that judgments about competence do not destroy the credibility of data collection; 4) focused upon formative rather than summative evaluation, at least in the early stages as the methodology and instruments are being validated; and concerned with the criteria to be used in making judgments.

References

Ellett C. "Understanding and Using the Georgia Principal Assessment System (GPAS)," *CCBC Notebook,* Vol. 7, No. 2, 1978.

Erlandson, D. *Evolution: Hypothesis Testing,* LM-43 of ILM Series, Salt Lake City.ILM Publishers, 1974.

Hersey, P. *et al. NASSP's Assessment Center.* Reston, Virginia: National Association of Secondary School Principals, 1977.

McCleary, L. and Miller, B. *Report of the Project to Assess Needed Competencies in Community Education Administration.* Tempe, Arizona: Southwest Regional Center for Community Education Development, Arizona State University, 1977.

McGregor, D. *The Human Side of Enterprise.* New York: McGraw-Hill, 1960.

Olivero, J., *et al. Self Performance Assessment Record.* Tulsa, Oklahoma: CARE, 1978.

Plath, K. *The Annual School Plan.* Reston, Virginia: National Association of Secondary School Principals, 1976.

Provus, M. *Discrepancy Evaluation.* Berkeley, California: McCutchan, 1971.

Pol, G., and McCleary, L. "Quadrant Assessment Model (QAM) for Assessment of Competencies," *CCBC Notebook,* Vol. 2, No. 3, 1973.

Scriven, M' "Goal-free Evaluation," *School Evaluation: The Politics and Process.* Berkeley, California: McCutchan, 1973.

Stake, R. "The Countenance of Educational Evaluation," *Teacher's College Record.* Vol. 68, No. 7, 1967.

Stufflebeam, D. "Toward a Science of Educational Evaluation," *Educational Technology.* (July) 1968.

Evaluating
Middle-Management Personnel

George B. Redfern

Written for the present book, George B. Redfern's article emphasizes the need for school districts to use the kind of competency-based evaluation system, meticulously discussed here, in assessing the performance of so-called middle managers. He says, however, that the techniques used with this group are perfectly adaptable to administrators at all levels. Thoroughly, yet succinctly, Dr. Redfern explains the evaluative process which he advocates. He has appended to the article a number of useful forms. Former Deputy Executive Director of the American Association of School Administrators, George B. Redfern is currently a consultant in educational personnel management.

Most of the attention in administrator evaluation has been given to two levels of administrators: principals and superintendents. Much less emphasis has been placed upon the evaluation of the so-called middle-level administrators and supervisors. For this reason, this article puts most of the stress upon the evaluation of deputy, associate, and assistant superintendents; directors, supervisors; coordinators; other specialists in central and area offices, and department heads in schools.

It is important to understand, however, that the approach, procedures, and format for evaluating all administrators and supervisors are similar. The differences are in job content, reporting relationships, and limits of responsibility and authority.

APPROACH TO EVALUATION

The evaluation process described herein rests upon the proposition that school administrators need to be better able to account for their performance in more specific and concrete ways than is the case in most school systems. The public increasingly is asking for more precise information about how well its schools are doing in providing educational services. While program evaluation is the customary method to make this determination, the evaluation of personnel services is also important.

An accountability approach to personnel evaluation requires a thrust quite unlike that so widely used in school systems throughout the country. In fact, unless there is a willingness to discard the typical procedures now widely used, it will be more difficult to account effectively for the performance of all administrative and supervisory personnel.

Competency-based evaluation measures performance by (a) clearly indicating the kinds of competencies required for the position, (b) determining where and how these competencies can be further refined and enhanced, (c) deliberately devising a plan for doing so, (d) assessing effectiveness in terms of results achieved.

This leads to some premises. First, inspectional, checklist rating procedures are inadequate for competency-based programs. Second, school systems, if they choose to adopt a more effective approach, must design evaluation procedures which are compatible with competency-based philosophy. Third, evaluation must be comprehensive and cover all categories of personnel. Fourth, a new orientation is necessary. It should be primarily a means of providing feedback information which can be used to refine and improve performance rather than be used as a tool to classify practitioners into scaled levels of competence or incompetence. Finally, the adoption of a competency-based program of evaluation must be accompanied by a carefully planned and continuing program of orientation and training so that those involved may fulfill their roles and responsibilities with understanding and skill.

From the point of view of the person being evaluated, the concept of evaluation, advocated herein, is one that sees it as a means to enable competent persons to enhance their competencies and to help individuals who are performing below the acceptable level to correct deficiencies and become satisfactory in performance.

Perhaps the best way to present this concept of evaluation is in the form of a model. This is done on the following page.

MODEL
A Competency Based Program of
Performance Evaluation

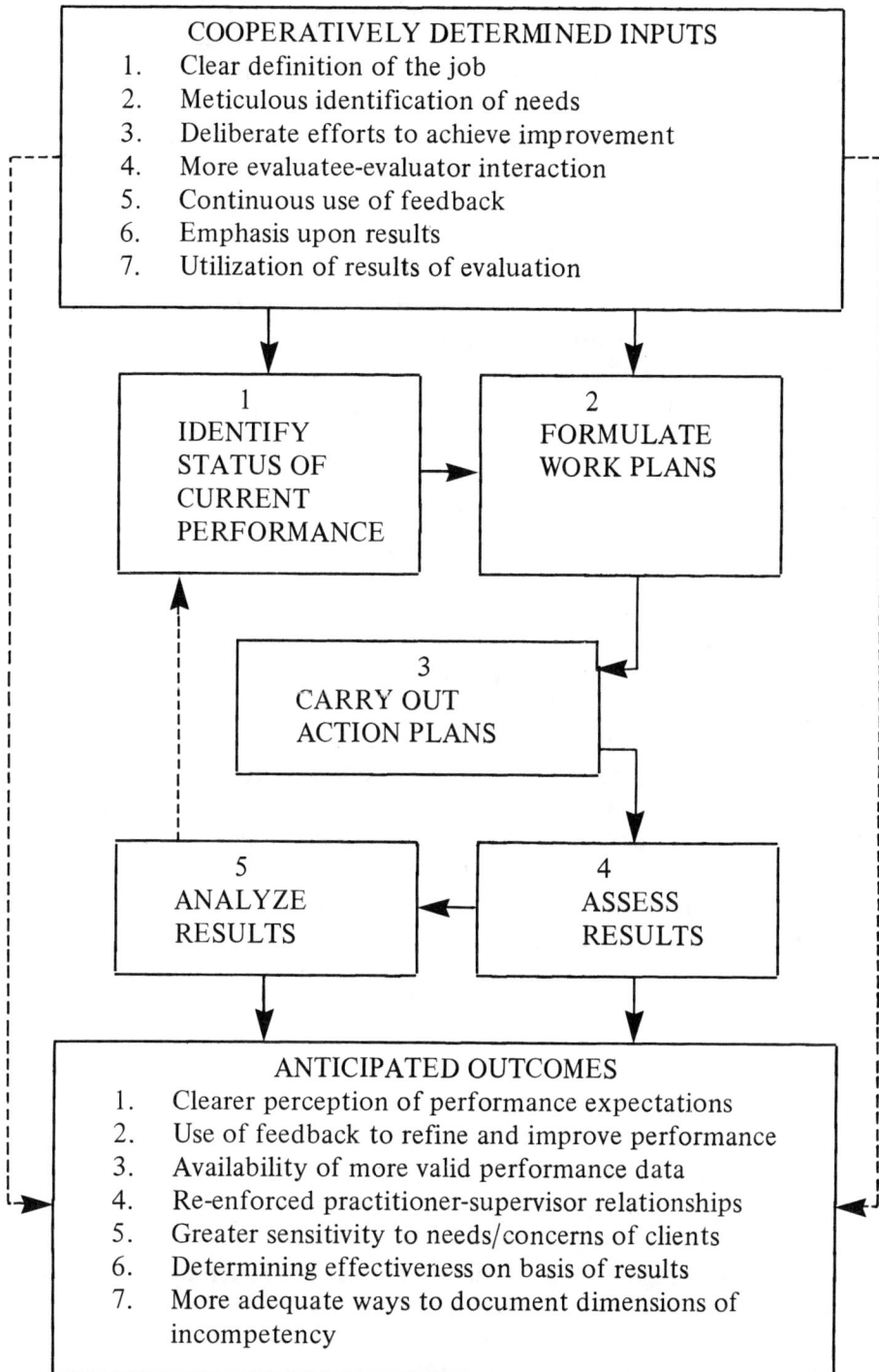

COOPERATIVELY DETERMINED INPUTS
1. Clear definition of the job
2. Meticulous identification of needs
3. Deliberate efforts to achieve improvement
4. More evaluatee-evaluator interaction
5. Continuous use of feedback
6. Emphasis upon results
7. Utilization of results of evaluation

1
IDENTIFY
STATUS OF
CURRENT
PERFORMANCE

2
FORMULATE
WORK PLANS

3
CARRY OUT
ACTION PLANS

5
ANALYZE
RESULTS

4
ASSESS
RESULTS

ANTICIPATED OUTCOMES
1. Clearer perception of performance expectations
2. Use of feedback to refine and improve performance
3. Availability of more valid performance data
4. Re-enforced practitioner-supervisor relationships
5. Greater sensitivity to needs/concerns of clients
6. Determining effectiveness on basis of results
7. More adequate ways to document dimensions of
   incompetency

THE MODEL

Inputs

There are three components in the model. The inputs are essentially "how to do it" qualities. In one sense, the seven inputs are prerequisites for making a competency-based program work well. It has been said that *"what is done in evaluation is important, but how it is done is crucial."* These co-operatively developed inputs provide the qualitative foundation necessary to make the evaluation process effective.

Evaluation Cycle

There are five steps in the process. (a) based upon the status of current performance, needs are identified; (b) work plans to respond to the needs are developed; (c) appropriate action plans are carried out, (d) results are assessed; and (e) the implications of the results are discussed and appropriate follow-up action taken.

Outcomes

Given the cooperatively determined inputs plus the successful fulfillment of the five evaluation steps, it is likely that the seven outcomes, indicated in the model, will be achieved.

Some may feel that this approach to evaluation is too complex and too time-consuming. It will take more time and will require more involvement than conventional, post-performance rating techniques. The justification for investing the extra time and effort in the process is the greater dividends that will accrue to the person being evaluated and to the school system itself. Evaluation should be perceived as a *means* for achieving desirable ends rather than being an *end* in itself. Evaluation, effectively done, produces information which can be used by both the administrator and the supervisor to enable the former to become a more effective person.

THE PROCESS

Job Definition

Clear definition of the job is absolutely essential. This is the starting point in the evaluation process. The fact is that middle-level leadership personnel hold a wide variety of specialized positions, ranging from cabinet-level generalists to individual specialists. It is impractical to use a single, standard set of performance criteria to define job content of such a diversified group of administrators and supervisors.

An accurate, up-to-date position description should be used to define the specialized nature of the job. In addition, a common list of performance criteria should be used to supplement the position description. The latter are likely to have wide application to all types of middle management positions.

    1.   **Position Description** (for specific positions) The conventional format is suggested. The headings might be:

       (a)   Name/Administrator
       (b)   Position Held
       (c)   Work Location
       (d)   Supervisor (Evaluator)
       (e)   Persons Reporting to Administrator (by positions)
       (f)   Major Function of Position
       (g)   Specific Duties and Responsibilities

    2.   **Performance Criteria** (applicable for all administrators)

Beginning in 1975, the National Association of Secondary School Principals, Reston, Virginia initiated its NASSP Assessment Center Program.* *Author's note.)* This was a new and innovative approach for identifying administrative leadership candidates and has, since that time, expanded into a nationwide, field-tested process to identify promising candidates for educational posts, primarily at the school level.

In conducting assessment centers throughout the country, NASSP identified twelve behavioral qualities which appear essential to successful performance in administrative positions. Validation studies have confirmed the reliability of these qualities.

These twelve qualities are suggested for use as general performance criteria to be used in the evaluation process for all administrative and supervisory persons regardless of the level of position or area of specialization.

a.	Problem Analysis	g.	Range of Interests
b.	Judgment	h.	Personal Motivation
c.	Organizational Ability	i.	Educational Values
d.	Decisiveness	j.	Stress Tolerance
e.	Leadership	k.	Oral Communication Skills
f.	Sensitivity	l.	Written Communication Skills

(Specimen copies of the suggested position description and general performance criteria are provided in the Appendix of this article.)

EVALUATION CYCLE

Determining Needs (Step 1.)

In order to bring about change or improvement in performance, it is

(Author's note: For additional information regarding the NASSP Assessment Center Program, contact NASSP, 1904 Association Drive, Reston, Virginia 22091.)

necessary to identify needs or areas that should be strengthened or enhanced. Both the person being evaluated and the one doing the evaluating should make the identification. Generally, the administrator does a self-analysis of the status of current performance, using the position description and the list of general performance criteria. This may be done informally merely by thinking about all aspects of the administrator's job. It may, however, be done more systematically by doing an item analysis of specific duties in the position description and for each of the performance criteria.

Once the administrator completes the self-analysis and identifies needs, a conference is held with the supervisor (evaluator). Obviously, the latter, in anticipation of the conference, should have also completed an analysis of the administrator's current performance. In the conference, both parties discuss the analyses and hopefully reach consensus regarding appropriate areas in which the administrator can concentrate to achieve specific improvements in performance.

Formulating Work Plan(s) (Step 2.)

Once it has been decided that there are areas or aspects of the administrator's job that need improvement, it is the responsibility of the administrator to prepare a written performance improvement plan which will indicate:
      a.   Area(s) needing improvement
      b.   Action plan (activities) to achieve the improvement
      c.   Methods by which results will be measured
A copy of the performance improvement plan is given to the supervisor (evaluator). If the latter has suggestions or recommendations, they are given to the administrator so that modifications can be made in the work plan.

Carrying Out the Action Plan (Step 3.)

The content of the work plan controls the nature of the implementing activities. The administrator has the major responsibility for carrying out these activities. The supervisor, in performing regular supervisory contacts, provides assistance, advisement, and periodically conducts progress reviews of the administrator's overall performance. It is during the implementing stage that the supervisor provides both oral and written feedback for the administrator. It is important for the latter to be made aware of the former's viewpoints about the administrator's performance. Progress reviews vary in number, ranging from one midway in the evaluation cycle to as many as three or four during the year.

Assessing Results (Step 4.)

Assessment is a dual responsibility. The administrator usually does a self-assessment of the extent to which goals and objectives, in the work plan, are achieved. These self-assessments are reviewed by the supervisor who may concur or disagree with the self-assessments. If the latter, reasons for disagreeing should be given as well as recommendations.

The supervisor completes an assessment of the administrator's performance effectiveness based upon the general performance criteria.

The form of the assessments may vary due to preferences of the administrator and supervisor. Some form of rating may be used by both parties with supplementary comments and recommendations. On the other hand, narrative assessments have many advantages. They can be made very personal and descriptive of the results achieved.

Discussing the Implications of Assessments (Step 5.)

The culminating step in the process is the conference to discuss the implications of the assessments. The conference provides an opportunity for a frank interchange of ideas about the implications of the results attained. This conference is *not* a time to spring surprises. In fact, there should be no surprises in the culminating conference.

Most conferences will be pleasant and productive occasions because the administrator will have had a successful year and the evaluation results will have been very positive. When the opposite is the case and when the administrator's performance has been less than satisfactory, the conference can be less pleasant. In fact, it may be uncomfortable for both parties.

While most of the conference will likely be devoted to a discussion of evaluation results, some attention should be given appropriate follow-up action and preliminary planning for the next evaluation cycle.

EVALUATION PROCEDURES

Reporting Relationships

The general rule is that the administrator's immediate supervisor serves as the primary evaluator because it is assumed that the latter will have the most direct knowledge about the administrator's performance. The organizational structure of the school system may dictate who will evaluate whom. There should be no doubt, however, who will serve as primary evaluator. A few simple guidelines may be useful in making these determinations.

    a.   The person directly supervising the administrator should serve as the primary evaluator.

    b.   Wherever possible an administrator should have only one primary evaluator.

    c.   Each primary evaluator should not have an excessive number of evaluatees. A ratio of 10-12 evaluatees per primary evaluator is an optimum number.

d. If the organizational structure calls for an administrator to report to more than one supervisor, it is essential that evaluator roles be clearly defined. It is preferable to designate one as the primary and the other as a consulting evaluator.

Frequency of Evaluations

Normally administrators are evaluated annually. Sometimes, a rotation plan is prescribed by which administrators in their first three to five years of service are evaluated annually. Thereafter, they are evaluated periodically as long as their performance is regarded as being satisfactory or higher. Those whose performance is judged to be below the satisfactory level are evaluated annually until performance becomes satisfactory.

Use of Goals and Objectives

Most competency-based evaluation programs utilize goals and objectives in the pursuance of improvement in performance. Where school systems establish district goals annually, it is not uncommon for administrators and supervisors to develop performance improvement plans that include district-wide, departmental, and individual goals and objectives.

Perception Inventories

Some school systems are beginning to use perception inventories, completed by subordinates, to convey to administrators how their performance is perceived by those whom they supervise. An instrument is developed that will cover items which subordinates may be able to provide very useful information that will enable the administrator to "see self as subordinates sees him/her." Usually, the use of a perception inventory is optional — not mandatory. A supervisor might urge an administrator to use the instrument, however.

Subordinates would fill out the inventories without signing them and all responses would be combined into a composite report. This summary can be best used in Step 1 of the evaluation process when the status of current performance is being reviewed.

IMPLEMENTATION OF PROGRAM

Most successful administrator evaluation programs are developed co-operatively by a committee of administrative and supervisory personnel, representative of all categories which will be affected by the program. Such a committee has a dual responsibility: (a) to develop sound procedures and

(b) to concern itself with the introduction and implementation of the program.

It is essential that the board of education and top administration of the school system are kept aware of developments, as the program is being formulated. It is also a wise practice to have the board adopt the procedures before they are introduced to the staff.

It isn't sufficient just to develop a good program; introducing and implementing it is just as important. It should be recognized that some administrators and supervisors may have apprehensions and negative feelings about being evaluated by a competency-based program. These feelings can be honest and sincere and should be accepted as such. The evaluation process should be discussed candidly. Its purposes should be clarified and potential advantages both to the person being evaluated and the school system should be pointed out.

The process must be explained thoroughly. Any misconceptions should be cleared up. Copies of the evaluation procedures should be provided all persons affected by them. Above all, established procedures must be adhered to. "Free-lancing" is an unwise practice.

Integrity should be made the cornerstone of all evaluator-evaluatee interactions. A high trust level is absolutely essential and it is created by example more than by exhortation.

Patience is imperative. It takes time to build a conducive climate in evaluation relationships and to make the program operate smoothly.

A CONCLUDING COMMENT

In many respects, the supervisor can perform a Pygmalion-like role in working with administrative and supervisory staff members. Some supervisors treat their subordinates in a manner that leads to greater achievement and productivity. On the other hand, others treat their assistants in ways that lead to lower performance than they are capable of achieving. It is largely a matter of expectations – high expectations tend to generate high productivity. Low expectations often cause a low level of performance. The implication of this observation for the evaluation process is self-evident. If supervisors expect top-level performance and work with their assistants in ways to attain it, the likelihood is that it will occur.

APPENDIX

POSITION DESCRIPTION

Name/Administrator:	John Doe
Position Held:	Department Head (Guidance)
Work Location:	XYZ High School
Supervisor (Evaluator)	High School Principal
Persons Supervised:	Guidance Personnel
Major Function:	Provide, under direction of principal, supervision and give direction to the guidance/counseling services for the high school and work with teaching personnel in their efforts to contribute to the guidance program.

Specific Responsibilities:

A. ORGANIZATIONAL DUTIES
1. Provide part-time departmental services.
2. Perform part-time counseling responsibilities.
3. Carry out such other duties as assigned.

B. COMMUNICATIONS
1. Provide an on-going information program to create public awareness of the services and activities of the counseling program including:
   (a) Career programs
   (b) College night
   (c) Honor assembly
   (d) Student/parent orientation meeting

C. PERSONNEL
1. Assist principal in selection and placement of new guidance personnel.
2. Conduct orientation for new personnel.
3. Conduct observations of guidance personnel.
4. Make recommendations regarding re-employment.
5. Make recommendations regarding advancement on salary schedule.
6. Make recommendations regarding dismissals.
7. Plan, organize, and manage departmental meetings.
8. Plan and conduct inservice activities.

D. PUPIL SERVICES
1. Assist principal with student registration.
2. Assist principal in preparation and organization of materials for course registration and class selection.
3. Maintain an on-going program to keep students, parents, teachers, and administrative personnel informed on the status of each student.

Terms of Employment: 10½ months contract

Evaluation: In accordance with established policies and procedures governing the evaluation of administrative personnel.

PERFORMANCE IMPROVEMENT PLAN

DIRECTIONS: List below the objectives chosen to respond to identified needs and indicate the activities to achieve them. Use the third column to report results attained. Encircle the appropriate symbol and supplement it with supporting comments and recommendations. (Use separate page for more space.) Symbols: FA=Fully Achieved; PA=Partially Achieved; NA= Not Achieved. Column three is filled out by the Administrator.

Objective/s/	Action Plan	Results Achieved
		FA PA NA
		FA PA NA
		FA PA NA
		FA PA NA

Review by Evaluator (Check)
☐ Concur
☐ Disagree
    Comments.

Signatures:

Administrator _____

Evaluator _____

Date/Conference _____

(Signatures indicate that conference was held, not necessarily concurrence)

Use additional page for comments.

PERFORMANCE CRITERIA (*)

A. *Problem Analysis* Ability to seek out relevant data and analyze complex information to determine the important elements of a problem situation; searching for information with a purpose.

B. *Judgment* Skill in identifying educational needs and setting priorities; ability to reach logical conclusions and make high-quality decisions based on available information; ability to evaluate critically written communications.

C. *Organizational Ability* Ability to plan, schedule, and control the work of others, skill in using resources in an optimal fashion, ability to deal with a volume of paper work and heavy demands on one's time.

D. *Decisiveness* Ability to recognize when a decision is required and to act quickly. (Without an assessment of the quality of the decision.)

E. *Leadership* Ability to recognize when a group requires direction, to get others involved in solving problems, to interact effectively with a group, to guide it to the accomplishment of a task.

F. *Sensitivity* Ability to perceive the needs, concerns, and personal problems of others, tact in dealing with persons from different backgrounds; skill in resolving conflicts, ability to deal effectively with people concerning emotional issues; knowing what information to communicate and to whom.

G. *Range of Interests* Competence to discuss a variety of subjects (educational, political, economic, etc.): desire to participate actively in events.

H. *Personal Motivation* Showing that work is important to personal satisfaction; a need to achieve in all activities attempted, ability to be self-policing.

I. *Educational Values* Possession of well-reasoned educational philosophy; receptiveness to change and new ideas.

J. *Stress Tolerance* Ability to perform under pressure and opposition; ability to think on one's feet.

K. *Oral Communication Skills* Ability to make a clear oral presentation of ideas and facts.

L. *Written Communication Skills* Ability to express ideas clearly in writing, to write appropriately for different audiences, students, teachers, parents, colleagues, and other administrators.

(*) Adapted and used with permission of The National Association of Secondary School Principals, *NASSP* Bulletin, Vol. 61, No. 410, September 1977, pp. 81-82. *(Author's note.)*

EVALUATION REPORT

DIRECTIONS: Supervisor (evaluator), using the rating scale shown below, encircle the number that best represents the effectiveness of the administrator's performance on each of the performance criteria. Use the lower part of the page for comments and recommendations.

Rating Scale:

```
     5    4    3    2    1
     |    |    |    |    |
   High            Low
```

Performance Criteria	Evaluation
A. Problem Analysis	5 4 3 2 1
B. Judgment	5 4 3 2 1
C. Organizational Ability	5 4 3 2 1
D. Decisiveness	5 4 3 2 1
E. Leadership	5 4 3 2 1
F. Sensitivity	5 4 3 2 1
G. Range of Interests	5 4 3 2 1
H. Personal Motivation	5 4 3 2 1
I. Educational Values	5 4 3 2 1
J. Stress Tolerance	5 4 3 2 1
K. Oral Communication Skills	5 4 3 2 1
L. Written Communication Skills	5 4 3 2 1

Comments and Recommendations

SIGNATURE: Administrator: _____

Evaluator: _____

Date/Evaluation Conference: _____

COPIES:
1st-Personnel
2nd-Admin.
3rd-E'uator.

PERCEPTION INVENTORY

DIRECTIONS: This optional inventory may be used by the Administrator to obtain from those supervised viewpoints regarding their perceptions about his/her performance with reference to the items listed below. The respondent need NOT sign the inventory. *Scoring key:* 5=Always; 4=Most of the time; 3=Usually; 2=Sometimes; 1=Rarely; 0=Not sure.

Performance Factors	Assessment (Encircle)
1. Recognizes achievements of staff	5 4 3 2 1 0
2. Shows concern for staff morale	5 4 3 2 1 0
3. Works well with staff	5 4 3 2 1 0
4. Promotes cooperative working relationships	5 4 3 2 1 0
5. Leads by example	5 4 3 2 1 0
6. Utilizes skills and talents of subordinates	5 4 3 2 1 0
7. Demonstrates efficient management skills	5 4 3 2 1 0
8. Shows flexibility in dealing with staff members	5 4 3 2 1 0
9. Deals fairly and equitably with staff members	5 4 3 2 1 0
10. Shows sensitivity in human relations	5 4 3 2 1 0
11. Supports subordinates in their decisions	5 4 3 2 1 0
12. Is respected by subordinates	5 4 3 2 1 0
13. Keeps self available to staff members	5 4 3 2 1 0
14. Communicates well with staff members	5 4 3 2 1 0
15. Handles pressure well	5 4 3 2 1 0

Strongest Qualities:

Weakest Qualities:

PLEASE DO NOT SIGN FORM

Management by Objectives Can Be Meaningful For School Administrators, Others

J. I. Durham

J. I. Durham attempts to apply the principles of management by objectives to the school business office, so that every member of the office "is involved in the exchange of thoughts related to his individual job as well as the total output from this office." Establishing goals, writing job descriptions, and determining a plan of action and a timetable are among the author's recommendations as he sets out a number of guidelines for use in putting such a program for evaluation into effect. Mr. Durham, now retired, was formerly Assistant Superintendent for Business in the Hinsdale, Illinois, Public Schools.

The theory of managing by objectives has been in effect for a long time but the application of these fundamentals to the school business office is worth exploration and consideration.

In the current pressures of negotiation for salaries of the certified personnel the business administrator finds himself forced to put a lot of his time into coping with problems created in this area. He also is forced to cope with pressures arising from demands of non-certificated staff members. As the salaries of the non-certified staff increase it becomes apparent that there is also a need for an improved method of staff evaluation.

It has been my experience that evaluations for non-certified staff are for the most part superficial and of little constructive value to the employee or to the employer. The staff members often feel that little or no attention is given to their needs, their job performance or their improvement.

This lack of communication would be a primary concern for the business administrator. A basic need exists for improvement of communications between all staff members and supervisory personnel. The improvement of relationships and productivity should be a concern to all.

Such improvement can only occur when staff and supervisory personnel are concerned with what they seeking to accomplish. Each has a specific role to play in the improvement pattern. That role must be determined and a course plotted to improve results and encourage personal growth and productivity. Therefore, a system must be developed whereby every member of the business office is involved in the exchange of thoughts related to his individual job as well as the total output from this office.

The only logical approach is to involve all members of the business office staff in a systematic plan to implement and evaluate the results. There is a need for an analysis of what is expected of a job and how the best results can be obtained. Contributions from the employees are interlaced with guidelines from the supervisor.

As the procedure unfolds through co-operative planning, the business administrator must keep in view the whole plan and whole picture so that each segment may be developed in its appropriate significance. This can be an orderly procedure by establishing goals as objectives for improvement.

In organizing or re-organizing the business office, careful attention must be given to utilize the strengths and abilities of each person into areas where he may make his most complete contribution. For this reason, it must be assumed that planning for a goals program will include provisions for the individual to set personal goals so that they represent a commitment on his part.

Identify Problems

Problem situations may arise as they often do when one is dealing with personalities. In dealing with problem situations each problem must be identified without regard to personal opinions, emotional reaction, or preconceived ideas. The ultimate solutions must deal strictly with the facts of the situation in a manner that will insure the most success as well as the greatest contributions so that the continuation of the productive organization will be improved. It must be understood and is essential that placement of personnel in a supervisory or management position must be done in such a manner as to insure that continuity is maintained. Continued improvement through planned cooperative endeavor should be a high priority goal for the Business Office. The individual, the group, and the entire Business Office can be more effective when the desired expectations and needs are understood by all.

All persons involved are managers — managers of their specific responsibility and should strive to improve and develop their contributions. Appraisal of these contributions is absolutely essential to determine attainment. Commitment on the part of the business office staff is essential. Accountability becomes an outgrowth of this technique.

When all these facets are established the pay structure should become established within the goals and their achievement.

Goals can be established for working relationships within the office or outside groups for self improvement and professional growth. Attention to strengthen the weak areas needs to be recognized and coped with.

Goals Are Personal

The individual, therefore, needs to base his own goals upon his own personal assessment of needs. Once the goals are established develop the plan of action for accomplishing them. Regular meetings and conferences that lead to modifications and changes may take place. This flexibility prevents hopeless frustrations that could evolve out of a selection of unrealistic goals.

To achieve a workable goals program the machinery set up must be closely observed and carefully steered to achieve the desired results.

What is a goal? Here are five as a start for business administrators to contemplate:

1. Regular responsibilities for himself and subordinates.
2. Improvement of methods, systems, procedures.
3. Improvement of relationships with other organizations as well as with parts of the Business Office.
4. Up-grading and development of subordinates.
5. Self development — supervisor and subordinate.

The first step in a goals oriented Business Office is a job description for each employee. This should be the out-growth of a job description written by the employee as well as a job description written for the same position by the supervisor. A study should be made of these descriptions and a composite job description should be the ultimate result. This should eliminate future misunderstanding related to the duties of any job.

After job descriptions are completed there should be meaningful discussions between the supervisor and each one doing the job. Each person doing the job should establish, through a systematic approach, measurable goals for his area of responsibility. As these goals are discussed the supervisor should stress the improvement of individual performances within the framework of the goals.

The objectives of such a discussion are to set up conditions that enable established goals to be achieved and sustained.

Plans of Action

The accomplishment of these goals should be achieved within a given period of time. This is important to the success of any goal program. Attention to and interest in any goal diminishes if the time is too long. Set forth a plan of action, a timetable, an evaluation point and a meeting time to analyze and discuss the progress with each employee. Show facts and information by which the accomplishment is measurable.

There are specific benefits to be expected from such a program. The total process is geared to achieve desired results. Solutions are provided to the many problems of combining the major area of responsibility. There is enhancement of the possibility of obtaining coordinated efforts. There is a meaningful way of measuring time contribution of management and professional personnel. There should be an elimination of the need for meeting changes in personalities when there are personnel changes.

Guidelines for supervisor for working with the subordinate who is turning in his goals and plan for evaluation:

1. List major areas of responsibilities for subordinate.
2. What are the goals for the year as listed?
3. How realistic are these goals?
4. Are these goals challenging?
5. Can performance be measured?
6. Are the target dates to accomplish these goals set forth?

Guidelines for the subordinate to use in preparing for a discussion of his work with his supervisor:

1. Major area of responsibility or responsibilities.
2. Description of goals — what you expect to accomplish.
3. Time Table.
4. How do you measure achievement toward goal?

Suggestions for Preparing Manager Responsibilities.

1. Identify the major work areas wherein the Business Manager should expect to achieve results. List briefly the order of significance. Use only nouns.
2. Omit qualifying adjectives.
3. Do not combine two major responsibilities.
4. Keep your list of major responsibilities to less than ten. Greater efficiency is affected for subsequent use.
5. Give careful attention to the responsibility of development for relationship with others.
6. Develop separate responsibility for:
    a. Self development
    b. Development of subordinate personnel
7. Be sure to place the most important responsibility at the top of the list. Be realistic — actually this is a first step in self-evaluation.

Goals are end results to be achieved within a scheduled period of time. The following are suggestions in preparing a list of goals:

1. Set a goal for each identified responsibility. Allow for exceptions. If sufficient data or experience is not available to set a meaning-goal it is advisable to set a different goal. The goal should not be too easy or too difficult but it should be challenging.
2. State the goals in terms of end results anticipated.
3. Be sure goals are challenging enough to force each person to extend himself.
4. State the goals precisely.
5. Be sure the goals are measurable. The more measurable the better.
6. Conditions for attainment of goals may not be completely under the control of the subordinate. However, it is advisable to set the goals with this in mind and endeavor to reach them.
7. Do not let planning difficulties inhibit or restrain you from participation.

SUGGESTED TIME TABLE

Time	Action
Begin goals program	Prepare goals lists
	Subordinate prepares list
	Management review
End of each quarter	Review program
	Subordinate and management review program together
	Discuss problems
	Consider plan modification if failure seems imminent. Be reasonable and open-minded
End of year	Annual program review
	Subordinate prepares detailed program report
	Management & Subordinate:
	Review progress
	Discuss problems
	Consider methods of improvement
	Prepare new goals
	Evaluate what has been accomplished

Systemic Appraisal of Educational Leadership Personnel

Joseph W. Licata

Believing that teacher assessments of the performance of principals are helpful to the latter, Joseph W. Licata describes how such assessments can be done both efficaciusly and with confidentiality. He lists and examines a number of propositions dealing with such concepts as the use of "external observers," the use of developmental conferences involving a trio of persons, the creation of a development plan articulated in terms of performance objectives, the actual evaluation (as opposed to development) process, and the Principal Performance Description Survey (PPDS). In this excerpt, the author presents a number of graphs and forms (some designed by Chad Ellett, Vice President of Performance Assessment Systems, Inc., Athens, Georgia) that will assist in the implementation of his "systemic appraisal" process that relates professional development to evaluation. Dr. Licata is Associate Professor of the Academic Faculty of Education Administration and of the Senior Faculty of the Mershon Center at Ohio State University, Columbus.

1.1   Teacher Assessments

The professional development appraisal subsystem or cycle begins with a diagnostic scanning of the principal's performance based on subordinate or teacher ratings. The assessments would be conducted at regular intervals, quarterly, biannually or annually by the principals themselves or by a central data gathering source in the school district with the trust of all involved. For instance, principals could select a data collector in their schools to distribute and collect the assessment instruments. The data collector would be someone that teachers know will maintain their anonymity and that principals know will keep the assessments confidential. Once all instruments are completed, the data collector returns them to the principal unscored. The principal scores the instruments and builds the diagnostic profile. In this way, only the principal knows the findings and only the principal owns the data.

The data could also be collected by a central agency, e.g., principals' association, a leadership academy, a special central office unit, a regional services center like BOCES in New York. While this organizational pattern has some advantages such as a centralized data base and reduced paperwork for principals, the principals would have to be assured that the data on specific princiapls would never be shared with their superiors or the public at large. Whether teacher data is collected in a centralized fashion or by principals themselves, the point is that such data collection can be organized to provide accurate, helpful and confidential diagnostic profiles for professional development.

Yes, the gathering of teacher data may be initially threatening, perhaps even controversial. Many principals would argue that teachers are not an accurate source of information about administrative performance. Some would argue that the administration of organizational sanctions inevitably causes certain hostility that might negatively bias these data. In fact, it may well be that those principals that are just in the administration of sanctions, sooner or later will disappoint or anger everyone in their organization rather than a select group. While there is evidence to suggest that teacher assessments of the principals' performance do relate significantly to school climate and certain school outcomes,[1] many principals and supervisors of principals may always doubt the legitimacy of these assessments. For this reason, the teacher data is considered tentative. Anything suggested by teacher assessments of their principal is always subordinate to direct observations of the principal's performance by selected observers with administrative or leadership expertise.

1.2 Self-Assessment of Teacher Data

The diagnostic profile produced by teacher ratings of the principal's performance would include comparison of various dimensions of performance or comparison of individual performance with the average performance of all principals in the district.[2] After completing a personal profile, each principal could send an anonymous copy of his or her profile scores to each principal in the district. Identities would be hidden, yet averages could be determined. If a central agency were collecting the data, the agency could easily compute these averages and supply them as part of the entire profile package. From these comparisons, principals can make tentative decisions about areas of strength or weakness upon which they wish to focus appraisal and development activities. For instance, a principal noting weak ratings on instructional leadership skills as compared to other performance areas and average ratings of principals in the district, might wish to set up observation and subsequent development in this area.

1.3 Self-initiated External Observation

In a recent study of the principalship, principals tended to interact informally with other principals they thought had specific expertise about the principalship as well as demonstrated ability to maintain the confidentiality of the interaction.[3] This set of findings may be relevant to the means by which a principal initiates external observation. Two issues appear to become important in such a step. "Who shall do the observation?" or "What are the necessary characteristics of the observers?" and "What observation tools will be employed by the observers?" While possible instruments for the entire syscemic appraisal system will be discussed later in this text, it may be helpful to focus on the essential characteristics of observers as a way of describing the principals' responsibilities in initiating external observation. Toward this general purpose, let's consider some theoretical propositions:[4]

P1: As an external observer's understanding of the contextual idiosyncrasy of a leader's system increases, so does the leader's confidence in the accuracy of the observer's appraisals of the leader's performance.

P2 The more an external observer's status characteristics (expertise) render him/her more capable of appraising the performance of the leader than the leader him/herself, the more confidence the leader is likely to have in the accuracy of the observer's appraisals.

In other words, in order for outside opinions about the principal's performance to have an impact on that principal's self perceptions and future behavior, the observers must be viewed by that principal as understanding his/her particular work context or role and be seen as being better qualified to appraise that principal's performance than the principal him/ herself. For example, a principal who as a result of teacher assessments and personal perceptions feels the need to appraise his/her pupil personnel skills might try to organize a three-person observation team composed of the following types of individuals: (1) another principal in the system with a thorough understanding of what it is like to be a principal in that district and a reputation of exemplary performance with respect to pupil personnel services, (2) a university professor familiar with that particular type of work context and expert in pupil personnel services, and (3) the principal being observed.[5]

P3: There is an inverse relationship between the number of prior expectations held by the external observer for the leader's performance and the amount of confidence the leader has in the accuracy of the observer's appraisals of the leader's performance.

The principal must select observers, as P3 notes, that have relatively few expectations (positive or negative) for the principal's behavior. To select a person who knows and in the past has either positively or negatively evaluated that principal's performance, may present the principal with doubts about the objectivity and accuracy of the observers' appraisals. While it may be impossible to always recruit total strangers, the principal's avoidance of those individuals who have a reputation for an inability to control prejudgements about performance is probably a wise strategy.

> P4: As the leader's trust in the observer's ability to keep his/her appraisals of the leader's performance confidential increases, so does the leader's willingness to accept the observer as part of the appraisal process.

The characteristic of confidentiality in the relationship between principal and observer is crucial to maintaining the nonthreatening dimensions of this part of the appraisal system. As noted earlier, principals routinely interact with peers they trust to maintain confidentiality.[6] In organizing the observations, the principal should emphasize the need for confidentiality.

Further, in organizing the external observation process, the principal should necessarily advise observers about times, places, areas of concern to which they can give intense consideration. This could probably be accomplished over the phone or in an initial meeting of the observation team. If necessary, training in the use of the observation instruments can be arranged. Recall, throughout this process, the principal is the initiator and organizer of the external observations.

1.4 External Observation

The actual observation of the principal's performance or the products of performance constitute the next step in the developmental appraisal subsystem. The observers should observe independently of each other, observers and observations can be spread over a week, or a month. The important aspect of these observations is the need to access multiple sources of data, e.g., interviews with various groups, documents, student achievement and attendance records. In gaining access to this information, the observers might consider the following propositions:

> P5: As the leader's (and significant other's) trust in the observer's ability to keep his/her appraisals of the leader's performance confidential increases, so does the observer's access to information essential to accurate appraisal of the leader's performance.

> P6: As the observer's access to information increases, so does the quantity and quality of the data available in the appraisal of the leader's performance.

As noted previously, the ability of an observer to maintain

confidentiality and the subsequent trust of the principal may be a crucial observer characteristic, crucial not only to initial selection but also for access to data. Not only is it important that this be true of the observer – principal relationship, but it must be true with respect to the relationship between observers and members of the principal's organization. Nothing will increase the intensity of social defense mechanisms among teachers and others in the school more than the presence of a stranger asking questions. If observers are to be effective, the principal must prepare his/her organizational members for the visitors, testify to the observers' trustworthiness, inform organization members of the visits, and assure organizational members that their cooperation is needed and appreciated.

1.5 Developmental Conference

Once observations are completed and the observers have summarized the data and their thoughts, a developmental conference should be scheduled. Each observer must be present and the meeting should be held in a place that provides for a lack of interruption. The purposes of the conference are to give feedback and make recommendations for personal and professional development of the principal based on this feedback. The interaction might best be explained in terms of the following propositions:

P7: As the quality and quantity of the data used in the appraisal of the leader's performance increases, so does the leader's confidence in the observers' appraisals of the leader's performance.

P8: The more the observers' appraisals of the leader tend to focus on status characteristics (expertise) which favorably differentiate the observers from the leader, the more confidence the leader is likely to have in the accuracy of the observers' appraisals of the leader's performances.

The conference involves the principal and two external observers both of whom are perceived by the principal as having more expertise than the principal him/herself with respect to the targated areas of observation. The principal has the responsibility of determining the nature of the data and data sources the observers used to complete their appraisals, and to keep the observers' comments focused on those topics about which the observers can give expert advice and feedback. If these conditions are met, the following predictions or propositions might be helpful in understanding the subsequent interaction:

P9: In the conference, if both observers make a similar or congruent appraisal of the leader's performance, the leader will tend to agree with that appraisal and respond appropriately in terms of personal and professional development.

P10: In the conference, if the observers make differnt appraisals of the leader's performance the leader will tend to distribute agreement between the observers and value these appraisals less than appraisals that have unanimous agreement (particularly in planning for personal and professional development).

Triad social interaction and the tendency toward coalition development is well known in the social sciences;[7] interaction patterns in the developmental conference would probably be similar. Given two observers or interactors that the principal believes are better able to appraise his performance than the principal him/herself, on those occasions in which both observers agree on a particular appraisal, the principal is likely to agree also. Even in the face of disagreement between the observers, the principal's agreement with either would produce appraisal decision. Clearly, in terms of the latter, the disagreement of "experts" may well diminish the value and impact of that appraisal for development programming. These tendencies produce definitive decisions as well as decisions about needs that allow for the development of priorities.

In the developmental conference, the principal should take the leadership role, asking each observer to share assessments of performance, item by item. Once each observer has shared his/her perception, the principal would share his personal assessment and compare and contrast it to those of the observers. The process of developing generalizations about needs should be inductive in nature. Attempts at generalization should be reserved until all specific appraisals have been discussed. Discussion should be noncritical, allowing participants to express their opinions openly and without threat of rebuttal. Critical analysis of the data should take place at the end of the meeting. At this time, a general diagnostic profile serves as the central product of the meeting and the basis for personal and professional development.

1.6 Developmental Program

The principal would apply diagnostic data generated by the external observers to the creation of a development plan. The plan might best be articulated in terms of performance objectives.[8] These objectives would state conditions or learning alternatives, expected outcomes and criteria for successful completion. The school district might consider the development of an access capability to identify various relevant learning alternatives, critiques by previous users, and programmed learning systems. Ideally, if a central data bank was available, cumulative data from diagnostic profiles could be used to evaluate resources listed or held in the center.

Over a specific time period, the principal would implement this development plan by taking courses, reading, counseling with others or whatever activities the plan specifies. The broken line in figure 1 moving from 1.2 to 1.6 notes the possibility that teacher assessment data might be available during the duration of the development plan. If this is the case, the principal might simply use these data as a partial feedback mechanism and modify or continue the plan accordingly. The principal always has the option of moving to external observation (1.2 to 1.3) or developmental programming after teacher assessment (1.2 to 1.6).

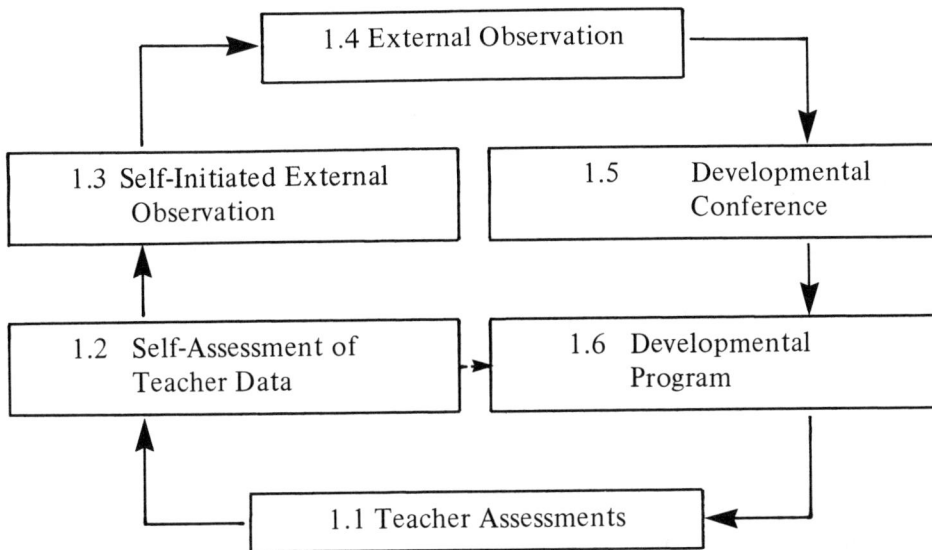

Figure 1. Professional Development Subsystem for School Administrators.

Evaluation

Since there is almost always an inherent threat involved in evaluation, the propositions (P1-P10) relevant to development might not initially appear applicable to the evaluation process. Certainly, during evaluation, the evaluator would be subject to a degree of defensiveness and data access would be limited to a greater extent that it would be as part of the development process. Often, the evaluator would hold prior expectations for a principal's behavior.

Keeping these considerations in mind, it would probably be a mistake to abandon the propositions just because they may be harder to apply in evaluation. Those doing evaluation appraisal must possess the same kinds of characteristics noted in the propositions presented above, i.e., contextual knowledge, specific expertise, a reduced number of prior expectations and the trust of those being observed. Those doing evaluations must work to establish this credibility among those being evaluated. With systemic appraisal, organizations that place people with questionable credibility in evaluator positions can no longer afford such luxury. Hopefully, systemic appraisal will provide an organizational mechanism to hinder the "Peter Principle" circumstance that sometimes allows the least able to move to evaluation or supervisory positions.

With systemic appraisal patterns, development concentrates on those same dimensions of professional performance that evaluation addresses. Since the principal's immediate superior or supervisor knows that appraisal for development is being employed in the development subsystem, evaluation is the central issue. The supervisor makes "no bones about it," the supervisor evaluates performance and distributes rewards and incentives accordingly. There is no need to experience the development — evaluation role conflict.

If the principal chooses to use the evaluation as a cross-check of the development appraisal results he/she owns, fine, but the purpose of the evaluation subsystem remains solely in the realm of producing data by which the organization can make personnel decisions. While this may seem rather harsh and final, participants would soon note the absence of development — evaluation tension. Further, the system would also be systemically related to a grievance subsystem to resolve possible disputes between supervisor and principal through the process.

Figure 2 presents a diagram of the evaluation subsystem. It mirrors the development subsystem configuration and uses the same teacher assessment data employed in the development subsystem. In essence, 1.1 in the development cycle is in part 2.1 in the evaluation cycle. This is the point of systemic linkage between the two subsystems which will be discussed later.

2.1 Teacher Assessments

Instead of receiving specific teacher assessment data on each principal or a copy of each principal's diagnostic profile, the principals' immediate supervisor receives a district-wide profile based on principal "averages."

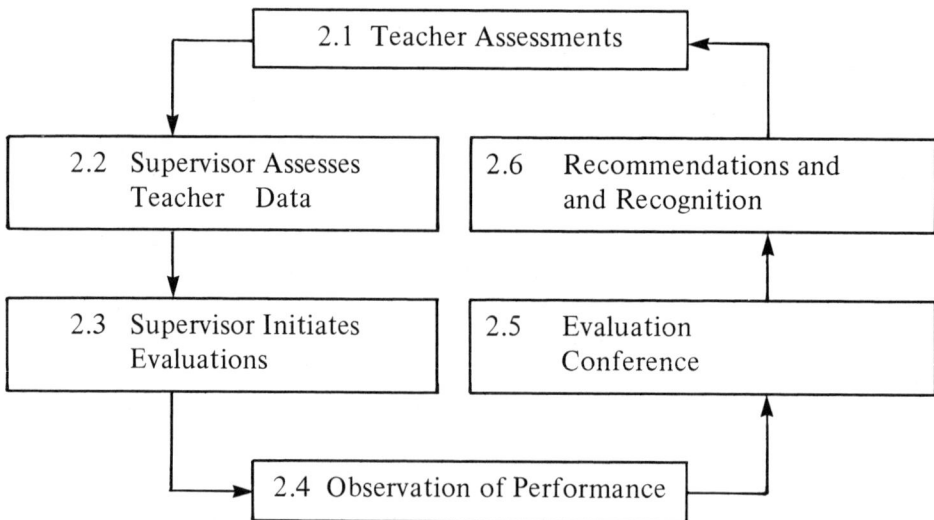

Figure 2. Professional Evaluation Subsystem for School Administrators.

The diagnostic profile would tell the supervisor about teachers' perceptions of the "average" principal in the district. To compute such a profile, principals would have to anonymously send the supervisor the numerical information used in computing scores for the individual profiles (an averaging of averages would not be sufficient). Ideally, this district-wide diagnostic profile would include various measures of central tendency and comparisons with assessments done at other times. If a central data bank existed in the system, the paperwork for the supervisor could be decreased. The purpose of this diagnostic profile is to graphically depict district-wide trends that need to be addressed and emphasized in evaluation.

2.2 Supervisor Assesses Teacher Data

Suppose the immediate supervisor notes on the district-wide profile that teachers in the district are relatively dissatisfied with supervisory relationships with respect to school discipline. This variable has the lowest average teacher rating as compared to other variables in the profile. Further, this variable rating appears to be declining over the past five years. On the other hand, instructional leadership skills received relatively positive ratings and these same kinds of ratings have been apparent over the past five years. Based on such information, the immediate supervisor might develop an evaluation strategy to determine whether or not these results could be verified. These areas of interest might be ripe for supervisor use of organizational rewards for excellent performance and incentives to improve questionable performance.

2.3 Supervisor Initiates Evaluations

Once the supervisor develops an evaluation strategy, the supervisor should arrange observations of the principals. These observations would employ the same external observation instruments used in the developmental cycle. The most preferable type of external observation instrumentation would probably focus on products or formal physical evidence of performance.[9] Since the people in the organization may instinctively attempt to defend their principal in the face of a superior's evaluation, data based on testimony may not be as valuable as data based on products. It is this author's experience that teachers will tend to defend a principal against any *outside* evaluation — even if they personally dislike that principal or feel that the principal needs help. This tendency appears to be almost instinctive in nature, simply a cultural reaction to outsiders. Although, the principal should let teachers and others know of the supervisor's visit in advance and ask their cooperation in the evaluation process, one cannot assume such cooperation would necessarily be forthcoming.

2.4 Observation of Performance

Because of the resistance predicted above and in propositions 4 and 5, let's take a closer look at product evaluation emphasis. For instance, examination of a principal's documented plan for teacher supervision, the principal's written evaluations of teacher performance, the documentation of inservice efforts planned for teachers may be better measures of the principal's supervisory skills than teacher or principal testimony. Such instrumentation is available and will be discussed later.

The evaluation process would involve the principal being observed, the principal's immediate supervisor and a third party whose selection and presence would be agreeable to both the principal and the supervisor. This third party would necessarily possess relevant status characteristics, but could not be someone involved in the principal's development appraisal activities. If the supervisor wished to emphasize instructional skills, people with a high degree of expertise in this area might be nominated as possible third-party observers. While this writer can easily think of a rationale for and against the use of a third-party, for field-test purposes, it might be worth experimenting with this form rather than the more traditional one on one, supervisor-principal interaction. The advantage of the third-party presence might be the reduction of problems inherent in an appraisal based on insider perceptions only.

Since the emphasis is on products, it might be helpful for the supervisor to advise each principal in advance of the products needed. This would not necessarily result in principals scrambling around at the last minute to develop products. Recall, these same products are part of the consensual definition of performance that the entire appraisal system addresses. It is quite likely that these products have been part of the principals' development programs in the past and are in place.

2.5 Evaluation Conference

While the introduction of this work seemed to malign evaluation conferences and much of the description to follow will seem similar to those in serendipitous patterns, there is a difference. This conference is based on data about specific performance, performance which is continually in the process of development. The conference is not a lone act of supervision, but part of a system which relates development to evaluation. In effect, principals are evaluated on those things they have been working to improve. Reduced to a degree is the role conflict of traditional evaluation conferences.

The supervisor should ask the principal to complete a self evaluation of the same product evaluation instrument employed in observation. While the principal cannot share the developmental appraisal data he/she owns, this self-evaluation might be an indirect representation of such a data base. The interaction between supervisor and principal should focus on a comparison of the principal's self-evaluation with the supervisor's and the third-party's evaluations, item by item. This process is inductive and generalizations about performance or improved performance should be reserved until all the data is on the table. These generalizations are made solely by the supervisor based on an evaluation profile completed as a result of the conference. Recommendations about subsequent rewards and/or incentives for performance would be made later in the absence of the third party.

2.6 Recommendations and Recognition

One of the main features of systemic appraisal is its ability to distribute organizational rewards and incentives particularistically. In some school districts, regardlesss of evaluation results, everyone receives the same privileges, pay increase and recognition. With systemic appraisal, the supervisor now has a data base by which excellent performance can be rewarded and less effective performance can be identified. What rewards? These are limited only by the organization's resources and its leaders' creativity, e.g., special operating autonomy, funds for innovative programs, recognition or promotion. Necessarily, when all else has failed, the supervisor may need to make a personnel decision to dismiss an individual. However, in doing so, the supervisor and the individual knew in advance what was expected, specified development activities were continuously provided and time to correct problems was made available. As the last arrow in Figure 2 shows, the cycle begins again with new teacher assessments (2.1).

Systemic Linkage

As noted above, the development and evaluation subsystems are systemically related through teacher assessment of the principals' performance. The linkage is more than this operational procedure. Required for such linkage is (1) a consensual definition of effective performance for principals and (2) instrumentation to operationally measure that definition. The two are necessarily interrelated.

Developing Consensus About Performance

As a precondition to systemic appraisal, system participants must develop consensus about a definition of effective practice. The definition necessarily would focus on performance descriptors that could be operationalized in terms of subordinate or teacher perceptions and products of performance. The definition should focus on those things principals *do* in operating an effective school. Operational definitions like, "Works with teachers to identify student needs" are preferable to statements like "Shows enthusiasm for the job." With the former, teacher ratings and a documented needs assessment relevant to students could be employed to substantiate this performance. In the latter, teacher rating might be relevant, but it might be difficult to find a product for "enthusiasm."

There are probably several ways to develop consensus; the delphi technique, the nominal group process and other organizational development processes would seem to be applicable to the task.[10] Everyone involved in appraisal, principals and their immediate supervisors, should be involved in the selection or development of the consensual definition of effective practice.[11] There are three ways to proceed. First, the participants could develop consensus on a general definition of performance such as the one presented in Figure 3. Note the relative simplicity and generality of this

---

Principals in this district must effectively and frequently perform the following as a means of operating an effective school:

1.   Principals must provide leadership with respect to *curriculum and instruction* in their schools.
2.   Principals must administer the *staff personnel* program in their schools.
3.   Principals must administer the *pupil personnel* program in their schools.
4.   Principals must implement *system-wide policies and procedures* in their schools.
5.   Principals must administer the *fiscal management* of their schools.

Figure 3. Sample Consensus Definition

simple definition. From this general definition, a committee of participants and/or consultants would then need to develop more specific, behavior descriptors of what a principal would do to accomplish those things noted in the consensual definition. So that these could be rated and scored in the development of diagnostic profiles, these behavioral descriptors would be linked with scoring scales, i.e., rating each performance on a 1–5 continuum, the higher the score, the better the performance. Because of the number of developmental tasks, this is probably the most complex and difficult means to an operational definition of effective performance.

The second possibility would simply be to tentatively adopt both a conceptual and operational definition that has been previously developed. These definitions might be already in place in the organization or school district adopting systemic appraisal. There may be an instrument already being used to assess the performance of school principals. If it employs behavioral descriptors and has a sound theoretical base, why not use it or adapt it?

Often such definition and instrumentation is not available, particularly for school administrators. If this is the case, the participants should consider the possibility of tentatively adopting or adapting a definition and set of instruments that have already been developed elsewhere. As an example of such instrumentation, the Principal Performance Description Survey (PPDS) provides such a possibility.[12] These instruments measure the principal's performance in terms of teacher perceptions and external observer ratings of the products of performance. The items in the instruments are conceptually based on an extensive review of the literature, time-motion studies of practicing principals and verification by hundreds of practicing professionals. These behaviors or items are known to be related significantly to teacher and student perceptions of school climate and to student achievement and attendance.[13] While these instruments may not be totally congruent with the nature of practice in the principalship from one district to another, this author would argue that there is more in common between these measures and differential practice in the principalship than there is different. Further, these instruments would provide at least a starting point for field-testing and adaption to a specific district. Items might need to be modified, some eliminated, some added, but at least the instrumentation is in hand and consensus can be built through practical trial and error rather than extended theoretical and philosophical disucssions that often lead nowhere.

One other issue needs to be noted relative to consensus building. While consensus should be based on the input of all system participants, there probably needs to be an external cross-check on the consensus building process. Without such a cross-check or devil's advocate role in the process, those involved may overlook new ideas in favor of the status quo. An external consultant or an organizational member whose job it would be to play the devil's advocate could provide input to avoid "watered-down" or inadequate definition of effective performance.

Instrumentation

In place, the consensual definition of effective performance would provide a focus for the development and evaluation subsystems. Principals could employ appraisal and development activities to the same performance definition that evaluation would address. To do this, two operational definitions would be needed to provide measures for the consensual definition of performance. With principals, an instrument to measure teacher perceptions of their principal's performance and an external observation tool to assess the products of principals' performance would need to be developed or identified.

As noted above, the Principals' Performance Description Survey, particularly the teacher form and the external observer form are examples of possible operational definitions. These instruments assess a principal's performance through teacher perceptions of the principal and external observer ratings of the products of the principal's performance. This battery of instruments addresses several functional areas of responsibility, i.e., curriculum and instruction, staff personnel, pupil personnel, system-wide policies and procedures and fiscal management (fiscal management is on the external observer form only). Also, as a way of showing how a consensus definition could be specified operationally, these PPDS measures could be possible examples of the operational measures of the definition noted in Figure 3.

Items on the teacher form of the PPDS ask the respondents to rate both the "effectiveness" and "frequency" with which the principal performs certain tasks in the school. Each item is scored on a 1—5 continuum. The higher the score, the more effective or more frequent the performance is rated by respondents. Since high effectiveness and frequency ratings are known to be related to meaningful school outcome measures,[14] the higher the scores, the better the performance rating. All item scores under each functional area, e.g., curriculum and instruction, are totaled to produce a general measure for that area. Figure 4 presents a sample part of the teacher form of PPDS, specifically from the section on curriculum and instruction responsibilities.[15]

Recall, the teacher form would be used to present a diagnostic profile to each principal to initiate the development cycle. The profile would graphically compare teacher ratings of different functional areas of responsibility with one another or with average scores for all principals in the school district. Figure 5 presents an example of such a diagnostic profile. As part of the evaluation cycle, average teacher ratings for this entire school district on the various functional areas could be compared to one another or average teacher ratings from the most recent assessment can be compared to assessments done at other times. Figure 6 presents an example of a district-wide profile which the principal's immediate supervisor can use in planning an evaluation strategy. These profiles would serve as the systemic linkage between development and evaluation subsystems. In essence, principals will be working on the very same thing that their immediate supervisor will be observing during evaluation.

The external observer form of the PPDS focuses on observed evidence or products of a principal's performance. Each performance descriptor or item on this form must be substantiated in terms of a scale ranging from "informal" to "product (formal)" evidence of performance. Again, items measure a principal's performance in terms of the same five functional areas of responsibility that are addressed in the teacher form of the PPDS. A sample item and response scale that an external observer or evaluator might employ during appraisal is presented on page 296.[16]

PERFORMANCE STATEMENT SHEET

RATING SCALE

Frequency With Which Principal Performs Task	Effectiveness With Which Principal Performs Task

1   2   3   4   5
NEVER   VERY
                       OFTEN
	1 2 3 4 5
	INEFFECTIVE VERY
	                       EFFECTIVE

CURRICULUM AND INSTRUCTION

1. Evaluates the instructional climate by observing in the classroom.

2. Works with teachers in formulating grading practices and procedures.

3. Encourages teachers to consider individual differences when evaluating student performance and progress.

4. Discusses changes in the educational program with teachers.

5. Encourages teachers to work together in planning and modifying the curriculum.

6. Informs teachers of general teaching practices and skills for which they are responsible.

7. Encourages teachers to try new and innovative teaching methods in helping the consistently failing student.

8. Discusses problems of consistently failing students with teachers.

9. Discusses classroom goals and procedures with teachers.

10. Works with teachers in understanding and using results of the school testing program.

11. Plans a variety of instructional programs to meet individual learner needs.

12. Works with curriculum committees to establish educational goals of the school.

13. Works with faculty committees to review curriculum content and organization.

14. Works with teachers in establishing student performance standards.

15. Works with teachers in evaluating the classroom instructional climate.

FIGURE 4. Sample part of the PPDS teacher form.

1. Keeps information about new research and methods in education on-hand for personal and staff use.

Source	NA	Informal	Input	Process	Product
_____	_____	1	2	3	4

Product Description _____

_____

Let's assume a principal is being interviewed by one of the external observers he/she has selected for the development cycle or the principal's immediate supervisor during the evaluation cycle (each using this external observer instrument). Once rapport is established and a general explanation of the procedure and how it is to be administered has taken place, the interview and observations may begin. While there are specific interview or observation questions on the form, the observer is not restricted to only questions on the form in trying to determine the meaning of the principal's response.

Scoring of each item or question involves the following procedure. If the respondent identifies another individual in the school who has responsibility for a given performance (e.g., secretary, an assistant, a department chairman, etc.), this person is to be noted in the space provided under "source." These persons are to be interviewed later. If the respondent understands the question but states that it is not applicable to principal's job description in that district, the observer checks the space under NA and proceeds to the next question or item.

Recall that in the process of producing a product score, the scale varies from 1 – INFORMAL to 4 – PRODUCT. If the respondent agreed that he performs a particular behavior, but could not provide the external observer with direct observable evidence, but claims it is done informally, he/she is given a score of 1 for the INFORMAL category. If he/she had on hand materials relevant to a particular performance, but had done nothing with them, e.g., personality profiles for students that had never been used in assessing student needs, the observer scores a 2 for INPUT. If, in the observer's judgment the respondent was in the process of carrying out a particular performance beyond the input stage, e.g., asking teachers to critique personality profiles before use in policy making he/she is given a score of 3 for PROCESS. The highest score of 4 for PRODUCT is given for only directly observable evidence relevent to a specific criterion or procedure beyond the process stage.[17]

Under the product scale is an open-ended section entitled "Product Description." The observer is to use this section to note any and all informal

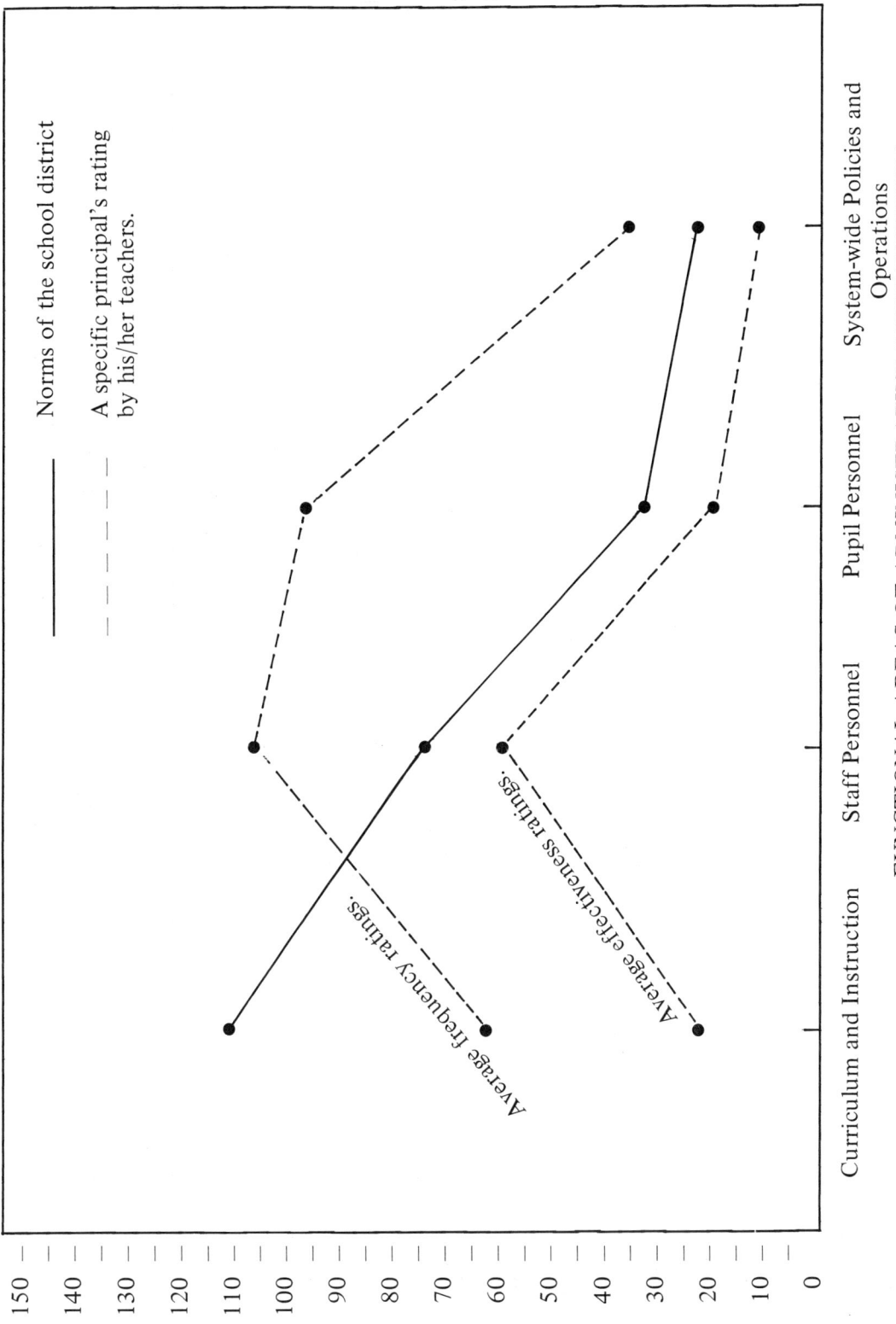

FIGURE 5. Sample diagnostic profile based on teacher ratings.

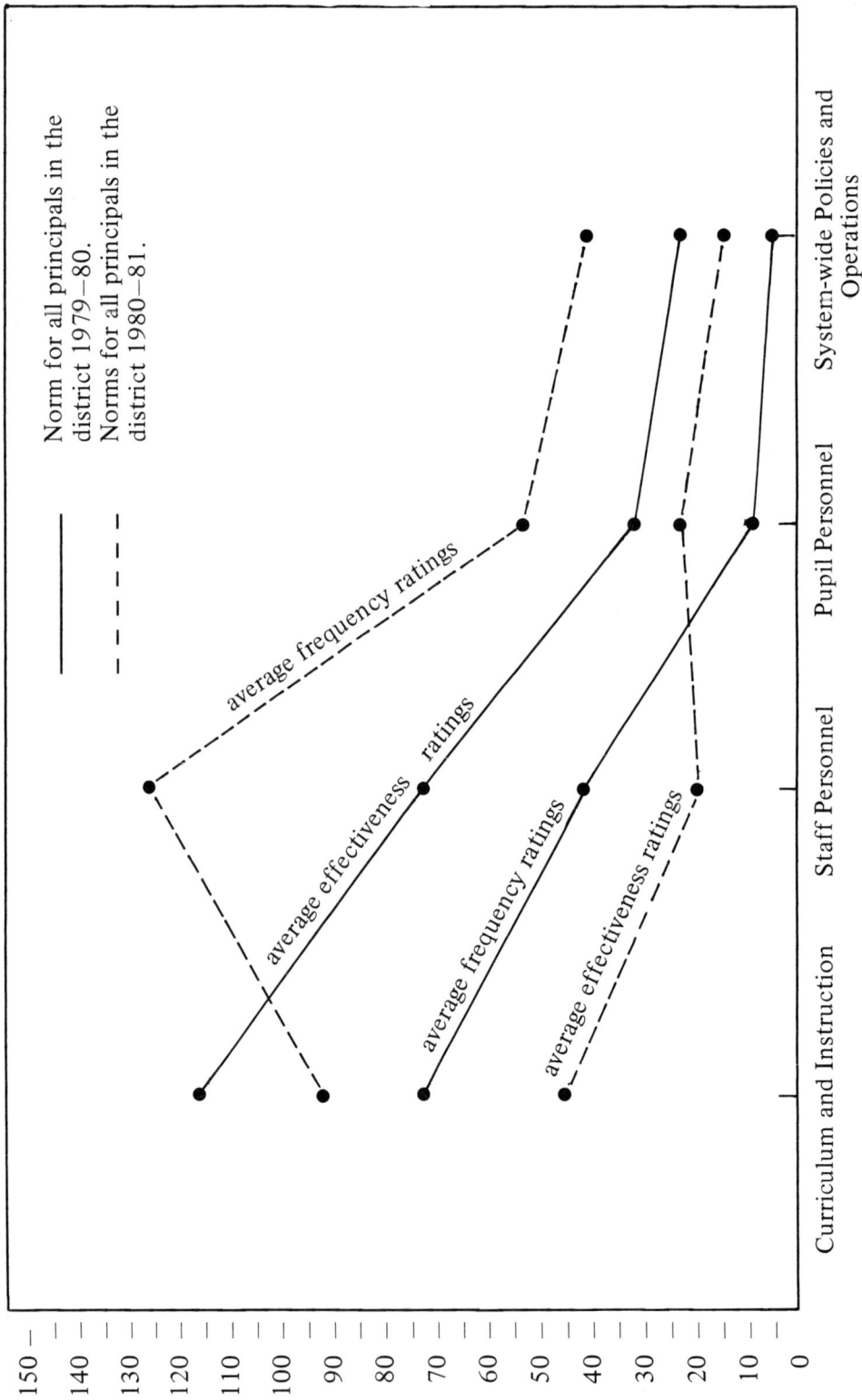

FUNCTIONAL AREAS OF ADMINISTRATIVE RESPONSIBILITY

FIGURE 6. Sample evaluative profile based on teacher ratings.

or subjective information derived from the interview. For instance, if the respondent produces a list of advisory committee members and minutes of their last meeting, these products would be noted in this section as well as any informal comments that might be used in making qualification judgments. If, when asked about identification of qualified minority group candidates for teaching positions, the respondent reports that this is a "word of mouth" or informal process, a description of this informal process would go under Product Description. In this way the observer is able to get both verification of formal procedures in practice and specific information relative to *informal* processes. Figure 7 presents a sample part of an external observer form of the PPDS, specifically from the section on staff personnel responsibilities.[18]

This particular or external observer instrument would be completed by the principal him/herself prior to the observers' visits or at least prior to the developmental conference and the observers selected by the principal to participate in the developmental cycle. This instrument would be completed by the principal him/herself and evaluators during the evaluation cycle. While the PPDS does feature a self-rating instrument that can be used with both the teacher and external observer forms, this author's suggestion would be that in systemic appraisal the external observer instrument would provide the best vehicle for interaction and comparison during development or evaluation conferences. This would allow the teacher data to be kept separate from the observation process. Figure 8 presents a sample profile that might be the result of external observation in either the development or evaluation subsystem.[19]

STAFF PERSONNEL

8. Matches employee qualifications and job descriptions in selecting new employees.

    Source   NA   Informal Input   Process   Product
    _____   ____   1   2   3   4
                               Product Description _____
                                                   _____

9. Maintains written job descriptions for employees.

    Source   NA   Informal Input   Process   Product
    _____   ____   1   2   3   4
                               Product Description _____
                                                   _____

10. Informs teachers of guidelines to be followed in reporting student disciplinary problems.

    Source   NA   Informal Input   Process   Product
    _____   ____   1   2   3   4
                               Product Description _____
                                                   _____

11. Evaluates staff participation in formulating school policies and procedures.

    Source   NA   Informal Input   Process   Product
    _____   ____   1   2   3   4
                               Product Description _____
                                                   _____

12. Maintains written policies concerning school rules and regulations for students and teachers.

    Source   NA   Informal Input   Process   Product
    _____   ____   1   2   3   4
                               Product Description _____
                                                   _____

FIGURE 7. Sample part of the PPDS external observer form.

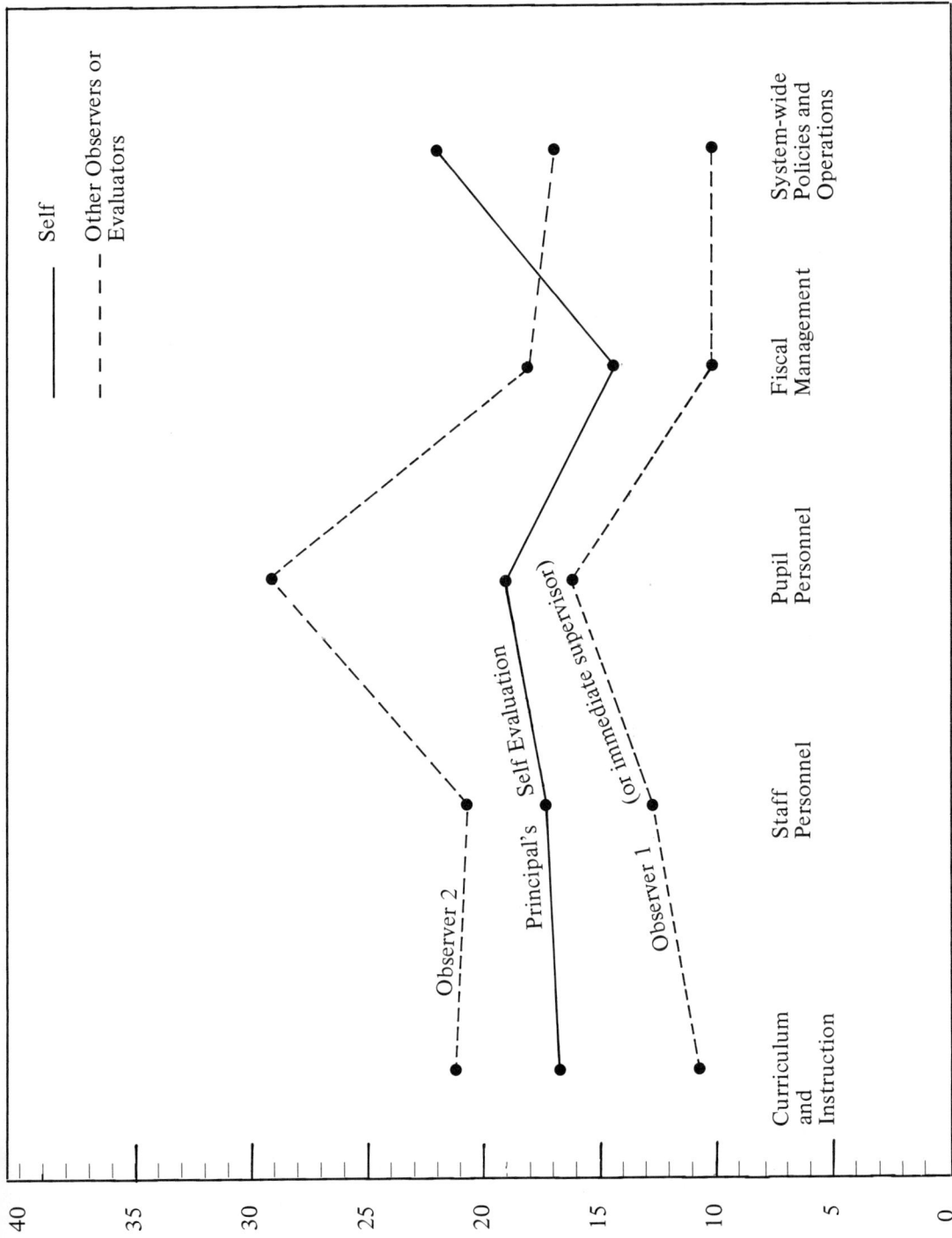

FUNCTIONAL AREAS OF ADMINISTRATIVE RESPONSIBILITY

FIGURE 8. External observer profile from evaluation or development subsystems.

FOOTNOTES

1. C.D. Ellett, et. al., "The Relationship of Principal's Competencies and Meaningful School Outcome Measures: a Field Test of the Georgia Principal Assessment System," *CCBC Notebook, 3.* 5, 1976.

2. See C.D. Elllett and D.A. Payne, *Principal Performance Description Survey* (Athens, Georgia: Project ROME, 1977) for an example of an instrument measuring teacher perceptions of their principal's performance.

3. J.W. Licata and W.G. Mack, "School Administrator Grapevine Structure," *Educational Administration Quarterly*, in press.

4. These propositions have been modified from statements about evaluator characteristics noted in M. Webster, Jr. and B. Sobleszek, *Sources of Self-Evaluation* (New York: John Wiley and Sons, 1974), 1–64 and 156-166.

5. See J.W. Licata and R.L. Norman, "The Triangulation Interview Form." *Education 99,* 3 (1979), 321–325 for an explanation of this type of observation strategy.

6. Licata and Mack, "School Administrator . . ."

7. T. Caplow, *How to Run Any Organization* (New York: Holt, Rinehart and Winston, 1976), 1–38.

8. See Vern Cunningham, "An Academy for Professional Development," Educational Administration, The Ohio State University, Columbus, Ohio, 1980 or J.W. Licata and E.C. Ellis, Project ROME-FOCUS *Field Manual, ERIC* Clearinghouse on Educational Management, 1980 for examples of developmental plans for educational leadership personnel.

9. D.A. Payne, et. al., "The Development and Validation of an Observation instrument to Assess Competencies of School Principals," *Educational and Psychological Measurement, 36* (1976), 945–952.

10. For instance, such procedures are explained in texts like R.A. Schmuck and P.J. Runkel, *Handbook of Organizational Development in Schools* (National Press, 1972), 115–116.

11. Schmuck and Runkel, 259–260.

12. C.D. Ellett and D.A. Payne, *Principal Performance* . . . Figure 4 through 8 are in part taken from these documents and are used by permission of the authors.

13. C.D. Ellett, et. al., "The Relationship . . ."

14. C.D. Ellett, *The Continued Refinement and Development of the Georgia Principal Assessment System and Its Application to a Field-Based Training Program for Public School Principals,* Project ROME Final Report, 1, Georgia State Department of Education, Thomas County Public Schools (Ga.) and College of Education, University of Georgia, 1976.

15. Ellett and Payne, *Principal Performance* . . . See "Teacher Form," 6, Used by permission of authors.

16. Payne, et. al., 947.

17. Payne, et. al., 947–948.

18. Ellett and Payne, *Principal Performance* . . . See "External Observer Form," 6, Used by permission of the authors.

19. Again, the profile forms used in figures 4–8 are in part taken from Ellett and Payne, *Principal Performance* . . . "Principal Form," 16–2 and "External Observer Form" 12. Used by permission of the authors.

Completing the Appraisal Cycle

Ronald R. Booth and
Gerald R. Glaub

The following excerpt is from the handbook, Planned Appraisal of the Superintendent, *described as a "performance-based program for school boards and superintendents." The book serves to acquaint them with procedures used in appraising performance. The authors discuss in specific terms such topics as developing measurable objectives, setting guidelines for appraisal meetings, annual performance review, and the link between appraisal and compensation. Emphasizing that a board of education's commitment to the appraisal process implies a willingness to "expect the superintendent to be open and honest regarding the board's strengths and weaknesses," the authors stress that "mutual understanding can occur only when all of the participants share their concerns in the open climate free from threat and coercion." Ronald R. Booth is Assistant Executive Director of the Illinois Association of School Boards in Springfield, Illinois; Gerald R. Glaub is the Association's Director of Communications in Springfield.*

COMPLETING THE APPRAISAL CYCLE

The First Appraisal

A board that has thoroughly analyzed the superintendent's job has the following information:
1) The district functions and management tasks that make up the superintendent's job.
2) The nature of the superintendent's role, whether it is to recommend, implement, develop, direct, etc.

3) A statement of purpose which provides the superintendent with an indicator of effectiveness for each responsibility.

4) The above information broken down into minimum responsibilities and reasonable and special expectations.

The board and superintendent are now ready for their first performance appraisal. This initial appraisal is different from all that will follow in subsequent years in at least one important respect: the superintendent probably has had no advance notice as to what the school board expects of him. This may be the first time that the board has really said what his responsibilities are. This initial appraisal, therefore, is apt to produce some surprises for everyone. The superintendent may be surprised to find that the board is not as happy (or unhappy) as he has supposed. The board will be surprised to learn the many forces which restrict the superintendent's activities (laws, workload, public pressure).

The results of the initial appraisal should not be regarded as final or as an ending to the appraisal process. This first effort is, in fact, a beginning. From this point forward, the board and superintendent will have a common understanding and clear set of standards upon which to base appraisal judgments.

In the first appraisal, the board and superintendent should go through the following steps:

1) Discuss and reach agreement on the superintendent's strengths and weaknesses in performing minimum responsibilities. Is the superintendent presently achieving the "indicator of effectiveness" for these responsibilities? If not, is there any reason to believe he cannot easily do so now that he knows what the board expects? These functions and tasks which the superintendent handles adequately can be evaluated by exception, assuming the board feels that it need not monitor them on a regular basis.

2) Make a list of minimum responsibilities representing problems that the board wants corrected. For these the board and superintendent will later write performance objectives.

3) Through open and honest discussion — possibly using a checklist as a springboard — identify those skills, personal traits, or behaviors of the superintendent which the board as a while feels are problems. These weaknesses also can be brought under performance objectives.

4) Reach agreement on the superintendent's strengths and weaknesses in handling the reasonable expectations of the board. Except for those which the superintendent is already handling at or beyond board expectations, add them to the list of responsibilities calling for performance objectives.

5) Review the board's special expectations — its hopes for long-range district improvements. Are there any critical issues which the superintendent should be pursuing?

From the above categories, the board and superintendent compile a list of functions, tasks, and characteristics which represent board concerns or areas needing improvement. The next step is to put the items into a priority order. For one thing, the superintendent needs to know what comes first in the view of the board. For another thing, the list may contain more items than the superintendent can reasonably handle the first year. He should handle the most important problems first and leave others for following years.

The final steps have the board and superintendent agreeing on performance objectives and then meeting from time to time to assess progress toward those objectives. A year later, the board has a sound basis for making a performance appraisal — that is, how well did the superintendent do in meeting his objectives?

Developing Measurable Objectives

An objective states the desired results of a specified activity with a definite purpose in mind. An objective related to performance also states expected results.

A good objective tells:

> What is to be done
> By whom
> By when
> The expected results

For example.

> To enable the school board to maintain current policies which are up-to-date, the superintendent shall recommend for board adoption those new or revised policies required by new legislation or court decisions no later than April 1.

For this particular objective, the board will be able to judge the superintendent's performance in two ways — first, by whether he does or does not present recommendations by April 1 and second, by whether the policies prove to be adequate in guiding the district.

Most people have difficulty preparing useful objectives — especially the first time they try it. There are many things that can go wrong. Many of the potential pitfalls have already been avoided by the school board and superintendent who have carefully analyzed their respective roles and arrived at a list of priorities for improvement. They should know by now what they want to accomplish, and that is the biggest hurdle in writing objectives.

Some objectives will not lend themselves to the appraisal of effectiveness. The board will have to measure such objectives merely by determining whether something was done — such as the filing of a report or the making of a recommendation to the board. The most useful objectives, however, are those that include an indicator of effectiveness.

Writing Objectives

In most districts, the board will ask the superintendent to draft an objective for each responsibility or deficiency calling for action. Regardless of who does the actual writing, both the board and superintendent have certain responsibilities in the process.

The superintendent should:
1) Examine the problem and determine what actions he can take to meet the board's expectations.
2) Write an objective in specific, measurable terms. Make it clear what is to be accomplished and by when.
3) Be certain that the objective advances the school system and that it is both reasonable and yet high enough to demand his best efforts.
4) Accept responsibility for reaching the objective.

The school board should:
1) Be prepared to provide resources and guidance to help the superintendent develop and reach objectives.
2) Be sure that the objective is appropriate to the board's expectations, to the district's goals, and to the superintendent's growth. Avoid objectives which are trivial or too easy.
3) Discuss the obstacles that might prevent the superintendent from achieving the objectives on schedule. Allow for problems requiring alterations.
4) Establish intermediate meeting dates for checking progress. Changing conditions may dictate changes in objectives.
5) See that both the board and superintendent are fully committed to the objectives.

For boards that follow the entire development process outlined in this book, most of the work in writing objectives has already been done. The person doing the writing merely needs to combine the elements already identified into a clearly worded statement and add a completion date. It may be necessary in some cases to clarify the indicator of effectiveness or write a new one.

For example:
Superintendent's responsibility: "To develop and recommend

an employee compensation plan."

Indicator of Effectiveness: "To attract and maintain a high quality staff."

To convert this to a performance objective, simply add a deadline:

By January 15, the superintendent will develop and recommend to the school board an employee compensation plan designed to attract and maintain a high quality staff.

By January 15, both the board and superintendent will know whether the commitment to provide recommendations was met. In addition, the board has agreed upon the major criterion for evaluating the superintendent's recommendations — that is, will the plan attract and maintain a well-qualified staff?

It can be argued whether the superintendent should be held fully responsible for the eventual outcome of his recommended plan if it is adopted by the board. If the board adopts the plan, it can reasonably be said that the superintendent did his job. But what if the plan fails to achieve the desired result? What if the quality of the staff is not satisfactory? (What is meant by "high quality?" What factors besides compensation influence staff quality?)

Certainly, the board and superintendent will want to monitor the progress of the plan so that the superintendent can be held responsible for its implementation. But the board must share the responsibility for the effectiveness of the plan itself — for it was the board that agreed that there is some relationship between staff compensation and staff quality.

This is one of these many situations where the board cannot hold the superintendent responsible for the outcome of decisions which the board makes. But the board can hold the superintendent responsible for the quality of his advice, particularly on matters where the board gives the superintendent extensive flexibility.

Both in developing objectives and in evaluating the outcome, the emphasis has to be on dialogue and district improvement. The board is always free to say that the superintendent's advice is no good. But that does not get at the source of the superintendent's performance problem (if he has one) and it certainly doesn't help the district improve. For the objective cited here, the board and superintendent might want to conduct some research to determine how to best improve staff quality before jumping to the conclusion that a new compensation plan is the answer.

The superintendent, as the only professional school manager in the group, must advise the board in these matters. Only the superintendent can be expected to know the results he can reasonably obtain. He should not promise more than he can deliver.

Obviously, there are opportunities here for the superintendent to cop-out, to make things easier for himself. That is why performance appraisal has to have an open and honest relationship between board and superintendent if the school district itself is to benefit. Otherwise, some members of the board may become inclined to use performance objectives as booby traps and the superintendent may want to use them to cover up mistakes.

Performance objectives do not remove subjectivity or personal judgment from appraisal. Therefore, they can be abused.

Appraisal Meetings

The superintendent's performance should be reviewed periodically with input from all of the members of the board. Committees should not be assigned this important responsibility. The frequency of these sessions may vary from district to district and may be affected by the contractual relationship with the superintendent.

In Illinois, an annual cumulative review of performance, including documentation, should be held prior to April 1, because contractual commitments are required by that date (unless the contract provides otherwise). For multi-year contracts, this applies to April 1 of the year in which the contract expires. It would be advantageous to hold additional review sessions at other times to consider progress and/or to alter expectations based on experience. At least one review session and preferably two should be held to assess progress prior to the final review of performance. Keep in mind that some objectives will take several years to accomplish and may even be written in a series of stages.

The Objective-Setting Session

The initial session when standards of performance are established cooperatively with the superintendent involves a great deaf of effort by both the board and superintendent. It will be difficult and demanding, because setting standards is not easy. Without guidance, it can become a traumatic once-a-year project.

The superintendent and all board members must be committed to appraisal if the process is to be successful. Everyone must avoid the following:

1) Dominating the conversation, attempting to tell rather than listen.
2) Providing little input and blindly agreeing to adopt whatever goals or decisions that others propose.
3) Setting goals too low or unrealistically high.
4) Attempting to leave out certain objectives on the grounds that they are not precisely measurable. Many worthwhile objectives do not lend themselves to precise measurement.
5) Trying to cover up and rationalize failures, shifting the blame, and not accepting appropriate responsibility.

6) Presenting goals inconsistent with board and district goals or not related to the needs of the district.

7) Arguing that the board does not have the background nor training to tell a professional what he is supposed to accomplish.

If the ingredients of *priorities, outcomes,* and *commitments* are present, these things will not occur and the process should be beneficial and rewarding to both the board and the superintendent. Board members must be aware that their commitment to the process means that they expect the superintendent to also be open and honest regarding the board's strengths and weaknesses. Mutual understanding can occur only when all of the participants share their concerns in an open climate free from threat and coercion.

Progress Reports

At appropriate times throughout the year, the superintendent should provide the board with progress reports on each agreed-upon objective. Aside from keeping the board informed of what is going on, this is an opportunity for the superintendent to report on any unforeseen difficulties. The board may agree to modifications in some objectives to reflect changing conditions.

Annual Performance Review

If the board and the superintendent have honestly and openly committed themselves to evaluate measurable and attainable objectives, have scrutinized and/or reviewed them periodically at appraisal review meetings, and have a reasonable "feel" for results expected, they should be ready to engage in the annual performance review. The annual review conference must include:

1) The superintendent's self-evaluation of expected results, justification or explanation of how and to what degree objectives were realized, and suggestions for revising or altering objectives based on outcomes (results).

2) The board's evaluation of the superintendent's performance in meeting specified objectives.

3) A point discussion of the board's evaluation compared to the superintendent's observations. Each objective should be analyzed to determine whether it has been realized, needs revising, or is unrealistic.

4) A written summary and documentation of the evaluation.

The way these sessions are organized will vary from district to district. The best way will be through procedures with which the board feels comfortable. Some boards may want to neet first without the superintendent to arrive at group concensus or to neutralize diverse criticism. Such boards may also want one board member to summarize and act as a spokesperson for the whole board at the review session.

Other boards may ask individual board members to comment in writing and/or complete individual evaluation forms prior to meeting jointly. Others may be perfectly comfortable in holding all discussions in the presence of the superintendent. Of utmost importance is that all board members are candid and have input. If they cannot do so in the presence of the superintendent, then some form of pre-session should be initiated by the board to obtain total input.

The biggest problem for both board and superintendent will be determining how well or to what degree objectives were or were not accomplished. It is human nature to expect a "grade" rather than a discussion. This should be avoided. The process is more important than the grade, since a lay board is not endowed with the skill or time to assess educational outcomes. All outcomes may not meet expectations and results may come in various shades of gray, no matter how well they were proposed. Boards caught in this dilemma must consider the superintendent's responses as the major criteria for evaluation. If the reasons are logically explained, departures from expected results justified, and the response reasonably explained by data or circumstance, the process of evaluation by objectives has been successful. Clear-cut results cannot be guaranteed even with well-stated objectives — and rightly so, because if they were all clearly met, they were either too easy and lacked "stretch" or were unnecessary or trivial. These "gray areas" provide material for revising and rewriting objectives for the next year.

The degree to which the board is satisfied with results forms the basis for the board's evaluation of the superintendent. No scorecard is required; however, an evaluation summary should include these items which have been accomplished, those which not (a form of remediation), and those which, although justified, require more work.

The summary should also specify those areas or problems which need attention next year and for which new objectives should be established. Direction should also be given by the board, in writing, in areas of concern not previously specified or stated as objectives for evaluation. Any minimal expectations not met by the superintendent also should be recorded, in writing if obvious or substantiated, since this document will become the basis for remediation and future employment decisions. All of these should be made known to the superintendent. The board president or his designee should be responsible for a final written document which has an attachment for the superintendent's response. These should be kept as permanent board records.

Some boards may also use this session to establish objectives for next year, evaluate the board, direct the superintendent to prepare an agenda for an objective-setting session, or determine the superintendent's compensation and contract. None of these are absolutely necessary and can be done at later meetings. Each board should, however, establish a policy and procedure for accomplishing these important tasks.

Guidelines for Appraisal Meetings

A performance-based appraisal can be successful where procedures are agreed upon and where the errors and pitfalls in the process are understood. Here are some guidelines for the appraisal review.

1) Concentrate on performance rather than personality.
2) Concentrate on action for improvement.
3) Encourage genuine participation – let the superintendent take the initiative.
4) Let performance review influence salary review only indirectly, because other factors are included in salary determination.

Questions to be asked during appraisal:

1) Are practical and realistic standards identified for each of the superintendent's major responsibilities?
2) Are the board's expectations clearly stated?
3) Have indicators of effectiveness been identified for each major responsibility?
4) Are suggestions for improvement noted?
5) Were problems stated accurately?
6) Were objectives stated using measurable terms (or at least observable)?
7) Were objectives practical and realistic, yet challenging?
8) Will appraisal achieve desired results?
9) Are target dates realistic?

Don'ts for appraisal review:

1) Don't dictate what someone should do or think.
2) Don't manipulate by trying to get predetermined conclusions.
3) Don't talk too much – listen!
4) Don't display bias for your own ideas and suggestions.
5) Don't attack or attempt to alter the views of others.

Errors in appraisal meetings:

1) Traits or personality emphasized.
2) Emphasis on incidents — nagging.
3) Hiding one's own views.
4) Focus on activities, not results.
5) Focus on items which cannot be controlled.
6) Being too rigid.
7) Implied emphasis on "pleasing me."
8) Discussion of salary.

In the process of appraisal, the following rules of fairness and consideration should be followed:

1) Strive for fair and equitable treatment of the superintendent.
2) Make competence and performance the keys.
3) Make decisions when they are needed without undue delay.
4) Be consistent and do not vacillate — but admit it when you're wrong.
5) Be understood.
6) Keep your word.
7) Find time to show concern for misfortune, to commend excellence, and to offer encouragement during stress and difficulty.
8) Be warm, humane, and operate with the smallest possible ego.
9) Follow through and remember significant details. Sort out for insignificance.
10) When a big decision is coming up, hear all sides.

Compensation and Appraisal

Some educators insist that appraisal and salary remain separate on the assumption that any "merit" emphasis destroys the honesty of the evaluation and is threatening to those being evaluated. Although in some cases this may unfortunately be true it also indicates a generalized fear about evaluation with or without compensation included. This general reluctance on the part of school boards to consider performance-related compensation is the major reason that educational management has lagged behind the private sector in evaluating effectiveness and has helped to create the demand for schools to be more businesslike.

It is inconsistent to encourage effective performance in an appraisal process and at the same time separate appraisal from compensation. Performance appraisal is bound to have a psychological impact on salary decisions. Those who do not perform do not deserve to be rewarded. Anything else defies logic.

Performance, however, is only one factor in setting salary. Basing salary decisions exclusively on performance appraisal is unrealistic. Other considerations are: comparisons of salary with those of other employees; the responsibility level of the particular job; comparisons of salary with similar positions in other districts; the employee's market value outside the district; past practice in individual compensation; the compensation policy of the district, the district's ability to pay; and economic conditions in the community.

Salary policies and procedures must be specified clearly and will undoubtedly include factors other than performance. However, to reward a poor performance at the same level as a superior performance may effectively negate performance evaluation and even discourage the high performer.

Evaluating Administrative Personnel in School Systems

Dale L. Bolton

In this lengthy excerpt from his book of the same title, Dale L. Bolton meticulously lays out a number of guidelines for setting up an evaluative process. He speaks of the need to establish purposes and specific objectives for evaluation, variables to be considered as the process unfolds, ways of collecting data, and other elements of evaluation. Sensitive to the complexity of the task of judging administrative performance, Dr. Bolton outlines some of the problems inherent in the process — many of which result from human fallibility. Finally, the excerpt concludes with an analysis of scales used in measuring performance. Dale L. Bolton is Chairman of the Department of Education at the University of Washington, Seattle.

Reprinted by permission of the publisher from Dale L. Bolton, EVALUATING ADMINISTRATIVE PERSONNEL IN SCHOOL SYSTEMS. (New York: Teachers College Press. Copyright © 1980 by Teachers College, Columbia University. All Rights Reserved.), pp. 47—76.

Establishing Purposes of Evaluation

If the local school situation has been thoroughly analyzed and all

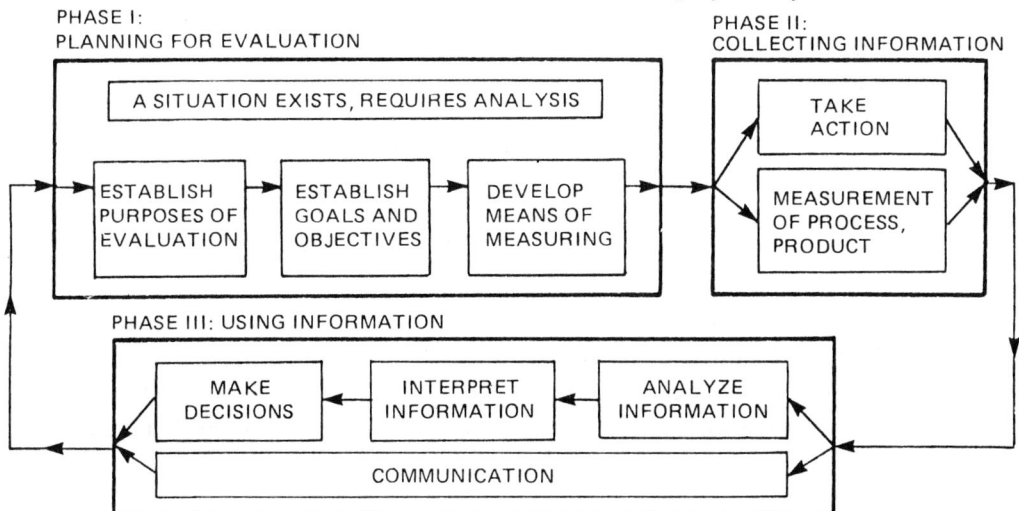

seemingly pertinent variables examined, the next step is to establish the purposes for evaluating administrators. If the evaluation system is to be successful, these purposes must be identified, discussed, and agreed upon by all who are involved in the process. This is important so that the additional phases of the process will be given direction and a reason for existence. Without purpose, activities have a tendency to be generated or omitted on the whim of those involved.

Some statements of purposes for evaluating administrators include a philosophical statement, indicating what the adopting body believes to be true about such things as behavior, the nature of man in general, the way adults learn, and motivational factors for adult behavior (Bolton, 1977:72). Also, assumptions are sometimes stated regarding such things as whether individuals desire change in themselves, what constitutes fairness among employees, or what productivity a person can be responsible for. At other times, these must simply be inferred from procedures and criteria described; but it is helpful if these values and assumptions are explicitly stated and discussed.

The real problem in stating all purposes is that the group involved tends to become embroiled in meaningless arguments or discussions over whether one purpose is primary or more basic than another. Yet, the key question is not whether one is more important than another, but whether a system can be designed that will allow all purposes which are important to the individuals and the organization to be accomplished. Another problem is in stating the underlying assumptions and value system of the evaluation process without becoming so ponderous and/or so general that the statements become meaningless to anyone except the initial author. In providing background information for the statement of purposes, it would be helpful to state what assumptions are made about the need to restrict the administrator's behavior and whether one is to assume that each administrator in the organization desires to improve her or his performance.

There appear to be differences among people regarding whether the evaluation system should function as a major source of motivation for administrators. Pharis (1973:37) advocates that evaluation programs be designed around basic motivators for human behavior. However, if the evaluation system is primarily a feedback mechanism to determine if one is "on course," then it would not necessarily be designed for the purpose of reward or award. Indeed, motivation would have to come from another source if this were the case. This issue cannot be decided from outside an organization but most depend on the value system of those who have responsibility for design and implementation of the system.

Sometimes conflicts are generated when evaluation systems are designed around multiple purposes, especially when a reasonable balance is not maintained between purposes designed to help the administrator and other purposes designed to maintain standards of the school system. Glaynor discusses the need to keep in focus the principal's behavior in relation to organizational complexities.

Mainly, the intent of evaluation should be to help the principal to understand better the complexities of the bureaucratic, cultural-political, legal, and fiscal environment of the school and to mirror for the principal her/his behavior in relation to that environment. The prime focus should be upon helping the principal to determine what changes in task priority and administrative style are likely to work better, to help the principal to gain the knowledge and skills necessary to make those changes, and to provide formative feedback on the process over time (1977:46).

Since the purposes for evaluation are multiple and must be determined for specific local situations, a list which fits all situations cannot be recommended. However, Bolton (1974:172) believes that consideration should be given at least to the following:

- changing goals or objectives
- modifying procedures
- determining new ways of implementing procedures
- improving performance of individuals
- supplying information for modification of assignments
- protecting individuals or the school system
- rewarding superior performance
- providing a basis for career planning and individual growth and development
- validating the selection process
- facilitating self-evaluation

Changing Goals or Objectives

There are times when it is not obvious that direction should be changed, or that sights should be raised or lowered. It is at these times that systematic evaluation can assist in making decisions about change of goals or objectives. Sometimes administrators will set goals that are too ambitious, considering the reality of the situation and the constraints in effect. When this happens, they may become discouraged, frustrated, or even give up and reduce their activities. An examination of data in light of the objectives may cause them to reassess the situation within which they are working and agree on more reasonable goals. Also, goals may be revised upward when evaluation of results warrants it. As significant as adjusting one's objectives either upward or downward is the dropping of them altogether. This is a matter of periodically examining objectives in light of the situation in which one is functioning and determining whether objectives are still as appropriate as they were when initially written. Although this is a very simple matter to do, it may easily be overlooked if evaluation does not occur.

Modifying Procedures

Sometimes there are resistances to modification of procedures when an administrator has been involved in designing those procedures. For example, the administrator who has been involved in designing a new scheduling procedure for students may resist a suggestion that it be changed. However, if data are gathered to show how well the procedure is functioning, how well it is liked by parents and students, and how teachers think it affects their jobs, the administrator may well be encouraged to consider alternative scheduling procedures. Without evaluation of the specific results or outcomes, procedures used by administrators may acquire an unwarranted momentum and permanency.

Determining New Ways of Implementing Procedures

There are times when a procedure is not faulty but simply implemented inappropriately. If such is the case, the procedure should not be rejected; the implementation should be controlled more precisely. The key to evaluation in relation to implementation is a careful examination of the exact nature of the processes used (as opposed to those planned). It may be that inadequate resources were used, or that support from higher levels of the school district were lacking, or that there were breakdowns in communication. There may be a variety of reasons that a good procedure was not properly implemented, but the correction for poor implementation is considerably different from correction of a faulty procedure. For example, a faulty scheduling procedure may be replaced or drastically modified; but if it has never been implemented fully, one should not conclude that such action is warranted.

Improving Individual Performance

The first three purposes cited above are concerned with ways of changing the environment within which an administrator works, but this purpose is concerned with providing information that will allow the individual to change. Evaluation provides the information base, supervision procedures or self-teaching provides the mechanism for change. The information acquired for this task should indicate the relationship between the processes used by the administrator and the results (products) of these processes. Precise knowledge of the process-product relationship should provide clues to the nature of actions that need to be taken to correct outcomes. If new skills are needed, either the supervisor or the administrator should be in a position to know what these are and how they may be acquired.

Supplying Information for Modification of Assignment

There are times when a given assignment is not suitable for a particular administrator or when the administrator would be better suited for another assignment. Evaluation can play an important role in helping to make decisions in such cases. Modifications may include a change in load (by increasing or decreasing the tasks required), a shifting to another building or level of the organization, changes in those being supervised, promotions, demotions, change in type of assignment (e.g., from a personnel job to one involving curriculum or finance), or release. While these decisions must be made in all organizations, morale tends to suffer if the procedures for determining such decisions are not systematic and if the emphasis is on elimination of the weak and ineffective. Consequently, the negative emphasis should be avoided. When dismissal or demotion procedures are necessary, they should be orderly, systematic, and understood by all in the organization.

Protecting Individuals or the School System

Administrators and the school districts they represent are particularly vulnerable to criticism, some of which may be unjust. At the same time, they are held accountable for establishing and maintaining a system of education that accomplishes goals established by the board of education. Since school boards have the right to establish the kind of school system they want, as long as it remains within constitutional limits (Howsam, 1963; Heald & Moore, 1968), including the prerogative of setting up any form of evaluation they desire, the evaluation of administrators' actions and results can protect both the school boards and administrators from being criticized unjustly. Arguments about factual information are unprofitable; criticism of systematically evaluated individuals, when they are performing in accordance with agreed-upon goals, will largely go unheeded. If unjustified and disruptive elements pursue legal means for accomplishing their purposes, systematic evaluation procedures will provide protection of either the individuals involved or the school system.

Rewarding Superior Performance

Rewarding superior performance financially has generally been resisted by the teaching profession, however, there probably is less resistance among administrators than among teachers. Regardless of the extent of acceptance of practices for differentially paying administrators according to performance, there is an almost universal concern that any such practice should rely on precise measurements and open systems of communication regarding expectations. With increasing pressures from people outside the schools to pay for services in accordance with quality and quantity of performance, there are likely to be more school systems accepting the purpose of rewarding superior performance with increased salaries.

Other types of rewards for superior performance should be considered, also. If, indeed, the underlying motive for reward systems is to provide an incentive to the individual to produce more, then perhaps a school system should look beyond the monetary. For example, feelings of accomplishment, satisfaction with nature of work, professional growth, recognition, responsibility, and advancement are all considered to be true motivators (Herzberg, Mausner, & Snyderman, 1959, Herzberg, 1968), whereas pay, benefits, and working conditions are considered to be sources of dissatisfaction if withheld rather than motivators when provided. If motivation is really what is being sought, school districts should seek creative means of using evaluation procedures for helping administrators to recognize their achievements and analyze means for achieving more.

Providing a Basis for Career Planning and Individual Growth and Development

One evidence of a good administrator is that she or he develops the talents of the individuals being supervised. If this is to be done effectively and if one assumes that each administrator desires to improve, evaluation becomes the information basis for development of talent. Development and growth should occur within the context of the long-range career goals of the administrator in order to be meaningful. In addition, it should be beneficial to the school district to know of the ambitions and desires of its administrators. Diagnosis and interpretation of evaluation information will help administrators view themselves realistically; this may or may not cause the long-range plans to be adjusted. When evaluation is done properly, in a spirit of guidance and sincere desire for the well-being of the administrator, there should be opportunity for growth, meshing of long-range goals with reality of performance and capabilities, and a harmony of individual aspirations with the goals of the organization. These results are not likely to occur unless the system of evaluation explicitly incorporates this purpose.

Validating the Selection Process

Here is another purpose of the evaluation system that is often overlooked. Not only should the criteria used for the selection of administrators be consistent with those used to evaluate administrators, but the evaluation of administrators selected should provide the feedback necessary to analyze whether selection information (e.g. that obtained from examinations, placement papers, and other written documents, interviews, and assessment centers) was beneficial in making decisions. Evaluation information can also be helpful in determining whether certain interviewers are effective, whether decision strategies being used are appropriate, and whether certain information tends to be overlooked or stressed too much in the selection process. If evaluation information is not used to validate the selection process, there is a tendency to evaluate selection decisions at the time they are made; this is analogous to determining whether one made a good decision in the purchase of a house at the time of buying the house rather than after living in it for a while.

In addition, there is a need for all who are involved in administrator evaluation to understand the relationship of evaluation to selection. When administrators are involved in both selection and evaluation of those whom they supervise, they see the necessity of selecting someone who will respond to the type of supervision provided. In addition, they are more likely to feel responsible ·for the individual when they see how the feedback provides information to the selection procedures. This does not necessarily mean that supervisors should make the final decisions regarding the selection of administrators, but their intimate involvement in the determination of criteria and attributes should help the selection process and at the same time contribute to their own understanding of the interrelationship of selection and evaluation.

Facilitating Self-Evaluation

One of the functions of external evaluation is to facilitate self-evaluation. The value of self-evaluation, of course, is that it allows administrators to continuously diagnose what is happening and to make minute adjustments in terms of the information available. The better the external evaluator, the more sensitive administrators will become to surroundings and the more willing they will be to view events realistically. Both sensitivity and realism are beneficial to making judgments about actions to be taken in the day-to-day activities.

In conclusion, then, it can be said that all purposes for evaluation of administrators should be discussed openly and clarified in writing so that all who are involved may understand the bases for the evaluation program. Such discussion and writing should help to alleviate any unknowns that would lead to fear, hostility, resistances, and low morale and should promote commitment of administrators to the activities involved. In essence, evaluation programs that have written statements of purposes that are clear, precise, and complete are more likely to produce a sound basis for open communication and cooperative relationships than programs designed around ambiguous, or unwritten purposes (Bolton, *Selection and Evaluation of Teachers*, 1973:26).

ESTABLISHING GOALS AND SPECIFIC OBJECTIVES

Surely one of the more important aspects of administrator evaluation, and one that captures the attention of most people, is determining *what* should be evaluated. Various headings are used for this, including establishing goals and objectives, setting targets, specifying standards of performance, and determining criteria. Regardless of what one calls it, there is the necessity to determine a standard against which comparisons can be made. Certainly this task precipitates the largest number of differences among people who are intimately involved, including differences as to perceptions of role expectations, how goal statements should be written, the setting of priorities, and the determination of variables to be considered.

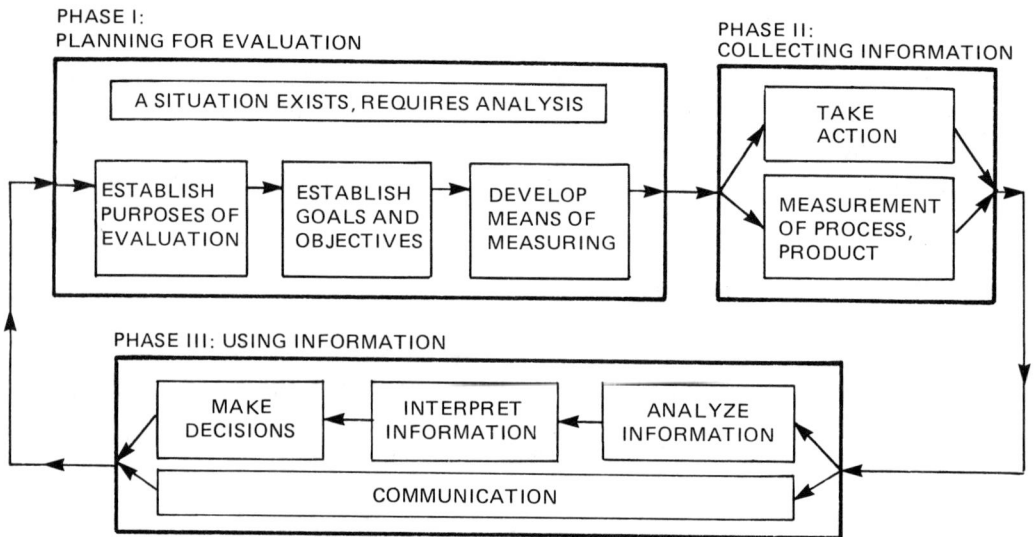

PHASE I:
PLANNING FOR EVALUATION

PHASE II:
COLLECTING INFORMATION

A SITUATION EXISTS, REQUIRES ANALYSIS

| ESTABLISH PURPOSES OF EVALUATION | ESTABLISH GOALS AND OBJECTIVES | DEVELOP MEANS OF MEASURING |

TAKE ACTION

MEASUREMENT OF PROCESS, PRODUCT

PHASE III: USING INFORMATION

| MAKE DECISIONS | INTERPRET INFORMATION | ANALYZE INFORMATION |

COMMUNICATION

Role Specification

Role theory may not be as popular today as it was in the sixties. For example, Griffiths indicates other approaches may be more valuable. He says:

> I submit that the concept of role as *the* set of expectations held for a position has little value in today's complex organizations. We would be better off if we described behaviors and perceptions and dropped the role spectacles (1977:7).

However, Beer and Ruh (1976:60–61) think that is valuable to consider the triple role of managers in dealing with subordinates: as *managers*, they are responsible for achieving organizational goals; as *judges*, they must evaluate performance and make decisions about salaries; and as *helpers*, they must develop subordinates into more effective and promotable employees. In many cases the judge role (in the sense of affecting salary) is eliminated from the role of educational administrators, and the helper role is paid lip service only. This leaves the managerial role, where many times the precise definition of achievement is left to one's imagination rather than put in writing.

If educational administrators are expected to be involved in all three of these roles, there should be clear recognition that sometimes one of the roles interferes with another. For example, the judge role may interfere with the helper role. In addition, it should be made clear precisely what is expected in each of these roles. If this is put in writing in the form of general goals or specific objectives, and if communication is open and authentic between an administrator and the evaluator, then the potential conflict between these roles may be alleviated somewhat.

Writing Objectives

Goals or purposes are rather general outcomes that one desires to accomplish. For example, a personnel director may want to establish a new teacher evaluation process. This is a general outcome, but there may be no time specification connected with the goal at the initial statement of it. As one begins planning for the goal, there may be several parts of it that can be specified in the form of objectives. These objectives are much more specific than the general goal and include deadlines for accomplishment. Two general criteria are important when considering objectives;: they should be worth doing (in terms of the organizational goals), and they should be well written.

If an objective is worth doing, it is because someone has conceived it and someone has approved it. Usually the conceptualization of the objective is the responsibility of the person who also must see that the objective is accomplished (in the major part), but the approval is the responsibility of the person supervising the administrator who initially conceived the objective. For example, the personnel director may have conceived the general goal of establishing a new teacher evaluation process. She or he may have several objectives in mind in relation to this goal, but the supervisor of the personnel director is the person who must make the judgment regarding whether this set of objectives is worthwhile in relation to other needs of the school district and the demands on the personnel director's time. In making this judgment, the supervisor may lean heavily on the expertise of the personnel director, but she or he may also obtain information (or ask that the personnel director obtain it) from teachers, department chairpersons, curriculum specialists, principals, and the budget division. Research information may be sought as well regarding the benefits of evaluation for improved performance.

It appears obvious that if an objective is judged to be worthwhile, the administrators have given considerable thought to what their true mission is, what will be the cost to them and their division in order to accomplish the objective, and what the results are likely to be. Otherwise, administrators may simple compile a list of routine activities that they plan to pursue (McConkey, 1972). In essence, one should first focus on the results desired and then begin writing objectives.

Sometimes administrators begin with a rather hazy idea and take this idea to a group of people for discussion and consensus regarding initation of it. A problem with this procedure is that it may be easy to obtain consensus on the vaguely stated objective without having a clear idea of the implications in terms of commitment of time and energy. In addition, an eclectic collection of activities may result rather than a set of actions based on clear theory of what one is attempting to do (Lawrence, 1974:300). The value of consensus procedures is that a true discussion of the idea may lead to an understanding of diverse views regarding the idea and an acceptance of both the objectives and the underlying theory base. The choice of whether one uses such a procedure may depend on the nature of the objective and the stake which the discussants have in the outcome. Use of consensus procedures does not mean that there has been fuzzy thinking on the part of the leader, however. Clear thinking of the details and the underlying theory may be done prior to a meeting in order to help clarify the thinking of the group during the consensus process.

Development of consensus related to objectives is similar to the involvement of other administrators in the development of objectives. In their discussion of collaborative MBO procedures, French and Hollman (1975: 15) suggest there is a need for this kind of involvement but very little evidence of it among the companies they studied:

> Eight of the nine companies (four British, five American) require that forms be filled out in the MBO programs, but in only one company's form is there any space for the manager to specify the extent to which his objectives require involvement of other managers.

Any necessary support and involvement of other personnel should be taken into account by an administrator during the planning phase. For example, if the personnel director needs the cooperation and assistance of the principals in order to implement a new teacher evaluation process, then it will be beneficial to specify this on the form that states the objective. This will allow the supervisor of the personnel director to know more about whether to approve the objective.

Another technique an administrator may find beneficial is to do some type of task structure breakdown. For example, Keegan (1975:37) suggests the following sequence for developing performance objectives:

1. Identify purpose or reasons for evaluation of administrators, keeping the number to a minimum.

2.   Identify the characteristics or job functions that relate to the position being evaluated.
3.   Identify the "indicators" or "tasks" that are necessary to carry out in order for the job function (characteristic) to operate smoothly.
4.   State the indicators (tasks) in performance terms.

It should be noted that this is a hierachy and that the eventual indicators could be written after forming a breakdown of characteristics or job functions, which are themselves a breakdown of the purpose chosen. The number of eventual indicators would depend on the number of functions, and the number of functions would depend on the number of purposes.

Raia (1974:65–66) provides us with a set of guidelines that relate directly to whether an objective is worth doing:

1.   It should be realistic and attainable.
2.   It should be both relevant and important.
3.   It should be challenging.
4.   It should be consistent with organization plans, policies, and procedures.

Each of these guidelines is worth examining prior to making any judgment regarding whether an objective should be accepted.

In addition, an objective should be well written so that all who are being asked to commit themselves to it will understand what is to be done. The following are criteria for a well-written objective:

1.   It should be clearly written, avoiding such relative terms as "adequate, sufficient, reasonable," since they lead to countless misunderstandings and make measuring practically impossible.
2.   It should focus on an identifiable outcome or result as a target.
3.   It should specify the action to be taken, the activities to be engaged in.
4.   It should specify who should accomplish the objective.
5.   It should be time limited, specifying not only when it is to be accomplished but also any time constraints.
6.   It should specify cost, in terms of all resources needed.
7.   It should be stated so that it is verifiable. (Author's note: the following sources all discuss guidelines or criteria for writing objectives: Arikado and Musella, 1975; Campbell et al., 1970.107–108, Carroll and Tosi, 1973:40; McConkey, 1972:16; and Raia, 1974:65–66.)

Raia (1974:65) suggests that any statement of "why" or "how" should be omitted from the goal-setting process and included, instead, in a separate statement of rationale. This would mean that a separate "action plan" would need to be devised that would include a discussion of the advantages and disadvantages of various alternatives for accomplishing the stated objective. There are advantages and disadvantages to the procedure proposed by Raia. It may work best for an administrator who has the habit of hastily choosing an alternative without considering a complete analysis of the situation. On the other hand, for more mature and responsible administrators, the action plan may simply be discussed in the goal-setting conference (or conferences) and only the process to be used may be written. The choice appears to be one that should be individualized on the basis of the behavior pattern of the administrator.

Setting Priorities

There may be times when an administrator sets a group of goals, each of which in turn has a group of objectives involving a variety of activities. At the same time, the supervisor may identify one or more objectives that have been overlooked by the administrator. Or perhaps the administrator may simply identify too many objectives to be accomplished in a given period of time. Under such circumstances, it is necessary to establish priorities in order to reduce objectives to a manageable number. Unless this is done, frustration will result because of not being able to accomplish all that is written down.

In calculating the time needed to accomplish certain objectives, it may be beneficial to have both the administrator and the supervisor estimate minimum and maximum times. This may give a better idea of the real time needed. In addition, one should allow enough leeway in the total time schedule for emergencies and discretionary time, since the complete scheduling of one's time can be another source of frustration when emergencies occur.

Another reason for setting priorities is to establish which objectives are to be met first in case some cannot be accomplished. Thus the administrator and the supervisor may identify those areas where extra resources may be used in order to complete a project and to specify what will be set aside if it becomes apparent that what was originally planned cannot be finished (Keegan, 1975:38). Ritchie emphasizes that it is important for both the administrator and the evaluator to be willing to modify objectives during the school year, but that this must be done by mutual agreement in order to assure successful operation of the administrator's unit (1976:34). Such modification, of course, allows flexibility for adjustment of the priorities of both the administrator and the supervisor as it becomes apparent that problems that were unimportant or unapparent at the beginning of the year have suddenly become more pressing because of either internal or external changing conditions.

Variables to Consider

Various types of criteria can be described, and there is a general lack of agreement in the profession regarding the relative significance of each type. For example, it is generally recognized that the following can be evaluated: (a) characteristics or personal qualities of administrators (such as emotional stability, appearance, and sociability), (b) functions performed (such as implementation or maintenance), (c) procedures used by administrators (such as conducting in-service programs for teachers, planning with Parent Teacher Student Association (PTSA) groups, or initiating a change in some aspect of the curriculum), and (d) results of behavior (such as changes in teacher behavior, or changes in school climate or parental satisfaction). It is important to keep in mind that any one of these variables may be expressed as a general goal or a specific objective to be attained, but considerable confusion occurs when goal expectations are not clarified.

In addition, problems arise in relation to the amount of detail to be specified in any statement of performance standards (Bolton, 1977:74). Because of the almost unlimited number of behaviors and results of behaviors that might be specified, it is difficult to determine a level of generality that is likely to be most helpful to evaluator and evaluatee. Statements should be specific enough to give direction and allow judgments regarding excellence and progress to be made. However, one should be wary of too much detail; it may become cumbersome paperwork, cause a lack of attention to important tasks, and tend to stifle creative, assertive people while attracting only the passive and conforming.

One further statement of warning may be necessary regarding determination of what should be evaluated. One should not confuse the following:

1. The mission of the school system as a whole (e.g., to maximize the learning of all students attending school, considering their interests and abilities as well as societal needs).
2. The purpose of the evaluation system (e.g., to improve the performance of all administrators in the school system).
3. The specific objective of a particular administrator (e.g., to use an individualized supervision and evaluation system that will cause each teacher being supervised to initiate at least two new projects during an academic year).

The total school system should be designed to accomplish the mission of the district, and the administrators' actions should be taken on the basis of goals and objectives designed to facilitate this mission, but not to accomplish it directly. If the mission of the school district or the purposes of the evaluation system are not being accomplished, the administrator may or may not be effective. Certainly there may be problems in the school system, but an examination of the integral parts of the system is needed; an administrator should be held responsible for individual objectives rather than for the more general overall mission to which many contribute.

What is the significance of the discussion thus far in regard to establishing goals and objectives?

1. Each individual administrator has a responsibility for establishing objectives that are compatible with and contribute to the overall mission and goals of the school district. It is not the responsibility of the supervisor of an administrator to establish objectives that are unique to the given administrator, even though the school district may establish some which are common to a given group of administrators.
2. The objectives of the individual administrator are not synonymous with the goals of the district or the objectives of teachers. The processes and products of the administrator are unique to the role of the particular administrator being evaluated.
3. The supervisor of each administrator has the responsibility for approval of the objectives; when this occurs, it is presumed that the objectives are compatible with organizational goals.
4. Establishment of objectives by the administrator means commitment of time and effort, acceptance by the supervisor means approval and support via school district resources.

The emphasis of the writing thus far has been on individualizing the evaluation process by analyzing the individual situation and specifying goals and objectives in terms of the uniqueness of the situation. This is in alignment with much of the literature regarding administrative behavior and with the experiences of administrators in varying assignments. It runs counter to making global assessments based on limited information. Campbell et al. (1970: 124) indicate that global estimates of administrator effectiveness have little utility, especially in providing knowledge of specific problems or areas of effectiveness. They emphasize that people often make decisions about effectiveness on the basis of global impressions "formed from job-irrelevant factors reflecting society's stereotypes of success" rather than on the basis of factors directly pertinent to organizational goals. The same authors also specify that effective administrative behavior must be tested in specific situations rather than devised in speculative armchair fashion. They say:

> We freely believe we cannot overemphasize the essential inadequacy of opinions, hunches, speculations, and expertise as a basis for prescriptions concerning the prediction of effective executive behavior (Campbell et al. 1970:10).

In addition, research indicates that no single criterion can be considered as supreme or sufficient. Dunnette, for example, says:

> I would argue that as we talk about managerial effectiveness, we must continue to ask for and investigate many criteria, rather than seek any single elegant, "ultimate," or composite criterion. I do not believe that there is or can be such a thing as a single best criterion of managerial effectiveness (1967:12).

With these dangers in mind, it should be pointed out that the following variables must be considered locally — rather than used regardless of the values and constraints of a given situation. In addition the variables to be examined take into account more than merely the what and the how (i.e., the process and the product) of the role of educational administrators. (Author's note: Gaynor's position is more limiting than the one presented here. He says, "The role of the school principal, like any role, can be conceptualized in terms of two primary components. The task component of the role defines what the principal is expected to do. The style component of the role defines how the principal is expected to perform these tasks in a social context. Evaluation designs will probably need to facilitate description and analysis of role behavior on both of these dimensions" [1977:34–35].) A number of the variables have to do with the characteristics of administrators, while others deal with the functions and tasks of administrators. These latter variables are among the less frequently discussed; consequently, they are not found on some of the summary evaluation forms in use at the present time. This discussion, then, is intended as a supplement to the forms and examples provided previously and should provide assistance in the eventual decisions regarding what should be evaluated.

Cognitive Complexity.   This is one of the characteristics of administrators that should be evaluated. Cognitive complexity is directly related to the ability to process information and is necessary to decision making in a complex organization. In general, the integration of behavior with situation is a function of information, there is an increase of integration with increasing information load until an optimum performance is reached, beyond which the amount of integration decreases with further increasing information load. This can be visualized as an inverted U-shaped curve relating load of information to performance. However, differences in conceptual structure of individuals result in different levels of this inverted U-shaped function (Streufert & Schroder, 1965). This means that the optimum level of information processing varies from individual to individual, depending on the cognitive structure of the individual. Studies done by Streufert and Schroder indicate that the more flexible. integrative, complex and/or "abstract" the structure of the group members, the higher the level of integration involved in performance. This suggests that there is a need to select and/or train individuals who are high not only in ability to deal with concrete ideas but also with abstract concepts.

Silver (1975:62) found that principals with more abstract conceptual structures were more person-oriented in their leadership style. If cognitive complexity is desirable, Silver specifies that the following competencies are important:

1.   ability to search a broad range of information before making decisions.
2.   skill in perceiving the relevance of broadly diversified information to given problems or situations.
3.   ability to defer closure on decisions so as to remain receptive to new information.
4.   competence to view each situation from numerous alternative perspectives.
5.   techniques for creating diversity, divergence, and ambiguity in situations over which the individual has some control (1975: 63—64).

How significant this variable is depends on the role expected of an administrator in a specific situation. Where the organization is not very complex or where maintenance or stability is extremely important, this variable is reduced in significance. In a complex school system where creativity is valued, an administrator's cognitive complexity should most probably be evaluated.

Awareness.   Awareness is not discussed much in the literature regarding administrator evaluation. Perhaps it is implied or taken for granted in relation to other characteristics or behavior. For example, it seems evident that it would be very important in relationships with people. Levinson (1968: 253—254) attests to the importance of this variable, when he says, "In contemporary innovative organizations, the most successful executive is high in achievement motivation, low in power motivation, and keenly aware of himself, his employees, and the market." Being aware of oneself and having an awareness of one's employees contribute to healthy human relations, and having an awareness of the market (in business organizations) indicates a real concern for productivity of the organization.

Levinson provides a cue as to how this awareness can contribute to the success of a leader in an organization. He indicates that motivation studies show

. . . that a good superior gives recognition to his subordinates, helps them grow in the job, represents their interests to higher management, looks out for their interests, corrects them justly and in private, and does not exploit them for his own gain. In this country the major objective of parents is to help their children grow to independent responsibility. The executive implicity is expected to do the same in the course of fulfilling the objectives and goals of the organization (1968: 18–19).

This parent figure concept of leadership (where the leader shows awareness of needs of subordinates) is different from paternalism, however, in that a paternalistic leader actually acts as if he really were the parent. Under such circumstances, the paternalistic leader provides things for the subordinates that they might better do themselves, e.g., recreation programs. Awareness that leads to consideration and good human relations, but stops short of paternalistic smothering, appears to warrant evaluation.

Deciseveness. My interest in this variable has persevered since the time of an earlier study in which I found that the measure of certainty an administrator experienced in making teacher selection decisions was a function of the format of the information provided. In the experiment conducted, there was significantly more certainty expressed with audiovisual than with audio interview information (Bolton, 1968:36). In effect, administrators choosing teachers after interviewing them via telephone would be less certain of their decisions than when they interviewed them in person. The certainty variable was included in the experiment because it was assumed that uncertainty can lead to indecision, vacillation, and wasted motion. It is interesting that House, Filley, and Gujarati (1971:431) came to a similar conclusion. They report that:
> . . . deciseveness emerges as an important variable with both a high degree of pervasiveness and generality. Surprisingly, little attention is or has been given to deciseveness as an independent variable in organization theory or studies concerning leadership behavior.

It seems that this variable would be most significant in situations where there is pressure of time and heavy work loads. It may be valued as a personal quality in other circumstances but it would affect outcomes of the organization most where time and work loads require speed of operation.

Personality. Certainly this variable has precipitated considerable discussion. Many consider it as important but are wary of it because of the problems of measurement. It may be helpful to examine some of the more measurable qualities or behavior which are a part of personality.

Consideration. A concern for and interest in those with whom one is working generally thought to be desirable in a leader and has been analyzed and measured by a number of studies. It is a valuable quality without regard to other variables. For example, Cummins (1971) found that the impact of initiating structure on the part of leaders was moderated by consideration, i.e., indicating structure did not have as much impact unless accompanied by consideration. However, he found that this was true in relation to quality of work performance, but not in relation to total productivity as the results are generalizable, it would appear that initiating structure (or thrust productivity) is sufficient for acquiring productivity but must be accompanied by consideration if quality also is desired. I presume that such results would be particularly important for education, since the quality of work is always of great importance.

Emotional maturity, cooperation, and tact. Campbell et al. reported on reasons that indicated that peer judgments of emotional maturity, cooperation, and tact were unrelated to subsequent promotion (1970:114). However, at the same time, such traits as independence of thought, leadership qualities, and ability to think analytically were strongly related to promotion. Perhaps the reason for the lack of correction is that the variables are difficult to differentiate or discriminate among subjects. For example, Peres and Garcia (1962:285) reported that in letters of recommendation the variables of "urbanity" and "cooperation-consideration" were least incriminating among those studies, whereas those dealing with "mental agility" were most discriminating. If, therefore, a variable like cooperation is rated virtually the same for all individuals, it is unlikely that it would be found to be related to any dependent variables such as productivity or quality of output.

However, if they are valuable in themselves, one should be wary of eliminating these variables from consideration in the evaluation process. If among twenty-five administrators only one of them is uncooperative or tactless, the correlation with some measure of productivity would be approximately zero. Yet, it may be important that all he evaluated on the variables in order to correct undesirable behavior was only the one person. This is a matter of validity as well as differentiation. One might desire to include variables that are considered to be high validity and low differentiation because of the utility with the exceptional case (Bolton, *Selection and Evaluation of Teachers*, 1973:157–158).

Perceptual accuracy and interest. Along with the nature of the administrator's interests, their ability to assess others and situations may be of concern when considering the broad category of personality. Campbell et al. (1970: 129) indicate that both of these are predictive of proficiency in executive and managerial jobs.

Persuasion, verbal interest, interpersonal contact. These qualities are common to effective managers, but they are not very well defined at present. They should be discussed and agreement should be reached among local leaders before they are included in evaluation systems (Campbell et al.

1970:133). It may be that persuasion is really an evidence of power need, that verbal interest is inherent in communication skills, and interpersonal contact is a part of consideration; if so, they may be better measured under different headings.

Conflict Resolution and Bargaining.   This function or task of administrators has increased in significance as organizations have become more complex and as teachers and administrators have viewed professionalism as more important. Griffiths (1977:15) believes that in the future, "The key administrative process in organizations is very likely to be *bargaining* and not necessarily collective bargaining." If such is the case, many more administrators are likely to be involved in bargaining activities.

Although there are many strategies that can be used for the purpose of receiving conflicts, Sayan and Charters (1970:43) indicate that many people overlook one of the most important strategies used by school administrators when faced by conflict situations, viz., acting to alter the expectations or demands of the parties involved. Only when the people holding the competing expectations are seen as intractable does the administrator search for other means of resolution. If this strategy is successful, it resolves the conflict by eliminating it. It may be that this type of conflict resolution is very similar to the bargaining discussed by Griffiths. At any rate, it is evident that this variable should be considered by most school districts for inclusion in an evaluation system; the exact behavior in terms of strategies to be used may be expected to vary from district to district.

Using Judgment.   Some of the literature makes very little distinction between using judgment and making decisions; however, judgment is somewhat less systematic than decision making. Odiorne describes it in this way:

> Judgment is that untheoretical and apparently intuitive (at least often described as such) reaction to questions which are presented without much warning and to which almost immediate responses are demanded. The quality of this reaction to an inescapable demand for decision forms the quality of judgment which we attribute to the manager (1969:124–125).

Although a decision is involved in the situation described by Odiorne, there is no opportunity to collect data, devise alternatives, predict consequences, or examine value systems in relation to the consequences predicted as an administrator would ordinarily do in making more substantive decisions. It may be that judgment is simply a special case of decision making in which time is short and yet a creative selection of alternatives is needed. If such is the case, "good" judgment may be directly related to prior experience with similar circumstances, intelligence and ability to assimilate quickly all of the relevant cues involved in the situation, and the creative ability to devise several alternatives in a short period of time. It may also involve the ability to determine whether a short delay, which would allow more systematic and comprehensive procedures to be used for making the decision, would prove detrimental to the organization.

The extent to which the local school district expects administrators to use their own judgment in relation to their jobs should be specified in the job description. The nature of the behavior to be exhibited could be specified in a summary report device applicable to a set of administrators, or in an individualized MBO statement.

Boundary Spanning.   The function of an administrator identified by Gaynor (1975:2—3) as *boundary spanning* is probably recognized intuitively by most school personnel. Its significance is probably incorporated in the outcome area for which many administrators have some responsibility, viz., school-community relations and the process of communication that is often emphasized in relation to this outcome area. But Gaynor discusses it as a role rather than either an outcome area or process and indicates that the principal and the superintendent are in particularly critical positions in relation to the interface between the school system and the community. This role allows them to be sensitive in evolutionary changes in the school environment. Gaynor says:

> It can be hypothesized that in those school systems still operating in placid-clustered environments, the role of the principal remains internal and primariily bureaucratically oriented; however, as school systems find themselves in increasingly turbulent environments, the role of the principal should become more externally and politically oriented . . . it seems critical for us to understand precisely what the relationship is between the role expectations held for the school principal and the nature of the changing environments of schools (Gaynor 1977:2—3).

It would appear, then, that this variable would be most important to consider under circumstances where the community is dynamic rather than stable. Since the information provided by the interface would aid the school district in adopting and responding.

Being an Entrepreneur.   One does not ordinarily think of an educational administrator as an entrepreneur. However, as one thinks of adapting and responding to the environment, the words of Drucker concerning the business administrator are pertinent. He indicates that the manager has to be an entrepreneur as well as an administrator, in the following sense:

> He has to redirect resources from areas of low or diminishing results to areas of high or increasing results. He has to slough off yesterday and to render obsolete what already exists and is already known. He has to create tomorrow (Drucker, 1968:45).

If the entrepreneur's significant activities include (a) redirecting resources to improve results, (b) eliminating the obsolete in order that the move pertinent may prevail, and (c) creating changes that make the future more significant than the past, then certainly many school districts should consider this function as they design administrator evaluation systems. It may be considered as a separate function, or it may be included in more traditional tasks such as coordination, leadership, and planning.

DEVELOPING MEANS FOR MEASURING

Determining the means for collecting data and for measuring the procedures and results of procedures for administrators is more difficult than for the evaluation of teachers. Basically, this is true because of the difficulty of observing many of the actions of administrators. Developing means for measuring includes determining what information will be collected, understanding the limits involved in collecting data, and agreeing on the data-collection procedures to be used. An important consideration is that the development of measurement should occur before action is taken t(that is, before the administrator implements any procedures) and before information is collected. This prevents the outcomes from influencing the criteria for judging.

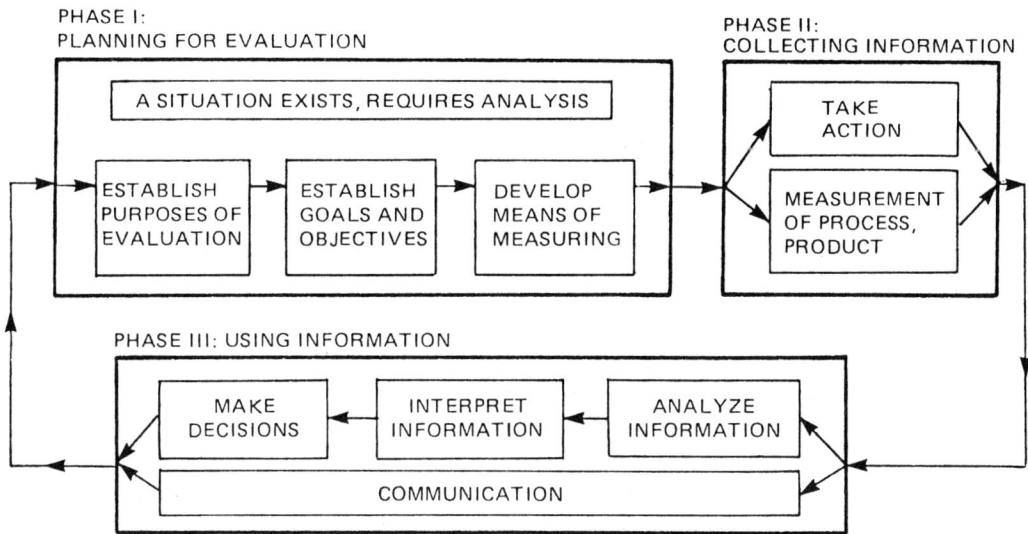

PHASE I:
PLANNING FOR EVALUATION

PHASE II:
COLLECTING INFORMATION

A SITUATION EXISTS, REQUIRES ANALYSIS

| ESTABLISH PURPOSES OF EVALUATION | ESTABLISH GOALS AND OBJECTIVES | DEVELOP MEANS OF MEASURING |

TAKE ACTION

MEASUREMENT OF PROCESS, PRODUCT

PHASE III: USING INFORMATION

| MAKE DECISIONS | INTERPRET INFORMATION | ANALYZE INFORMATION |

COMMUNICATION

Basic Ways of Collecting Information

Information can be collected in one of three ways: observing behavior, asking questions, and examining written documents. Each of these ways may be used in the evaluation of administrators, but agreement on the type of data collection to be used with each objective should be made during the planning period. Certain processes used by teachers are difficult to observe (e.g., the handling of emergencies), but many people consider most of the processes used by administrators unobservable or difficult to observe without severely altering the situation by the presence of the observer. For this reason, more emphasis is likely to be placed on information from records and from questions asked of the evaluatee and clients of the evaluatee such as students, teachers, and parents. Simply because questions and written records may be easier to obtain does not mean that creative means should not be used to observe administrators, since observation can be a very beneficial source of information. For example, faculty meetings, parental conferences, public meetings, and teacher conferences can all be observed for the purpose of evaluating performance, but this is seldom done systematically.

Dimensions to Consider

As one considers the collection of data, there should be an attempt to reach agreement regarding what data will be collected, how it will be collected, who will collect it, and when and where it will be collected.

What. The basic question most people have regarding their work is "what works for me, in my situation?" The question itself furnishes clues to what information should be collected. The "what" refers to the processes to be used; therefore, one should collect information regarding those processes. The "works" has to do with the results or outcomes of the processes; therefore, one should collect information regarding the products. It is this interest in process-product relationship which is at the heart of the evaluation process. Information about the product is needed in order to determine whether desired results were obtained, information regarding the process is needed in order to know how to replicate or to modify so that desired results can be obtained.

How. There are many ways of classifying how one collects data, but one should at least consider whether it is to be collected on an individualized or a uniform basis. If it is to be collected on a uniform basis, a common data collection form may be used for a group of administrators. If an individualized procedure is to be used, it will be beneficial for a school district to develop a group of data collection forms that may be useful in a variety of situations. This will assist an evaluator and an administrator to determine which data collection form might be most appropriate for use. Care should be taken to avoid choosing a recording form simply because it is available, however (Bolton, *Selection and Evaluation of Teachers*, 1973.34, 111–112). Instruments should not be chosen solely on the basis of the evaluator's familiarity with the document, its availability, or the fact that other districts are using it! Considerations should include:

- relevance to the goals and objectives established.
- acceptability to those who are involved, including the administrator, the evaluator, and anyone who may be responsible for responding to a self-report device.
- accessibility of information to those who will complete the device.
- time needed to acquire the information.
- the cost of information.

Who.   Deciding who should be involved in the collection of information involves many of the same considerations as the question of how it should be collected. Certainly of major consideration should be the nature of the goals and objectives and the type of information to be collected. The possibilities of who should be involved include the administrator, the evaluator or some other person(s) external to the evaluatee, and a combination of the evaluator and external people. With a single objective one is likely to choose either self or external collectors; but with the total evaluation process, a combination is more likely.

When and Where.   If one has decided on the what, how, and who regarding the collection, many times the when and where will be self-evident. For example, if a principal has an objective which relates to his or her effectiveness in conducting faculty meetings, the following may have been decided:

1.   The *what* will include procedures used in the meeting, with particular interest in the amount of participation by all members of the faculty. In addition, the product will involve the faculty's feelings of inclusion in the decision process and their satisfaction with the process.
2.   The *how* will be individualized. An observation guide will be developed and used to determine how many people participated, the frequency and time taken by each participant, the percentage of time taken by the principal, what decisions were made, and how long it took to make each decision. In addition, a self-report device will be developed to obtain the reactions of the faculty to the faculty meeting.
3.   The *who* will include the evaluator as an external observer of the meeting, using the structured observation guide developed by the principal and the evaluator. In addition, the faculty will respond to the short self-report device designed by the principal and the evaluator. The principal will be responsible for duplication of the device and for designing procedures for collecting them after they have been completed anonymously.

Once all of this has been determined, it is evident that the observation will need to occur *during* the meeting and the self-report device will need to be completed *immediately following* the meeting. It would not be beneficial to have the faculty complete the device a month after the meeting because their views may be altered by other circumstances; in addition, they may forget certain information about the meeting. However, a decision will need to be made regarding whether the faculty is to complete the device at the location of the meeting or whether they will be given the option to complete it elsewhere (e.g., at home or in their own classrooms) and turn it in the following day. Note that usually the information collection procedures as well as goals and objectives, should be determined mutually. The only exception would be in cases where an administrator is unwilling to face behaviors that are detrimental to organizational goals.

A final idea should be emphasized in relation to these dimensions to be considered in the collection of information. In evaluating administrators, the emphasis should be on making judgments in relation to established objectives, not on judging the personal worth of individuals. Judging the personal worth of an administrator is in another realm (perhaps in the legal or even the spiritual) not in the realm of the evaluator. If the evaluator is concerned with the administrator being an appropriate model for teachers or students, then the appropriate behavior should be put in the form of an objective and evaluated accordingly; but this does not involve the question of personal worth of the individual.

Some Problems of Measurement

Regardless of whether the measurement planned will be based on direct observation, asking questions of others, or examination of written records, certain problems can occur. Most of these problems are inherent in the capability and training of the person gathering the information. This person must translate raw data into usable format, and she or he can affect the translation in ways that cause problems.

Prejudice, Bias, or Poor Judgment. For example, a person's prejudices or biases regarding behavior may affect the translation of raw data. If a person who is observing an administrator (in a faculty meeting, or in a face-to-face conference) has an aversion to certain personal characteristics of the administrator, it may affect the measurement of how a discussion is conducted or how the administrator reacts to questions. Or, because the observer thinks that nonverbal behavior is extremely important in communication, he or she may improperly measure the substantial element of a conversation.

Inconsistency of Reaction to Behavior. A person who reacts positively to a given behavior or fact on one day and negatively on another day is reaching inconsistently. Likewise, a person who indicates that an administrator "seldom" behaves in a particular way and the next day indicates that the administrator "occasionally" behaves that way is being inconsistent. The reasons back of such inconsistency may be diverse, but regardless of the reason(s) the inconsistency poses a problem of measurement.

Ratings and Classifications Requiring High Interferences. Rating devices that require an individual to come to a conclusion about several bits of information and to respond to a single scale can sometimes cause problems. For example, to ask one individual to rate another on the function of "communication" by marking a pont on the scale below requires him or her to make an inference from many observations of the individual.

poor .... fair .... satisfactory .... good .... excellent ....

In addition, the scale forces the observer to attach a value to the sum total of the observations. The combined task of summarizing the information collected and attaching a value to it by coming to a conclusion about which classification is appropriate can cause inconsistency — both within and among measurers.

Outside and Inside Influences. Each person who is responsible for measuring any process or product of an administrator is influenced by his own physical and mental health (internal feelings) as well as by surroundings. When a person is frustrated or engaged in a conflict immediately prior to collecting data, these external influences can have dramatic effects on results.

Attempts to Measure Too Much. Undoubtedly all school administrators can remember their first attempts to observe a classroom full of students and a teacher. It probably was during the time they were training to become teachers, and there was the attempt to observe everything that happened in the classroom. After some experience of teaching, and perhaps some training in observational techniques, the administrator learned which cues were important for the particular objective being sought by the teacher. Consequently, this cue reduction process enabled the administrator to focus on a limited number of things to observe. When one attempts to measure too much, only some type of global impression is obtained — which may not be very helpful in terms of measurement.

Continuation of a Prior Viewpoint. Sometimes impressions of an individual gained from a particular situation tend to carry over into other situations even though the behavior of the individual changes. For example, in a superintendent's cabinet meeting an evaluator may form an impression of an administrator based on a discussion of teacher evaluation procedures. Because of what is said, the impression may be created that the administrator does considerable classroom observation followed by individual conferences with teachers. If this impression persists when the evaluator is examining the teacher-observation reports completed by the administrator, it may affect the reaction of the evaluator to the number of observations and conferences completed. The prior viewpoint should continue only if the new information warrants it, in essence, the two measures should be independent.

Consistent Over- or Under-valuation. Some people have a tendency to be consistently lenient while others tend to be harsh. These tendencies naturally affect the measurements they make and may be directly related to optimism-pessimism tendencies. Stores of such people exist in profusion. One of my favorites consists of three characters: a dean of a college of education and two professors. It happened that at the end of one quarter the dean was examining the grade distributions of each professor's classes. As he examined these grades, he noticed that the professors had rather unusual distributions of their grades. Professor "A" had given a large number of As, a few Bs, two or three Cs, and no Ds or Fs. Professor "B" had a distribution that was the reverse of Professor "A"; no As, no Bs, two or three Cs, a few Ds, and a large number of Fs. Since these two professors had such different grade distributions, the dean decided to discuss it with them. To Professor "A" he said, "I notice that you have a rather skewed distribution of grades, with many As, a few Bs, two or three Cs, and no Ds or Fs. I wonder if you could explain this to me." "Why, of course," said Professor "A" "That is merely due to my superior teaching." The dean then encountered Professor "B" and posed a similar question: "I notice your grade distribution is rather skewed, with no As, no Bs, two or three Cs, a few Ds, and a large number of Fs. I wonder if you can explain this to me." With a slight pause, Professor "B" declared, "Well – you can't flunk 'em all." Over- and under-valuation can be a real problem of measurement.

Types of Scales

It may be recalled that measurement is described as "the quantification or quasiquantification of events, behaviors, or results of behaviors; as such, it does not incorporate any judgment making or require any value system to be applied." The only value required for measurement to occur is for someone to desire that something be measured. Classical scaling theory discusses nominal, ordinal, equal interval, and ratio scales. However, for our purposes another classification of scales may be more beneficial. In examining documents in use by school systems, one finds rank ordering, forced distribution, absolute categories, verbal descriptors, degree of existence, and extent of agreement scales (Bolton, "Collecting Evaluation Data," 1973:80–82).

Rank Ordering. Rank ordering uses a scale for ranking individuals in a group according to some item or characteristic. For example consider the item and the scale below:

Ability to communicate with groups of people in structured situations. Superior ...... Above Aver. ...... Aver. ...... Below Aver. ...... Inferior ......

Note that this ranking is against a reference group, but rank ordering may also be against an absolute standard or criterion. For example, the scale may be:
Excellent ...... Good ...... Satisfactory ...... Poor ...... Inadequate ......

This latter scale requires only that one define each point on the scale in terms of behavior that would represent the point; whereas, the first scale requires that some reference group be known well enough to determine each point. On the first scale, one could not have 90 percent of a group in the "Superior" category, since that would violate the meaning of average (Author's note: If the reference group in all of the administrators in a state, one might well have 90 percent of the administrators in a given district in the "Superior" category, but not if the reference group is the given district.) However, one might well have 90 percent of the administrators of a group in the "Excellent" category, since they could conceivably satisfy that criterion or standard.

If one desires to use a rank ordering scale, care should be taken not to mix criterion referenced scales and norm referenced scales. For example, the following scale is mixed:
Poor ...... Average ...... Good ...... Very good ...... Superior ......

Since poor, good, and very good are absolute standards and average and superior require a norm group, the scale is confusing to anyone trying to use it, error of measurement is "built into" the scale itself.

The rank ordering scale may be used with specific items (as illustrated with the communication item above) or with general and overall type items, which may be illustrated as follows:

General item: Professional responsibility.
Overall item: Indicate your estimate of the service rendered by this administrator by placing a check in front of the most appropriate term.

Forced Distribution. A forced distribution requires that a certain percentage of the people being considered be placed in each descriptive category. For example, consider the specific item which we combined with the norm referenced scale:

Ability to communicate with groups of people in structured situations.
Superior ...... Above Aver. ...... Aver. ...... Below Aver. ...... Inferior ......

If we required that the categories include ratios of 10 percent, 20 percent, 40 percent, 20 percent, 10 percent, we would in fact be changing the item to:

Ability to communicate with groups of people in structured situations.
Upper 10% ..... Next 20% ..... Mid 40% ..... Next 20% ..... Lowest 10% .....

As with the norm-referenced rank ordering scale, it would be necessary to define the norm group.

The forced distribution scale may also be used with general areas or overall items; the items could be similar to those used to illustrate the rank ordering scale.

Absolute Categories.   Absolute category systems describe individual behaviors or total behavior of an administrator by placing incidents into discrete descriptive categories. For example, a *specific* item combined with this scale might be:

The administrator provides background information from official school district policies or procedures.

...... (count the number of times this occurs during the meeting observed)

It appears that this type of scale does not readily combine with a *general* type of item, but it may combine with an *overall* item; for example:

My recommendation for this administrator for the coming year is:

_____ should remain in the present position
_____ should have a parallel change of assignment
_____ should receive a promotion
_____ should request leave of absence
_____ services should be terminated

Verbal Descriptors. Verbal descriptors are used to express what has been perceived and may be used in sentence, phrase, single word form, or scaled with bipolar adjectives. The example below uses a *specific* item combined with bipolar adjectives.

The manner in which the principal evaluates teachers can best be

described as (put a check in the space you consider to be appropriate):
continuous ...... : ...... : ...... : ...... : ...... : ...... : ...... erratic
rational ...... : ...... : ...... : ...... : ...... : ...... : ...... irrational
systematic ...... : ...... : ...... : ...... : ......: ...... : ......disorganized

For a more *general* item, the following might be required:
Write a brief paragraph describing characteristics that are most pertinent to the administrator's potential for promotion to the next higher
level.

An *overall* item may simply ask for comments regarding areas needing improvement. The examples used in this category indicate that the specific
items merely supply the descriptors and the behavior or characteristic to be
described, but the more general item or the overall item leaves the responsibility for devising these descriptors to the person doing the measuring.

Degree of Existence.   The degree of existence scale is concerned with
how often an event or type of behavior occurs. An example of a *specific*
item would be:

Exhibits confidence in teachers' doing a professional job
always ...... often ...... occasionally ...... seldom ...... never ......

The same type of scaling could be used with a more *general* type of item
such as "uses good judgment," but it does not appear to be appropriate for
the overall type of item.

Extent of Agreement.   This type of scale usually makes a statement with
which a person may express an amount of agreement or disagreement. For
example, teachers may be asked to respond to the following *specific* item:

The evaluation procedure used by my principal has encouraged me to
initiate and maintain a systematic procedure for self-evaluation.
SA .... A .... U .... D.......... SD ....
in this case, SA = Strongly Agree, A = Agree, U = Undecided, D = Disagree,
and SD = Strongly Disagree.

A more *general* item might be:
The principal of this school is well organized.
Strongly Agree ...... : ......: ...... : ...... : ...... Strongly Disagree

An *overall* item might be:
This administrator should be retained in the present position next year.
Yes .... No ....

It is probable that this type of scale will be more useful for the specific item, but some may find it beneficial for either the general or the overall type of item.

The scales and types of items that have been described are not intended as a prescription for use in specific school districts. However, under conditions where administrators in a school district desire to construct their own measurement or information recording devices (rather than borrowing them from another district or having them designed by a consultant), the classification scheme may be of benefit. Care should be taken to choose the types of scales and items that contribute most to the purposes for evaluation. For example, the use of a forced distribution scale on an overall item may be quite beneficial for making administrative decisions about reduction in force, however, under conditions where such decisions are not being made, the scale may induce anxiety, apprehension, and even hostility.

Sources of Information

It has been mentioned that the behavioral sciences obtain information from three sources: observation, asking questions, and written records. And all of these can be used for obtaining information for the evaluation of administrators.

Observation. Observation of administrators by external evaluators can occur in both a systematic and an incidental way. Systematic observation of administrators may occur in certain structured situations such as faculty meetings, departmental or level meetings, or meetings with groups of parents. In addition, one might systematically observe the office routines used by an administrator or an observer could keep an accurate log of the way an administrator manages his time. Less systematic observation is likely to occur in meetings of administrators, superintendent's cabinet meetings, individual conferences with a supervisor or another person, committee meetings, or task force meetings. In these situations all individuals are likely to be concentrating on the substance of the encounter and only incidentally observing the behavior of the participants.

Because an evaluator may have many more contacts of an incidental nature with an evaluatee than contacts where systematic observation is designed and carried out, there should be a conscious effort to review criteria, circumstances where information might be collected, and critical incidents occurring in these circumstances. Where the review occurs between the evaluator and the administrator, not only is communication likely to be improved between the two of them, but also both are likely to become better observers of events contributing to the evaluation.

Asking Questions. Asking questions of others can occur via interviews or structured self-report devices. Questions may be asked of subordinates, peers, or clients. For example, subordinates of principals would be teachers and vice principals, peers would be other principals who may interact with each other on projects or in coordination of programs; and clients would include students, parents, and voters. An assistant superintendent in charge of personnel would have a different set of subordinates, peers, and clients, however.

Suppose, for example, that an assistant superintendent has responsibility for a series of meetings in homes where the purpose is to provide information about a school levy for operations during the coming school year. He may desire to acquire information from those who attend the meetings (clients) in order to evaluate his own effectiveness in conducting the meetings. The self-report device might include such items as the following:

A. Please respond to the following items by placing a checkmark in the space you judge to represent your views.
    1. The ideas presented and discussed, in relation to my own concerns regarding the school levy, were
        pertinent ...... : ...... : ...... : ...... : ...... : ...... : ...... missed the point
    2. The presentation was
        valuable ...... : ...... : ...... : ...... : ...... : ...... : ...... worthless
    3. The question and answer period was
        interesting ...... : ...... : ...... : ...... : ...... : ...... : ...... dull
        worthwhile ...... : ...... : ...... : ...... : ...... : ...... : ...... worthless
        clear ...... : ...... : ...... : ...... : ...... : ...... : ...... hazy
    4. There were opportunities today for me to clarify my thinking
        considerably ...... : ...... : ...... : ...... : ...... : ...... : ...... not at all
    5. The combination of the presentation and the question-and-answer period allowed me to feel
        free to
        participate ...... : ...... : ...... : ...... : ...... : ...... : ...... stifled

B. Complete the following sentences:
    6. I would like   _____
    7. The main problem   _____
    8. I found out   _____

C. Please respond to the following:
    9. What questions or topics were not discussed as fully as you would have liked?   _____
   10. Please indicate how you think meetings of this type would be of more benefit to voters   _____

Such information may be used to (a) facilitate communication between the administrator and his supervisor (probably the superintendent) regarding the exact nature of the meetings and how they are perceived by those who attend, (b) suggest changes in format or content of meetings during the levy campaign, (c) assess information regarding differences in reactions in different parts of the community; and (d) compile summary information for use in planning future information dissemination.

An additional advantage of this type of information is that it can be acquired and analyzed quickly; ten items such as those suggested above can be completed in five to seven minutes by those who attend; a clerk can summarize a set of twenty-five in approximately fifteen minutes; and the administrator and supervisor can analyze and interpret the results in fifteen minutes or less. The major time factor would be in devising the precise questions. However, one could soon accumulate sets of items that could be used in a variety of situations, and then a questionnaire could be devised in a fairly short time.

Written Records.   An administrator's written records fall into two categories: those which result from the normal activities of the administrator and those made by the administrator in order to answer some question of an evaluative nature. An example of the first category is the records a principal may keep of all observations of classrooms during a school year. An example of the second category is the record a principal may decide to keep of the number of telephone calls received from parents — classifying them by nature of the inquiry, duration of call, and when they occur, in order to determine how this places a constraint on use of time. In each case, the written records would be subject to analysis and interpretation by both the administrator and the evaluator in relation to certain objectives established prior to the data collection (or at least prior to the analysis).

Use of Forms

Forms are used to collect information and to summarize the information for reporting purposes. The collection of information is basically a measuring process, and general conclusions may not be needed. However, summary report forms usually require conclusions to be stated.

One of the major problems with forms currently in use by many school districts is that these two functions (i.e., collecting and summarizing/reporting) are combined in the same form. When this happens, it is often the case that the summarizing/reporting overshadows the collecting function rendering the form inadequate for use in collecting information. A solution to this problem is to design a summary report form and use it for that purpose only. It may then be necessary to design individual information collection devices in terms of the needs of specific administrators. A "bank" of devices is helpful for designing these forms.

SUMMARY

Planning for the evaluation of administrators is considered to be the first phase of a three-phase, cyclical process that also includes collecting information and using information. The information used during the third phase becomes the basis for planning as the cycle repeats itself. The *planning for evaluation* phase includes analysis of a specific situation, establishing purposes for evaluation, setting goals and specific objectives, and deciding on means for measuring the processes used and the eventual outcomes.

The planning phase may involve primarily one-to-one relationships between an evaluator and evaluatee, but it is more likely that some parts of the planning phase will occur with groups of administrators. For example, as the situation within which administrators function is analyzed fully, both the external and the internal variables are likely to be examined by groups of administrators. They may be reviewed by individual evaluators and evaluatees, but the initial examination may be by groups. The same may be true of other parts of planning.

There is some evidence that the level of an administrator's position and the nature of subordinates supervised have an impact on the type of cognitive skills needed in a position. In addition, at least the following variables should be considered by administrators analyzing local situations: (a) the number of individuals and groups that have an impact on the commitment and support of schools, (b) the size of the organization, and (c) the value system and expectations of those with whom the administrator works.

Job descriptions for administrators vary from organization to organization — in substance as well as extent of use. The three areas of responsibility often included in job descriptions are (a) performance of regular and/or routine duties, (b) achieving satisfactory solutions to problems, and (c) completing new and innovative projects. The job description is generally considered a beneficial tool in managing an organization when used as a basis for discussion about priorities, significant elements of the job, and elements that have changed since prior discussions.

Studies of the expectations others have of administrators in local situations appear to offer clues to what type of behavior causes people to be satisfied with the functioning of schools. Since others' expectations regarding such things as thrust for productivity and attention to the concerns of people vary among situations, it appears important for school districts to identify locally what characteristics and behaviors are valued by subordinates, administrators, and clients. Such empirical evidence may be quite beneficial in planning for evaluation of administrators.

BIBLIOGRAPHY

Arikado, Marjorie and Donald Musella. "Toward an Objective Evaluation of the School Principal." *Ontario Council for Leadership in Educational Administration* (January 1975).

Beer, Michael and Robert A. Ruh. "Employee Growth Through Performance Management," *Harvard Business Review* 54:59–66 (July-August 1976).

Bolton, Dale L. "Collecting Evaluation Data." *The National Elementary Principal* 52:77–86 (February 1973).

————. "Evaluating School Processes and Products: a Responsibility of School Principals." In *Performance Objectives for School Principals: Concepts and Instruments,* ed. Jack A. Culbertson, Curtis Henson, and Ruel Morrison. Berkeley, Calif.: McCutcham Publishing, 1974.

————, "Problems and Issues in the Evaluation of Administrative Performance." In *NSPER: The Evaluation of Administrative Performance: Parameters, Problems & Practices,* ed. William J. Gephart, Robert B. Ingle, and W. James Potter. Bloomington, Ind.; Phi Delta Kappa, 67–92, 1977.

————, *Selection and Evaluation of Teachers.* Berkeley, Calif.: McCutchan Publishing, 1973.

————, *Variables Affecting Decision Making in the Selection of Teachers.* Seattle: University of Washington, Cooperative Research Project No. 6-1349, 1968.

Campbell, John P., Marvin D. Dunnette, Edward E. Lawler, III, and Karl E. Weick, Jr. *Managerial Behavior, Performance, and Effectiveness.* New York: McGraw-Hill, 1970.

Carroll, S.J., Jr. and H.L. Tosi, Jr. *Management by Objectives: Applications and Research.* New York: Macmillan, 1973.

Cummins, Robert C. "Relationship of Initiating Structure and Job Performance as Moderated by Consideration." *Journal of Applied Psychology* 55:489–490 (October 1971).

Drucker, Peter. *Management: Tasks, Responsibilities, Practices.* New York: Harper and Row, 1968.

Dunnette, Marvin D. "Predictors of Executive Success." In *Measuring Executive Effectiveness,* ed. Frederic R. Wickert and Dalton E. McFarland. New York: Appleton-Century-Crofts, 1967.

French, Wendell L. and Robert W. Hollman. "Management by Objectives: The Team Approach." *California Management Review* 17:13–22 (Spring 1975).

Gaynor, Alan K. "The Multidemensional World of the School Principal." A paper presented at the annual meeting of the American Educational Research Association, Washington, D.C., April 3, 1975.

————. "The Role of the School Administrator: Perspectives for a Conference on Administrator Evaluation." In *The Evaluation of Administrative Performance: Parameters, Problems and Practices,* eds. William J. Gephart, Robert B. Ingle, and W. James Potter, *Phi Delta Kappa,* (1977).

Griffiths, Daniel E. "The Individual in Organization: a Theoretical Perspective." *Educational Administration Quarterly* 13:1–18 (Spring 1977).

Heald, James E., and Samuel A. Moore, Jr. *The Teacher and Administrative Relationships in School Systems.* New York: Macmillan, 1968.

Herzberg, Frederick. "One More Time: How Do You Motivate Employees?" *Harvard Business Review* (January-February 1968).

————, Bernard Mausner, and Barbara Block Snyderman. *The Motivation to Work.* New York: John Wiley, 1959.

House, Robert J., Alan C. Filley, and Damodar N. Gujarati. "Leadership Style, Hierarchical Influence, and the Satisfaction of Subordinate Role Expectations: A Test of Likert's Influence Proposition." *Journal of Applied Psychology* 55:422–432 (October 1971).

Howsam, Robert B. "Teacher Evaluation: Facts and Folklore." *National Elementary Principal* 43:7–18 (November 1963).

Keegan, John J. "Performance Based Staff Evaluation: A Reality We Must Face." *Educational Technology* 15:35–38 (November 1975).

Levinson, Harry. *The Exceptional Executive, a Psychological Conception.* New York: New American Library, 1968.

McConkey, D.D. "Writing Measurable Objectives for Staff Managers." *Advanced Management Journal* 37:10–16 (January 1972).

Odiorne, George S. *Management Decisions by Objectives.* Englewood Cliffs, N.J.: Prentice-Hall, 1969.

Peres, Sherwood H., and J. Robert Garcia. "Validity and Dimensions of Descriptive Adjectives Used in Reference Letters for Engineering Applicants." *Personnel Psychology* 16:279–286 (Autumn 1962).

Pharis, W. L. "The Evaluation of School Principals." *National Elementary Principal* 52:36–38 (February 1973).

Raia, Anthony P. *Managing by Objectives.* Glenview, Ill.: Scott, Foresman, 1974.

Ritchie, Douglas S. "Management System – Madison Public Schools." *The Administrator* 6:33–36 (Spring 1976).

Sayan, Donald L. and W.W. Charters, Jr. "A Replication Among School Principals of the Gross Study of Role Conflict Resolution" *Educational Administration Quarterly* 6:36–45 (Spring 1970).

Silver, Paula F. "Principals' Conceptual Ability in Relation to Situation and Behavior." *Educational Administration Quarterly* 3:49–66 (Autumn 1975).

Streufert, Siegried and H.M. Schroder. "Conceptual Structure, Environmental Complexity and Task Performance." *Journal of Experimental Research in Personality* 1:132–137 (1965).

PART IV

Some Useful Forms for the Evaluation Process

An Appraisal and Evaluation System
For Teachers and Administrators

Carmelo V. Sapone

Carmelo V. Sapone, Associate Professor of Education at Niagara University, Niagara Falls, New York, presents in this article an appraisal and evaluation model that can be used for administrators. It is his contention that using the model, which he suggests can be altered to suit the needs of individual school districts, can answer questions about whether or not an effective appraisal system can be implemented in a particular district, lead to more effective performance, demonstrate greater accountability to the community, or make a difference in student growth and school achievement. His hope is that the eighteen tersely-worded steps listed in his model can help school organizations move towards greater educational effectiveness.

Today, as never before, the public is demanding educational and fiscal accountability. The message is clear that new dollars for education will not be forthcoming until the taxpayers' confidence is restored in what is currently happening in schools and until they can expect a reasonable return from additional investment.

It is, therefore, incumbent upon educational leaders to develop specific appraisal and evaluation systems for assessing the process and products of education. What citizens are requiring is *proof* of increased effectiveness of teacher and administrative performances as they influence pupil growth and school achievement.

Boards of education, administrators, and teachers must collaboratively develop a meaningful appraisal and evaluation system to facilitate school effectiveness. This system must provide opportunities for all to learn. The system must insure that the desired educational outcomes are actually being achieved.

The model, as presented in Figure 1 and Table 1, is representative of specific programmatic components, or steps, which bear relationship to one another. Some of these components are based primarily on issues of attitude change or personal development. Other components in the system are based primarily on issues of process change or instructional development. The third set of components is based on issues of structural change or organizational development. Included in the total system are the concepts of leadership behavior and style.

One missing link in most appraisal and evaluation systems is the lack of negotiated leadership among those involved in the appraisal process. Most appraisal and evaluation systems assume the role of "supervisor vs. subordinate." Consequently, there is little feeling of ownership of the total system at the grass-roots level. The major purpose of any organization must be to coordinate the activities of its personnel toward greater educational efficiency and effectiveness. The components and/or guidelines, as used in this system, represent one attempt to help the organization focus on that purpose.

What is also missing in most appraisal and evaluation systems is a method for assessing the health of the organization. The proposed system addresses itself to the process of improving the health of the organization through a systematic approach to defining the parameters needed in any appraisal and evaluation plan. It also attempts to deal with the attitudes of the participants as well as with related values, philosophies, and self-perceptions.

What may be needed in any synergistic system is the desire to validate local school appraisal and evaluation plans with the author's suggested model. Where local components/guidelines are lacking, the incorporation of some or most of the author's components may become desirable.

Additionally, the proposed systematic model might insure answers and solutions to many of the pressing questions in the field of appraisal and evaluation systems:

1. Can an effective appraisal and evaluation system be developed and implemented with the strong endorsement of all involved in the total process?
2. Can meaningful criteria be established and used as the agreed-upon basis for performance measurement?
3. Can the appraisal and evaluation system demonstrate to the community greater accountability in terms of goal achievement?
4. Will the appraisal and evaluation system lead to increased and effective administrator and teacher performances?
5. Does improved performance (if any) make any difference on student growth and school achievement?
6. Will a negotiated leadership style emerge that can be identified as appropriate for the local appraisal and evaluation system?

7. Can a meaningful and effective appraisal and evaluation system be replicated and disseminated to other school systems with a minimum of effort and cost?

It is the author's contention that answers to the above questions can be in the affirmative, if local school officials incorporate and improve upon the author's model. Its implementation resides with those who desire to improve their appraisal and evaluation systems.

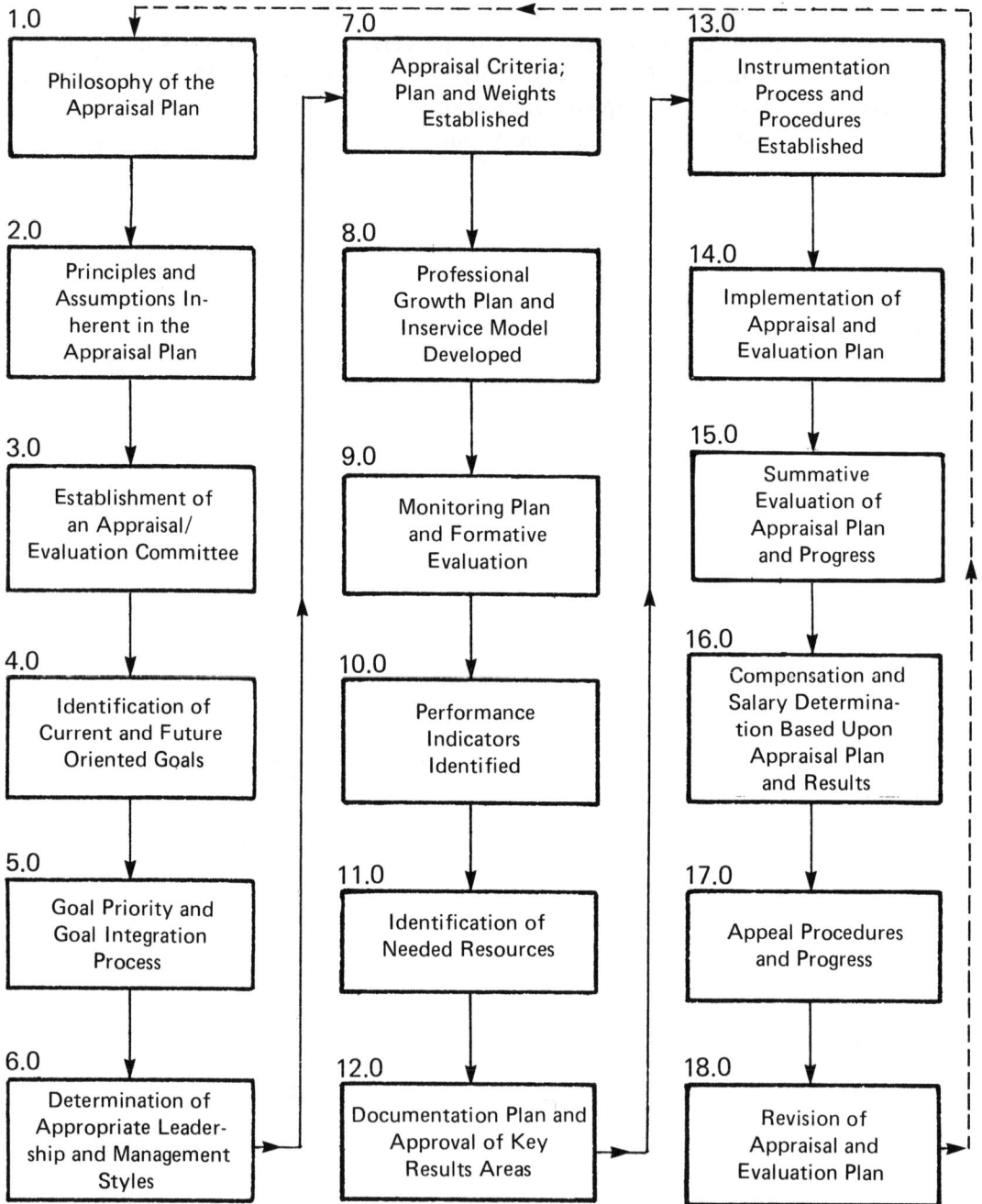

FIGURE 1
An Alternative Model for Administrative and Teacher Appraisal

1.0 Philosophy of the Appraisal Plan

2.0 Principles and Assumptions Inherent in the Appraisal Plan

3.0 Establishment of an Appraisal/ Evaluation Committee

4.0 Identification of Current and Future Oriented Goals

5.0 Goal Priority and Goal Integration Process

6.0 Determination of Appropriate Leadership and Management Styles

7.0 Appraisal Criteria; Plan and Weights Established

8.0 Professional Growth Plan and Inservice Model Developed

9.0 Monitoring Plan and Formative Evaluation

10.0 Performance Indicators Identified

11.0 Identification of Needed Resources

12.0 Documentation Plan and Approval of Key Results Areas

13.0 Instrumentation Process and Procedures Established

14.0 Implementation of Appraisal and Evaluation Plan

15.0 Summative Evaluation of Appraisal Plan and Progress

16.0 Compensation and Salary Determination Based Upon Appraisal Plan and Results

17.0 Appeal Procedures and Progress

18.0 Revision of Appraisal and Evaluation Plan

TABLE 1
An Appraisal and Evaluation Model for Teachers and Administrators

Step 1:   Philosophy of the Appraisal Plan
Weight: ...... A.   Compensation
          ...... B.   Merit
.... C.   Growth (personal and organizational)
          ...... D.   Position requirements and up-date
          ...... E.   Improve performance standards
          ...... F.   Develop leadership potential
          ...... G.   Improve the decision-making process
          ...... H.
          ...... I.
          ...... J.

Step 2:   Principles and Assumptions Inherent in the Appraisal Plan
Weight: ...... A.   The appraisal plan must integrate goals and objectives
                      of the organization and the targeted goals of the ap-
....   praisers.
          ...... B.   The appraisal plan must encourage leadership to emerge
                      and be recognized.
          ...... C.   The appraisal plan must be diagnostic in its scope and
                      in its planning.
          ...... D.   The appraisal plan must contribute toward mutually
                      acceptable goals and to the growth of all those in-
                      volved in the process.
          ...... E.   The appraisal plan should establish a plan of action at-
                      tainable by all involved in the design, implementation,
                      and evaluation.
          ...... F.   The appraisal plan should be based upon substantial
                      evidence of agreed-upon performance.
          ...... G.
          ...... H.
          ...... I.

Step 3:   Establishment of an Appraisal/Evaluation Committee
Weight: ...... A.   Representation selection procedures
          ...... B.   Investigation of appraisal plans
.... C.   Literature search of effective appraisal plans
          ...... D.   Development of pilot appraisal plan
          ...... E.   Approval of appraisal plan by all involved in the imple-
                      mentation and evaluation
          ...... F.   Inservice model developed for appraisal plan

	G.	Role of appraisal/evaluation committee after implementation phase defined
	H.	Use of resource expertise
	I.	Establishment of board policy and approval of appraisal and evaluation plan
	J.	
	K.	
	L.	

Step 4:   Identification of Current and Future Oriented Goals
Weight:
...... A.   Phi Delta Kappan goal oriented model
...... B.   Management by objectives and results model
.... C.   Competency-based education model
...... D.   State mandated goal model
...... E.   Local school and district goal setting model
...... F.
...... G.
...... H.

Step 5:   Goal Priority and Goal Integration Process
Weight:
...... A.   Federal and state mandates
...... B.   District goals
.... C.   Superintendent's goals
...... D.   Local school goals
...... E.   Instructional goals
...... F.   Teacher and student goals
...... G.
...... H.
...... I.

Step 6:   Determination of Appropriate Leadership and Management Styles
Weight:
...... A.   Maslow's Self-Actualization Concept and Theory
...... B.   Herzberg's Hygiene Theory (Motivational)
.... C.   McClelland's Achievement Theory
...... D.   Homan's Interaction, Activities, and Sentiment Theory
...... E.   Arygris' Immaturity and Maturity Theory
...... F.   Berne and Harris' Transactional Analysis Theory
...... G.   Blake, Shepard, and Mouton Management of Inter-Group Conflict
...... H.   McGregor's Theory X and Theory Y
...... I.   Tannenbaum and Schmidt's Leadership Continuum Theory
...... J.   Cartwright and Zander's Group Dynamics Studies and Theory

...... K. The Michigan Leadership Studies and Theory
...... L. Ohio State Leadership Studies and Theory
...... M. Blake and Mouton's Managerial Grid Theory
...... N. Likert's Pattern of Management Theory
...... O. Fiedler's Leadership Contingency Model and Theory
...... P. Lawrence and Lorsch's Differentiation and Integration Model
...... Q. Hersey and Blanchard's Situational Leadership Theory
...... R. Kurt Lewin's Field Analysis Theory and Model
...... S. Guest's Socio-Technical Cycle Theory
...... T. Kelman's Mechanism for Change Theory
...... U.
...... V.
...... W.

Step 7: Appraisal Criteria; Plan and Weights Established

Weight. ...... A. Successful and meaningful appraisal integrates the goals and objectives of the organization and the targeted goals of the appraisee
....
...... B. Determination and agreement of the leadership style required in the appraisal plan
...... C. Identification of needs to be used as a diagnostic measure for personal and organization growth
...... D. Commitment of growth as the fundamental principle in the appraisal process
...... E. Determination of weights to be used for area in the appraisal process
...... F. Appraisal process should enchance and result in defined plans, directions, or sets of goals that outline and guide future growth
...... G. Appraisal findings, judgments, and/or decisions should be based upon substantial evidence of performance as agreed
...... H. Focus of appraisals should be based upon performance, appropriate behaviors, and relevant strengths of the appraisee
...... I. Appraisal process should be shared with equal responsibility equated to those involved in the execution of the appraisal plan
...... J.
...... K.
...... L.

Step 8: Professional Growth plan and Inservice Model Developed

Weight: ...... A. Assessment of district goals integrated with school and individual goals.

.... B. Assessment of school curicula

...... C. Assessment of individual's strengths and weaknesses

...... D. Selection of inservice staff committee

...... E. Development of professional growth plan and inservice model congruent with assessment needs

...... F. Approval of professional growth and inservice model by staff

...... G. Pilot of professional growth plan and inservice model

...... H. Computerize data for professional growth plan and inservice model

...... I. Adopt plan on a school and/or district basis

...... J.

...... K.

...... L.

Step 9: Monitoring Plan and Formative Evaluation

Weight: ...... A. Reporting procedures developed

...... B. Evidence of appropriate performance established

.... C. Timetable established for performance review

...... D. Feedback model established and implemented

...... E. Revise goals and objectives as needed for updating and improvement of appraisal and evaluation plan

...... F. Computerized data of progress and attainment of goals and objectives of appraisal and evaluation plan

...... G.

...... H.

...... I.

Step 10: Performance Indicators Identified

Weight: ...... A. Achievement results (test, behaviors, etc.)

...... B. Key results areas of agreed-upon goals to be used during
.... the appraisal review

...... C. Agreed-upon evaluative performance indicators

...... D. Progress of achievement of goals

...... E. Motivation toward achievement of goals

...... F. Identified areas of improvement as a result of the achievement of agreed-upon goals and objectives

...... G.

...... H.

...... I.

Step 11: Identification of Needed Resources

Weight: ...... A. Resource personnel as identified to assist in goal attainment
.... B. Materials
         ...... A. Print
         ...... B. Non-Print
...... C. Secretarial assistance
...... D. Computer usage and related services
...... E.
...... F.
...... G.

Step 12: Documentation plan and Approval of Key Results Areas
Weight. ...... A. Identification of materials to support appraisal plan
         ...... 1. Minutes of meetings
.... 2. Personnel involvement
         ...... 3. Evaluation and research progress
         ...... 4. Material selection and utilization for appraisal plan
...... B. Regular progress to review achievement of goals
...... C.
...... D.
...... E.

Step 13: Instrumentation Process and Procedures Established
Weight: ...... A. Identification of appropriate instruments and procedures to be used during the appraisal process
         ...... 1. Micro-teaching and analysis
.... 2. Tuckman's school climate rating scale
         ...... 3. Flander's interaction analysis
         ...... 4. Rating scales
         ...... 5. Observation
         ...... 6. Student evaluation
         ...... 7. Peer evaluation
...... B. Detailed procedures established
         ...... 1. Reporting mechanism
         ...... 2. Scheduling of meeting
         ...... 3. Timetable development
         ...... 4. Progress review
         ...... 5. Agreement of procedure
...... C.
...... D.
...... E.

Step 14: Implementation of Appraisal and Evaluation Plan
Weight: ...... A. Starting and ending timetable
          ...... B. Trial pilot phase
.... C. Evaluation procedures reviewed
          ...... D. Final debugging of appraisal plan
          ...... E. Implementation of final appraisal plan
          ...... F.
          ...... G.
          ...... H.

Step 15: Summative Evaluation of Appraisal Plan and Progress
Weight: ...... A. Benchmark dates set and accomplishments stated
          ...... B. Appropriate evidence presented
.... C. Review of progress to date
          ...... D. Assistance needed and provided
          ...... E. Suggestions and recommendations given
          ...... F. Written and oral evaluation presented
          ...... G. Signatures of all parties on all documents
          ...... H. Areas of agreement and disagreement noted
          ...... I. Reivew of current position and incumbent
          ...... J. Compensation reward denied or given
          ...... K.
          ...... L.
          ...... M.

Step 16: Compensation and Salary Determination Based Upon Appraisal
Weight: Plan and Results
          ...... A. Salary plan and compensation factors presented and
....   agreed
          ...... B. Identification of monies to be distributed based upon
                      weights of goals and accomplishment in each key
                      results area as approved
          ...... C. Distribution of monies
          ...... D. Revision of compensation plan as needed
          ...... E.
          ...... F.
          ...... G.

Step 17: Appeal Procedures and Progress
Weight: ...... A. Appeal plan finalized and approved
          ...... B. Appeal procedures defined
.... C. Notification of appeal results
          ...... D. Final level of determination agreed

...... E.   Relationship of appraisal and evaluation plan to negoti-
              ated contract
...... F.   Review of appeals and relationship to total appraisal
              and evaluation model
...... G.
...... H.
...... I.

Step 18: Revision of Appraisal and Evaluation Plan
Weight: ...... A.   Review of each step of plan by appraisal and evaluation
                      committee
.... B.   Committee recommendations made and procedure for
                      implementing recommendations established
          ...... C.   Committee recommendations implemented
          ...... D.   Approval by appraisal committee and all participants of
                      revised appraisal and evaluation plan
          ...... E.   Approval by superintendent and board of education
          ...... F.
          ...... G.
          ...... H.

Principal's Performance Style

Josephine C. Barger

Josephine C. Barger is an Executive Assistant at Eastern Illinois University, Charleston, Illinois. The form reproduced here is part of a paper she presented at a meeting of the Rocky Mountain Educational Research Association in Tucson, Arizona, in 1979. Designed for use in evaluation of administrators by the teaching staff, the form may also be useful to the administrator as a self-appraisal questionnaire.

Appendix 1 of *A Model Instrument for the Evaluation of School Administrators* by Josephine C. Barger. Copyright 1979 by the author. Reprinted by permission.

DIRECTIONS: On each of the items, you are asked to decide which of the five possibilities, using the key below, best describes your principal. Draw a circle around the letter corresponding to your choice. Please omit your name from the questionnaire.

- A. Almost always
- B. Frequently
- C. About as often as not
- D. Sometimes
- E. Almost never

1. He/she is able to answer questions about the total program with which he/she is working.   A   B   C   D   E
2. He/she seems to be an emotionally stable person.   A   B   C   D   E
3. He/she seems to be self-confident about his/her work.   A   B   C   D   E
4. He/she seems preoccupied with his/her own personal problems.   A   B   C   D   E

5.	He/she shows genuine concern about the personal problems of the personnel.	A	B	C	D	E
6.	He/she welcomes ideas that are contrary to his/her own.	A	B	C	D	E
7.	He/she is willing to discuss with me any individual problems I may have in performing my duties.	A	B	C	D	E
8.	He/she asks for and uses suggestions from other personnel concerning the operation of the school program.	A	B	C	D	E
9.	He/she encourages personnel to employ useful innovations.	A	B	C	D	E
10.	He/she plans activities carefully and adequately.	A	B	C	D	E
11.	He/she works hard to accomplish the goals of the educational program.	A	B	C	D	E
12.	He/she meets emergencies effectively and competently.	A	B	C	D	E
13.	He/she possesses insight into the problems encountered by the professional staff in the performance of their teaching duties.	A	B	C	D	E
14.	He/she actively promotes good public relations.	A	B	C	D	E
15.	He/she keeps His/her staff informed.	A	B	C	D	E
16.	He/she gives constructive criticism to staff members.	A	B	C	D	E
17.	He/she attempt to promote good staff morale.	A	B	C	D	E
18.	He/she gives credit for ideas initiated by other people.	A	B	C	D	E
19.	He/she is available to counsel and assist other members of the staff.	A	B	C	D	E
20.	He/she accepts his/her share of the blame when things go wrong.	A	B	C	D	E
21.	He/she does not give unwarranted criticism to individual staff members.	A	B	C	D	E
23.	He/she does not shame and embarrass personnel in the presence of other staff members, students, or outsiders.	A	B	C	D	E
24.	He/she gives support to teachers in the face of criticism.	A	B	C	D	E
25.	He/she has a genuine concern for the students in the school.	A	B	C	D	E

26.	He/she is more interested in the school program than in his/her personal desires and advancement.	A	B	C	D	E
27.	He/she is friendly and personable.	A	B	C	D	E
28.	He/she accepts criticism about his/her members of the staff.	A	B	C	D	E
29.	He/she is sufficiently concerned about teachers' salaries and fringe benefits.	A	B	C	D	E
30.	He/she rules with an iron hand.	A	B	C	D	E
31.	He/she finds time to listen to staff members.	A	B	C	D	E
32.	He/she keeps to himself/herself.	A	B	C	D	E
33.	He/she gives advance notice of changes.	A	B	C	D	E
34.	He/she refuses to explain his/her actions.	A	B	C	D	E
35.	He/she acts without consulting the staff.	A	B	C	D	E
36.	He/she asks that staff members follow standard rules and regulations.	A	B	C	D	E
37.	He/she makes staff members feel at ease when talking with them.	A	B	C	D	E
38.	He/she lets staff members know what is expected of them.	A	B	C	D	E
39.	He/she makes plans carefully and adequately.	A	B	C	D	E
40.	He/she is honest and dependable in dealing with his/her staff.	A	B	C	D	E
41.	He/she displays unwarranted favoritism to some staff members.	A	B	C	D	E
42.	He/she affords teachers the opportunity to participate regularly and actively in making policies concerning curriculum.	A	B	C	D	E
43.	He/she allows teachers an appropriate amount of autonomy in the performance of their duties.	A	B	C	D	E
44.	He/she makes provisions to permit good communication both upward and downward.	A	B	C	D	E
45.	He/she protects the authority of the teacher.	A	B	C	D	E
46.	He/she supports teachers in disciplinary matters.	A	B	C	D	E
47.	He/she makes certain extra assignments are distributed equally.	A	B	C	D	E
48.	He/she sets an example by working hard himself/herself.	A	B	C	D	E

49. He/she performs an adequate number of classroom visitations during the school year.

A   B   C   D   E

50. He/she has the office organized in such a manner that it meets the needs of the staff.

A   B   C   D   E

Administrative Characteristics

Edmund L. Lewis

Edmund L. Lewis is Director of Board Policy Services for the California School Boards Association in Sacramento. He has devised a form which can be used both by the superintendent and the board in the course of evaluation. Lewis lists the items for evaluation under several headings. "Relationships with the Board," "Administration of the School District," "Community Relationships," "Staff and Personnel Relationships," "Educational Leadership," "Business and Finance," and "Personal Qualities." The form is useful to the superintendent in analyzing his own job performance and to the board in determining what questions it should be asking as it seeks to scrutinize and make judgments about the superintendent's effectiveness.

Evaluation should be an on-going process utilizing both formal and informal methods. Evaluation can be a positive or negative experience. For the benefit of both the superintendent and the district, it should occur and be conducted in the most positive manner possible at least once a year.

The process and criteria to be used in evaluation should be mutually acceptable to the board and the superintendent. Throughout the evaluation process it should be remembered that the purpose of evaluation is to improve the critical elements that are valued.

By using Parts I and II* of this document, a board should be able to establish a reasonable and fair evaluation system for the superintendent.

It is recommended that Part II be discussed in executive session when the actual evaluation of the superintendent is under consideration.

*Only Part II is reproduced here. — *Editor's note.*

Your Choice 1 2 3 4		RELATIONSHIP WITH THE BOARD	Board's Decision 1 2 3 4
... ...	1.	Keeps the board informed of issues, needs, and operation of the school system.	... ...
... ...	2.	Offers professional advice to the board on items requiring board action, with appropriate recommendations based on thorough study and analysis.	... ...
... ...	3.	Interprets and executes the intent of board policy.	... ...
... ...	4.	Seeks and accepts constructive criticism of his/her work.	... ...
... ...	5.	Supports board policy and actions to the public and staff.	... ...
... ...	6.	Has a harmonious working relationship with the board.	... ...
... ...	7.	Understands his/her role in administration of board policy, makes recommendations for employment or promotion of personnel in writing and with supporting data, and accepts responsibility for his/her recommendations. If the recommendation is questioned by the board, he/she finds another person to recommend.	... ...
... ...	8.	Receives recommendations for personnel from board members with an open mind but applies the same criteria for his/her selection for recommendation as his/her applies to applications from other sources.	... ...
... ...	9.	Accepts his/her responsibility for maintaining liaison between the board and personnel working toward a high degree of understanding and respect between the staff and the board.	... ...
... ...	10.	Remains impartial toward the board, treating all board members alike.	... ...
... ...	11.	Refrains from criticism of individual or group members of the board.	... ...
... ...	12.	Goes immediately and directly to the board when he/she feels an honest, objective difference of opinion exists between him/her and any or all members of the board in an earnest effort to resolve such differences immediately.	... ...

Your
Choice
1 2 3 4

Board's
Decision
1 2 3 4

... ...   13. Feels free to maintain his/her opposition to   ... ...
matters under discussion by the board until
an official decision has been reached, after
which time he/she subordinates his/her own
views to those of the board as long as he/she
remains in its employ.

ADMINISTRATION OF THE SCHOOL
DISTRICT

... ...   1. Distinguishes between prime problems and   ... ...
trivialities.

... ...   2. Plans his/her own time so that matters of   ... ...
greatest importance are dealt with thoroughly.

... ...   3. Has organized the staff so that appropriate   ... ...
decision-making may take place at various
levels as contracted with most decisions being
made at the superintendent's level.

... ...   4. Periodically reviews and reorganizes staff   ... ...
duties and/or responsibilities to take full
advantage of the staff's special competencies and interests.

... ...   5. Has developed a system that assures that all   ... ...
significant activies or duties are performed
regularly or administered promptly.

... ...   6. Encourages research and creativity among   ... ...
employees.

... ...   7. Informs the board and general public in an   ... ...
annual report or in a series of reports of the
state of the schools in the district.

... ...   8. Provides the board with a written agenda   ... ...
and appropriate back-up material by the
determined date before each board meeting.

COMMUNITY RELATIONSHIPS

... ...   1. Has gained the respect and support of the com-   ... ...
munity on the functioning of the district's
operation.

... ...   2. Solicits and gives attention to problems and   ... ...
opinions of all groups and individuals.

... ...   3. Develops friendly and cooperative relation-   ... ...
ships with news media.

Your
Choice
1 2 3 4

Board's
Decision
1 2 3 4

... ... 4. Participates actively in community life and affairs. ... ...

... ... 5. Achieves status as a community leader in public education. ... ...

... ... 6. Works effectively with public and private agencies. ... ...

STAFF AND PERSONNEL RELATIONSHIPS

... ... 1. Develops and executes sound personnel procedures and practices. ... ...

... ... 2. Develops good staff morale and loyalty. ... ...

... ... 3. Treats all personnel fairly, without favoritism or discrimination, while insisting on performance of duties. ... ...

... ... 4. Delegates authority to staff members appropriate to the position each holds. ... ...

... ... 5. Recruits and assigns the best available personnel in terms of their competencies. ... ...

... ... 6. Encourages participation of appropriate staff members and groups in planning, procedures, and policy interpretation. ... ...

... ... 7. Evaluates performance of staff members, giving recommendation for good work as well as constructive suggestions for improvement. ... ...

... ... 8. Takes an active role in development of salary schedules for all personnel, and recommends to the board the levels which, within budgetary limitations, will best serve the interest of the district. ... ...

... ... 9. At the direction of the board, establishes, meets and confers with the negotiating council, representing to the best of his/her ability and understanding the interest and will of the board. ... ...

EDUCATIONAL LEADERSHIP

... ... 1. Understands and keeps informed regarding all aspects of the instructional program. ... ...

... ... 2. Implements the district's philosophy of education. ... ...

Your Choice 1 2 3 4		Board's Decision 1 2 3 4
... ...	3. Participates with staff, board, and community in studying and developing curriculum improvement.	... ...
... ...	4. Organizes a planned program of curriculum evaluation and improvement.	... ...
... ...	5. Provides democratic procedures in curriculum work, utilizing the abilities and talents of the entire professional staff and lay people of the connumity.	... ...
... ...	6. Exemplifies the skills and attitudes of a master teacher and inspires others to highest professional standards.	... ...

BUSINESS AND FINANCE

... ...	1. Keeps informed on needs of the school program – plant, facilities, equipment, and supplies.	... ...
... ...	2. Supervises operations, insisting on competent and efficient performance.	... ...
	3. Determines that:	
... ...	a. Funds are spent wisely.	... ...
... ...	b. Adequate control and accounting are maintained.	... ...
... ...	4. Evaluates financial needs and makes recommendations for adequate financing.	... ...

PERSONAL QUALITIES

... ...	1. Defends principle and conviction in the face of pressure and partisan influence.	... ...
... ...	2. Maintains high standards of ethics, honesty, and integrity in all personal and professional matters.	... ...
... ...	3. Earns respect and standing among professional colleagues.	... ...
... ...	4. Devotes time and energy effectively to job.	... ...
... ...	5. Demonstrates ability to work well with individuals and groups.	... ...
... ...	6. Exercises good judgment and the democratic processes in arriving at decisions.	... ...
... ...	7. Possesses and maintains the health and energy necessary to meet the responsibilities of the position.	... ...

Your Choice 1 2 3 4		Board's Decision 1 2 3 4
... ...	8. Maintains poise and emotional stability in the full range of professional activities.	... ...
... ...	9. Is customarily suitably attired and well groomed.	... ...
... ...	10. Uses English effectively in dealing with staff members, the board, and the public.	... ...
... ...	11. Writes clearly and concisely.	... ...
... ...	12. Speaks well in front of large and small groups, expressing ideas in a logical and forthright manner.	... ...
... ...	13. Thinks well when faced with an unexpected or distrubing turn of events in a large group meeting.	... ...
... ...	14. Maintains professional development by reading, course work, conference attendance, work on professional committees, visiting other districts and meeting with other superintendents.	... ...

An Up-Front Approach
to Administrative Evaluation

Jerry J. Herman

Jerry J. Herman explains a three-fold evaluation system that is used, and apparently works, in his schools in Orchard Lake, Michigan. Stressing objectivity, deep involvement on the part of both the administrator and the evaluator, and open communications, the system takes a management by objectives approach, utilizing a comprehensive job description and a self-evaluation guide to enhance the effectiveness of the whole process. Jerry J. Herman is Superintendent of the West Bloomfield Schools in Orchard Lake, Michigan.

A tri-fold approach to administrative evaluation which stresses objectivity, deeply involves the evaluator and evaluatee, and provides for eyeball-to-eyeball open communications seems to be succeeding in the West Bloomfield School District. The three tools successfully utilized for the past five years are: West Bloomfield's own version of MBO (Management by Objectives); a comprehensive job description based on tasks to be performed; and a self-evaluation guide that serves as a discussion tool during evaluation conferences.

COMPREHENSIVE JOB DESCRIPTIONS

The total administrative team (principals, assistant princiapsl, central office administrators, and the superintendent of schools) spent months in analyzing the total management functions to be performed in the school district in order to create and maintain an effective management operation. Once the functional analysis was completed, each administrator's portion of the total function was analyzed and a task-oriented comprehensive job description was written. Once the total management team reached consensus on the job descriptions, they were forwarded to the board of education for official approval.

The job descriptions were widely distributed, and they became an integral part of the evaluation methodology — comprising approximately 50 percent of the standard for evaluation. An example of the specific duties and responsibilities for the position of senior high assistant principal for student services is printed below:

Specific Duties and Reponsibilities
1. Acts as school principal in the absence of the principal when the principal so assigns this duty.
2. Directly supervises all building level guidance and counseling personnel and programs including:
    a. Program scheduling, planning, development, and evaluation.
    b. Student scheduling.
    c. Student records and reports.
    d. Dropout and follow-up studies.
    e. Testing.
    f. Transcripts.
    g. Attendance, with consistent student attendance problems referred to the assistant principal for administrative and co-curricular development.
    h. College and job placement services.
    i. Coordinating referrals to outside agencies which serve students, i.e. courts, youth assistance, etc.
    j. Preparing a list of graduates and keeping the building principal informed of senior students' progress.
    k. G.E.D. testing.
    l. Scholarship programs.
    m. Work permits.
3. Directly supervises all building level career and vocational education personnel and programs including:
    a. Program scheduling, planning, development, and evaluation.
    b. Vocational education and job placement.
    c. Dropout and follow-up studies.
    d. Testing.
    e. Coordinating referrals to outside agencies which serve student career education and vocational education needs.
    f. Liaison functions related to the area vocational school.
4. Directly supervises all building level special education personnel and programs including:
    a. Program scheduling, planning, development, and evaluation.
    b. Placement services.
    c. Coordinating internal and external referrals and screening.
5. Directly supervises the driver education program.

6. Coordinates the itinerant staff assigned to his building, i.e. social workers, speech therapists, nurses, etc.
7. Assists the principal in the screening, selection, placement and evaluation of certified and paraprofessional building staff in the areas of guidance and counseling, reading, career education and special education.
8. Plans the calendar and implements building events as they relate to pupil personnel, guidance and counseling, career education and vocational education, and special education.
9. Supervises and makes all arrangements for commencement activities including rehearsals, speakers, programs, caps and gowns, special awards, etc.
10. Assists building principal in the preparation and control of the budget related to his assigned functions.
11. Substitute teaches between two (2) and four (4) days yearly in order to maintain knowledge of on-line procedures and problems.
12. Prepares an annual progress report to be submitted to the principal, assistant superintendents for personnel and instruction, and superintendent. Said report to be distributed in May of each year shall include an assessment of the past year's activities and future objectives for program improvement for the succeeding year together with a five (5) year projection of needs in his areas of responsibility.
13. Provides the principal at least yearly with a written evaluation of all professionals and non-certified personnel assigned to his supervision, with at least two (2) yearly written evaluations provided for probationary personnel. Said evaluation to include a recommendation for employment and placement in the succeeding year. Copies are also to be submitted to the assistant superintendent for personnel, assistant superintendent for instruction, and the superintendent.
14. Agrees to accomplish the performance objectives as established for the year by the principal and himself.
15. Performs other tasks as assigned by the building principal.
16. Operates, and sees that staff assigned to him operate, within the letter and intent of legal mandates, Board of Education policies, and superintendent's rules and regulations.
17. Performs with integrity in all instances as a subordinate officer of the building principal, honoring the confidences and loyalties ascribed to and required of this administrative position.

Performance Objectives:
Yearly performance objectives are written for each administrator. They

are limited to a maximum of 10 in number, and they may evolve from the suggestions of the administrator being evaluated, his supervisor, or as a portion of the districtwide objectives given the superintendent by the board of education. They may also evolve from the subsequent year because of a weakness in performance of the basic tasks listed in the job description. They are designed to be high priority tasks and are self-correcting and recycled from year-to-year. This tool comprises approximately 50 percent of the standard for evaluation.

The fact that all performance objectives are weighted in priority order can be emphasized by reviewing the three primary objectives agreed to for one principal for a school year.

PRIORITY NO. 1.

Objective: To plan, implement, and evaluate reading instruction in your building in such a manner that by June 1, the building's students have achieved the following: (1) a decrease by a minimum of three percent the percentage of students in grades two through four whose reading scores fall below grade level, (2) a gain of at least one month (by June 1) beyond the normal reading achievement pattern established by the pupils who remain below grade level in grades two through four, and (3) an achievement rate increase in reading, on a group basis, of at least one month beyond the normal reading pattern of achievement by students in grades one and five who are below grade level on the original measurement.

Sub-Objectives:

1a. To assist in the hiring and placement of one developmental reading consultant for your building.

1b. To assist in the hiring and placement of one reading aide for your building.

1c. To work with the assistant superintendent for instruction in devising a comprehensive testing and evaluation program in reading for grades K–5.

1d. To cause the developmental reading consultant assigned your building to program his efforts in such a manner that he becomes a "teacher of teachers."

1e. To initiate, operationalize, and evaluate a comprehensive plan of lay resident volunteer tutorial services within your building.

1f. To devise, operationalize and evaluate a comprehensive plan of parent involvement in the home. This plan to provide specific information on helping the child read, listing of interesting books and materials for home use, etc.

1g. To devise, operationalize and evaluate a plan which utilizes the physical education staff assigned your building in the development of perceptual skills related to reading.

1h. To assist in the meaningful transfer of those teachers who have a great deal of training in reading into the most crucial lower elementary grades, and to assist in the hiring of new staff who possess a wealth of reading training for elementary, especially grades one through three.

li. To develop, implement and evaluate an instructional mode which fosters a full academic program in reading at the kindergarten level for those children who by observation and testing display a readiness for formal reading instruction.

Resources: (1) your own knowledge, skills and motivational ability; (2) a developmental reading consultant, reading aide, and parent volunteers; (3) the assistant superintendent for instruction and all other administrators; (4) your building's share of the $5,000 allocated for this purpose.

Measurement: (1) all students' achievement commitments have been met as determined by test measurement, (2) all program commitments are met by the target dates agreed upon.

PRIORITY NO. 2.

Objective: To draft by August 1 a handbook to be used by parent volunteers in the reading program in such a manner that the draft is deemed acceptable by the assistant superintendent for instruction.

Resources: (1) Your own abilities, and the assistance of the assistant superintendent for instruction, and your staff; (2) Available model materials from school districts and commercial publishers.

Measurement: The draft is completed by August 1, in a manner acceptable to the assistant superintendent for instruction.

PRIORITY NO. 3.

Objective: To involve your entire teaching staff in a series of no less than five inservice workshops centered on the implementation of West Bloomfield's Drug Education Guide before December 15.

Resources: (1) Your ability, the drug education planning committee, assistant superintendent for instruction, assistant principal for co-curricular activities; and (2) The Drug Education Guide.

Measurement: A minimum of five (5) inservice workshops for your total teaching staff are completed by December 15.

ADMINISTRATIVE EVALUATION GUIDE SHEET:

Although this document does not figure in final evaluative standards, it does accomplish the following:

1. It provides a discussion guide for two-way communication.
2. It identifies areas that might well be appropriate for the subsequent year's performance objectives.
3. It accepts the fact that all humans, and certainly all administrators, possess both strengths and weaknesses.

4. It causes suggestions to be made related to improving a variety of functions, invluding budgeting, transportation, secretarial services and many more.
5. It causes a dual evaluation of all administrators, including the superintendent, to become a routein portion of the evaluation system.

This specific document, that was devised by the superintendent but agreed to as an element of the evaluation process by all administrators, follows.

ADMINISTRATIVE EVALUATION GUIDE SHEET

DIRECTORS: Read and react to the following questions. These will serve as the basis for the evaluative discussion between yourself and the superintendent. This will be a two-way evaluation.

1. Professional growth: What have you done in the past year?
2. What local school related programs and activities have you participated in and how did this benefit you and the district?
3. Analyze your working relationship with the following: Why?
   a. Nonprofessional staff
   b. Teachers
   c. Students
   d. Other administrators – building, central office
   e. Lay people
   f. Board of Education
4. I have demonstrated the following:
   a. Dependability
   b. Initiative
   c. Creativity
   d. Give and take suggestions
   e. Self-confidence
   f. Ethical behavior
5. I have (improved, stayed the same) communications – name the specific ways – with:
   a. Nonprofessional staff
   b. Teachers
   c. Students
   d. Other administrators – building, central office
   e. Lay people
   f. Board of Education
6. In the area of instruction, I have:
   a. Visited classrooms – For what purposes? What did I gain? How did my visits help teachers and kids?
   b. I have studied the following instructional innovations this year: _____

    c.   I have made education in West Bloomfield better this year by doing the following things with my staff: _____

_____

    d.   I feel I have made the following contributions to a district-wide approach this year: _____

_____

7. In the area of management, I have:
    a.   Carried out assigned tasks accurately.
    b.   I have made the following "hard" decisions in the past year:

_____

    c.   I have modified my role because of negotiations in the following ways (positive and/or negative): _____

    d.   I have demonstrated the following:
        (1) Implementation of Board policies and District rules and regulations
        (2) Management within the existing Master Contract agreements
        (3) Monitored and controlled my unit budget
        (4) Was a team member in support of other administrators' decisions

8. If I had complete authority, I would make the following changes for next year in the area of:
    a.   Budgeting
    b.   Custodial service
    c.   Purchasing service
    d.   Maintenance service
    e.   Secretarial service
    f.   Transportation
    g.   Administrative decision-making authority and responsibility
    h.   Curriculum
    i.   Personnel
    j.   Any others (please list)

9. I feel that the following things I have done this year could have been done as well by a lay person: _____

_____

SUMMARY AND CONCLUSIONS

10. I feel that my greatest contribution in the past year has been:

_____

11. I feel my greatest area of weakness in the past year has been:

_____

12. I intend to do the following things to improve myself next year:

_____

13. I feel that I can contribute the following to the administrative team next year: _____

14. My hopes for improving my building's and/or West Bloomfield School District's instructional situation next year are: _____

_____

15. Your opinion of the superintendent is:
    a. Strengths (incidents)
    b. Weaknesses (incidents)
    c. Recommendations
16. Your opinion of the assistant superintendent for business is:
    a. Strengths (incidents)
    b. Weaknesses (incidents)
    c. Recommendations
17. Your opinion of the assistant superintendent for instruction is:
    a. Strengths (incidents)
    b. Weaknesses (incidents)
    c. Recommendations
18. Your opinion of the assistant superintendent for personnel is:
    a. Strengths (incidents)
    b. Weaknesses (incidents)
    c. Recommendations
19. Any other comments you wish to make: _____

_____

_____

CONCLUDING THOUGHTS

If you are willing to work as a team, are willing to attempt objectivity in evaluation, are willing to be open and honest, you can benefit from a system similar to that utilized by West Bloomfield School District. The major element, however, is the acceptance of the fact that each administrator can be valued as a member of a total management team while agreeing that everyone has strengths and weaknesses. This methodology of evaluation will cause measurable improvement in the weaknesses identified.

Performance Evaluation of School-Based Administrators

Baltimore City Public Schools

The following excerpts from the performance evaluation system of the Baltimore, Maryland, public schools gives a detailed outline of some performance criteria to be used in evaluating. These are followed by a list of "recommended actions" to be taken, depending upon how the administrator measures up against the criteria. An evaluation form and a performance rating scale are also reproduced here.

Excerpts from *Performance Evaluation of School-Based Administrators* by the Baltimore City Public Schools, Baltimore, Maryland. Reprinted by permission.

PHILOSOPHY

Administrators in Baltimore City Public Schools are responsible for maintaining a sound educational climate in each school. Such a climate includes the implematation of policies and goals set by the Board of School Commissioners and the Superintendent.

Careful planning by the administrator requires interaction with students, staff, parents and other community representatives. As a result of effective community action and involvement of appropriate persons, school-based goals are used to provide the best possible educational program for each student.

A school atmosphere conducive to learning is also the responsibility of the building level administrator. The successful administrator must constantly assess programmatic situations and render just and equitable decisions. Professional growth and individual development must be encouraged, counseled and nurtured through a carefully designed program of pre-service/in-service activities. Use must be made of school-based, city-wide, and community-oriented resource personnel.

Professionally, the administrator is constantly obligated to seek knowledge concerning current programs and practices in education. All administrators must become role models for their schools, accentuating those positive behaviors necessary and acceptable in a productive society.

ADMINISTRATOR EVALUATION PROCEDURE
Evaluatee's Worksheet for Submittal to Superiors

Each administrator will submit a statement of goals and objectives for the area of responsibility between August 15 and September 30. In the case of newly appointed administrators this statement will be submitted on a date mutually agreed upon by the administrator and the immediate supervisor but in no case later than sixty (60) days after the administrator assumes the position to which she or he is appointed. These goals will be agreed upon by the administrator and the immediate supervisor.

First Conference Report

Objectives and goals are subject to modification upon mutual agreement in writing or in a conference between the parties concerned no later than September 30. By this date, the First Conference Report form will be completed and copies retained by the evaluatee and the evaluators.

Second Conference Report

The second appraisal session between the administrator and the immediate supervisor will be held no later than January 15. The appraisal session will measure performance of the administrator in meeting responsibilities as well as progress toward attainment of the established goals and objectives. At this time, the Second Conference Report form will be completed.

Continuing communication between the administrator and the supervisor is desirable and necessary. Further formal conferences until the end-of-year conference may be held at the discretion of the administrator and/or the immediate supervisor. The result of such conferences will be summarized in writing and signed by both parties.

End-of-Year Conference Report

The final evaluation session will involve the same procedure as the second appraisal session and will be conducted between May 1 and June 30.

Exception to the Administrative Evaluation

Should the administrator take exception to the performance evaluation, the administrator may seek redress available via the appropriate administrative procedures.

(1) ASSESSES THE IMPLEMENTATION OF THE INSTRUCTIONAL PROGRAM CONTINUALLY AND ACHIEVES EFFECTIVE WAYS TO BRING ABOUT IMPROVEMENT
Indicators:
(a) Meets with instructional leaders in the building (e.g., department heads/senior teachers) on a regular basis to discuss the instructional program
(b) Meets with teachers to discuss instructional program
(c) Oversees the grouping of students for effective instruction
(d) Interacts with students to aid in determining the effect of the instructional program

(2) EVALUATES THE EFFECTIVENESS OF THE INSTRUCTIONAL PROGRAM IN TERMS OF STUDENT NEEDS AND GROWTH
Indicators:
(a) Visits classrooms to monitor programs
(b) Analyzes formal and informal test results in terms of total school outcomes
(c) Monitors pupil growth on a class-by-class and/or subject-by-subject basis
(d) Analyzes formal and informal test results in terms of individual program components

(3) CONTINUALLY SEARCHES FOR OPPORTUNITIES TO INITIATE AND IMPLEMENT PROGRAMS AND PROCEDURES WHICH SHOW PROMISE OF ENHANCING STUDENT GROWTH
Indicators:
(a) Keeps abreast of current trends in education
(b) Is aware of programs going on within the school system
(c) Seeks ideas from educators, parents and community people for suggestions that will meet the educational needs of each student
(d) Evaluates proposed new program carefully before putting it into operation

(4) WORKS COOPERATIVELY WITH TEACHERS AND RESOURCE PERSONNEL IN THE DEVELOPMENT OF THE INSTRUCTIONAL PROGRAM
Indicators:
(a) Assesses, together with teaching and resource personnel, the educational needs of the students relative to the philosophy, goals and objectives of the school
(b) Plans programs in view of the assessed needs of students
(c) Plans with staff and resource personnel instructional modes to meet identified exceptional needs of students

(5) SUPERVISES TEACHER PERFORMANCE (E.G., GIVES FAIR AND ACCURATE APPRAISAL AND EFFECTIVE SUPPORT)
Indicators:
(a) Defines with staff the instructional expectations which are required of all staff
(b) Gives fair and accurate appraisal in the observation of teaching performance
(c) Provides guidance and support for the improvement of identified areas of weakness
(d) Communicates to the teacher positive as well as negative critique
(e) Provides guidance and support for teachers and staff to carry out their creative ideas

(6) ORGANIZES AND USES HUMAN RESOURCES TO AID STUDENT ADJUSTMENT AND MEET STUDENT NEEDS
Indicators:
(a) Utilizes, to the fullest extent possible, individual staff skills and interests in making teaching assignments
(b) Creates within the school day opportunities for inter- and intra-disciplinary instruction
(c) Utilizes resources citywide and within the immediate community to aid in student adjustment and meet student needs
(d) Makes use of the strengths and skills of students within the building to aid in the growth and development of the entire student body

(7) DEVELOPS, PLANS, AND ENCOURAGES PROFESSIONAL GROWTH ACTIVITIES
Indicators:
(a) Makes available to staff information relative to workshops offered by the school system and offerings in education made by colleges and universities
(b) Recognizes areas of skill needs and strengths within the faculty and plans staff development programs in accordance
(c) Recommends areas of study to individual staff members as needed
(d) Encourages professional growth activities through staff use of professional materials and resources, and staff exchange of professional ideas

Management Ability

(1) BUDGETS TIME TO PROVIDE A BALANCE BETWEEN ADMINISTRATIVE AND SUPERVISORY DUTIES
Indicators:
(a) Delegates responsibilities to appropriate staff persons
(b) Accomplishes written reports with dispatch and efficiency

(c) Exhibits a command of supervisory skills which permit effective use of time allocated to supervisory tasks

(d) Allocates time on a given day in accordance with the demands of the day-to-day situation

(2) MAKES DECISIONS IN LINE WITH SYSTEM POLICY

Indicators:

(a) Is conversant with the goals of the System as outlined by the Superintendent

(b) Is aware of operational policies and procedures as described in the Administrative Handbook

(c) Is familiar with the school system's administrative organization and therefore able to direct questions concerning policies and procedures to the appropriate staff person

(d) Carries out System policies as they are communicated

(3) MONITORS THE IMPLEMENTATION OF A DECISION EFFECTIVELY ONCE IT HAS BEEN MADE

Indicators:

(a) Assigns decision implementation roles to appropriate staff persons

(b) Provides assistance and encouragement as needed during the implementation process

(c) Requires and seeks out feedback as to the progress of the implementation process

(d) Provides active leadership in readjustment of the implementation process as the situation warrants

(4) ANALYZES PROBLEMS EFFECTIVELY AND DETERMINES APPROPRIATE ACTION FOR THEIR SOLUTION

Indicators:

(a) Identifies and articulates well the parameters of a problem situation

(b) Breaks a problem into its component parts

(c) Identifies several possible solutions to a given problem

(d) Perceives the short-range and long-range ramifications of a decision

(e) Justifies the reasoning behind a given decision

(5) SEEKS AND USES WHEN APPROPRIATE THE ADVICE AND INSIGHTS OF STAFF, STUDENTS, AND COMMUNITY FOR BALANCED INPUT IN DECISION MAKING

Indicators:

(a) Establishes both formal and informal groups within the building to serve as both "sounding boards" and originators for decision formulation

(b) Defines carefully those decision situations where student input is needed and then seriously seeks out such input

(c) Defines carefully those decision situations where community input is needed and then seriously seeks out such input

(d) Weights carefully the input from all groups concerned in a decision situation before arriving at a final decision

(6) ORGANIZES AND UTILIZES EDUCATIONAL AND CALSSIFIED STAFF EFFICIENTLY AND EFFECTIVELY IN THE PURSUIT OF PROGRAM GOALS AND OBJECTIVES
Indicators:
(a) Makes reasonable requirements of staff
(b) Assigns staff resources (both quantitatively and qualitiatively) to program requirements without regard for personal bias and inclination
(c) Assesses staff assignments for possible changes in deployment in light of changing program needs
(d) Makes it possible for students, staff, parents, and community to maintain an effective physical building environment
(e) Allocates funds and keeps accurate records to assist in the implementation of program goals and objectives

(7) ESTABLISHES POSITIVE RELATIONSHIPS WITH THE COMMUNITY IN ORDER TO MAKE THE SCHOOL SYSTEM'S MISSION EFFECTIVE
Indicators:
(a) Assists parents in the formation and maintenance of parent organizations within the school
(b) Develops relationships with community leaders which extend awareness of the school's mission into the community at large
(c) Promotes staff interaction with the community through assemblies, special programs and other events to which the community is invited

Organizational Climate

(1) ESTABLISHES AND MAINTAINS COMPREHENSIVE AND SYSTEMATIC PROCEDURES FOR COMMUNICATION WITH STUDENTS, STAFF, AND PARENTS
Indicators:
(a) Develops needed expectations with students, staff, and parents
(b) Reviews expectations orally as needed with students, staff, and parents
(c) Communicates in writing the routine building policies and procedures
(d) Communicates policy and procedural changes in clear and concise written language
(e) Establishes formalized procedures for receiving input from students, staff, and parents

(2) WORKS FOR INTERACTION BETWEEN THE SCHOOL AND COM-MUNITY TO ACHIEVE MUTUAL UNDERSTANDING AND AS-SISTANCE

Indicators:

(a) Communicates school concerns and needs to community members on an informal and formal basis

(b) Lends support to community concerns which directly or indirectly affect the school

(c) Participates in community events and programs

(d) Develops professional and personal relationships with community opinion leaders

(e) Meets on a regular basis with parents of students

(f) Seeks to have representative members of the school community to give input to the school

(3) WORKS SKILLFULLY WITH DIVERSE GROUPS TO ACHIEVE PURPOSE, CLARITY AND RESOLUTION OF CONFLICTS

Indicators:

(a) Is accessible to students, staff, parents and community

(b) Serves as mediator between conflicting interest groups within the school organization

(c) Identifies potential conflict situations and initiates steps which will prevent the situation from developing

(d) Involves disparate interest groups within the building in the formu-lation of all major policy and programmatic decisions

(4) CREATES AN ENVIRONMENT WHICH PERMITS AND ENCOUR-AGES FULL UTILIZATION OF BOTH STAFF AND STUDENTTAL-ENTS AND CREATIVE ENERGIES

Indicators:

(a) Seeks to discover and use the strengths of each staff member

(b) Establishes an open atmosphere where it is acceptable for teachers to try new techniques

(c) Identifies methods for helping students to discover and develop their strengths and talents

(d) Offers positive reinforcement for students and staff

(5) FACILITATES A FREE AND OPEN FLOW OF COMMENTS, CRITI-CISMS AND SUGGESTIONS

Indicators:

(a) Encourages suggestions, ideas, and feedback from students, staff, parents, and community

(b) Listens with an open mind to suggestions

(c) Accepts divergent thinking

(d) Maintains in meetings with groups of staff an atmosphere which permits free and open expression of teacher concerns and opin-ions

(e) Exhibits professionalism in keeping confidences

Personal and Professional Development

(1) HAS GOOD PHYSICAL AND EMOTIONAL HEALTH, STRONG WORK CAPACITY, AND RESILIENCE FOR DEMANDING AS-SIGNMENTS
Indicators:
  (a) Shows evidence of sound emotional adjustment; is calm, poised and mature in reactions
  (b) Possesses the health and vitality needed to meet the responsibilities of the job
  (c) Deals with difficult or unpleasant problems
  (d) Shows initiative and displays enthusiasm
  (e) Meets frustration without becoming hostile toward teachers, pupils, administrators, clerical personnel, and others
  (f) Works effectively with others

(2) EVALUATES SELF CONTINUOUSLY IN AN EFFORT TO IM-PROVE EFFECTIVENESS
Indicators:
  (a) Participates with the teachers and other staff members in the analysis of self-progress
  (b) Makes use of the results of the evaluation for continuous development
  (c) Maintains an efficient procedure for self-evaluation
  (d) Makes use of an effective procedure for securing, recording, and using information about the school and its progress
  (e) Recognizes the importance of all employees to the school system and deals understandingly with those employees
  (f) Displays sustained effort and enthusiasm in the quality and quantity of work accomplished

(3) SETS AN APPROPRIATE EXAMPLE FOR STUDENTS AND TEA-CHERS IN BOTH APPEARANCE AND DEMEANOR
Indicators:
  (a) Presents appropriate professional appearance
  (b) Shows genuine respect, concern and warmth for others — for both children and adults
  (c) Is sensitive to the reactions of other persons; deals with them understandingly
  (d) Accepts suggestions or criticism intelligently and in spirit of mutual goodwill

(4) AVAILS SELF OF THE OPPORTUNITY FOR IMPROVEMENT BY ATTENDING WORKSHOPS, GRADUATE SCHOOL, PROFESSION-AL MEETINGS AND CONFERENCES
Indicators:
  (a) Demonstrates adequacy in professional background

(b) Takes advantage of opportunities for professional growth that are available beyond the requirements of the System

(c) Attempts to use ideas and suggestions gleaned from professional magazines and bulletins

(d) Continues professional study, attends professional meetings regularly and reads current professional literature

(5) COMMUNICATES EFFECTIVELY BEFORE GROUPS, SPEAKS DISTINCTLY, USES STANDARD ORAL AND WRITTEN ENGLISH

Indicators:

(a) Interprets the school program and policies to the community as occasion permits

(b) Is alert to the specific needs of the community which relate to the schools served and program offered

(c) Serves as a model for teachers and students by observing the conventions of oral standard English

(d) Keeps the community informed concerning the school program

(e) Speaks clearly and effectively

(6) PARTICIPATES IN SYSTEM AND REGIONAL ACTIVITIES AND SHARES RESPONSIBILITY FOR THE GOOD OF THE TOTAL SCHOOL SYSTEM

Indicators:

(a) Is active in professional activities related to work

(b) Makes self available to the staff and patrons of the school system for discussion of problems

(c) Works cooperatively with all departments of the school system

(d) Complies with rules and regulations

Recommended Actions

EVALUATION	FIRST YEAR	SECOND YEAR
Outstanding Performance	— Certificate — Travel opportunity(ies) for professional enrichment — Recognition as resource person for the system	— Certificate — Travel opportunity(ies) for professional enrichment — Recognition as resource person for the system
High Quality Performance	— Letter of commendation — Recognition as resource person for the system	— Letter of commendation — Recognition as resource person for the system
Professionally Competent		
Needs Improvement	— Retain with support — agreed upon courses of action to be outlined in the first conference report; said report may include suggested university courses, administrative workshop, pre-scribed procedures for communication. Mandatory monthly conferences with directions and guidance. — Transfer, based upon needs of the system.	— Permit staff member to return voluntarily to the next lower classification without prejudice. — Retain with support. — A less than "professionally competent" rating for the third year will result in mandatory application of the recommended action for second year "unacceptable performance." — Transfer, based upon needs of the system.
Unacceptable Performance	— Retain with support — agreed upon courses of action to be outlined in the first conference report; said report may include suggested university courses, administrative workshops, pre-scribed procedures for communication. Mandatory monthly conferences with directions and guidance. — Transfer, based upon needs of the system. — Permit staff member to return voluntarily to the next lower classification without prejudice.	— Permit staff member to return voluntarily to next lower classification with prejudice. — Upon receipt of "unacceptable performance," the staff member shall be demoted.

Performance Rating Scale and Criteria

PERFORMANCE RATING NOTION	SYMBOL	PERFORMANCE RATING CRITERIA
Outstanding Performance	O	Consistently exceeds expected performance in accomplishing stated objectives and position requirements and manifests a discernable degree of initiative and innovation.
High Quality Performance	HQ	Exceeds expectations and demonstrates high level performance in accomplishing objectives and position requirements.
Professionally Competent	PC	Meets stated objectives and satisfies position requirements in a manner resulting in expected performance.
Needs Improvement	NI	Performs most position requirements in an acceptable manner, but needs improvement in designated areas.
Unacceptable Performance	U	Unsatisfactory, does not perform at an acceptable level of accomplishment.

EVALUATION FORM

PERFORMANCE CRITERIA	U	NI	PC	HQ	O	SUPPORTING STATEMENTS
Educational Leadership — Assess the implementation of the instructional program continually and achieves effective ways to bring about improvement.						
Evaluates the effectiveness of the instructional program in terms of student needs and growth.						
Continually searches for opportunities to initiate and implement programs and procedures which show promise of enhancing student growth.						
Works cooperatively with teachers and resource personnel in the development of the instructional program.						
Supervises teacher performance (e.g., gives fair and accurate appraisal and effective support).						
Organizes and uses human resources to aid student adjustment and meet student needs.						
Develops, plans, and encourages professional growth activities.						
Management Ability — Budgets time to provide a balance between administrative and supervisory duties.						
Makes decisions in line with system policy.						
Effectively monitors the implementation of a decision once it has been made.						
Analyzes problems and determines appropriate action for their solution.						
Seeks and uses when appropriate the advice and insights of staff, students, and community for balanced input in decision making.						
Organizes and utilizes educational and classified staff efficiently and effectively in the pursuit of program goals and objectives.						
Establishes positive relationships with the community in order to make the school system's mission effective.						
Organizational Climate — Establishes and maintains comprehensive and systematic procedures for communication with students, staff, and parents.						
Works for interaction between the school and community for their mutual understanding and assistance.						
Works skillfully with diverse groups to achieve purpose, clarity, and conflict resolution.						
Creates an environment which permits and encourages full utilization of both staff and student talents and creative energies.						
Facilitates a free and open flow of comments, criticisms, and suggestions.						
Personal/Professional Development — Has good physical and emotional health, strong work capacity, and resilience for demanding assignments.						
Evaluates self continuously in an effort to improve effectiveness.						
Sets an appropriate example for students and teachers in both appearance and demeanor.						
Avails self of the opportunity for improvement by attending workships, graduate school professional meetings and conferences.						
Communicates effectively in front of groups, speaks distinctly, uses standard oral and written English.						
Participates in system and regional activities and shares responsibility for the good of the total school system.						
TOTALS						25

ANY CHECK IN THE **U, NI,** OR **O** COLUMN REQUIRES A COMMENT IN THE **SUPPORTING STATEMENT** COLUMN WITH APPROPRIATE DOCUMENTATION AVAILABLE.

Final Rating Determination

When U or NI performance ratings have been given, the rating is determined by the following table.

When no U or NI performance ratings have been given, the rating is determined by the following table.

Number of U's	Number of NI's	RATING
7 or more	0 or more	U
6	2 or more	U
	1 or less	NI
5	4 or more	U
	3 or less	NI
4	6 or more	U
	5 or less	NI
3	8 or more	U
	7 or less	NI
2	10 or more	U
	9 or less	NI
1	12 or more	U
	11 or less	NI
0	14 or more	U
	13	NI
	12 or less	PC

Number of HQ's	Number of O's	RATING
0-1	6 or less	PC
	7-17	HQ
	18 or more	O
2-3	5 or less	PC
	6-16	HQ
	17 or more	O
4-5	4 or less	PC
	5-15	HQ
	16 or more	O
6-7	3 or less	PC
	4-14	HQ
	15 or more	O
8-9	2 or less	PC
	3-13	HQ
	14 or more	O
10-11	1 or less	PC
	2-12	HQ
	13 or more	O
12-13	0	PC
	1-11	HQ
	12 or more	O
14-25	0-10	HQ
	11	O

PART V

Managerial Evaluation in the Business World:

Fresh Perspectives for Educators

Performance Review - A Mixed Bag

George A. Rieder

George A. Rieder, Senior Vice President of Human Resources at the Republic of Texas Corporation in Dallas, examines the concept of "perform-ance review" as he has experienced it from the vantage point of a personnel manager. First he analyzes the flaws "both in program design and in prac-tice." He then gives a series of suggestions on how we can "breathe new life into a misused management tool." Finally, Rieder reports on how the firm of which he was senior Vice President at the time this article was written adopted what he calls a "results management" approach to the question of performance review.

Mention the two words "performance review" and out gushes a torrent of associated words — ambulances, shotguns, blue forms, hero worship, professional basketball players, Lucy, Douglas McGregor, Persian rugs, onions, punch cards, mosaics, Weight Watchers, and car repair. What? Odd but true, the practice of performance review, which in theory holds out so much promise for management effectiveness evokes unpredictable responses. Some comments are downright damning. Others point to qualified successes. For the most part, left unfulfilled are the high expectations spelled out on scholarly articles, personnel manager rhetoric, performance review manuals, and training sessions.

The results? Disappointment. Disillusionment. Confusion. A loss of confidence in a tool of management. Sometimes a frantic race to resuscitate or modernize an ailing program.

APPARENT DEFICIENCIES

Suffering from managerial performance review battle fatigue myself, I made a down-to-earth personal analysis which revealed six apparent flaws both in program design and in practice.

1. *Reward/punishment*

All too many recipients of reviews perceive this vehicle as a reward/ punishment process. Sometimes, the "butter 'em up, ram it in" approach is employed. At other times, generous coats of whitewash are applied, often giving an individual false security and false hope for promotion. Occasional interviews are unadulterated fault-finding sessions, featuring exaggerated statements about behavior and stale, yet previously uncommunicated, bad news about performance. Infrequently applied are General Electric's research findings concerning the negative aspects of criticism, the neutral effect of praise, and the positive power of specific performance goals.[1]

Picture two businessmen striding down a city sidewalk when an ambulance whizzes by with red lights flashing. One turns to the other and says with a wry grin: "Someone must have just had his annual performance review."

Now note the assumption made by the businessman — namely, that there was only one casualty in the ambulance. Why not two? Remember Douglas McGregor's insights into the discomfort and distress of a manager who is placed in the position of "playing God" by judging the personal worth of a fellow man. McGregor observed: "Yet the conventional approach to performance appraisal forces us, not only to make such judgments and to see them acted upon, but also to communicate them to those we have judged."[2] It is not difficult to see, then, why managers also tend to perceive the review as a reward/punishment instrument. It is no small wonder that countless managers keep dragging their feet in keeping their reviews on schedule.

2. *Eclectic hodgepodge*

List the avowed objectives of performance review and a Rube Goldberg configuration takes shape. Performance evaluation, personal development planning, appraisal of potential, coaching and counseling, placement review, and sometimes salary administration are lumped together — in an eclectic hodgepodge of historical personnel programs, plus odds and ends delegated from top management. "Why not get it all in one fell swoop" is the cry. "Right on, get out the shotgun and we'll hit something at least" is the reply.

The shotgun approach has made fuzzy the rules of the game. Indeed, reviewers and reviewees alike are not clear as to the real game they are playing. And, when that occurs, caution and defensiveness result. Flanks become protected. Performance improvement takes a back seat.

3. *Misdirected emphasis*

Formal appraisals demand too much and too little from managers.

There is too much paperwork and ritual. As one manager said. "I wonder how many pounds of paper it takes to produce a dollar of profit." At the same time, too little is demanded in terms of mutual goal setting which pays off in better results.

All too often performance review is portrayed as a Personnel Department plan, something to be done to keep the staff specialists happy. It is viewed as an addition to — not a part of — the process of management. Stereotyped procedures coalesce into company dogma. Neatly typed blue-colored forms completed yearly tend to become the end rather than a means. Surely, these are attractively packaged in a story line which goes something like this: "Top management wants to know how you and your people are doing." Nevertheless, the emphasis seems to be on form and administration (doing things right) as opposed to process and management (doing the right things).

4. *Hero worship*

Many Americans take their cues from their heroes. In business, the successful executive and professional are most often emulated. When a top manager uses performance review to build competencies and develop potentials, and when he reinforces business values and beliefs, others follow. His managerial style may also cause inaction if he does not use the review instrument with those reporting to him. Even when practicing the "do as I say, not as I do" philosophy, hero worshippers imitate.

Performance review also suffers from the Liza Doolittle complex, wherein there is a concerted attempt to mold duplicates or to redo others. By calculated design, naive newcomers to management and even some experienced performers fashion their career paths after the paths of those occupying august positions. They thereby limit their choices and reside in a world of yesterday rather than tomorrow. Oftentimes, heroes do not realize what is happening to their admirers until it is too late.

5. *Reactive behavior*

The word appraisal or review implies judgments, measurements, and absolutes. Realities, emotions, intangibles, and imprecision seem foreign to the monikers affixed to this instrument. Human beings react to the system creatively, though not necessarily productively.

For example, a former company colleague who is now general manager of a professional basketball team commented: "When I'm negotiating with a ball player, for every statistic I've got to prove he's not worth more money, he's got ten to prove he is. All those training deals on performance review don't get the job done."

Perhaps emotions and tough bargaining do not surface in business as in professional athletics. Perhaps more leveling between individual and manager is one vital answer. What is clear, however, is that the review must be something done with the individual, not to him. Otherwise, be prepared for reactive behavior.

6. *Obscured focus*

The tendencies to talk about personality traits and to give advice on methods have obscured the focus on qualitative and quantitative results. In fact, character and personality ethics have tended to demean rather than to elevate the importance of the individual within an organization.

Instead of banking on the resourcefulness and ingenuity of individuals to accomplish meaningful performance-related goals, managers and staff specialists have dispensed the five cents psychiatry of Charles Schultz's famous cynic, Lucy. One graphic display of Lucy's managerial advice came in retort to Charlie Brown's question about the difference between being modest and being wishy-washy. Lucy pontificated: "The difference is you are wishy-washy and I am modest." Get the picture?

SUCCESSFUL FUNDAMENTALS

All the foregoing salvos aimed at performance review's apparent deficiencies should not signal abandonment. Certainly, Harold Mayfield, in his article "In Defense of Performance Appraisal,"[3] makes a persuasive case with which, in principle, many practicing managers can agree. The pivotal concern centers on future application. We must ask ourselves: How can we return to successful fundamentals? How can we breathe new life into a misused management tool, using as twin bases our past experience and perceptions of probably futures?

Partner relationship

Where do we begin? With Douglas McGregor, of course. His insights regarding managerial assumptions about people are timeless.[4] In designing any performance review vehicle, whether or not that descriptive term is used, look to candid notions about human resources. Most current review programs appear to be shaped according to Theory Y assumptions – check on everyone periodically, do thinking on important matters for subordinates, employ carrot-and-stick techniques as well as manipulate people in situations. The alternative provided in Theory Y stresses the wide distribution of creativity in the population, the need of people at all levels to achieve, the importance of high standards, and the capacity among most people for self-discipline and self-control.

Douglas McGregor once commented to a group of management development staff specialists that the "best performance review form" he had ever seen was a "blank piece of paper." Aside from reaffirming his belief in individual differences and Theory Y, this remark homed in on the partner relationship of manager and associate in making joint progress. No prescribed form or formula can substitute for thinking and planning together.

One's basic mental set about people, or indeed about a particular individual, comes through loud and clear, despite the verbiage he uses. As an example, one of our own managers who turned supposed misfits into above-average performers articulated his secret to success this way: "I just gave them jobs worth doing — tough jobs — let them know I believed that they could make the grade, and let them know they were a part of the team." His assumptions showed through his words. The self-fulfilling prophecy does work.

Individual accountability

Recognize that not all individuals want to pay the price of major job growth today. Maybe later but not today. Recognize also that company objectives are normally broad enough to permit substantial creativity in goal setting. Alternate paths of accomplishment which build on personal goals can be strong motivational stuff.

Part of the Lazarus Department Store legend is a tale of the rug buyer who decided to purchase a heavy inventory of expensive Persian rugs. His bosses, up to and including the store manager, questioned his judgment and tried to dissuade him by offering reasonable alternatives. He remained commited to his strategy. His management supported the buyer's brand of risk taking. The result? The ownership of Persian rugs per 1,000 family units in Columbus, Ohio, is the highest of any major city in the United States. And this was accomplished without heavy discounting or massive advertising budgets.

Management by objectives and performance development go hand in hand as long as the individual can be a true part of the action. As one study shows, performance improvement stands almost triple the chance of attainment with the use of goal setting (versus traditional performance review).[5] Remember, too, that the principle of accountability involves not so much the individual's "scorecard" in the manager's eyes, but his testing of himself, his own pride of accomplishment — in other words, his accountability to himself.

'Build on strengths'

This is the shibboleth personnel and other managers teach and preach. Seldom do these preachments manifest themselves in practice because, like the onion, strengths have a way of changing substance and surroundings alike. Onions give flavor and are healthful. They also cause tears and sneezes. In large doses, they can become unbearable. So it goes with the mighty strengths of people, too.

Who remembers the base running or fielding of Ted Williams? In terms of winning baseball games, what difference did his stormy press relations make? In fact, the bad publicity swelled gate receipts. To take a page from

Peter Drucker's 10/90 theory, the "Splendid Splinter"'s 10% contribution to the team — the use of his strengths — probably produced 90% of the Boston Red Sox's business results. The club could live with Ted's weaknesses as long as the home runs rattled off his bat. It could have been disastrous to attempt to redo his fielding or to alter his running on the base paths.

Harry B. Henshel, a courageous, risk-taking CEO, has put it this way: "Like the skier, we use our weaknesses at Bulova to turn us toward our strengths. We do not spend our time attempting to bolster our weaknesses; we bypass them and work from our strengths."[6]

The well-rounded man is not a necessity. Trying to become replicas of someone else can prove hazardous. Reinforcement of strong performance breeds more strong performance. Goal setting must place the premium on what an individual can or could do uncommonly well — and the individual is most often in the best position to locate and exploit the opportunities for positive growth.

Yet be prepared for the onion effect — that is, occasional discomfort along with distinctiveness. Also, recognize the diligent work required in in-dividualizing a development plan and making the organization function for the contributor.

Managerial support

The daily world of work tells the tale of corporate as well as individual success. Normally, no single masterstroke alters the course of performance. A yearly appraisal pales by comparison with supportive managerial relations on a regular basis. Coaching in a spirit of openness and mutual growth places priority on development results, not just direct results. This is consistent with the wishes of many of the "new breed" as well as mature managers and professionals moving up the hierarchy of needs that A.H. Maslow wrote about decades ago.[7]

In my experience, the premier manager in building a personal develop-ment atmosphere was always armed with blank punch cards. (He lifted them from the EDP machine room.) Whenever he and one of his people estab-lished a goal and target date, out would come the individual's card. On it, he would make a rough note, nothing facy. As other priorities interposed them-selves or uncontrollable delays occurred, he would make necessary adjust-ments on the running scorecard.

Two questions kept popping up in his dialogues: What are your plans? How can I help? There was little apparent pressure or criticism. As one of his subordinate managers said: "I never got the feeling things (the goals) are written in stone. Still I know he will be around to see how we're coming."

At annual review time, the manager would assemble all the completed cards he had accumulated on each of his people and engage in what he termed a "lay of the land" chat. A favorite query of his was: What can you do for the company that I haven't given you a chance to do? And he listened more than he talked.

Flexible systems

Some people honestly believe that, as individual groups, all bankers or engineers or secretaries or scientists are alike. Still lingering around business are vestiges of the melting-pot theory, which holds that in sameness there is strength. Not so. Progressive companies have "mosaics" of human resources. Some people are highly innovative while others thrive on routine and problem solving. Some are ingenious in designing computer systems; and others, in designing marketing strategies.

A wide spectrum of skills, abilities, potentials, aspirations, levels of existence, and personalities are represented in a corporate community — and that is a big plus. Appraisal systems must take this into account. Slavish adherence to rating forms, strict procedures, and limited hard-copy reports can place obstacles in the road to unleashing human talent. The significant early returns in job-enrichment experiments speak loudly for the need for flexible systems which reload responsibility into jobs and accept individual differences as natural and desirable.

Quantitative feedback

Ever explore the key to success of Weight Watchers? My observation isolates feedback as being critical. The individual sets a realistic target within a specified time frame. The weight-in confirms achievement or lack thereof. Once progress is set in motion, bite-size improvements become more probable. Even without initial progress, some choose to keep trying. Others drop by the wayside. So it goes in business too.

The startling $600,000 net cost reduction Emery Air Freight has realized from a program design and communications investment of $5,150 also tells us something about correct feedback and reward systems. In utilizing motivators, Emery's management builds on a full range of frequent non-pecuniary rewards. It stresses quantitative feedback directly to the individual and in relation to a goal. Its schema could have as its theme song Johnny Mercer's lyrics: "You've got to accentuate the positive. Eliminate the negative. And, don't mess with Mister In-between."

Action commitment

Meaningful personal relationships are being jealously guarded today, mainly because of their erosion in contemporary society. Large institutions, temporariness, and accelerated change place heavy pressures on people. They pose relevant questions about performance, development, pay, and promotion. Replies like these are frequent:

*"Wait until your next performance review in two months and we'll discuss how you're doing."

*"Sorry, it's company policy. I'm not allowed to talk about promotional opportunities."

*"That's a good suggestion. Remind me again, when things slow down."
*"Pay? Oh, that's up to the Salary Committee. I can't discuss it."

Human nature being what it is, we think of ourselves in terms of intentions and of others in terms of actions. Our intentions are to level with our associates, to be honest, and to be helpful. Developmental frameworks require more. There must be leveling, honesty, and helpfulness in actuality.

Like the auto mechanic who labored for more than two hours on a friend's car in diagnosing the problem and outlining the complicated solution, individual and manager must wrestle with practical concerns. And like that honest mechanic who charged 35 cents for his Sunday labors, the manager must show his personal involvement and freedom from strictly mercenary considerations. Corporate systems must support this type of philosophy as well.

'RESULTS MANAGEMENT'

To come to grips with the realities of the multipurpose performance appraisal vehicle, my bank is moving toward a pliable, responsive communication process that is geared to "results management." This system strives to do the following:

1.   Approach identified needs on a concentrated basis while, at the same time, trying not to be mutually exclusive, Segmented are —
. . . *management by objectives,* which includes personnel development goals and strategies,
. . . *salary administration dialogues,* which discuss past performance in terms of objectives met, exceeded, or missed as well as the rationale for the individual's pay in relation to performance,
. . . *planning for development* by those who wish manager or staff assistance, which stresses individual goal setting and the individual's primary responsibility for growth;
. . . *lay-of-the-land chats,* which are initiated by either the individual or the manager, to explore present status, future potentials, and alternative career paths;
. . . *"let's talk,"* a formal procedure for ideas, suggestions, and complaints,
. . . *coaches* for younger management people, provided on a voluntary basis for completely confidential dialogues,
. . . *task enrichment,* initiated by managers, with specialized assistance to heighten responsibility and make fuller individual jobs.
2.   Keep paperwork at a minimum, with most files retained by managers. The managerial guidepost is to have sufficient notes to make for effective performance. No checking of form is necessary. Results are determining.
3.   Use the Personnel Division alternately as a helper, internal consultant, systems designer, and formal trainer. Most new or revised programs

are first field-tested and/or critiqued by opinion panels. Periodically, attitudes and opinions are sampled in order to redesign systems.

4. Demonstrate that underlying the total effort is the belief that people at every level function best and grow most within an environment of genuine participation, high performance standards, prompt feedback, and proper rewards.

CONCLUDING NOTE

Profitable business practice dictates more effective use of human talents. Though the practice of performance review has delivered modest measurable results, its intent remains valid. A recovery of confidence in using the vehicle cannot come solely from remembering ambulances, shotguns, and Lucy, nor from thinking of onions, mosaics, and punch cards. Douglas McGregor's assumptions still cast the longest shadow. Fundamentals will carry the day. Managers at every level must be committed to discovering innovative ways to let people do their own thing — and within a responsible, decent corporate environment. From these discoveries will likely emerge the processes fostering accelerated human growth and business contribution.

NOTES

1. See Herbert H. Meyer, Emanuel Kay, and John R.P. French, Jr., "Split Roles in Performance Appraisal," HBR January-February 1965, p. 123.
2. "An Uneasy Look at Performance Appraisal," HBR May-June 1957, p. 90.
3. HBR March-April 1960, p. 81.
4. *The Human Side of Enterprise* (New York, McGraw-Hill, 1960), pp. 33-89.
5. See Herbert H. Meyer, Emanuel Kay, and John R.P. French, Jr., op. cit.
6. "The President Stands Alone," HBR September-October 1971, p. 42.
7. See *Motivation and Personality* (New York, Harper & Row, 1954), pp. 35-46.

What To Do About Performance Appraisal

Marion S. Kellogg

Marion S. Kellogg, Vice President for Corporate Counselling Services with the General Electric Company, says in this excerpt from her book that no system of appraisal can work unless certain pre-conditions exist: the employee must respect the evaluator the evaluator must respect himself; the manager's "style" must be such as to create a climate of "growth"; the relationship between employee and manager must be sufficiently solid to permit employee receptivity to managerial suggestions for the improvement of employee performance. The author cites a number of cases to illustrate her points and lists some factors that influence the receptivity which she deems so essential.

An organization may install the world's most effective system of appraisals, provide streamlined forms for documenting judgments, and train managers in the art and the skill of discussion, but if the man does not show his respect for the employee, the results will fall short of the mark. And unless the employee is receptive to feedback, wants to improve, and feels some sense of dissatisfaction with his work or progress, efforts to counsel him are unlikely to pay off. These issues are critical to making appraisal judgments and taking effective action based on them.

SELF-RESPECT, SELF-KNOWLEDGE

In any relationship, one person's lack of respect for the other is usually apparent, although it is not always identified as such. Respect is so important that its presence will surmount many problems and permit the two to function cooperatively. Its absence for whatever reason almost always prevents the two from successful joint efforts. A manager and those who report to him organizationally must work as a team in order to achieve their mission. Hence the critical nature of mutual respect.

To respect others, however, a manager must respect himself. He must accept what he is, understand his own strengths and deficiencies. This self-knowledge or insight is in no case more important than in making appraisal judgments and deciding on implementation. For our view of others is distorted by what we are like and how we see ourselves. Moreover, the confidence we are able to exhibit in others depends on our own self-confidence. To help someone else grow involves risk, and only when our inner security is strong enough are we able to undertake such risks.

Before making appraisal judgments and implementing them, therefore, managers should make an effort both to know themselves better and to foster a team relationship with employees.

Team effort stems from shared objectives for the organization and clarification and understanding of the roles and responsibilities of each member. Within this framework, performance appraisal judgments have more meaning and higher acceptability.

MANAGERIAL STYLE

Issues of managerial attitude and style cannot be ignored. Some managers display a self-interest and ambition that color their words and actions adversley. Others are more clearly interested in employee growth and organization achievement. It is not enough to have this interest. Such managers must let others see it and must demonstrate it in their day-to-day actions. If a manager is encouraging and suportive of others, thus displaying confidence in the ability of employees to progress, if he positively stimulates their willingness to take well-calculated risks, he creates a climate for growth and development. In this climate, his appraisals and subsequent discussions and actions with employees have an enriching, counseling character.

If, however, he surrounds them with a climate of criticism, warns them "not to rock the boat," and focuses his and their attention on the gap between what is desired and what was in fact accomplished, he often suppresses or limits growth. Some employees view appraisals in this climate as threatening, and discussions take on a harsh, punitive character.

In a growth climate, the relationship between the two parties is strengthened; there is more likely to be trust and therefore more openness. Managers are often unaware of the climate they create. A third-party professional can be of help in providing feedback on this important matter.

With respect to style, managers in most instances need to undertake self-awareness programs. They should ask themselves these questions and obtain professional help as needed.

1. Do I have a reasonable understanding of how others see me?
2. Do I have the inner confidence to risk growth and development of others?

Is the organization I manage working as a team — do we understand our mission, are our roles and responsibilities clear?

3.   Do I *show* my interest in others and my expectations for high team accomplishment?

If such questions can be answered positively, the manager is ready to build his share of the relationship.

EMPLOYEE'S VIEW OF THE MANAGER

Only if the employee respects the manager's knowledge or know-how in the performance area in which the manager is trying to encourage change and only if he believes the manager is sincerely interested in helping him do a better job is he likely to respond favorably to direct discussion of appraisal and improvement recommendations.

Unfortunately managers frequently tend to overestimate the soundness of the relationship between employees and themselves. This is true not only because a manager's own evaluation of himself is involved but also because employees often hide inner resentment, dislike, disparagement, and other unfavorable attitudes that might hurt them with the boss.

While the relationship between two individuals is necessarily unique, here are a few illustrative, generalized types of relationships.

CASE 1. GOOD GIVE-AND-TAKE WORKING RELATIONSHIP.

Joe and his boss have worked together long enough to know each other's ways and pretty well accept each other on an "as is" basis. Joe feels his boss knows his job. Joe's manager feels Joe performs well. From time to time, of course, the manager sees things that he feels could be improved. But he has found that he can usually talk them over with Joe, and Joe will try to make the desired changes. Joe, for his part, feels his manager really wants to help him do a better job.

In this situation, which is almost ideal for working together, the manager has a pretty easy time of it. Provided he really has worthwhile suggestions to make to Joe, the chances are good that Joe will make the effort to change and to improve within the limits of his natural abilities and at a rate determined by them.

CASE 2. THE FEARED BUT RESPECTED MANAGER.

Pete believes his boss knows his job but is a very hard man to work for. He is extremely demanding and expects such perfection that Pete tends to hide his mistakes, his problems, and any obstacles he encounters. In addition, Pete feels his boss is interested only in getting the work done and has little if any interest in Pete himself.

In this situation, in which an employee often gives the impression of hanging on to the manager's every word, it is relatively easy for the manager to convince himself the situation is better than it really is. The best clues to the existence of this kind of relationship are the infrequency of employee-initiated contacts with the manager, the relatively few problems and obstacles described by the employee as needing attention, the few times the employee disagrees with a manager's decision or argues the merit of another course of action, and the occasional, unexpected discovery that work thought to be on target is considerably off schedule.

The manager who suspects this kind of relationship should realize that implementation of his appraisal decisions will probably have to be within the framework of the already existing relationship. Any sudden about face, any sudden approach to the employee on the basis of helping him, will undoubtedly be viewed with suspicion. Since, however, the employee does respect his manager's work competence and is a little afraid of him, he will probably accept suggestions and try to put them into practice, particularly if he feels the manager will check up on him later. The manager's suggestions had better be good, however, otherwise the employee may adopt them only as long as the manager is watching.

CASE 3. THE "NICE GUY," THE SLIGHTLY INCOMPETENT MANAGER.

Bill works for a boss everybody likes — a "nice guy." Bill doesn't think much of his boss's technical or management know-how and feels he got where he is primarily because he's a good politician. Bill and his associates frankly find it easy to snow their boss and view his suggestions for their own improvement with something less than respect, although they feel the suggestions represent a sincere effort to help.

The manager in this situation may not be able — and may not want — to recognize the nature of his relationship with his employees. If he does, however, he may note possible clues in such things as finding out that employees have said they will do one thing but have actually done another, thinking a work situation is in good shape, but hearing from the top manager or an associate that this is not the case; or having employees introduce irrelevant topics at a meeting that take time and attention away from the purpose of the meeting. The most likely way of recognizing the situation, however, is with the help of an objective third party — perhaps a management development specialist or a management consultant.

The manager who detects this relationship needs to face up to the fact that his suggestions for work improvement will probably not carry much weight. Employees will listen to him good-humoredly, make their own appraisal of the worthwhileness of his ideas, discounting the value of his ideas somewhat because of their lack of respect for his competence (except perhaps in getting along with others), and then accept or reject pretty much on the basis of what they feel like doing.

This manager needs to double-check his coaching appraisal decisions to be sure they are sound. Perhaps his own boss can be of help here, or again, the use of a competent management development specialist or an outside consultant may add a great deal to the quality of both his appraisal decisions and their implementation. In all likelihood, discussion of the performance area in need of improvement and possible ways of improving it will not be fruitful, and another form of implementation should be selected.

CASE 4. AN OVER-THE-HILL MANAGER.

Tom works for an older manager who is close to retirement. In his younger days he was very successful, and his total career contribution to the firm has been high. At the moment, however, Tom feels he no longer represents current management thinking — his knowledge, skill, and standards of performance belong to another era. Though he considers the manager well-meaning, Tom feels trapped and in the position of taking direction from someone who is, for the most part, no longer qualified to give it.

Many managers in this position are keenly aware of the existence of this kind of relationship. They may feel the employee's analysis is wrong and go on trying to prove that their management judgment is as good as it ever was. Another reaction is to give up on this generation of workers and "let them sink or swim."

Other managers fight awareness of this relationship in spite of such clues as diffident and respectful agreement on almost all matters instead of the more normal, occasional differences of opinion; lack of shared enthusiasm over successes and disappointment over failures, and infrequent questions regarding evaluation of courses of action except as a matter of form.

The soundest assumption that an older manager, close to retirement, can make is probably that his employees feel he is no longer the best person to give them guidance and direction. Whether this assumption is in fact true or not, he should probably avoid face-to-face discussion of performance improvement needs and deliberately choose other ways of implementing his appraisal decisions.

CASE 5. THE INCOMPETENT, DISLIKED MANAGER.

Bob works for a manager who is considered ruthless, interested only in getting work out, and possessed of little, if any, knowledge about the work for which he is responsible. Bob is sure he knows more about his job than his manager does. He feels that because of his manager's lack of knowledge he sometimes makes impossible demands and then is unjust in evaluating performance. Bob feels, moreover, that his manager's suggestions are usually worthless or, if they have merit, are given only to make the manager himself look good in the eyes of his superior.

The manager in this situation probably sees it a little differently. Although he is aware that he lacks the specialized knowledge his employees have, he probably feels that his general knowledge of business, business methods, and ways of getting work done are all he needs to do his job.

If he is aware of how employees feel about him, he may believe it makes no difference to the total productivity of the group. If he is unaware of their reaction, such clues as high turnover among his employees, unwillingness on their part to sacrifice personal time in order to get work done, and covering up of mistakes and failures may help him.

In cases such as these, discussion of appraisal conclusions is not likely to be productive. Either the manager should check out what he is expecting of employees with a specialist in the work he is managing or he should give the employees themselves more say in what they are to do. When he sees the need for performance improvement, some method other than discussion should probably be chosen to bring it about.

Note that in each of these cases the employee's perception of the manager's competence and interest in helping him do a better job is the critical factor. Since the manager is admittedly able to get only an imperfect grasp of this view, it will always be safer, when it comes to implementing appraisal decisions, to assume that a poorer relationship exists than may actually be the case.

EMPLOYEE RECEPTIVITY

Clearly there is a strong connection between employee receptivity and employee-manager relationship. If the relationship between the two is poor, the employee will not be receptive even to the most meaningful and well-meant suggestions for his performance improvement.

However, the employee-manager relationship is not the only factor affecting the employee's receptivity, and the manager who seriously wishes to help the employee do a better job needs to be aware of other common determinants. Some of these also contribute to the kind of relationship existing between the two. None of these factors guarantees employee receptivity. The manager should see them as frequent contributors only.

FACTOR 1. DIFFERENCES IN AGE AND EXPERIENCE.

If the employee is considerably older than his boss or has had considerably more experience in doing the assigned work, his receptivity to his manager's suggestions will probably be low. On the other hand, if the manager is a little older than the employee and has had more directly related experience, the employee's receptivity will probably be high.

FACTOR 2. RIVALRY.

If the employee expected or hoped to be promoted to the position held by the current manager, his receptivity to suggestions made by the manager chosen in his stead will almost certainly be low — at least in the beginning. If, on the other hand, he was hired from outside the company by his manager or if his manager selected him for promotion to his present job, his receptivity should be high.

FACTOR 3. UNUSUAL WORK PRESSURES.

When the employee is faced with unusual work demands requiring considerable attention on his part — for example, peak volume of work, changes in work system or method, complex technical problems needing solution, or staffing problems if he supervises others — his receptivity to suggestions from his manager may be low unless they have immediate application to the problem at hand. But when his work is in good shape and there are no unusual pressures, his receptivity should be high.

FACTOR 4. HEALTH.

An employee who does not feel fit for either physical or emotional reasons, and who is concerned about his condition, is not likely to be receptive to a discussion of his performance.

FACTOR 5. OFF-THE-JOB PRESSURES.

Unusual family demands, such as illness at home or problems with children, will interfere with receptivity. So will any personal problem that absorbs an employee's attention or causes him worry and anxiety.

FACTOR 6. LENGTH OF TIME ON JOB.

If the employee is relatively new in his position or has just been given a new responsibility, his receptivity is ordinarily high.

FACTOR 7. DESIRE FOR ADVANCEMENT.

The employee who is interested in promotion in the near future is more likely to be receptive than the one who has no such ambition.

FACTOR 8. RECENCY OF SALARY INCREASE OR OTHER RECOGNITION.

Following a merit increase he views as substantial or some honor that indicates the high regard his manager has for his work, the employee will doubtless accept performance improvement suggestions in good spirit.

FACTOR 9. CHANGE IN MANAGERIAL ATTITUDE.

The manager's way of making suggestions may represent a marked change in his attitude toward the employee. Where this is so, the employee can hardly be blamed if he is not as receptive as he otherwise might be.

FACTOR 10. HISTORICAL MANAGERIAL ACTIONS.

If, in the past, the manager has suggested that improvement or change is desirable or has pointed out the need for added knowledge and skill and then has shown little follow-up interest in the employee's efforts to measure up, the employee probably will not welcome further discussion of his shortcomings. But if the manager has recognized and rewarded past efforts, the employee can be expected to cooperate once more to the best of his ability.

If, after considering these ten factors, the manager is still unsure of the employee's receptivity, he can:

a.   TEST IT OUT. Make a small suggestion and observe the employee's reaction.

b.   ASK THE EMPLOYEE HOW HE FEELS. Make a few suggestions

for performance improvement and ask the employee whether he is willing to act on them.

c.   WAIT FOR THE EMPLOYEE TO ASK. If there is no urgency about the matter, ask the employee to say when he is ready to discuss performance improvement.

d.   PROCEED ON THE BASIS OF PAST EXPERIENCE. If, in the past, the employee has responded well, assume he will this time, otherwise, choose an indirect approach.

Before a manager undertakes serious employee appraisal decisions and actions, he should understand and accept himself to the extent possible. He should recognize both his strengths and his limitations. He should make sure he has taken leadership in welding employees and himself into a team. Within the context of his personal style he should display his commitment to team results and the excellence of all team members. He should test the adequacy and nature of the relationship with an employee who is to be appraised and choose implementation methods and timing that will enhance the person's receptivity.

Some Common Factors Affecting Receptivity to Performance Improvement Suggestions

The employee is MORE likely to be receptive to his manager's performance improvement suggestions if:

He feels his manager is competent in these performance areas and wants to help him do a better job.

He is younger than his boss and has had less directly applicable experience.

He was hired or promoted to his present position by his boss.

His work is in good shape and there are no unusual work pressures.

He is new in his position or has just been given a new responsibility.

He is eager for promotion soon.

He has just been rewarded with a merit increase or other honor.

Past experience shows the manager will recognize and reward efforts to follow suggestions.

The employee is LESS likely to be receptive to his manager's performance improvement suggestions if:

He feels his manager is incompetent in these performance areas.

He is older than his boss and has had more directly applicable experience.

He competed for his boss's position and lost.

He is under unusual pressure at work.

His physical or emotional health is not good.

He is faced with unusual off-the-job pressures.

The manager displays a marked change in attitude toward the employee.

Past experience shows the manager has little interest in the employee's response to suggestions.

Integrating Behaviorally-Based and Effective-Based Methods

Craig Eric Schneier and
Richard W. Beatty

Starting with the premise that most organizations are unhappy with the results of their performance appraisal process, especially as it relates to administrative position, the authors take a "good, hard look" at appraisal. They begin by examining and defining job performance and performance appraisal, stressing that human behavior is really what is being observed and measured. They go on to state that in order to provide feedback and improve performance, performance appraisal must have certain characteristics: clarity about job expectations, utilization of behavioral terminology, use of a "problem-solving focus," and others. Various behavior-based and effective-based formats are compared against performance appraisal objectives to determine the validity of the former. Problems that tend to plague appraisal systems are examined in some detail and suggestions for improving such systems are given. Craig Eric Schneier is Associate Professor of Personnel Administration and Organizational Behavior at the University of Maryland. Richard W. Beatty is Professor of Management and Organization at the University of Colorado.

Reprinted from the July, 1979 issue of *The Personnel Administrator*, 30 Park Drive, Berea, Ohio 44017, $26 per year.

Most organizations are dissatisfied with their performance appraisal (PA) process, particularly for administrative/managerial positions. They have concerns about its objectivity, its relevance and its validity. In many cases the complaint is that the appraisal system simply does not work! In a three-part series on this topic which begins with this article, we take a good, hard look at appraisal. First the objectives and legal requirements for appraisal systems are discussed and potential problem sources are identified. Appraisal is seen as a process involving key decisions and having important consequences. PA is not simply a form or a rating scale, but an integral managerial tool which can improve performance of individuals and units....

Performance appraisal (PA) is required for it forms the rationale for key decisions regarding promotion, wage and salary administration and selection for training programs. However, despite noteworthy advances in scaling techniques to reduce such psychometric errors as leniency, many organizations still feel their appraisal systems are ineffective[1] and still have problems removing subjectivity and bias of raters. They have given up the search for perfect form, hoping to develop any acceptable one.

WHAT IS JOB PERFORMANCE?

Much of the activity observed on a job results in an evaluation of the performance of a person, team, unit, or an entire organization. In order to understand how such evaluations are made, the distinction between the following three terms is essential: behavior, performance and effectiveness (see also Figure 1).[2]

BEHAVIOR is simply what people do on a job — their activity. Writing reports, holding meetings, analyzing documents and conversing with others are possible behaviors exhibited on the job. Effective behavior is a function of the interaction between ability and effort — the behavior initiated to put one's ability to use. PERFORMANCE is the term used for the evaluation of these behaviors as to their desirability or efficacy on the job. For example, writing reports in a specific style is evaluated as desirable performance. The report writing is evaluated according to a set of standards, or *criteria,* used by the evaluator. Certain behaviors or groups of behaviors are evaluated as good performance, others as fair performance and still others as unacceptable performance. Performance is the evaluated behavior and is what is measured in appraisal systems.

EFFECTIVENESS refers to the outcomes or results of various degrees of performance at the individual, unit, or organizational level. Did the behaviors which produced an excellent report actually result in a desired organizational outcome, such as more efficient spending or the development of more relevant programs? Did holding a meeting with appropriate persons actually result in a more effective plan?

A key aspect of judgment in the appraisal setting thus involves drawing cause and effect inferences between behaviors and effectiveness. For example, if a rater observes that profit in a unit has gone down (i.e., the unit has become less effective), he or she must draw a conclusion concerning whether behaviors exhibited by management or others responsible were inappropriate or whether other factors may have caused the decline, such as a drop in demand for the product. As will be discussed in subsequent sections, Management by Objectives (MBO) appraisal systems, designed to measure outcomes or effectiveness, are deficient if they are unable to identify and measure the effectiveness of the behaviors which produced (or failed to produce) the outcomes.

FIGURE 1
WHAT IS JOB PERFORMANCE?

BEHAVIOR is simply activity on the job ⟶	**BEHAVIORS**: Checking all sick leave balances, preparing a tabular summary and report, and distributing to entire staff, along with new leave policy statements.
Which is evaluated or appraised by the organization according to set of CRITERIA and termed PERFORMANCE ⟶	**PERFORMANCE**: To what degree was the report accurate, thorough and timely?
Which can result in desired individual, unit or organizational outcomes and hence degrees of EFFECTIVENESS. ⟶	**EFFECTIVENESS**: Report proves useful, as leave and associated costs have been reduced.

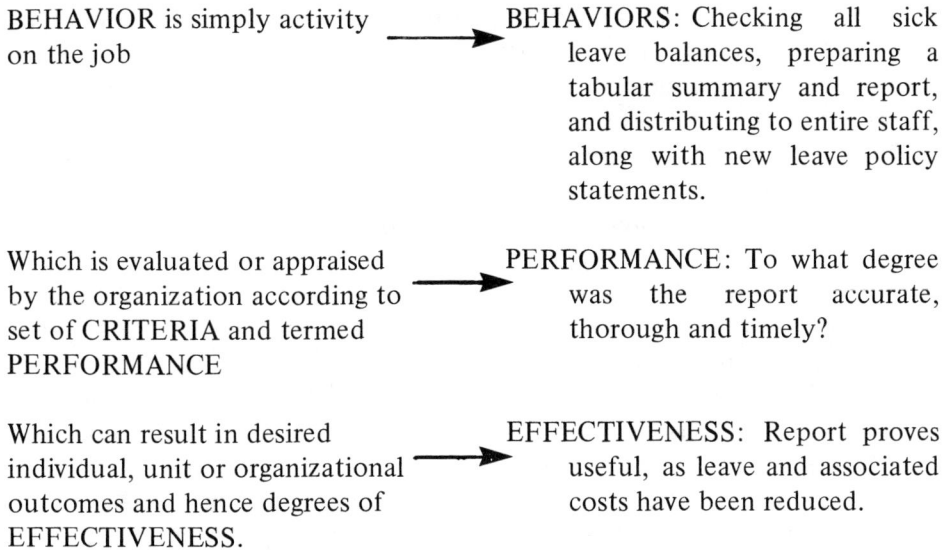

WHAT IS PERFORMANCE APPRAISAL?

Performance appraisal or evaluation is the *process of identifying, measuring and developing human performance* in organizations. An effective appraisal system must not only *accurately measure current performance levels,* but also contain mechanisms for *reinforcing strengths, identifying deficiencies* and feeding such information back to rates in order that they may *improve future performance.* This second, developmental aspect of appraisal is as important as the measurement aspect.

As noted in the preceding section, the term performance itself denotes judgment — behavior which has been evaluated. Performance appraisal is thus the process of OBSERVING and IDENTIFYING, MEASURING and DEVELOPING human behavior in the organization. These activities are described as follows:

OBSERVATION and IDENTIFICATION refers to the process of viewing or scrutinizing job behaviors. It consists of choosing what job behaviors to look at among all that are emitted by a ratee, as well as how often to observe them. The choices inherent in this process add subjectivity to appraisal.

MEASUREMENT refers to ascertaining the extent, degree, level, etc., of a behavior. After raters choose what information to examine, they compare this information about ratee behavior against a set of organizational or personal expectations for each job. The degree to which observed behavior meets or exceeds the expectations determines its desirability, or the level of performance it reflects, such as excellent or satisfactory.

DEVELOPMENT refers to performance improvement over time. An appraisal system must contain mechanisms to communicate the expectations and measurement process to persons being appraised, motivate them to remove any deficiencies uncovered and reinforce them to build on strengths in order to improve future performance.

When PA is considered in terms of its utility to an organization, several operational PA objectives seem critical. These include 1) the ability to provide adequate feedback to employees to improve subsequent performance, 2) the identification of employee training needs, 3) the identification of criteria used to allocate organizational rewards, 4) the validation of selection techniques to meet Equal Employment Opportunity (EEO) requirements and 5) the identification of promotable employees from internal labor supplies (see Figure 2). In order to accomplish these objectives, the PA system must, of course, be an accurate measure of performance.

A PA's adequacy to *provide feedback and improve performance* requires that it possess the following characteristics: be unambiguous and clearly specify the job-related performance expected, use behavioral terminology, set behavioral targets for ratees to work toward and use a problem-solving focus which culminates in a specific plan for performance improvement. If PAs are to identify training needs, the format must specify ratee deficiencies in behavioral terms, include all relevant job dimensions, and identify environmental deterrents to desired performance levels.

PAs are also used in the *allocation of organizational rewards* such as merit pay and punishments, such as disciplinary actions. Effective reward allocation may require a valid PA which ranks employees according to a quantifiable scoring system. Sufficient variance in scores is essential to differentiate across performers. In allocating rewards, PAs must have credibility with employees. The same PA format must also be used for disciplinary action, which may range from warnings to termination. Thus, the documentation required for such decisions must also be facilitated by the PA format. With the recent passage of Civil Service Reform Act and its provisions tying performance to merit pay and bonuses, the importance of PAs in the public sector has been greatly heightened.

PAs must be designed to facilitate the *validation of selection* techniques. This process requires, in general terms and at a minimum, measures of employee output or job-related dimensions that tap the behavioral domain of the job obtained through systematic job analysis, the facilitation of interrater reliability measures, professional and objective administration of the PA and continual rater observation of ratee performance.[3]

The *identification of promotion potential* requires that job-related PAs have several dimensions in the incumbent's job, the same, or similar to, the job to which the incumbent may be promoted. This indicates the incumbent's ability to assume increasingly difficult assignments. The PA must also rank ratees comparatively, measure the contribution to departmental objectives and perhaps capture a ratee's career aspirations and long-term goals.

The final but perhaps most important PA objective is its accuracy in measuring performance. In some ways it could be conceived as essential for meeting the PA objectives mentioned above. The issues of concern here would include PA formats which minimize rater response set errors (e.g., leniency, restriction of range, halo), those which agree with other measures of performance using alternative formats (e.g., direct indices such as salary or number of promotions), those which obtain reliability across raters, those which have the flexibility to reflect changes in the job enviornment and those possessing credibility with raters such that they complete the format seriously.

FIGURE 2
OBJECTIVES OF PERFORMANCE APPRAISAL SYSTEMS

1 FEEDBACK/ DEVELOP- MENT REQUIRES:	2 ASSESSING TRAINING NEEDS REQUIRES:	3 IDENTIFYING PROMOTION POTENTIAL REQUIRES:	4 REWARDS ALLOCATION REQUIRES:	5 VALIDATION OF SELEC- TION TECH- NIQUES REQUIRES:	6 MEASURE- ACCURACY REQUIRES:
Specifying behavioral terminology on the format	Specifying deficiencies in behavioral terms	job-related criteria	Ability to rank order ratees or results in quantifiable, performance scores.	job relatedness and a comprehensive list of dimensions tapping the behavioral domain of the job	Reducing rater response set errors (e.g., leniency, restriction of range, halo)
Setting behavioral targets for ratees to work toward	Rating on all relevant job dimensions.	job dimensions dealing with ability to assume increasingly difficult assignments built into the form	Facilitating a variance or spread of scores to discriminate between good bad, fair, etc., ratees.	Systematic job analysis to derive criteria	Agreeing with other performance measures not on the format (e.g., direct indices such as salary, number of promotions.)
job-related problem-solving performance review which ends with a plan for performance improvement	identifying motivation/attitude and environmental conditions as causes of inadequate performance.	Ability to rank ratees comparatively	Measuring contributions to organization/ department objectives	Assessing inter-rater reliability	Reliability across multiple raters.
Reducing ambiguity/anxiety of ratees regarding job performance required and expected by raters/organization.		Measuring of contribution to organization/department objectives	Accuracy and credibility with employees	Professional objective administration of format	Flexibility to reflect changes in job or environment
		Assessing of ratee's career aspirations and long-range goals.		Continual observance of ratee performance by raters.	Job-related criteria.
					Commitment of raters to observe ratee performance frequently and complete format seriously.

FIGURE 3. GENERALIZED EVALUATION OF PA FORMATS COMPARED TO PA OBJECTIVES

FORMAT \ OBJECTIVE	FEEDBACK/DEVELOPMENT	ASSESSING TRAINING NEEDS	IDENTIFICATION OF PROMOTION POTENTIAL	REWARD ALLOCATION	SELECTION SYSTEM VALIDATION	MEASUREMENT ACCURACY
Global	Poor	Poor	Poor to Fair	Poor	Poor	Poor
Trait-based	Poor	Poor	Poor to Fair	Poor to Fair	Poor to Fair	Poor to Fair
Behavior-based (if behaviorally-anchored)	Very Good to Excellent	Very Good	Very Good	Very Good	Very Good to Excellent	Good
Effectiveness-based	Fair to Good	Fair to Good	Fair to Good	Very Good to Excellent	Fair to Good	Very Good to Excellent

FIGURE 4. SOURCES OF PROBLEMS IN APPRAISAL SYSTEMS

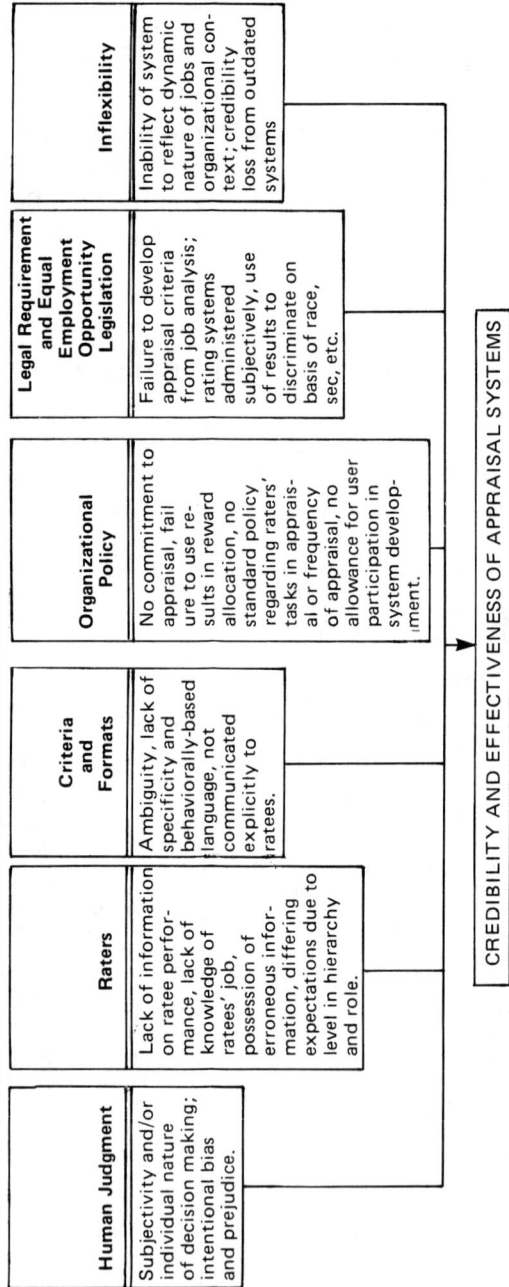

Human Judgment	Raters	Criteria and Formats	Organizational Policy	Legal Requirement and Equal Employment Opportunity Legislation	Inflexibility
Subjectivity and/or individual nature of decision making; intentional bias and prejudice.	Lack of information on ratee performance, lack of knowledge of ratees' job, possession of erroneous information, differing expectations due to level in hierarchy and role.	Ambiguity, lack of specificity and behaviorally-based language, not communicated explicitly to ratees.	No commitment to appraisal, failure to use results in reward allocation, no standard policy regarding raters' tasks in appraisal or frequency of appraisal, no allowance for user participation in system development.	Failure to develop appraisal criteria from job analysis; rating systems administered subjectively, use of results to discriminate on basis of race, sec, etc.	Inability of system to reflect dynamic nature of jobs and organizational context; credibility loss from outdated systems

CREDIBILITY AND EFFECTIVENESS OF APPRAISAL SYSTEMS

Thus, there are several criteria which PAs should meet to be fully operational. But which types of formats — those which measure worker behavior or those which measure the outcomes of that behavior — are more effective? No simple answer is available, but the utility of various types of behavior-based and effective-based formats can best be ascertained by comparing them against the PA objectives identified above.

COMPARISON OF FORMATS

GLOBAL RATINGS. The first PA format alternative is a uni-dimensional, global rating which uses a rater's overall estimate of performance without distinguishing between critical job elements or dimensions. There are numerous problems in the use of uni-dimensional formats and when compared to the six PA objectives described above, they generally fall far short (see Figure 3). Uni-dimensional PA formats are also questionable as measures of performance (i.e., criteria) from a legal standpoint because they are not based on job analysis and thus are not job-related.

TRAIT-BASED SCALES. There are numerous multi-dimensional (or graphic) approaches to measuring performance. They are more useful than global scales because they recognize that job performance consists of separate dimensions, or job elements. The first of these is the familiar trait-based scale using dimensions such as loyalty, dependability, etc. Other dimensions traditionally found on these formats are cooperation, initiative and self-confidence. There are problems in the use of trait-based scales centering around potential ambiguity and subjectivity. That is, specifically what is meant by "lack of cooperation"? Thus, many trait-based scales are generally evaluated as only poor to fair relative to PA objectives. Further, and perhaps most important, trait-based scales are typically not sufficiently job-related or based on a thorough job analysis. Thus an organization's vulnerability to Equal Employment Opportunity (EEO) litigation is not alleviated.

BEHAVIOR-BASED SCALES. A significant step beyond global and trait-based formats are behaviorally based scales. These are based upon a job analysis and attempt to determine what an employee actually does at work. A behavior-based scale provides specific feedback to employees because it is based on the activities required of the job. It captures specific information across employees for reward allocation and about each employee specifically in the assessment of training needs because it identifies the activities (dimensions) in which an employee may be deificient. For promotion potential, a dimension-based scale can certainly be useful because it may specify the kinds of behaviors incumbents are to demonstrate in their present jobs. Performance on these dimensions can then be compared to the dimensions required in the next job level (for which the employee is a promotion candidate). Behavior-based scales are often seen as more accurate than the previous two PA formats because of their job-relatedness and specificity. Thus we can expect less rater error and higher interrater agreement (and/or reliability). Finally, because dimension-based scales can meet the legal requirements for criterion measures, these certainly can be an improvement for the validation of selection procedures.

The major drawback with dimension-based scales is that although they provide specification of the particular activities of an employee, the scale points are of limited use if they are only numerically and/or adjective-anchored. They provide little specific feedback on what behaviors led to the particular rating given, even though the area of performance deficiency has been identified. Thus, a dimension-based PA may be deficient in assessing an employee's specific behaviors within job dimensions since only adjective or numerical anchors are used.

Behavioral expectation scales or *behaviorally-anchored rating scales* (BARS) are also dimensional scales.[4] The scale points are behavioral statements illustrating various degrees of performance, not merely adjectives or numbers. Thus, BARS are far more specific in terms of identifying employee behavior relative to performance on a specific job dimension. These are also more sophisticated than dimension-based formats and require more time to develop.

Behavior-based scales seem to provide excellent feedback to employees in specifying not only what activities employees are to engage in, but also the behaviors a rater perceives that a ratee has demonstrated during the performance period. In fact, performance improvement has been demonstrated through the use of behavior-based systems.[5]

EFFECTIVENESS-BASED SYSTEMS. Another multi-dimensional system is results, or effectiveness, based scaling. Effectiveness-based scales attempt to provide "objective" indicators for levels of performance and are, of course, typically called Management by Objectives (MBO) systems.[6] Although it is a multi-dimensional approach in that there are often many objectives which are to be accomplished, effectiveness-based scaling is unique in that what it provides is a measure of an employee's *contribution*, not an employee's *activities or behaviors.*

Ratees evaluated with effectiveness-based scaling are being evaluated not on what they *do* but what they *produce;* not on how they spend their time, but what they contribute. This is an important difference and a major shortcoming of the previously disscussed PA approaches. Obviously, it is difficult to develop specific indicators of employee contribution, but it can be done for many jobs. It is accomplished with more ease in lower level jobs and entry-level jobs within an organization than in higher level jobs.

Thus, effectiveness-based scales offer something that is critical and often overlooked in the assessment of performance appraisals. MBO systems are often used to measure unit productivity to which a manager presumably makes a contribution.

WHAT ARE THE CAUSES OF PROBLEMS?

Regardless of what format is used, problems can deter PA system effectiveness. The cause of the ineffectiveness of any particular PA system is a function of many variables, acting singly or in groups, which characterize the job, organizational setting and users. However, most often specific causes are located within the following broad problem categories: human judgment, raters, criteria and formats, organization policy, legal requirements and Equal Employment Opportunity (EEO) legislation and inflexibility. Each of these six broad categories contains several possible sources of PA problems (see Figure 4), discussed briefly below.

Problems in a PA system ultimately can only be judged as to their degree of severity and dysfunctional consequences in light of the original objectives developed for each system. For example, a PA system may sacrifice some degree of applicability across job-type (and would, possibly have higher developmental costs) in order to have a greater amount and specificity of information about performance available to a certain group of ratees. Hence, it may have greater ability to pinpoint performance deficiencies and thus reduce costs of unnecessary training programs. If the objectives of a PA system are predetermined and prioritized, the system can be designed to make such trade-offs rationally and at minimal cost. Further, after PA design and implementation, problems diagnosed can be judged as to seriousness and corrective action planned in light of objectives. This relationship between PA objectives and both the design and revision of PA systems, while considering various PA problems, is emphasized in the discussion to follow.

PROBLEM NO. 1: HUMAN JUDGMENT. A fundamental source of problems in PA is the *subjectivity and individuality* which accompanies the human judgment process. Individual differences among people influence their attitudes, values, perceptions, behavior and judgment, a fact as true in the PA setting as it is in all others. Intelligence, cognitive style, amount of education, age, sex and self-esteem are but a few of the individual level characteristics which have been found to influence the making of judgments of others. The expectations raters' supervisors hold for them, as well as a rater's own level of job performance and competence, have also been found to effect ratings.[7]

All of these factors, however, act in an implicit manner. They reflect "honest" or legitimate differences in personality, background or ability between participants in PA which influence their perception – their view of reality – and thus perceptions of the behavior of ratees. While these individual differences typically do not result in deliberate attempts to bias or prejudice ratings, their result on PA (e.g., inaccuracies) is similar.

Besides these *un*intentional PA errors resulting from individual differences, are those overt, deliberate attempts to distort PAs based upon personal prejudices and biases against others of a certain religion, national origin, race, sex, age, political ideology, etc. The result can be the setting of different performance standards for two people performing the same job or the distorting of PA results upward or downward to correspond to one's prejudices. Even when performance criteria are quantifiable and visible, figures can be distorted or interpreted erroneously by such judgmental factors as perceived amount of effort or initiative and hence intentional bias can still enter the process.

PROBLEM NO. 2: RATERS. PA problems stem from conscientious raters who possess *inadequate and/or erroneous information* about ratee performance. Many supervisors, due to their own job duties which may physically separate them from their subordinate ratees, are able to observe ratee performance too infrequently to accurately judge typical performance. Many must thus "sample" performance over a long period. But non-representative sampling or allowing a typical positive or negative performance occuring during their infrequent observation periods to bias their judgments of performance over the entire period can lead to inaccurate appraisals.

In addition, members of each hierarchical level within an organization may view a ratee's performance from a different vantage point or hold differing expectations for desired performance based upon their roles.[8] Thus a ratee's supervisor may be in an excellent position to judge the ratee's technical competence, but not his or her ability to effectively interact with others. Peer raters may possess the best information regarding a ratee's interpersonal effectiveness. Supervisors of ratees, as critics and evaluators of their subordinates, typically judge performance more harshly than do job incumbents themselves.

PROBLEM NO. 3: CRITERIA AND PA FORMATS. The identification of specific, consistent, performance criteria are the first objective of a PA system, as discussed earlier. The easiest way to assure that a ratee's performance can be evaluated based upon only the whim of a rater is of course to keep the criteria ambiguous and/or secret, to change them capriciously, or never to develop them at all! As discussed above, each type of appraisal format has advantages and disadvantages relative to this issue of defining the criteria against which to base evaluations. The overall objective, of course, is to develop a format which identifies and defines the criteria in explicit, concrete terms.

PROBLEM NO. 4: ORGANIZATIONAL POLICY. Problems in PA systems arise from the relationship between organizational policies regarding performance, promotion, merit raises and other decisions and the uses for which PA results are intended. If these types of decisions are actually to be made on the basis of performance, rather than on the basis of seniority or other criteria, results of a PA obviously assume a great deal of importance. Here problems arise when PA formats are ambiguous, criteria are not communicated to raters and ratees and/or if each of several degrees of performance (e.g., good, fair, etc.) do not have observable, behavioral referents.

For example, if a supervisor (rater) is given the authority to set merit raises for a group of subordinates (ratees) and the PA format which is used to measure performance is of the global type involving overall ranking, the supervisor can easily feel trapped. Of course, the supervisor might have a definite and accurate overall impression as to the relative performance of his or her ratees and can easily discriminate between the excellent and average performers. But if the top performers are given merit raises and the others are not, the supervisor needs a rationale for this action to give to those who were denied the merit raise. The global PA format provides little help since it does not specify and define the exact criteria used in PA or the different levels of performance within each criteria. To develop a formal, written rationale for each rating may not only be seen as too bothersome for many raters but they may find it difficult to articulate the exact criteria to ratees. The result is often that either extreme leniency is used on many ratings or that all ratees are rated about the same and hence each receives a smaller merit raise. Thus, expediency rather than discriminability between good and poor performers characterizes the PA system and its credibility is destroyed.

PROBLEM NO. 5: LEGAL REQUIREMENTS AND EQUAL EMPLOYMENT OPPORTUNITY (EEO) LEGISLATION. The risk of precipitating charges of discrimination as a result of policy decisions based upon PA results is now itself a serious cause of problems in PA systems. The ramifications of subjective, unsubstantiated PAs can be devastating to an organization. Recently, through several pieces of legislation, court decisions and guidelines of various Federal agencies, the issue of discrimination in employment as a result of PAs has become more visible and spelled out in more detail than ever before.[9]

Organizations must present PA forms and any instructions given to raters as part of the evidence for the validity of such selection techniques as employment tests. Thus, the use of, for example, an application blank, would be judged acceptable in certain situations only if answers to particular items on the blank were found to correlate highly with the probability of future job "success" of workers in the job. Job "success" is demonstrated typically by results of a PA system. The PA system is thus open to scrutiny by the courts and must therefore be thorough and as bias-free as possible.

Violations of civil rights legislation can also come from the use of PAs directly in promotion decisions . . . .

PROBLEM NO. 6: INFLEXIBILITY. The final cause of problems in PA systems is the dynamic nature of jobs and job performance and the static nature of any written PA document typically developed several months before it is to be used. As job responsibilities, duties, requirements and job environments change over time, a PA format may become obsolete before it is even used! Further, as workers' performance levels change over time, perhaps due to training and experience, the standards set in PA formats may be too low, geared only for newer workers. Even the same jobs within classes are not identical.

One solution is, of course, to continually develop new PA formats as all of the above factors change and to develop separate PA formats for each and every position. But this solution is an economic impossibility. A solution often used by organizations is to develop a few broad categories of formats— perhaps one format for operating-level workers, one for clerical workers, one for technical workers, and one for managers. A reasonable solution? Yes, provided raters are knowledgeable, competent, use identical standards, observe performance equally, are generally bias-free and are provided with specific, detailed criteria. But in the all too often instances when the "ideal" rater is unavailable, PA formats applicable across job types may lead to subjectivity and possibly to litigation for discrimination.

The view of PA systems presented above is, admittedly, problematic. Yet is is a realistic one as many organizations find their appraisal system to be the source of continual problems. As discussed, no system is capable of alleviating all appraisal problems completely. Yet there are a few things which can be done to enhance a system's effectiveness.

The first way to improve appraisal systems is to recognize that the appraisal process entails far more than measurement and the use of a form. It also includes observation and identification of performance, as well as development of performance. As discussed, PA systems have several objectives. They must be developed in light of both the trade-offs between these objectives and the potential problem sources in appraisal.

The second mechanism for improved appraisal is to integrate the best aspects of the various formats. Behavior-based systems, such as Behaviorally-Anchored Rating Scales (BARS), specify criteria in very concrete terms to improve accuracy, provide detailed feedback to ratees and help comply with legal requirements due to the job-relatedness of criteria. Effectiveness-based systems, such as Menagement by Objectives (MBO) are very popular due to their ability to measure and quantify results, redirect effort to important tasks and allow for ratee participation in goal-setting. The next article in this series demonstrates how and why BARS and MBO can be integrated to derive the benefits from both systems. The developmental procedure for BARS is explained and the sample of all required forms are included. The last article in the series describes the final, integrated system and explains its operation through an actual case study.

REFERENCES

1. Bureau of National Affairs,
   Management of Performance Appraisal Systems (Washington, D.C., BNA, 1974).
2. See also J.P. Campbell, et al.,
   Managerial Behavior, Performance, and Effectiveness (NY: McGraw-Hill, 1970).

3.   See "Uniform Guidelines on Employee Selection Procedures," *Federal Register*, Dec. 30, 1977; D.B. Schneier, "The Impact of EEO Legislation on Performance APPRAISAL," *Personnel,* 1978, 55 (4), 24-34.

4.   The development and utility of BARS is the subject of Part II of this series of three articles. See also C.E. Schneier and R.W. Beatty, *Personnel Administration Today* (Reading, MA, Addison-Wesley, 1978) and S.J. Carroll and C.E. Schneier, *Performance Appraisal* (Goodyear Pub. Co., forthcoming).

5.   R.W. Beatty, C.E. Schneier and J.R. Beatty, "An Empirical Investigation of Perceptions of Ratee Behavior Frequency and Ratee Behavior Change Using Behavioral Expectation Scales (BES)," *Personnel Psychology,* 1977, 30, 647-658.

6.   See S.J. Carroll and H. Tosi, *Management by Objective* (New York: Macmillan, 1973).

7.   See e.g., C.E. Schneier, "The Psychometric Characteristics and Operational Utility of Behavioral Expectation Scales (BES): A Cognitive Reinterpretation," *Journal of Applied Psychology,* 1977, 62, 541-548.

8.   See C.E. Schneier and R.W. Beatty, "The Influence of Role Prescriptions on the Performance Appraisal Process," *Academy of Management Journal,* 1978, 27, 129-134.

9.   See W.H. Holley and H.S. Field, "Performance Appraisal and the Law," *Labor Law Journal,* July, 1975, 423-429; "Uniform Guidelines on Employee Selection Procedures," *op. cit;* D.B. Schneier, *op. cit.*

Evaluating Managerial Performance: Is Your Assessment System Legal?

Thomas A. Basnight and Benjamin W. Wolkinson

The authors' experience in labor relations and with questions of compensation enables them to examine with insight some of the weaknesses of typical managerial merit pay plans: vagueness of standards, subjectivity, and inconsistency among appraisers. They also report on laws and litigation involving merit pay, detailing a number of cases involving discriminatory pay practices under the Fair Labor Standards Act and Title VII of the Civil Rights Act of 1964. They advise employers to apply merit pay plans with uniformity and without any hint of discrimination, to use assessment centers as "promotional determinants" rather than use only traditional performance criteria, and to avoid subjectivity by employing some form of management by objectives system; only in this way can litigation be avoided. What the authors say has application to the world of education where the concept of merit pay is playing an increasingly larger role. Thomas A. Basnight is an independent consultant in wage and salary administration in East Lansing, Michigan. Benjamin W. Wolkinson is Associate Professor of Labor/Industrial Relations at Michigan State University in East Lansing.

Organizations almost always will encounter employee morale problems when there is a noticeable discrepancy between organization policy and practice. Endorsement by an employer of equal employment opportunity, occupational safety, or the primacy of its human resources rings false in organizations with predominantly white male managements, persistently unsafe working conditions, or chronic resort to layoffs at the first hint of economic distress. But these types of policy-practice dichotomies often have a limited impact upon management personnel, who may not be affected as directly as members of subordinate ranks. All management personnel are affected, and perhaps upset, however, by a gap between advancement-by-merit policy and a practice that reflects other criteria. Closing the gap is difficult if the organization insists on making personality assessment a part of performance appraisal by weighting traits such as "loyalty" and "attitude" along with the quantity and quality of work. Such subjective appraisals may be the rule rather than the exception. Despite the publicity given "management by objectives" and other results-oriented appraisal systems, 64 percent of the companies responding to one survey, included personality traits in their performance-appraisal systems. This study examines the legitimacy of subjective management-appraisal systems under existing fair employment legislation and litigation.

In managerial compensation systems, "pay for performance" is a hard-sought, seldom-attained goal. Most organizations would like to pay the highest salaries to their most effective performers, but identifying those performers poses numerous problems. In this, managerial merit plans differ markedly from merit plans for clerical or production employees, among the latter group, jobs tend to be homogeneous and results easy to quantify, while merit pay increments may represent a very small proportion of base pay, and promotions may be based on objectively measured criteria unrelated to performance, such as seniority. In management positions, however, the supervisor's performance evaluation frequently is meant to govern both raises and promotions: It is performance, not time in rank, that is said to "merit" additional compensation and broader responsibilities. Managerial merit plans typically suffer from three weaknesses:

(1) VAGUENESS OF STANDARDS. In most organizations, the diverse nature and scope of managerial assignments make it hard to assess managerial performance through a single system of standards unless those standards are stated so broadly that they can be applied both to marketing executives and to maintenance foremen. There are really only two output standards that are sufficiently universal for this purpose: quantity and quality. Most evaluation plans, unfortunately, also attempt to measure *inputs* – personality traits, knowledge of job, potential for advancement – that are not necessarily related to performance.

(2) SUBJECTIVITY. Many compensation specialists bemoan the halo effect – the tendency of the appraiser, assigned to assess the employee's performance for the previous year, to focus on recent subordinate triumphs or tragedies and allow these to influence the over-all rating unduly.

(3) INCONSISTENCY AMONG APPRAISERS. Even where jobs are fairly homogeneous, and supervisors fairly objective, discrepancies in performance rating may occur. Smith and Brown may both be unit supervisors in the accounting department, but one never rates a subordinate "outstanding," while the other grants this maximum accolade every year. This is because one uses absolute, the other relative, standards: Smith reserves "outstanding" for that yet-to-be-seen subordinate whose performance embodies all the ideal qualities; Brown simply determines his ranking of subordinates'

performance and hands the "O" to the highest name on the list.

Although these problems seem to warrant management efforts to train appraisers in evaluation techniques to ensure consistency, one study[2]found that over half the organizations using performance-evaluation systems expended no effort toward this goal. Some employers are quite concerned with the form of the system, with frequent evaluation format revisions and obsessive attention to merit-review timetables. Other firms acknowledge the existing weaknesses of traditional performance-evaluation systems.

> Most, if not all, formal appraisal systems become ends unto themselves and in no way . . . fulfill the objectives of employee appraisal . . . (I)f the person doing the appraisal must submit appraisal data to his own organizational superior . . . (it) is made out to please the boss and not to be of any value to the employee . . . Any appraisal system tied into a merit system is valueless . . . made out only to justify the salary increases and not as an objective appraisal of performance.[3]

Merit-system problems — the degree to which pay increases for a given job can be made truly dependent upon performance lvel, the propriety of using performance in job x as a qualification for promotion to job x + I, the determination of a "best" performance-evaluation form, the validity of claimed ability to "measure" performance at all — have long been pondered by compensation specialists. They may have the solutions handed to them by the courts.

MERIT PAY AND THE LAW

Both the Fair Labor Standards Act (FLSA) and Title VII of the Civil Right Act of 1964 contemplate differences in pay based upon merit considerations:

> No employer . . . shall discriminate . . . between employees on the basis of sex by paying wages . . . at a rate less than the rate at which he pays wages to employees of the opposite sex in such establishment for equal work . . . except where such payment is made pursuant to
>
> i)   a seniority system
> ii) a merit system . . .[4]

Notwithstanding any other provision of this title, it shall not be an unlawful employment practice for any employer to apply different standards of compensation . . . pursuant to a bona fide seniority or merit system . . .[5]

There has been very little litigation involving merit systems under either statute. This probably has been due to four factors:

(1) Most merit systems involve management personnel, who were exempt from *all* provisions of the FLSA until 1972, when the equal pay standards were extended to otherwise exempt employees by section 906(b)(I) of the Higher Education Act.[6]

(2) Although the discriminatory denial or reduction of a merit raise is

unquestionably an injury to the employee involved, the damages may be so slight (a difference of a few percentage points in total compensation) as not to seem worth the social risks involved in bringing charges against an employer.

(3) Since individual performance ratings are usually confidential, an employee may not be aware that his or her own unfairly low appraisal caused a promotion to go to someone else.

(4) Merit system is an affirmative defense — that is, the employer claiming merit as the explanation of pay differentials has the burden of proving it. Some employers may conclude that their merit system is so subjective that there is no point in advancing it as a defense in litigation.

The issue has come into the courts, nonetheless, in cases involving non-managerial employees, as an outgrowth of investigations of other charges, or as one item in a list of discriminatory practices being charged. Where such challenges have occurred, the courts have taken different approaches: In FLSA cases, they have tended to look to form, in civil rights cases, to substance.

THE FAIR LABOR STANDARDS ACT CASES

The Secretary of Labor has had mixed success in prosecuting discriminatory pay practices under the FLSA when the defendant has claimed that the practices resulted from a merit increase system. An effort to develop a standard for evaluating the legitimacy of merit systems may have occurred in *Hodgson v. Brookhaven General Hospital.*[7] The defendant hospital, appealing a finding that its pay scales for male orderlies and female nurse's aides violated the Equal Pay Amendment to the FLSA, protested the district court's exclusion of supervisory testimony as to the performance of the cited employees. In commenting upon the hospital's contention that this exclusion did not allow it properly to develop its "merit pay" defense, the Court of Appeals noted:

> (T)he Act specifically provides that unequal pay for equal work is justified if administered pursuant to a "merit system." This statutory exception, if not strictly construed against the employer, could easily "swallow the rule." . . . *The employer must show that its "merit system" is administered, if not formally, at least systematically and objectively.* The merit system issue is so closely related to the equal-effort issue as to warrant the taking of additional evidence on the point if the hospital has anything better to offer than *highly subjective evaluations* of employee merit by hospital officals.(Emphasis added)

The case was remanded for further testimony on the nature of the merit system, as well as on the hospital's allegations that differences in effort expended by nurse's aides and orderlies justified the wage disparities between the two classifications. Apparently the hospital did not feel sure that its merit pay plan was that systematic and/or objective, because the testimony offered upon remand dealt with the equal-effort government.

While the scope of judicial review of a company's merit system would include, under the Brookhaven decision, examination of both the plan's objectivity and the uniformity of its administration, other courts have been satisfied with a less rigorous scrutiny. *Hodgson v. Golden Isles Nursing Home*[8] is a good illustration of a court's limited inquiry as to the systematic nature, but not the objectivity, of the merit plan. Here the district court sustained, on grounds of unequal effort and the effects of a merit system, the familiar pay dichotomy between orderlies and aides. The nursing home gave evaluations every three months. Criteria evaluated were "performance, reliability, initiative, responsibilities and fulfillments of responsibilities both to the patient and to the nursing home."

The court apparently was unconcerned by the manner in which "initiative" and "reliability" were assessed, and about the existence or absence of any standard by which these criteria could be measured objectively. As a result, the court did not inquire as to whether judgments concerning the performance of male and female employees were colored by considerations of sex. Relying on the fact that the nursing home's merit system had been maintained with quarterly punctuality, the court upheld its legality, notwithstanding its disparate results.[9]

At times the courts have even abandoned the requirement that merit plans be applied systematically and uniformly if they are to serve as a basis for wage disparities between male and female employees. In *Cupples v. Transport Insurance Co.*[10] the plaintiff, a woman, was promoted from a clerical position to that of underwriter trainee at a monthly salary of $450, while a man was hired for the latter job at $500. He was promoted to underwriter in six months at a salary of $560, and six months later he was raised to $600, while the woman waited a year for promotion to underwriter at a salary of $525. When she questioned the discrepancy, her supervisor replied that the man had come to the position with superior knowledge of the client industry (trucking) "since his dad was owner-operator for . . . North American Van Lines." In addition, the male employee was on a six-month salary review schedule, the woman on an annual schedule. Finally, the supervisor said, he had to consider the "law of supply and demand," which he felt dictated paying the man more. The defendant was also able to cite one complaint about the plaintiff's work. Reviewing the case, the court decided that the supervisor

> arrived at the conclusion that at the time, (the male employee) was worth more to Transport than the Plaintiff was. He arrived at that conclusion by permissible means, a merit system and a system that measured earnings and promotions by quantity and quality of production.

The court supported its approval of the defendant's system by noting that the man was promoted in a far shorter period of time than the woman. Here an apparent act of discrimination served as its own justification, as the court failed to consider the disparate review schedules to which the employees were subjected.

In *Brennan v. Victoria Bank & Trust,*[11] the Department of Labor challenged disparate pay levels between male and female bank tellers, which the defendant claimed were the product of a merit system. Under the bank's merit plan, a department head rated individuals on an increase worksheet, which then was submitted to the personnel manager. He entered proposed raises on the worksheet and forwarded it to an operating committee, which consulted department heads and then "adjusted" the increases prior to submitting them to a management committee for approval. The court characterized this as "a systematic, formal system guided by objective, written standards," although the decision reflects no evidence that the management committee used systematic or objective criteria in approving or disapproving the suggested increases. From these cases it is evident that merit systems challenged under the FLSA have been scrutinized for little beyond uniformity of administration. Minimal attention, if any, has been focused upon the degree to which subjective appraisals, unrelated to objective measures of job performance, may serve as a vehicle for the establishment and maintenance of discriminatory pay disparities between male and female employees.

CIVIL RIGHTS CASES

Given both a broader group of potential litigants and an enforcing agency whose exclusive purpose is its application, there is little surprise that Title VII of the Civil Rights Act of 1964 has produced cases which address performance revaluation in a more probing, less literal-minded fashion than the FLSA cases cited above. In the light of Title VII decisions regarding other employment practices, the problems of vagueness of standards, subjectivity, and inconsistency among appraisers will probably require substantial restriction − perhaps elimination − of the use of traditional, subjective performance evaluation in making both merit-pay and promotional decisions. While most cases to date have addressed themselves to the legitimacy of promotions, the principles established therein are applicable to the merit-pay system as well. The leading case in this area is *Rowe v. General Motors.*[12]

In *Rowe,* a black employee challenged a company's policy of promoting workers from hourly to salaried positions on the basis of supervisory recommendations. Given statistical evidence of a disproportionately smaller number of blacks thus promoted, the Fifth Circuit highlighted the following discriminatory aspects of the promotion procedure:
   − The foreman's recommendation is the single most important factor in the promotion process,

- Foremen are given no written instructions pertaining to the qualifications necessary for promotions,
- Those standards determined to be controlling are vague and subjective,
- Hourly employees were not notified of promotion opportunities or the qualifications necessary to get jobs,
- The procedure contained no safeguards designed to avert discriminatory practices.

Significantly, other courts have declared unlawful similar promotional practices.[13] Moreover, the attack on the legitimacy of subjective supervisory appraisals has not been limited to promotional cases. In *Hester v. Southern Railway*,[14] the Rowe criteria were followed in concluding that the defendant employer was violating Title VII in basing hiring decisions upon subjective employment interviews. Although reversing *Hester* for lack of proof of disproportionate impact, the appellate court noted that "the interview procedure comes uncomfortably close to the promotion procedure proscribed by *Rowe v. General Motors*."[15] It is arguable that merit increases based upon subjective supervisory performance evaluations could be challenged with similar results. Table 1 indicates the extent to which companies may be relying upon discriminatory performance evaluations in affording merit increases and promotions.

Rowe attacked vague and subjective standards having disparate effects upon minority promotions. Inconsistency among appraisers was found illegal in *Harper v. Mayor and City Council*.[17] Here, supervisory efficiency ratings generated 30 percent of a candidate's promotional score, with efficiency ratings generally correlated, by the city's own admission, with a candidate's time in rank. Although black firemen had, on the average, greater seniority than the whites with whom they competed for promotional opportunities, their efficiency ratings were no higher. Relying on the city's argument that efficiency ratings were related to seniority, the court concluded that the failure of the black firemen to receive higher ratings than less senior whites was caused by the inconsistent application of evaluation criteria. The court required, among other remedies, that "the Board of Fire Commissioners shall ensure that blacks and whites are graded equally by promulgation of regulations governing supervisors' efficiency ratings." The case is interesting because it demonstrates that a system's neutral results may not be a sufficient defense to charges of discrimination where the mechanics of the system are applied disparately. Thus, while in *Harper* blacks' ratings were not lower than whites', the evaluation and promotion system was unlawful because its objective application would have afforded blacks higher ratings and more promotions.

Personnel specialists frequently view the broad application of performance-evaluation results as one of the major sources of ineffectiveness of evaluation systems:

TABLE 1

Criteria found discriminatory in *Rowe v. General Motors*	Frequency of use of similar criteria in managerial performance evaluation[16]
1. Foreman evaluation most important part of promotion process	85% of employees use evaluation to justify salary adjustments 64% use it as basis for promotion decisions
2. Foremen given no written instructions re qualifications necessary for promotions	52% gave no special training in performance-appraisal techniques
3. Controlling standards are vague and subjective	64% require appraisal of "personality traits" 52% ask appraisal of "capacity for development or advancement"
4. Employee not notified of a) Openings b) Necessary qualifications	a) No parallel b) 9% of employers do not discuss evaluation with employee
5. No safeguards against discriminatory practice.	51% have no procedures to assure consistency among appraisers

The first major reason for (appraisal program) failure relates to program objectives . . . when it is necessary to determine which piece of the form is allotted to which interest group (management development, personnel records, wage and salary administration, training, etc.). It is this pressure of each group's desire to mold their portion of the same management tool to achieve their own end, that distorts the tool.[18]

They frequently suggest that different types of evaluation be developed consistent with specific goals: one review for merit increase purposes, another for training and development performance, another for promotional and manpower-planning considerations. Employers who adopt multiple-evaluation policies should be aware of the potential for inconsistencies of the type found discriminatory in *Allen v. City of Mobile*.[19] There, candidates for promotion were ranked partly upon their regular performance evaluation and partly upon special service ratings, an estimate of their expected performance if promoted. Both the regular and special ratings asked the candidate's superior to rate him as 1) unacceptable, 2) needs to improve, 3) good, 4) better than average, 5) outstanding. The ten areas rated are: 1) care of equipment, 2) quality of work, 3) initiative and ingenuity, 4) work habits, 5) personal appearance, 6) attitude, 7) judgment, 8) reliability, 9) quantity of work, 10) integrity and loyalty.

Finding that, under this system, blacks had a uniformly greater disparity between regular and special ratings than whites, the court concluded that "some objective controls must be placed on these *subjective reports*." (Emphasis added.) As a remedy, the court required that the "special" rating be prepared on all officers every six months regardless of their promotional prospects, that all supervisors receive instruction in rating, and that "the raters support their evaluations, in addition to the form used, with narrative reasons for their judgment of what sort of sergeant . . . the man would be."

An employer might try to protect its performance-evaluation program from the thrust of *Rowe* by providing written instructions, with objective criteria, for the preparation of the evaluations; however, if this evaluation program produces disproportionate numbers of merit increases and/or promotions for minority and female employees, it may still be found illegal under *Griggs v. Duke Power*[20] if it cannot be shown to be related to job performance.

The combined effects of the Rowe and Griggs decisions can be seen in *Muller v. U.S. Steel*,[21] where a Chicano challenged a company practice of promoting individuals to the rank of foreman on the basis of supervisory recommendations. Since no Chicano had ever been promoted to supervisor, the court, citing Rowe, found the promotional system discriminatory. The court went further, however, by considering the defendant's promotional system in the light of the *Griggs* standards for business necessity: "It has not been shown that efficiency or safety or any other of the company's interests are served by this system which depends on hunch judgments rather than specific criteria."

Not only are performance evaluations a poor defense to allegations of discrimination; they may confirm it. In *Marquez v. Omaha District Sales Office*,[22] the defendant, Ford Motor Company, included "promotability" as part of its performance appraisal. The Chicano plaintiff, a sales analyst, was rated as promotable to administrative assistant in 1961 and to field manager in 1962. In subsequent years, he was not rated promotable but continued to receive high performance ratings. Considering the company's failure to explain Marquez's removal from the promotable list, the absence of minority managers in the entire sales district, and the worker's favorable performance evaluations, the court concluded that this hierarchical immobility was due to discrimination.

CONCLUDING OBSERVATIONS

A review of the cases indicates that the impact of fair employment legislation upon the use of traditional managerial performance-evaluation systems in making pay and promotion decisions has been limited. Pay decisions have been challenged under the Equal Pay Amendments to the FLSA; frequently they have been defended successfully, especially when the evaluations were conducted systematically, even if not objectively. With the possible exception of *Marquez,* appraisal-based promotions to other than first-line positions have not yet been challenged directly in either FLSA or Title VII actions. Nonetheless, two factors may separately or jointly bring subjective managerial performance appraisal under direct legal attack:

(1) EXPANDED FLSA IMPACT. With the expansion of the Equal Pay Amendment's protection to otherwise exempt managerial employees by the Higher Education Act, the group of potential litigants on the "merit system" issue is greatly enlarged. Furthermore, employers may find it more difficult to quantify the duties, and thus defend disparate compensation, of male and female managers than was the case with nurse's aides and orderlies.

(2) EEOC OVERVIEW. Violations of the Equal Pay Amendment are ipso facto violations of Title VII. Additionally, while giving consideration to interpretations of the Department of Labor, the Commission is not bound by them and may apply more rigorous scrutiny to the challenged practice.[23] Finally, although none of the litigants in the Title VII cases previously discussed was a managerial employee, it is difficult to imagine that criteria found discriminatory in promotion to management ranks would be legal for promotion within them. The Rowe decision is applicable on a far broader scale than mere access to supervisory positions.

The opinions in both *Muller* and *Rowe* noted that there was nothing to prevent a bigoted foreman from wholesale discrimination in recommending candidates for promotion. If it is illegal to use subjective criteria for promotion, it should be equally unlawful to apply subjective criteria for more frequent transactions, such as merit increases. And the logic of *Griggs* seems to dictate that an employer, if challenged, most prove a "manifest relationship" between his evaluation system and actual performance on the job. To the degree to which the evaluation includes nonquantifiable criteria, that relationship may not be demonstrable.

The employer who currently utilizes subjective performance evaluation seems to have three options:

(1) ASSUME NO DISPROPORTIONATE IMPACT. Where there is no injury, there is no cause of action. If the employer can assume that the rewards of the evaluation system flow to minority and female managers in proportion to their numbers, it should not fear third-party scrutiny. This goal may prove difficult to attain, particularly in organizations that have practiced tokenism in their placement of minority and female managers;

where avoiding disproportionate impact requires artificially skewed evaluation or other special treatment, the employer is open to serious morale problems and the possibility of reverse-discrimination claims.

(2) DEVELOP NEW BASES FOR PROMOTION DECISIONS. Employers could avoid litigation, and practice sounder management, by basing promotions on more predictive criteria than performance evaluation. Assessment centers, wherein promotional candidates are evaluated upon their hnadling of a simulation of the types of problems encountered in higher-level positions, may prove better promotional determinants in this regard.

(3) RESTRICT OR ABANDON THE USE OF SUBJECTIVE PERFORMANCE EVALUATIONS IN MERIT INCREASE PLANNING. Merit increases might be better based on some form of "management by objectives," where superior and subordinate negotiate a mutual a priori determination of the goals to be achieved, the time frame for their accomplishment, and the indices of partial or total achievement of the goals. "Management by objectives" would at least provide internal EEO auditors an opportunity to review the performance expectations established for protected classes and, by comparison with goals established for white males, an opportunity to detect and correct discriminatory trends before any injury to the employee. Furthermore, such a system might better meet the Rowe standards by giving subordinates advance knowledge of the objective criteria by which their efforts are to be judged.

Following the latter suggestion would eliminate any reason to retain the traditional performance-evaluation plan. Organizations might bemoan the demise of the old way, might miss knowing whether a given employee's "attitude" or "loyalty" was rated outstanding by his superior, or merely satisfactory — but that problem may be preferred to a class-action lawsuit.

NOTES

1.   Bureau of National Affairs, *Survey No. 104: Management Performance Appraisal Program* (1974). Another survey from the same source (*Survey No. 108: Employee Performance: Evaluation and Control,* 1975) is generally supportive of the earlier survey's findings, but was not relied on, as it covered nonmanagerial personnel.

2.   *Id.*

3.   Director of Personnel for a manufacturing firm, quoted in *Survey No. 104, supra,* note 1, at 12.

4.   29 U.S.C. § 206 (d) (1) (1963).

5.   42 U.S.C. § 2000e (1972).

6.   20 U.S.C. § 1078 (1972).

7.   463 F.2d 719 (5th Cir. 1972).

8.   3 EPD ¶ 8108 (D. Fl. 1971), *aff'd,* 468 F.2d 1256 (5th Cir. 1972).

9. The court was oblivious of other problems: the fact that only males received excellent performance ratings; the fact that aides were hired at $1.40 per hour and progressed only to $1.70, while the lowest hiring rate for an orderly was $1.65; the fact that the duties performed exclusively by orderlies were of the type found inconsequential in *Brookhaven;* the fact that there were no orderlies on night shift. From a less pejorative view, and an attempt to harmonize the *Brookhaven and Golden Isles* decisions, see *Brennan v. Owensboro-Daviess County Hospital,* 10 EPD ¶ 10404 (6th Cir. 1975). The latter case notes that in *Golden Isles*, orderlies were assigned exclusively to certain duties such as driving cars. The *Golden Isles* decision, however, does not indicate that nurse's aides were incapable of driving.

10. 498 F.2d 1091 (5th Cir. 1974).

11. 493 F.2d 896 (5th Cir. 1974).

12. 457 F.2d 348 (5th Cir. 1972).

13. See *Wetzel v. Liberty Mutual Life Insurance*, 508 F.2d 239 (3rd Cir. 1975), and *Muller v. U.S. Steel Corp.,* 509 F.2d 923 (10th Cir. 1975).

14. 349 F. Supp. 812 (D. Ga. 1972).

15. 8 EPD ¶ 9582, at 5522 (5th Cir. 1974).

16. Bureau of National Affairs, *Survey No. 104.*

17. 359 F. Supp. 1187 (D. Md. 1972).

18. F. Fournies, *Management Performance Appraisal: A National Study*, at 81-82 (1973).

19. 331 F. Supp. 1134 (D. Ala, 1971).

20. 401 U.S. 424 (1971).

21. *Supra* n.13.

22. 440 F.2d 1157 (8th Cir. 1971).

23. *EEOC Guidelines,* C.F.R. § 1604.8 (1972).

DATE DUE